SAVED
by
GRACE

Anthony A. Hoekema

WILLIAM B. EERDMANS PUBLISHING COMPANY
GRAND RAPIDS, MICHIGAN / CAMBRIDGE, U.K.

First edition 1989
Paperback edition 1994

Wm. B. Eerdmans Publishing Company
2140 Oak Industrial Drive N.E., Grand Rapids, Michigan 49505 /
P.O. Box 163, Cambridge CB3 9PU U.K.
www.eerdmans.com

Printed in the United States of America

20 19 18 17 16 15   18 17 16 15 14 13

Library of Congress Cataloging-in-Publication Data

Hoekema, Anthony A., 1913-1988
Saved by grace / by Anthony A. Hoekema
p.   cm.
Bibliography: p. 257
Includes indexes.
ISBN 978-0-8028-0857-8
1. Salvation.   I. Title.
BT751.2.H58   1989
2234—dc19   89-30639
CIP

Unless otherwise noted, Scripture quotations are from the Holy Bible,
New International Version. Copyright © 1973, 1978, 1984 International
Bible Society. Used by permission of Zondervan Bible Publishers.

To the memory of my dear parents,
Peter and Jessie Hoekema,
who first taught me what it meant
to be saved by grace

Contents

Foreword: In Memoriam

SAVED BY GRACE IS ANTHONY HOEKEMA'S SEVENTH BOOK AND THE last of three expository studies in central topics of Reformed theology. The present examination of the doctrine of salvation completes a series encompassing books on eschatology (*The Bible and the Future,* 1979) and theological anthropology (*Created in God's Image,* 1986).

Tony completed the manuscript of the present study just before his seventy-fifth birthday. It was to be his last birthday and his last book. A few months later, on October 17, 1988, our husband and father died of a stroke he had suffered two days earlier. Thus did his life of teaching and scholarship come to an end and his experience of the saving love of Jesus Christ enter a new stage.

The author dedicated this book to the memory of his parents, a Frisian tailor and a strict but loving mother who shared their son's joy in his ministerial calling but passed away before his first book (*The Four Major Cults,* 1963) was published. Our sadness in the loss of a husband and a father is tempered by thankfulness for his forty-four years of ministry to the church through preaching, teaching, and writing, and in seeing this book to publication we add a rededication to his memory.

Anthony Andrew Hoekema was born in Drachten, Friesland, in 1913 and moved from the Netherlands to the United States with his parents and two brothers in 1923. Tony attended Baxter Christian School, graduated from Grand Rapids Christian High School, and received the B.A. from Calvin College in 1936—a path also followed by all four of his children, thirty years later. He received the M.A. in psychology from the University of Michigan in 1937 and the Th.M. from Calvin Theological Seminary in 1944. He went on to receive the Th.D. from Princeton Seminary in 1953. Following his ordination to the ministry in 1944 he served three Christian Reformed Churches as pastor: Twelfth Street in Grand Rapids, Bethel in Paterson, New Jersey, and Alger Park in Grand Rapids.

In 1956 Tony was called to continue his ministry through teaching, first at Calvin College and then, from 1958 until his retirement in 1978, at Calvin Seminary, where he held the chair of Professor of Systematic Theology. He is remembered by students and parishioners alike—so we have been reminded often in the months since his passing—for his clarity of mind, his precision of expression, his warm personal interest in all whose lives touched his, and his weakness for awful puns. All of these traits save the last, we hope, have been evident in his writing.

At Tony's passing the present study was already in production, and it was left to us only to complete a few editorial and proofreading tasks and to supply indices. It has been not a burden but a privilege to make this modest contribution to the completion of Tony's scholarly and pastoral work.

We do not know what joys our husband and father now enjoys in the presence of our Savior; but we hope and pray that his endeavor to articulate the Bible's teaching concerning salvation will deepen others' understanding of this richness of the gift of grace that we receive through God's boundless love.

February 18, 1989   RUTH BRINK HOEKEMA
                                                        DAVID A. HOEKEMA

Preface

THIS IS THE THIRD IN A SERIES OF DOCTRINAL STUDIES. THE FIRST, *THE Bible and the Future*, was a presentation of Christian eschatology, or the doctrine of the last things. The second, *Created in God's Image*, dealt with Christian anthropology, or the Christian doctrine of man.

This book concerns what theologians call soteriology, or the Christian doctrine of salvation. I have tried to draw answers to my questions in this area primarily from the Bible. My theological position is that of evangelical Christianity, interpreted from a Reformed or Calvinistic perspective.

The Reformed understanding of Scripture begins with a recognition of the sovereignty of God in all things, including our salvation. One of the central teachings of the Bible, sounded repeatedly, like the major theme of a symphony, is that we are saved wholly by grace, through the powerful working of God's Holy Spirit, on the basis of the all-sufficient work of our Savior, Jesus Christ.

At the same time, however, the Scriptures teach that God saves us not as puppets but as persons, and that we must therefore be active in our salvation. The Bible, in a way which is deeply mysterious, combines God's sovereignty with our responsibility in the process of our salvation. But we can only love him because he first loved us. To him therefore must be all the praise.

Again I should like to thank my many students at Calvin Theological Seminary, whose questions, challenges, and comments in the classroom helped to deepen my insights into this aspect of Scripture teaching.

I am grateful to the Calvin Theological Library for the use of its excellent resources, and for the privilege of occupying an office in the library during my retirement. I would like to give special thanks to the theological librarian, Peter De Klerk, for his exceptional helpfulness.

The editorial staff at the Eerdmans Publishing Company has provided the kind of expertise that is a joy to an author's heart. I wish especially to thank Jon Pott and Milton Essenburg.

I owe to my wife, Ruth, more gratitude than I can express for her constant interest and encouragement, for her many suggestions, and for her help with the bibliography. Without her, this book would have lacked sparkle.

Most of all, I owe thanks and praise to the God of all grace, who gave me the strength to write. Through this study I have become overwhelmed anew by the incomprehensible greatness of his mercy to undeserving sinners like ourselves. We look forward with eager anticipation to the final perfection of the work he has begun in us, when we shall see him face to face, and tell the story, "saved by grace."

Grand Rapids, Michigan   ANTHONY A. HOEKEMA

Abbreviations

ASV	American Standard Version
Bavinck, *Dogmatiek*	H. Bavinck, *Gereformeerde Dogmatiek*, 3rd ed.
Berkhof, ST	L. Berkhof, *Systematic Theology*
EDT	*Evangelical Dictionary of Theology*
Inst.	J. Calvin, *Institutes of the Christian Religion*
ISBE	*International Standard Bible Encyclopedia*, rev. ed.
JB	Jerusalem Bible
KJV	King James Version
NASB	New American Standard Bible
NEB	New English Bible
NIV	New International Version
RSV	Revised Standard Version
TDNT	*Theological Dictionary of the New Testament*
VGT	Moulton & Milligan, *Vocabulary of the Greek Testament*

(See Bibliography for full publishing information.)

SAVED
BY GRACE

CHAPTER 1

Orientation

BY HIS TOTAL OBEDIENCE TO THE FATHER AND BY HIS SUFFERING, death, and resurrection, our Lord Jesus Christ earned for us salvation from sin and from all its results. But this saving work of Christ will avail us nothing until it has been applied to our hearts and lives by the Holy Spirit. The study of the application of the work of redemption to the people of God is called *soteriology,* from two Greek words, *sōtēria* and *logos,* meaning "the doctrine of salvation."

Soteriology has not always been understood in the same way. Charles Hodge, for example, defines it as including the plan of salvation (predestination and the covenant of grace), the person and work of Christ, and the application of that work by the Holy Spirit for the salvation of believers.[1] William G. T. Shedd has a somewhat narrower view; for him soteriology includes the work of Christ (exclusive of his person) and the application of salvation by the Spirit.[2] In the present volume, however, soteriology or "the doctrine of salvation," as it is more commonly called, will be understood as including only the study of the application of the blessings of salvation to the people of God, and their restoration to God's favor and to a life of fellowship with him in Christ. It should be understood that this application is the work of the Holy Spirit, though it must be appropriated by faith.

The theological standpoint represented in this book is that of evangelical Christianity from the Reformed or Calvinistic perspective. Reformed soteriology has much in common with other evangelical soteriologies, but it does have certain distinctive emphases. Among these emphases are the following:

(1) The decisive factor in determining who is to be saved from sin is not the decisions of the human beings concerned, but the sovereign grace of God — though human decision does play a significant role in the process.

---

1. *Systematic Theology* (1871; Grand Rapids: Eerdmans, 1940), 2:313.
2. *Dogmatic Theology* (1889-94; Grand Rapids: Zondervan, n.d.), 2:353.

3

(2) The application of salvation to God's people has its roots in God's eternal decree, according to which he has chosen his people to eternal life, not on the basis of any merits on their part, but solely out of his good pleasure.

(3) Though all who hear the gospel message are invited to accept Christ and his salvation, and are earnestly summoned to such acceptance, the saving grace of God in the strict sense of the word is not universal but particular, being bestowed only on God's elect (those who have been chosen by him in Christ to salvation).

(4) God's saving grace is therefore both efficacious and unlosable. This does not mean that, left to themselves, believers could not drift away from God, but it does mean that God will not permit his chosen ones to lose their salvation. The spiritual security of believers, therefore, depends primarily not on their hold of God but on God's hold of them.

(5) Although the application of salvation to God's people involves, in the aspects distinct from regeneration in the narrower sense, human willing and working, this application is nevertheless primarily the work of the Holy Spirit.

These distinctive emphases shape Reformed soteriology all along the line. While stressing the sovereignty of God's grace in the application of salvation, however, Reformed theology does not negate human responsibility in the process of salvation.

In a previous study I have tried to develop an aspect of this thought in a chapter entitled "Man as a Created Person."[3] I there point out that the human being is both a creature totally dependent on a sovereign God and a person who makes responsible decisions. This combination of total dependence and freedom of choice constitutes the central mystery of man.[4] How does this view of man affect our understanding of the process of salvation? Though God must regenerate human beings and give them new spiritual life, believers have a responsibility in the process of their salvation: in the exercise of their faith, in their sanctification, and in their perseverance.

Since human beings are by nature dead in sin, God must make them

3. *Created in God's Image* (Grand Rapids: Eerdmans, 1986), pp. 5-10.
4. I use the word *man* here and frequently in what follows as meaning "human being," whether male or female. When the word *man* is used in this generic sense, pronouns referring to *man* (he, his, or him) must also be understood as having this generic sense; the same is true of the use of such masculine pronouns with the word *person*. It is a pity that the English language has no word corresponding to the German word *Mensch*, which means human being as such, regardless of gender. *Man* in English may have this meaning, though it may also mean "male human being." It will usually be clear from the context in which sense the word *man* is being used.

alive; regeneration in the narrower sense[5] must be exclusively the work of God. But in the aspects of the process of salvation which are distinct from regeneration both God and believers are involved—we could speak of salvation in this sense as being both God's work and our task. Sometimes these aspects—repentance, faith, sanctification, perseverance, and the like—are described as a work of God in which believers cooperate. The problem with this way of putting it, however, is that it seems to imply that God and we each do part of the work. It would be better to say that in these aspects of our salvation (distinct from regeneration) God works and we work. Our sanctification, for example, is at the same time one hundred percent God's work and one hundred percent our work. Paul gives classic expression to this "mysterious concurrence" of God's work and ours in Philippians 2:12-13, "Therefore, my dear friends, as you have always obeyed . . . continue to work out your salvation with fear and trembling, for it is God who works in you to will and to act according to his good purpose."[6]

THE CONCEPT OF PARADOX

We could say that we are here dealing with what is commonly called a paradox—that is, a combination of two thoughts which seem to contradict each other. It does not seem possible for us to harmonize in our minds these two facets of biblical truth: that on the one hand God must sanctify us wholly but that on the other hand we must work out our sanctification by perfecting our holiness. Nor does it seem possible for us to harmonize these two apparently contradictory thoughts: that God is totally sovereign over our lives, directing them in accordance with his will, but that nevertheless we are required to make our own decisions and are held totally responsible for them.

We must believe, however, that both sides of these apparently contradictory sets of thoughts are true, since the Bible teaches both. For example, the Bible clearly teaches God's sovereignty: "The king's heart is in the hand of the LORD; he directs it like a watercourse wherever he pleases" (Prov. 21:1); "In him we were also chosen, having been predestined according to the plan of him who works out everything in conformity with the purpose of his will" (Eph. 1:11); "Does not the potter have the right to make out of the same lump of clay some pottery [the reference is to human beings] for noble purposes and some for common use?" (Rom. 9:21). But

---

5. For the distinction between regeneration in the narrower and broader sense, see below, pp. 93-94.

6. For a fuller discussion of this passage, see below, pp. 201-202.

the Bible also clearly teaches human responsibility: "Whoever believes in the Son has eternal life, but whoever rejects the Son will not see life, for God's wrath remains on him" (John 3:36); "For the Son of Man is going to come in his Father's glory with his angels, and then he will reward each person according to what he has done" (Matt. 16:27); "Behold, I am coming soon! My reward is with me, and I will give to everyone according to what he has done" (Rev. 22:12).

In at least two passages these two aspects of biblical truth meet together: Luke 22:22 ("The Son of Man will go as it has been decreed, but woe to that man who betrays him"); and Acts 2:23 ("This man was handed over to you by God's set purpose and foreknowledge; and you, with the help of wicked men, put him to death by nailing him to the cross"). God had indeed decreed Christ's death; yet he who betrayed Christ and those who put him to death were held responsible for their wicked deeds.

If we wish to understand the Scriptures, therefore, we must accept the concept of paradox, believing that what we cannot square with our finite minds is somehow harmonized in the mind of God.

The need to accept paradoxical truths has been recognized by many Reformed theologians. John Calvin is a case in point. Calvin, so says Edward Dowey, was willing to combine doctrines which were clear in themselves but logically incompatible with each other, since he found them both in the Bible.[7]

> Calvin, then, was completely convinced of a high degree of clarity and comprehensibility of individual themes of the Bible, but he was also so utterly submissive before divine mystery as to create a theology containing many logical inconsistencies rather than a rationally coherent whole. . . . Clarity of individual themes, incomprehensibility of their interrelations — this is a hallmark of Calvin's theology.[8]

James Packer, an Anglican Reformed theologian, has some helpful things to say about this problem:

> God's sovereignty and man's responsibility are taught us side by side in the same Bible; sometimes, indeed, in the same text. Both are thus guaranteed to us by the same divine authority; both, therefore, are true. It follows that they must be held together, and not played off against each other. Man is a responsible moral agent, though he is *also* divinely controlled; man is divinely controlled, though he is *also* a responsible moral agent. God's sovereignty is a reality and man's responsibility is a reality too.[9]

7. Edward A. Dowey, Jr., *The Knowledge of God in Calvin's Theology* (New York: Columbia University Press, 1952), p. 37.
8. Ibid., pp. 39-40.
9. James I. Packer, *Evangelism and the Sovereignty of God* (Chicago: InterVarsity Press, 1961), pp. 22-23.

After warning against the danger of stressing one aspect while denying the other, Packer goes on to say,

> The antinomy which we face now [between God's sovereignty and man's responsibility] is only one of a number that the Bible contains. We may be sure that they all find their reconciliation in the mind and counsel of God, and we may hope that in heaven we shall understand them ourselves. But meanwhile, our wisdom is to maintain with equal emphasis both the apparently conflicting truths in each case, to hold them together in the relation in which the Bible itself sets them, and to recognize that here is a mystery which we cannot expect to solve in this world.[10]

In a magisterial essay on the subject Vernon Grounds puts it this way: ". . . In Christianity, as I see it, paradox is not a concession: it is an indispensable category, a sheer necessity—a logical necessity!—if our faith is to be unswervingly Biblical."[11] He ends his article by saying, "Let us emphatically assert 'apparently opposite truths,' remembering as a sort of criterion that very likely we are being loyal to the Bible as long as we feel upon our minds the tug of logical tension. Let us as evangelicals unhesitatingly postulate paradox."[12]

G. K. Chesterton's startling aphorism expresses this point in a sparkling way: ". . . Christianity got over the difficulty of combining furious opposites by keeping them both, and keeping them both furious."[13]

We must therefore affirm both God's sovereignty and man's responsibility; both God's sovereign grace and our active participation in the process of salvation. We can only do justice to biblical teaching if we firmly hold on to both sides of the paradox. But since God is the Creator and we are his creatures, God must have the priority. Hence we must maintain that the ultimately decisive factor in the process of our salvation is the sovereign grace of God.

INTERRELATIONS

Something further should be said about the interrelations between soteriology and other aspects of Christian theology. Soteriology is, of course, closely related to the doctrine of God, since it deals with the way God saves us from our sins. Inadequate understandings of God will result in an inadequate grasp of soteriology. A one-sided, exclusive emphasis on

10. Ibid., p. 24.

11. Vernon C. Grounds, "The Postulate of Paradox," *Bulletin of the Evangelical Theological Society*, Vol. 7, No. 1 (Winter 1964), p. 5.

12. Ibid., p. 20.

13. Gilbert K. Chesterton, *Orthodoxy* (1908; Garden City: Doubleday, 1959), p. 95.

God's sovereignty will imply that God saves his people the way computers control robots. An exclusive emphasis on human responsibility, on the other hand, will produce a God who is totally dependent on human decisions, so that he must simply wait in the wings, hoping that people will be so kind as to accept the gospel invitation but having no control over their acceptance. Both of these understandings of soteriology, however, are unbiblical.

Soteriology is also intimately related to theological anthropology, or to the Christian doctrine of man. One's understanding of man is decisive for his or her understanding of the way of salvation. To suggest that human beings are born in a state of moral and spiritual neutrality so that they do not need to be regenerated but only to be properly trained and to be surrounded by good examples would result in a Pelagian soteriology. To teach that human nature after the Fall is only partially depraved, so that human beings are not dead in sin but only diseased, must therefore take the first step in regeneration, and may lose their salvation after they have received it, implies a Semi-Pelagian soteriology. If, however, one believes that human nature after the Fall is totally or pervasively depraved (so that human beings are dead in sin by nature), that therefore people need to be regenerated or given new spiritual life by a gracious act which is the work of God alone, and that the salvation thus bestowed by God can never be lost, he or she will be committed to a Reformed or Calvinistic soteriology.[14]

Soteriology is also closely related to Christology, or the doctrine of the person and work of Christ. Only if one accepts the full deity of Christ can one understand the doctrine of salvation in the biblical sense; Athanasius, in fact, in opposition to Arius, who denied Christ's deity, is reputed to have put it as strongly as this: "Jesus, whom I know as my Redeemer, cannot be less than God." Only if one accepts the genuine humanity of Christ can one believe that Jesus is our Savior from sin since, as the Heidelberg Catechism, perhaps the best-known Reformed confession, affirms, "the justice of God requires that the same human nature which has sinned should make satisfaction for sin. . . ."[15] Further, a biblical understanding of Christ's atoning work is essential for a proper grasp of the doctrine of justification, and an understanding of Christ's continuing intercession for his people is indispensable for an adequate comprehension of the doctrine of the perseverance of the saints.

14. The theological understanding of human nature that underlies the soteriology presented in the present volume can be found in my *Created in God's Image*.
15. Heidelberg Catechism, Q. 16, as found in Philip Schaff, *The Creeds of Christendom* (1877; New York: Harper, 1919), 3:312.

Soteriology is also closely related to the doctrine of the Holy Spirit. The Holy Spirit inspired the writers of the Bible, and illumines our hearts as we read it, enabling us to understand the Scriptures. The Spirit regenerates us, sanctifies us, and enables us to persevere in the faith. In other words, the entire process dealt with in soteriology is a description of the work of the Holy Spirit as he applies to our lives the salvation earned for us by Christ.

There is also a close relationship between soteriology and eschatology (the doctrine of the last things). We should first distinguish between inaugurated and future eschatology. By *inaugurated* eschatology we mean the believer's present enjoyment of eschatological blessings. Since Christ's coming to earth inaugurated the "last days," we may say that the blessings of the salvation we receive through Christ are aspects of eschatology which we enjoy already in this life. The outpouring of the Holy Spirit on the Day of Pentecost—an outpouring which was the fruit of Christ's completed work—was the breaking in of the future into the present.[16] By receiving the Holy Spirit believers have become participants in the new mode of existence associated with the future age. The Spirit is the firstfruits (Rom. 8:23) and the deposit or pledge (2 Cor. 5:5; Eph. 1:14) of future blessings, the seal of our belonging to God (2 Cor. 1:22), and the guarantee of our sonship (Rom. 8:15-16), the full riches of which will not be revealed until Christ comes again (Rom. 8:23). In this sense soteriology is an aspect of eschatology.

By *future* eschatology we mean the discussion of eschatological events that are still to come. In various ways the soteriological blessings we receive in this life are a foretaste of greater blessings to which we look forward in the age to come. Our being raised with Christ now (Eph. 2:6; Col. 3:1), for example, anticipates and guarantees our final resurrection on the last day. Our justification by faith in this present life anticipates and guarantees our final and definitive justification before the judgment seat of Christ. The process of our sanctification on this side of the grave looks forward to its glorious perfection on the new earth.

All of this implies that our salvation, as long as we are in this life, is marked by a very real tension between the "already" and the "not yet." The believer is already a participant in the new type of existence associated with the new age, but he or she is not yet in the final state. Whereas we must now continually struggle against sin, we know that someday that struggle will be over. Although we are now *genuinely* new persons in Christ, someday we shall be *totally* new. We know that God has begun a

16. Neill Q. Hamilton, "The Holy Spirit and Eschatology in Paul," *Scottish Journal of Theology Occasional Papers No. 6* (Edinburgh: Oliver and Boyd, 1957), p. 26.

good work in us; but we are confident that one day he will bring that work to completion. Though we are already now citizens of the kingdom of God, we look forward eagerly and excitedly to the final phase of that kingdom in the life to come, when the earth shall be filled with the knowledge of God as the waters cover the sea.[17]

---

17. On the implications of this tension for our life today, see my *The Bible and the Future* (Grand Rapids: Eerdmans, 1979), pp. 1-75, particularly Chapter 6.

CHAPTER 2

The Question of the "Order of Salvation"

IF SOTERIOLOGY IS UNDERSTOOD AS "THE DOCTRINE OF SALVATION," the question we should take up first is whether there is a certain order in the application of the blessings of salvation to the people of God. On this question there has been a good deal of discussion in the history of theology. In 1737 Jacob Carpov, a Lutheran theologian, coined the phrase *ordo salutis* (literally, order of salvation) to describe what we are now discussing.[1] Many theologians, both Roman Catholic and Protestant, have suggested various "orders of salvation" both before and after this date.

Louis Berkhof describes the *ordo salutis* as

> the process by which the work of salvation, wrought in Christ, is subjectively realized in the hearts and lives of sinners. It aims at describing in their logical order, and also in their interrelations, the various movements of the Holy Spirit in the application of the work of redemption.[2]

It should be noted that Professor Berkhof describes the order as a logical rather than a chronological one, and that he speaks of the interrelations between the various activities of the Spirit in the process of salvation.

THREE DIFFERENT APPROACHES

We go on to note three recent approaches to the problem of the "order of salvation." At one extreme is the position of John Murray, who believes that we can draw a definite order of salvation from Scripture. In his *Redemption —Accomplished and Applied* he states: "There are good and conclusive reasons for thinking that the various actions of the application of redemption . . . take place in a certain order, and that order has been established by divine appointment, wisdom, and grace."[3] From Romans 8:30 Murray draws the fol-

---

1. G. N. M. Collins, "Order of Salvation," EDT, p. 802.
2. Berkhof, ST, pp. 415-16.
3. *Redemption—Accomplished and Applied* (Grand Rapids: Eerdmans, 1955), p. 98.

11

lowing order: calling, justification, and glorification.[4] He further finds Scriptural ground for putting faith and repentance prior to justification, and regeneration prior to faith.[5] Logical considerations based on Scriptural teachings lead him to add adoption, sanctification, and perseverance after justification. He therefore understands the biblical order of salvation to be calling, regeneration, faith and repentance, justification, adoption, sanctification, perseverance, and glorification.[6]

A mediating position on the question of the order of salvation is that of Louis Berkhof. In his *Systematic Theology* he affirms that the Bible does not explicitly furnish us with an order of this sort:

> When we speak of an *ordo salutis*, we do not forget that the work of applying the grace of God to the individual sinner is a unitary process, but simply stress the fact that various movements can be distinguished in the process, that the work of the application of redemption proceeds in a definite and reasonable order, and that God does not impart the fullness of his salvation to the sinner in a single act . . . The question may be raised, whether the Bible ever indicates a definite *ordo salutis*. The answer to that question is that, while it does not explicitly furnish us with a complete order of salvation, it offers us a sufficient basis for such an order.[7]

After indicating that the Bible often gives to the terms we use in systematic theology wider meanings than those to which we are accustomed, and after reviewing Scriptural teachings of various ways in which different aspects of the work of redemption are related to each other, he goes on to suggest the following order of salvation: calling, regeneration, conversion (including repentance and faith), justification, sanctification, perseverance, and glorification.[8]

At the other extreme from Murray's position is that of G. C. Berkouwer. He is quite unhappy with the concept of an *ordo salutis* or "order of salvation." He observes that theological preoccupation with this topic has often led to a greater concern for the various steps in our salvation than for the riches of salvation itself.[9] He goes on to insist that one cannot deduce a fixed order of salvation from Scripture, and that in Romans 8:30, for example, Paul's purpose is not to teach us a definite sequence of steps in the process of salvation.[10] He further affirms that faith should never be thought of as simply "one distinct point in the way of salvation"; faith should rather

4. Ibid., pp. 100-102.
5. Ibid., pp. 102-104.
6. Ibid., pp. 104-105.
7. Berkhof, ST, p. 416.
8. Ibid., pp. 416-18 (on the order of calling and regeneration, see pp. 454-56).
9. *Faith and Sanctification*, trans. Lewis B. Smedes (Grand Rapids: Eerdmans, 1954), pp. 25-26.
10. Ibid., p. 31.

be seen as permeating the Christian's entire life.[11] For these and other reasons, therefore, Berkouwer refuses to set up an *ordo salutis*, preferring to speak of "the way of salvation" rather than of an "order of salvation."[12]

DIFFICULTIES

What are some of the difficulties which confront us as we try to construct an "order of salvation"?

(1) The terms employed in constructing an *ordo salutis* are not used by Bible writers in the same way in which they are used in systematic theology. For example, the word *palingenesia* (regeneration) is used twice in the New Testament. Only in Titus 3:5 does the term (rendered "regeneration" in the KJV and the RSV, but "rebirth" in the NIV) mean what we usually understand by the word, namely, new spiritual life brought about in us by the Holy Spirit. In the other passage, Matthew 19:28, the word (translated "regeneration" in the KJV, "new world" in the RSV, and "the renewal of all things" in the NIV) points to the new order of things which will be ushered in at the time of Christ's return. Herman Bavinck, in fact, puts his finger on this difficulty when he says,

> Regeneration, faith, conversion, renewal, and the like, often [in the Bible] do not point to successive steps in the way of salvation but rather summarize in a single word the entire change which takes place in man.[13]

(2) The order in which the various steps in the process of salvation are said to occur is not always the same in the Bible. For example, whereas commonly sanctification is presented as a step which follows justification (see the orders suggested by Murray and Berkhof), in 1 Corinthians 6:11 sanctification is mentioned before justification: "But you were washed, you were sanctified, you were justified in the name of the Lord Jesus Christ and by the Spirit of our God."

(3) Even Romans 8:30, often used as a basis for constructing a segment of the *ordo salutis,* does not have as its primary purpose that of providing steps in the order of salvation. For the purpose of verses 29 and 30 is to give a reason for the statement made in verse 28, "And we know that in all things God works for the good of those who love him, who have been called according to his purpose." Verses 29 and 30 expand on the meaning of the phrase "those . . . who have been called according to his purpose," showing that these people have been foreknown, predestined,

11. Ibid., p. 32.
12. Ibid., p. 36.
13. Bavinck, *Dogmatiek,* 3:682 [trans. mine].

called, justified, and glorified. But the order in which these facets of their redemption are mentioned is secondary to Paul's main purpose. That purpose is to set forth in ringing words the security and everlasting blessedness of God's redeemed people.

(4) Faith should not be thought of as only one of the steps in the order of salvation; it must continue to be exercised throughout the believer's life. It is just as necessary in sanctification and perseverance as in justification.

(5) Justification and sanctification are not successive stages in the Christian life but are simultaneous. It is impossible to receive Christ for justification and not at the same time to receive him for sanctification, as Paul teaches in 1 Corinthians 1:30, "He [God] is the source of your life in Christ Jesus, whom God made our wisdom, our righteousness and sanctification and redemption" (RSV).

(6) The orders suggested by Murray and Berkhof are not complete. Love is not mentioned in either of them, and neither is hope. Yet surely love and hope are just as essential in the process of our salvation as is faith.

SHOULD WE SPEAK OF AN ORDER OF SALVATION?

Should we then still speak of an order of salvation? Before we take up this question, we should consider the relationship between regeneration and the other aspects of soteriology. By regeneration we mean that work of the Holy Spirit whereby he initially brings us into a living union with Christ and changes our hearts so that we who were spiritually dead become spiritually alive. It will be obvious that regeneration as thus defined must precede conversion (including faith and repentance), justification, sanctification, and perseverance, since these last-named experiences presuppose the existence of spiritual life. In this sense we could speak of a kind of order in the process of salvation: regeneration must be first.

But even this priority of regeneration is hardly to be construed as pointing to a chronological or temporal order. The relationship between regeneration and, let us say, faith is like that between turning on the light switch and flooding a room with light—the two actions are simultaneous, Similarly, when a person receives new spiritual life, he or she immediately begins to believe.[14] Perhaps the best way to put it is to affirm that regeneration has *causal priority* over the other aspects of the process of salvation: faith, repentance, sanctification, and the like.

But then how should we think about the various phases or aspects of

14. Note, for example, what Luke says about the conversion of Lydia in Acts 16:14, "The Lord opened her heart to respond to Paul's message." Here faith (responding to the gospel message) follows at once upon regeneration (the opening of the heart by the Lord).

the process of salvation? Should we speak about an order of salvation here, involving a series of successive steps? Is it true, for example, that justification follows conversion, sanctification follows justification, and perseverance follows sanctification? Obviously, this is not so. Conversion includes faith and repentance, and one is justified by faith and at the time of faith, not at some time after one has come to faith. That justification and sanctification are simultaneous has been shown above. Surely, further, we do not begin to persevere in the faith only after we have been believers for a length of time.

We recall Louis Berkhof's observation that the work of applying God's grace to the individual is a unitary process.[15] In the first edition of his *Dogmatics* Herman Bavinck said that all the benefits involved in salvation are given to the elect at the same time.[16] In the third edition he put it this way: "These benefits [involved in our salvation] can be distinguished but cannot be separated; like faith, hope, and love they form a triple cord which cannot be broken."[17] We should therefore abandon the concept of an order of salvation as an attempt to impose a chronological order on a unitary work of God which does not admit of being divided into successive steps.

It is true, however, that in applying to us the salvation we have in Christ the Holy Spirit does bring about various experiences which, though they may never be separated, must be distinguished from each other. We shall be studying these various workings of the Spirit and their corresponding human experiences. But, though we take them up one by one, we must remember that they never occur separately but always together. We will, for example, consider and discuss separately what we call justification and what we call sanctification, but we must never allow ourselves to forget that these two always occur together. We will take up separately what we call regeneration and what we call conversion, but these two never occur separately. Keeping this point in mind will help us avoid many a pitfall in the study of soteriology.

We should think, then, not of an *order of salvation* with successive steps or stages, but rather of a marvelous work of God's grace—a *way of salvation*—within which we may distinguish various aspects. These aspects, however, are not all of the same sort; they should not therefore all be placed into the same category. For example, some aspects of this way of salvation concern what *man does*, though only in God's strength (faith and repentance), whereas other aspects concern what *God does* (regeneration and justification). Some aspects are *judicial* acts (justification), whereas

---

15. Berkhof, ST, p. 416.
16. *Gereformeerde Dogmatiek*, 1st ed. (Kampen: J. H. Bos, 1898), 3:485.
17. Bavinck, *Dogmatiek*, 3:689 [trans. mine].

other aspects concern the *moral and spiritual renewal* of man (regeneration and sanctification). Some aspects are *instantaneous* actions (regeneration, conversion of the crisis type, definitive sanctification), while other phases are *continuing* actions (progressive sanctification, perseverance).

In summary, the various phases of the way of salvation are not to be thought of as a series of successive steps, each of which replaces the preceding, but rather as various simultaneous aspects of the process of salvation which, after they have begun, continue side by side.

To illustrate this understanding of the way of salvation, I add these diagrams. The process of salvation ought not to be understood as a series of successive experiences, like this:

regeneration | conversion | justification | sanctification | perseverance

Rather, the process of salvation ought to be understood as a unitary experience involving various aspects which begin and continue simultaneously:

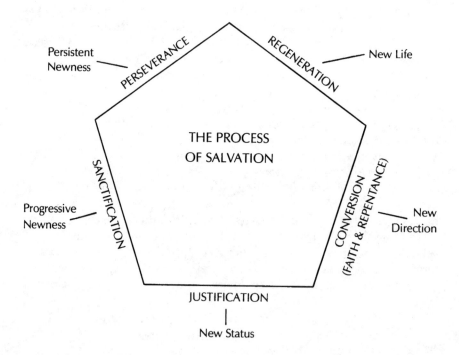

As an aid in interpreting this diagram, the following comments are offered:

(a) In this diagram, calling has been left out, since the gospel call precedes the actual process of salvation. Glorification has also been left out, since this is an aspect of eschatology.

(b) It is to be understood that these aspects of the process of salvation occur not successively but simultaneously. Though regeneration has causal priority over the other aspects, it has no chronological priority.

(c) Sanctification is here understood in its progressive sense. As will be shown later, however, there is also a sense in which sanctification is definitive or instantaneous.

IMPLICATIONS

What, further, are some of the implications for our theology of this understanding of the process of salvation?

(1) Though regeneration occurs at the beginning of the Christian life, its effects continue, as the believer lives a regenerate life. Although faith and repentance occur at the beginning, they must continue to be exercised throughout the Christian life. Though justification occurs as soon as one accepts Christ by faith, it is followed by a lifelong appropriation of its benefits. Sanctification continues throughout the believer's life, and is not completed until after death. Perseverance in the faith is also a lifelong activity.

(2) These aspects of the process of salvation are not only simultaneous; they are also interactive. Regeneration is bound to reveal itself in faith and repentance; it is also the beginning of sanctification. Faith is necessary throughout the Christian life as a means of appropriating the blessings of justification, of making progress in sanctification, and of persevering in fellowship with Christ. Regeneration, in fact, already implies perseverance; the new life received at the time of the new birth can never be lost. It is impossible to be justified without being sanctified, just as it is impossible to be truly converted and not to persevere in the faith.

(3) Although, as was said above, the glorification of believers belongs to that aspect of theology known as eschatology, and is therefore not here considered a part of soteriology, yet it must always be remembered that the process of salvation is not completed during this present life. Believers, as long as they are in this life, are in tension between the "already" and the "not yet": already they are in Christ, but they are not yet perfect. They are on the way which leads to glory, but they are still far from the goal. They are *genuinely* new persons, but not yet *totally* new.

This understanding of the process of salvation also means that certain soteriological views must be rejected. The views to be rejected include those of groups which posit the need for a distinct and recognizable second step after conversion, and those of groups which insist on the need for both a second and a third step subsequent to conversion. We could call these two-stage or three-stage soteriologies.

The following diagrams will help to illustrate these types of soteriology:[18]

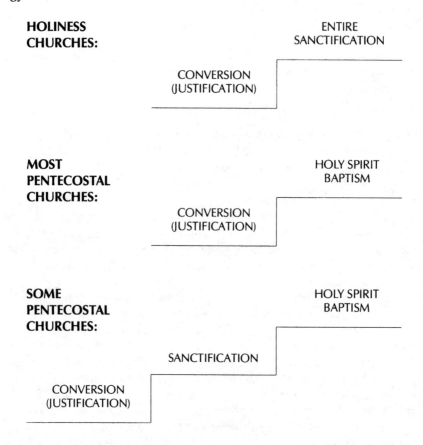

Why should these types of soteriology be rejected? We have already seen that a proper understanding of the process of salvation sees the various aspects of that process as simultaneous rather than successive. Advancement in the Christian life should therefore be understood as involving progressive and continuing growth rather than the mounting of

18. In later chapters these soteriological views will be set forth and discussed in greater detail.

specific steps after conversion. In addition, the following objection to the soteriologies in question may be raised:

(1) If one who is in Christ receives him for sanctification as well as justification, how can one be justified (the first "step") without being sanctified (the second "step")?[19]

(2) Since in the New Testament Holy Spirit baptism, as an experience other than the once-for-all outpouring of the Spirit on the Day of Pentecost, means the reception of the Spirit for salvation, all who are in Christ must see themselves as already having been Spirit-baptized. There is therefore no need for thinking of Holy Spirit baptism as a second or third step after conversion.[20]

(3) How can one tell when the second (or third) step or stage has been reached? In the case of Holy Spirit baptism, the evidence that one has reached this stage is commonly said to be the "initial physical sign of speaking with other tongues."[21] But there is no biblical evidence that speaking in tongues is either the necessary or highly desirable proof that one has received a postconversion baptism in the Holy Spirit.[22] In the case of "entire sanctification," one might say that the attainment of sinless perfection would be the evidence that a person had reached this stage. But such a claim would involve a weakened understanding of both sin and perfection.[23] If, however, as many holiness churches teach, "entire sanctification" must still be followed by further progress and growth in the Christian life, who is to tell when a sufficiently advanced level of sanctification has been achieved to warrant designating it as the required second step? And if this "second step" is something short of sinless perfection, why should it be called *entire* sanctification?

(4) These soteriologies suggest that there are two types (or three types) of Christians: ordinary ones, sanctified ones, and/or Spirit-baptized ones. There is, however, no biblical basis for such a distinction. Further, such a compartmentalization of Christians would seem to open the way for two

19. A. A. Hodge puts it this way: "You cannot take Christ for justification unless you take him for sanctification. . . . You can no more separate justification from sanctification than you can separate the circulation of the blood from the inhalation of the air. Breathing and circulation are two different things, but you cannot have the one without the other; they go together, and they constitute one life. So you have justification and sanctification; they go together, and they constitute one life." *Evangelical Theology* (1890; Carlisle, PA: Banner of Truth, 1976), pp. 310-11.

20. The meaning and significance of Holy Spirit baptism will be discussed in the following chapter.

21. Article 8 of the "Statement of Fundamental Truths" of the Assemblies of God, in *The Constitution and Bylaws of the Assemblies of God* (Springfield, MO: Gospel Publishing House, 1985), p. 108.

22. See my *Holy Spirit Baptism* (Grand Rapids: Eerdmans, 1972), pp. 30-46.

23. This point will be further developed on pp. 207, 214-25 below.

erroneous and spiritually harmful attitudes: depression on the part of those who still think of themselves as being on the lower level of the Christian life, and pride on the part of those who deem themselves to have reached one of the higher levels.

The understanding of the process of salvation which has been developed in this chapter also implies that we must reject a concept which is taught by certain evangelical groups, namely, that of the so-called "carnal Christian." This concept has been popularized for many years by the *Scofield Reference Bible.* From the *New Scofield Reference Bible* published in 1967 I cull the following quotation, found in a footnote to 1 Corinthians 2:14,

> Paul divides men into three classes: (1) *psuchikos,* meaning *of the senses, sensuous,* (Jas. 3:15; Jude 19), *natural,* i.e. the Adamic man, unrenewed through the new birth (Jn. 3:3, 5); (2) *pneumatikos,* meaning *spiritual,* i.e. the renewed man as Spirit-filled and walking in the Spirit in full communion with God (Eph. 5:18-20); and (3) *sarkikos,* meaning *carnal, fleshly,* i.e. the renewed man who, walking "after the flesh," remains a babe in Christ (1 Cor. 3:1-4). The natural man may be learned, gentle, eloquent, fascinating, but the spiritual content of Scripture is absolutely hidden from him; and the fleshly or carnal Christian is able to comprehend only its simplest truths, "milk" (1 Cor. 3:2).[24]

It will be observed that according to this note a "carnal man" is someone who, though he is in Christ and has been renewed, is still walking "after the flesh."

The concept of the "carnal Christian" has also been actively promoted by the interdenominational student Christian movement called "Campus Crusade for Christ." The diagrams on the following page have been taken from the *Lay Trainee's Manual* published by Campus Crusade. The diagrams are preceded by these words, addressed to the trainee:

> Explain [to the new convert] that, after he has invited Christ to come into his life, it is possible for him to take control of the throne of his life again. The New Testament passage, 1 Corinthians 2:14-3:3, identifies three kinds of people.

Note that the "carnal man" is called a "Christian who is not trusting God." Note also that the diagrams for the "natural man" and the "carnal man" are exactly the same, except that in the former the cross, standing for Christ, is outside the circle of the person's life, whereas in the latter the cross is inside the circle. The clear implication of these diagrams is that "carnal Christians" are persons who, though they have accepted Christ in some sense as Savior, live exactly the same way as they did before conversion.[25]

---

24. New York: Oxford University Press, 1967, p. 1234. The same note, with the exception of a few minor differences, appeared in the original *Scofield Reference Bible* of 1909, pp. 1213-14.

25. This teaching about the "carnal Christian" is further developed in a small booklet widely used by Campus Crusade workers called "Have You Made the Wonderful Discovery

NATURAL MAN | SPIRITUAL MAN | CARNAL MAN
(non-Christian) | (Christian who is | (Christian who is
 | trusting God) | not trusting God)

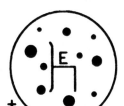
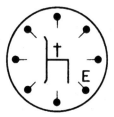
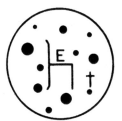

⊓ = throne or control center
E = ego or finite self
● = various interests in the life
† = Christ is either:
    1. outside the life
    2. in life and on throne
    3. in life but off throne[26]

This teaching about the "carnal Christian," however, must be rejected, because it describes a type of Christian the Bible nowhere recognizes. To be sure, Paul admits that there are Christians who are "mere infants in Christ" (1 Cor. 3:1), and the author of Hebrews writes about believers who must "leave the elementary teachings about Christ and go on to maturity" (Heb. 6:1). There are indeed levels of maturity among Christians, and all who are in Christ constantly need to press forward to perfection. But the concept of the "carnal Christian" as a separate category of believers is not only misleading but harmful. The following objections may be raised against it:

(1) This concept suggests that there are two types of Christians: carnal and spiritual. But there is no biblical basis for this distinction. The New Testament does distinguish between people who have been born again and those who have not (John 3:3, 5), between those who believe in Christ and those who do not (John 3:36), between those who "live according to the flesh" and those who "live according to the Spirit" (Rom. 8:5, RSV), and between the "unspiritual man" and the "spiritual man" (1 Cor. 2:14-

of the Spirit-Filled Life?" (San Bernardino, CA: Campus Crusade for Christ International, 1966).

The distinction between "carnal" and "spiritual" Christians can also be found in J. Robertson McQuilkin's chapter on the Keswick perspective in Melvin Dieter et al., *Five Views on Sanctification* (Grand Rapids: Zondervan, 1987), p. 160.

26. Chart taken from *Lay Trainee's Manual* (San Bernardino, CA: Campus Crusade for Christ International, 1968), p. 156. Used by permission of Here's Life Publishers.

15, RSV). However, it never speaks about a third class of people called "carnal Christians."[27] Whether the reference in 1 Corinthians 3:1 and 3 to those who are "yet carnal" (KJV) points to a separate class of Christians will be discussed later in this chapter.

(2) The concept of the "carnal Christian" implies the need for a second distinct and recognizable step beyond conversion. Apparently accepting Christ and becoming a Christian is not enough; *the* important change which needs to occur is the second step, which will make the convert a "spiritual Christian." What has been said earlier in this chapter in criticism of soteriologies which teach the need for a second step beyond conversion is also applicable here.

(3) The concept of the "carnal Christian" suggests that one can receive Christ as Savior without receiving him as Lord. In groups where this teaching is accepted, appeal is often made to the so-called "carnal Christian" to put Jesus on the throne and to "make him Lord" of your life. After this has been done, such a person is then told, he or she will no longer be a "carnal Christian." This teaching, however, is foreign to the New Testament. One cannot accept Christ as Savior and not accept him as Lord. Paul said to the Corinthians, "For we do not preach ourselves, but Jesus Christ as Lord, and ourselves as your servants for Jesus' sake" (2 Cor. 4:5). And to the Colossians he wrote, "So then, just as you received Christ Jesus as Lord, continue to live in him" (Col. 2:6). We do not make Christ Lord; God has made him Lord (Acts 2:36). It is, of course, true that we who are in Christ do not always follow him as Lord and need continually to grow in our obedience to him. But to suggest that one can be a Christian while self is still exclusively on the throne is to misunderstand New Testament teaching.[28]

(4) The concept of the "carnal Christian" suggests that a person can be walking or living according to the flesh (or according to the sinful tendencies which are still within us) and yet be thought of as a Christian. It will be remembered that the Scofield Bible note quoted above describes the "carnal man" as "the renewed man who, walking 'after the flesh,'

27. Bishop J. C. Ryle expresses this point vividly and unforgettably: "The Word of God always speaks of two great divisions of mankind, and two only. It speaks of the living and the dead in sin—the believer and the unbeliever—the converted and the unconverted—the travellers in the narrow way and the travellers in the broad—the wise and the foolish—the children of God and the children of the devil. *Within* each of these two great classes there are, doubtless, various measures of sin and of grace; but it is only the difference between the higher and lower end of an inclined plane. *Between* these two great classes there is an enormous gulf; they are as distinct as life and death, light and darkness, heaven and hell. But of a division into three classes the Word of God says nothing at all!" *Holiness* (London: James Clarke, 1956), p. xv.

28. On this point see Ernest C. Reisinger, *What Should We Think of "The Carnal Christian"?* (Carlisle, PA: Banner of Truth, n.d.), pp. 19-21.

remains a babe in Christ." In the Campus Crusade booklet entitled "Have
You Made the Wonderful Discovery of the Spirit-Filled Life?", one of the
Scripture passages used to describe the "carnal Christian" on page 6 is
Romans 8:7. This text, in the King James Version, reads as follows: "The
carnal mind is enmity against God: for it is not subject to the law of God,
neither indeed can be." The person Paul is describing in this passage,
however, is not a "lower-grade" kind of Christian, but someone who is
unregenerate and outside of Christ. For in verse 8 Paul says that those pictured in verse 7 are "in the flesh"; he then goes on to say, in verse 9, "But
ye [the Roman Christians to whom he is writing] are not in the flesh, but
in the Spirit" (KJV). Further, in Galatians 5:16 Paul writes: "Walk in the
Spirit, and ye shall not fulfill the lust of the flesh"; in verse 24 he adds,
"They that are Christ's have crucified the flesh with the affections and
lusts" (KJV). To be sure, all believers are still tempted by the flesh and at
times yield to it. But the thought that a person can be continually walking
or living in the flesh or "after the flesh" and still be considered a Christian
is not in agreement with biblical truth.

We go on now to see whether 1 Corinthians 3:1-3, a passage on which
both the *Scofield Bible* and the Campus Crusade writers base their teachings on the "carnal Christian," supports this doctrine. The passage in question follows, as it is found in the King James Version:

> 1 And I, brethren, could not speak unto you as unto spiritual, but as unto
> carnal, *even* as unto babes in Christ.
> 2 I have fed you with milk, and not with meat: for hitherto ye were not
> able *to bear it,* neither yet now are ye able.
> 3 For ye are yet carnal: for whereas *there is* among you envying, and strife,
> and divisions, are ye not carnal, and walk as men?

It is true that Paul here calls the Corinthians to whom he is writing "carnal" (*sarkinois,* rendered "of the flesh" in the RSV and "worldly" in the
NIV). The question is: Is he suggesting a third category into which Christians could be placed, in addition to those of the "natural man" (*psychikos
anthrōpos,* 2:14) and the "spiritual" man (*pneumatikos,* 2:15)? I do not think
so. My reasons for this judgment are as follows:

(1) Paul does not say that the Corinthians *are* not spiritual; what he
says is that he could not and cannot now *speak to them* as spiritual (v. 1).
He is not affirming that they do not fall into the class of "spiritual" persons he described in 2:15, nor is he saying that they belong to the category
of "natural" persons described in 2:14. Note, for example, that he begins
chapter 3 by addressing the Corinthians as brothers. Note also that in 6:19
he tells them that their bodies are temples of the Holy Spirit who is in them
—surely one of the distinctive marks of the "spiritual" person.

(2) After Paul writes that he had to speak to the Corinthians "as unto

carnal," he adds, "*even* as unto babes in Christ" (3:1). To be "in Christ" means nothing if it does not mean belonging to the category of the "spiritual" in distinction from that of the "natural" person.[29] The Corinthians are therefore indeed in Christ, but they are in Christ as infants— "mere infants," as the New International Version puts it. Following up the analogy, a baby or an infant is not a nonhuman being in an immature state.

(3) The thought that the Corinthians are immature is further stated in verse 3, where Paul says, "For ye are yet carnal," implying that they should grow beyond the state of spiritual infancy.

(4) What, then, does Paul mean when he calls his Corinthian readers "carnal"?[30] He means that there is still among them "envying, and strife, and divisions"[31] (3:3, KJV); in verse 21 he describes their behavior as "glorying in men." In chapter 1 Paul had shown what was going on in the Corinthian church: "One of you says, 'I follow Paul'; another, 'I follow Apollos'; another, 'I follow Cephas' [or Peter]; still another, 'I follow Christ' " (1:12, NIV). Instead of being a unified congregation, serving God together in mutual Christian love, the Corinthians were hopelessly divided into four quarreling and squabbling factions. Instead of glorying in the fact that they all belonged to Christ, they were boasting about the human leaders they were following, and looking down their noses at fellow church members who followed other human leaders. The Corinthians, in other words, were behaving for the most part in a "carnal" or fleshly way. They were "acting like mere men" (3:3, NIV)—that is, like unregenerate men. Later in chapter 3 Paul tries to correct their misbehavior by reminding them of the spiritual riches they have in Christ: "All things are yours, whether Paul or Apollos or Cephas . . ." (vv. 21-22). Instead of saying, "We belong to Paul" or "We belong to Apollos," you ought to be saying, "Paul, Apollos, and Cephas all belong to us; they are not our masters but our servants in Christ; instead of lining ourselves up under one or the other of these human leaders, we may learn from them all. They belong to us, and we belong to Christ!" If you fully realized your spiritual riches in Christ, Paul is saying, you would stop bickering about these leaders, and move out of your state of immaturity and carnality.

29. Further implications of what it means to be in Christ will be developed in Chapter 4.

30. The term "carnal" in these verses translates two Greek words, both derived from the word *sarx*, which means "flesh": *sarkinos* (v. 1) and *sarkikos* (v. 3). The former word is commonly understood as meaning "fleshy" (consisting of or resembling flesh), and the latter as meaning "fleshly" (allowing the flesh to work actively within). But the words are often used interchangeably (see H. Conzelmann, *1 Corinthians*, trans. J. W. Leitch [Philadelphia: Fortress, 1975], p. 72).

31. The word "divisions" *(dichostasiai)* is not found in most Greek manuscripts, and is therefore dropped from the more recent Bible versions.

The "carnality" of the Corinthians, therefore, is their spiritual immaturity—an immaturity which they should outgrow. It does not imply that in the lives of these Christians self is exclusively on the throne, or that they are totally enslaved by the flesh. The "carnality," in other words, is a behavior problem.

(5) That Paul considers the Corinthians, in spite of their behavior problems, as belonging to the category of "spiritual" persons is shown by the following statements that he makes about them:

(a) In 1 Corinthians 1:2 he addresses them in this way: "To the church of God in Corinth, to those sanctified in Christ Jesus." In the Greek the verb translated "sanctified" is in the perfect tense—a tense which pictures completed action with continuing result. Paul is here describing his Corinthian readers as those who have been and still are sanctified in the definitive sense. Definitive sanctification is an act of God which occurs at a point in time rather than along a time line.[32] Surely such a statement as that quoted above could not be made about people who are still "natural" persons.

(b) In 1:4 Paul thanks God for the grace which was given to the Corinthians in Christ Jesus—a comment which could not be made about those who are merely "natural."

(c) In 1:30 Paul says, "It is because of him [God] that you are in Christ Jesus, who has become for us wisdom from God — that is, our righteousness, holiness [or sanctification, KJV, NASB, RSV] and redemption." One cannot say, therefore, that the Corinthians were only justified and not sanctified; the Christ in whom they now exist became for them both their righteousness and their holiness or sanctification.

(d) In 3:21-23 Paul sums up in lyrical fashion the riches which are theirs in Christ—riches which no "natural" person could possess: "All things are yours, whether Paul or Apollos or Cephas or the world or life or death or the present or the future—all are yours, and you are of Christ, and Christ is of God."

(e) In 6:11 Paul writes: "But you were washed, you were sanctified, you were justified in the name of the Lord Jesus Christ and by the Spirit of our God." The Greek verbs are all in the aorist tense, which usually pictures instantaneous action. So here Paul again states that the Corinthians whom he had addressed as "carnal" in chapter 3 have both been sanctified (in the definitive sense) and justified.

(f) In 2 Corinthians 5:17 Paul sounds a trumpet call: "Therefore, if anyone is in Christ, he is a new creation. . . ." In his first epistle to them Paul had clearly stated that the Corinthians are in Christ; if this is so, then they are indeed new creations or new creatures. To be sure, much is wrong with

---

32. Definitive sanctification will be defined and discussed in Chapter 12.

their behavior, and they need to be rebuked, to be instructed, and to be encouraged to do better. They need to grow up into greater maturity of behavior, based on a better understanding of their riches in Christ and on a fuller exercise of their faith. But they are new creatures in Christ, and should not be put into a different category than that of "spiritual" persons.

The concept of the "carnal Christian," though it must be rejected for the reasons given, does contain an important element of truth. The "carnality" which Paul criticized in the Corinthians constitutes a danger to which all Christians are exposed and a type of behavior into which all believers may at times fall. We must always be on our guard against such behavior. We may often, like the Corinthians, be tempted to exalt human leaders above Christ. We are all constantly enticed to yield to other forms of "carnality": lustful thoughts, unchaste actions, envy, jealousy, pride, covetousness, gluttony, sinful anger, and slothfulness. According to the New Testament, the Christian life is a continual conflict with sin: it is described as a battle (James 4:1), a fight (1 Tim. 6:12), a struggle (Eph. 6:12; Heb. 12:4), a beating of the body (1 Cor. 9:27), and a resisting of the devil (James 4:7). When we disavow the doctrine of the "carnal Christian," therefore, we do not intend to deny the ever-present danger of slipping into carnal ways of living.

Earlier in the chapter reasons were also given for rejecting two-stage and three-stage soteriologies. The rejection of these soteriologies, however, does not imply an unwillingness to recognize the need for advancement and growth in the Christian life. In fact, we must be ready to acknowledge that many Christians may have what we might call "peak experiences"[33] or "mountaintop experiences" after conversion.[34]

We could cite the Apostle Paul as an example. Sometime after his conversion he asked the Lord three times to remove a painful "thorn in the flesh" (perhaps some type of physical affliction). The Lord did not remove the thorn, but revealed his grace so abundantly that Paul was now enabled to say, "I will boast all the more gladly about my weaknesses, so that Christ's power may rest on me. That is why, for Christ's sake, I delight in weaknesses, in insults, in hardships, in persecutions, in difficulties. For when I am weak, then I am strong" (2 Cor. 12:7-10). Surely this was a high point in Paul's postconversion Christian life.

Another example of such a postconversion peak experience can be

33. The expression is taken from Abraham Maslow's *Toward a Psychology of Being*, 2nd ed. (New York: Van Nostrand Reinhold, 1968), p. 270. Since Maslow is not a Christian psychologist, however, it should be remembered that his view of the nature of these "peak experiences" is quite different from a Christian understanding of such events.

34. See, for example, James Gilchrist Lawson, *Deeper Experiences of Famous Christians* (1911; New York: Pyramid Books, 1970).

found in the life of Blaise Pascal, a French scientist and religious thinker who lived from 1623 to 1662. He had what is usually thought of as his first conversion to Christianity in 1646. Eight years later, however, he experienced a dramatic "second conversion," which he described in his so-called *Memorial.* This second conversion was marked by total renunciation and total submission to Christ.[35]

Recently I heard about a Christian businessman who had a serious bout with cancer. Knowing how close he had come to death, and seeing himself now as a "brand plucked out of the fire," he sold his business and began to devote all his time to working for the church or for church-related organizations. A friend of mine who had been a Christian for many years was brought into a deeper commitment to Christ, a new joy in the Lord, and a much more active evangelistic ministry than before through observing fellow Christians whose close walk with God made him jealous. Examples of this sort could easily be multiplied.

We ought not to program such postconversion peak experiences into the structure of the "order of salvation," for the reasons given above. We may not insist that every Christian should have such an experience. God does not save all his children in exactly the same way. But we certainly must leave room for experiences of this sort in the lives of Christian believers.

Let me put it even more strongly. Spiritual growth in the lives of Christians is not just a luxury but a necessity. Such growth does not need to take the form of a crisis or peak experience, but it must be there. This the Bible clearly teaches. To his recent converts Peter writes: "Like newborn babies, crave pure spiritual milk, so that by it you may grow up in your salvation" (1 Pet. 2:2). At the end of his second epistle, Peter still insists on the need for spiritual growth: "Go on growing in the grace and in the knowledge of our Lord and Savior Jesus Christ" (2 Pet. 3:18, JB). And Paul sounds a similar note: "Speaking the truth in love, we are to grow up in every way into him who is the head, into Christ" (Eph. 4:15, RSV).

While recognizing, then, that the various aspects of the process of salvation are not successive steps but are simultaneous, we must always remember the need to keep on growing into a richer grasp and enjoyment of our salvation. Has anyone made greater progress in the Christian life than the Apostle Paul? Yet, near the end of his days on earth, he wrote, "One thing I do: Forgetting what is behind and straining toward what is ahead, I press on toward the goal to win the prize for which God has called me heavenward in Christ Jesus" (Phil. 3:13-14).

35. R. V. Pierard, "Pascal, Blaise," EDT, p. 827. For the text of the *Memorial*, see Hugh T. Kerr and John M. Mulder, eds., *Conversions* (Grand Rapids: Eerdmans, 1983), pp. 37-38.

CHAPTER 3

The Role of the Holy Spirit

AS WE CONTINUE OUR STUDY OF THE DOCTRINE OF SALVATION, OR soteriology, we look next at the role of the Holy Spirit in this process. Earlier it was said that the saving work of Christ will avail us nothing until it has been applied to our hearts and lives by the Holy Spirit.[1] It will be helpful now to review briefly the work of the Spirit in the process of our salvation.

THE SPIRIT'S ROLE IN THE PROCESS OF OUR SALVATION

In the words of the Westminster Confession of Faith, the Holy Spirit is "the only efficient agent in the application of redemption."[2] Paul teaches that God saves us, not because of the righteous things we have done, but through renewal by the Holy Spirit (Tit. 3:5); he assures the Galatians that we live by the Spirit (meaning not just physical but particularly spiritual life, Gal. 5:25). Jesus himself told his disciples that the Spirit gives everlasting life (John 6:63). As the one who applies redemption to our hearts and lives, the Holy Spirit lives or dwells with us and in us (John 14:17; Rom. 8:9; 1 Cor. 3:16; 2 Tim. 1:14).

The chief role of the Holy Spirit in the process of our salvation is to make us one with Christ. Paul expresses this thought most vividly in 1 Corinthians 12:13, "For we were all baptized by [or with, or in] one Spirit into one body" — it is obvious from the preceding context that this one body is the body of Christ. Paul, in other words, "ascribes the whole of the new life, in its origin as well as in its realization and communication, to the Spirit, to his operations, powers, and gifts."[3]

---

1. See above, p. 3. Cf. also point (5) on p. 4.
2. Westminster Confession, IX, 3, found in *The Confession of Faith of the Presbyterian Church in the United States*, 1861 ed. (Richmond: John Knox, 1956), p. 62.
3. Herman Ridderbos, *Paul: An Outline of His Theology*, trans. John R. De Witt (Grand Rapids: Eerdmans, 1975), p. 223.

In the next chapter I plan to discuss union with Christ as central to soteriology. At this point, however, it must be said that it is the Holy Spirit who unites us to Christ. The Holy Spirit is called the Spirit of the Lord (2 Cor. 3:17), the Spirit of Christ (Rom. 8:9; 1 Pet. 1:11), the Spirit of Jesus Christ (Phil. 1:19), or the Spirit of his (God's) Son (Gal. 4:6). When one participates in Christ, therefore, he or she also participates in the Spirit. Paul illustrates this point dramatically in his Epistle to the Romans. In 8:9 he describes believers as those who are not in the flesh *(en sarki)* but in the Spirit *(en pneumati).* He then goes on to call the Holy Spirit the Spirit of God and the Spirit of Christ. But in verse 10 he describes believers as those in whom Christ is. To be in Christ and to be in the Spirit, therefore, are not two different things but the same thing.

Hence we are not surprised to find that all the major elements in the process of salvation are ascribed to the Holy Spirit as their author. *Regeneration* or the new birth is said to be the work of the Spirit: "I tell you the truth," Jesus said to Nicodemus, "no one can enter the kingdom of God unless he is born of water and the Spirit" (John 3:5). Paul's statement in Titus 3:5 that God saved us "through the washing of rebirth and renewal by the Holy Spirit" similarly ascribes regeneration or the new birth to the Spirit.

How about *conversion?* Conversion, or turning to God, is commonly thought of as involving two aspects: *repentance* and *faith.* Both of these aspects are described in the Bible as gifts of the Holy Spirit. In Acts 11:15 Peter, describing to the believers in Jerusalem the conversion of the Gentile Cornelius, is reported as saying, "As I began to speak, the Holy Spirit came on them [Cornelius and his household] as he had come on us at the beginning." The response of the church at Jerusalem (consisting of Jewish Christians) is given in verse 18: "When they heard this, they . . . praised God, saying, 'So then, God has granted even the Gentiles repentance *(metanoia)* unto life.'" God gave these Gentiles repentance, however, through the Spirit who had come upon them.

Faith is also a gift of the Spirit. In 1 Corinthians 2 Paul points out that it is only through his Spirit that God has revealed his wisdom to us (v. 9), and that we may understand what has been freely given us by God (v. 12) —that is, the truths about Christ which the rulers of this age did not understand when they crucified the Lord of glory (v. 8). The same point is made explicitly in 1 Corinthians 12:3, "No one can say, 'Jesus is Lord' [words which can be uttered only by a believer], except by the Holy Spirit."

The Spirit also gives us the *assurance of salvation,* which is one of the most important marks of a healthy faith. Paul tells us in Romans 8:16, "The Spirit himself testifies with our spirit that we are God's children." Since the tense of the verb translated "testifies" *(symmartyrei)* is present, implying continuation, we conclude that this testimony of the Spirit is not just an occasional or once-for-all occurrence, but continues throughout the believer's life.

Does the New Testament indicate that *justification,* commonly understood as a work of God the Father, is associated with the Holy Spirit? Yes, in more than one way. Since we are justified by faith, the fact that faith is a gift of the Spirit, as was shown above, clearly links this blessing with the Third Person of the Trinity. No New Testament passage links justification more directly with the Holy Spirit than does 1 Corinthians 6:11, where we hear Paul telling his readers, "But you were washed, you were sanctified, you were justified in the name of the Lord Jesus Christ and by the Spirit of our God." Both concluding phrases (referring to Jesus and the Spirit) apply to all three of the preceding verbs: "washed," "sanctified," and "justified." In the original Greek each of these phrases begins with the word *en,* which is usually translated "in"; we could therefore render the second phrase "*in* the Spirit of our God" (ASV, NASB, RSV). The meaning is: "in union with" or "in connection with" the Spirit. Our justification, therefore, is inseparable from the work of the Holy Spirit.

One of the benefits of our justification is our *adoption* as children of God. This blessing, too, is closely linked with the Holy Spirit. We read about this in Galatians 4:4-6. God sent forth his Son, Paul here informs us, so that "we might receive the full rights of sons" (v. 5). The Greek word rendered "full rights of sons" is *huiothesia,* a term used in the papyri of the early Christian centuries to denote the legal act of adopting someone as a son.[4] Paul then goes on to say, "Because you are sons, God sent the Spirit of his Son into our hearts, the Spirit who calls out, '*Abba,* Father'" (v. 6). It is the Holy Spirit, in other words, who, as he lives in us, calls God Father, thus assuring us that we are indeed no longer slaves but sons and daughters of God.

The same point is made in Romans 8. In verse 15 Paul states, "You received the Spirit of sonship *(huiothesia).* And by him we cry, '*Abba,* Father.'" Here it is specifically pointed out that it is we believers who call God Father, though we do so by or through the Holy Spirit. Not only is this so, but it is through following the Spirit's guidance that we learn to live as sons: "those who are led by the Spirit of God are sons of God" (v. 14).

That our *sanctification* is ascribed to the Spirit does not come as a surprise. In fact, the very name "Holy Spirit" already suggests that the Spirit is associated with holiness or sanctification. In 2 Thessalonians 2:13 Paul thanks God for his readers "because from the beginning God chose you to be saved through the sanctifying work of the Spirit...." In Romans 15:16 Paul describes his work as that of being a minister of Christ to the

4. Moulton and Milligan, VGT, pp. 648-49.

Gentiles "so that the Gentiles might become an offering acceptable to God, sanctified by the Holy Spirit." But the ascription of sanctification to the Holy Spirit is not limited to Paul. Peter begins his first epistle by addressing his readers as those "who have been chosen according to the foreknowledge of God the Father, through the sanctifying work of the Spirit [or, in sanctification of the Spirit, ASV]" (1:2). In agreement with passages of this sort, the Westminster Confession calls the Holy Spirit "the sanctifying Spirit of Christ."[5]

The Holy Spirit is also indispensably involved in our *preservation* or *perseverance* in the faith. Two biblical figures now invite our consideration: "seal" and "pledge." The Spirit is said to be the seal of our final redemption in Ephesians 4:30, "Do not grieve the Spirit of God, with whom [or in whom, RSV] you were sealed for the day of redemption." In New Testament times a seal was often a mark of ownership; to be sealed with the Spirit means to be set apart as one who belongs to God. But in this passage to be "sealed with the Spirit" also means that the Spirit will keep us in fellowship with God until the final day of redemption.

Similarly, in Ephesians 1:13-14 Paul encourages us by saying, "Having believed, you were marked in him [Christ] with a seal, the promised Holy Spirit, who is a deposit guaranteeing our inheritance until the redemption of those who are God's possession." The word here rendered "a deposit guaranteeing" is *arrabōn*, which could also be translated "pledge." If we have the Spirit within us, Paul is affirming, we have the assurance that the future glory which is our inheritance in Christ will someday be ours—nothing can ever take that inheritance away from us.

The word *arrabōn* is used of the Spirit in two other passages. From 2 Corinthians 1:22 we learn that God has "set his seal of ownership on us, and put his Spirit in our hearts as a deposit, guaranteeing what is to come." And in 2 Corinthians 5:5 Paul instructs us that God, who is preparing for us a "building from God, an eternal house in heaven" (v. 1), "has given us the Spirit as a deposit, guaranteeing what is to come." The Holy Spirit, in other words, in a mysterious but wonderful way, enables us to persevere in the Christian walk until the day when we shall enter into our final inheritance on the glorified new earth.

THE GIFTS OF THE SPIRIT

Another way of studying the role of the Spirit in the process of salvation is to examine biblical teaching on the gifts of the Spirit and the fruit of the Spirit. These two must, of course, never be separated. Whatever gifts the

---

5. Westminster Confession, XIII, 3.

Spirit has given us should be exercised in love, joy, peace, and the other
aspects of the Spirit's fruit. Whenever we use our gifts without manifest-
ing the fruit, we shall be, as Paul says, only "noisy gongs" or "clanging
cymbals" (1 Cor. 13:1).

We look first at what the New Testament teaches about the gifts of the
Spirit. The most common word used by New Testament writers to
describe the Spirit's gifts is *charisma*. This word, however, has a wide range
of meaning. "Some twenty gifts are mentioned in connection with the
word [*charisma*]. The enumeration of the gifts in Romans 12 and 1 Corinthians 12 shows that they encompass a great breadth, from the administra-
tion of money to prophecy, from healing the sick to the state of celibacy."[6]
Commonly the word refers to some specific gift which God bestows on
his people. Bittlinger defines a *charisma* as follows: "A gratuitous manifestation of the Holy Spirit, working in and through, but going beyond, the
believer's natural ability, for the common good of the people of God."[7]

It is important to observe that the *charismata* mentioned in the New
Testament are not just the miraculous or spectacular gifts of the Spirit. Included among the *charismata* are the gifts of teaching, encouraging, giving
money (Rom. 12:8), helping others, and administering (1 Cor. 12:28). We
see, therefore, that there is something quite misleading about calling Neo-
Pentecostalism[8] the "charismatic movement." The New Testament *charismata* include far more gifts than the spectacular ones usually featured in
Pentecostal and Neo-Pentecostal circles, like tongue-speaking and healing. Every Christian has gifts with which he or she may and should serve
the Kingdom of God. In other words, not just Pentecostals and Neo-
Pentecostals, but the entire church of Jesus Christ is charismatic.

A common way of dividing the gifts of the Spirit is into miraculous
and nonmiraculous gifts. Among the nonmiraculous gifts are the gift of
teaching, of ruling, of giving, and of showing mercy. Among the
miraculous gifts are "gifts of healings" (*charismata iamatōn*, 1 Cor. 12:9);[9]
"workings of miracles" (*energēmata dynameōn*, 1 Cor. 12:10); and "speaking in different kinds of tongues" (*genē glōssōn*, 1 Cor. 12:10).

What is the function of the gifts of the Spirit? They enable believers
to perform specific types of service in the church, or to engage in some

6. Arnold Bittlinger, *Gifts and Ministries*, trans. Clara K. Dyck (Grand Rapids:
Eerdmans, 1973), p. 15.
7. Ibid., p. 18.
8. The movement beginning about 1960 in which Pentecostal teachings and practices
have spilled over into non-Pentecostal churches.
9. Note the double plural. J. Sidlow Baxter, in his *Divine Healing of the Body* (Grand
Rapids: Zondervan, 1979), understands this double plural as implying that no person ever
had a continuing gift of healing, but that every miracle of healing was a separate gift (pp.
282-83).

particular form of ministry in the Kingdom of God. Their purpose is to edify believers, to build up the church, and to serve the entire Christian community. They also have a missionary purpose: to bring those who do not believe into a saving knowledge of Christ, to strengthen new Christians in the faith, and to equip them for further witnessing.

There has been and continues to be considerable difference of opinion among Christians on the question of whether the miraculous gifts of the Spirit are still present in the church today. Both miraculous and non-miraculous gifts were in evidence in the Book of Acts, and are found in the lists of gifts given in 1 Corinthians 12. Christian theologians all agree that the nonmiraculous gifts of the Spirit are still with us today. Some theologians and Bible scholars, particularly those of Pentecostal and Neo-Pentecostal persuasion, say that the miraculous gifts are also still in the church today, whereas others question this.

It cannot be proved with finality that these miraculous gifts are still in the church today. Two weighty considerations strongly suggest that the miraculous gifts of the Spirit, like "gifts of healings" and speaking with tongues, are no longer to be looked for in the present-day church.

(1) Certain New Testament passages specifically associate the miraculous gifts of the Spirit with the work of the apostles as they laid the foundation of the church. One of these passages is Acts 14:3, "So Paul and Barnabas spent considerable time there [in Iconium], speaking boldly for the Lord, who confirmed the message of his grace by enabling them to do miraculous signs *(sēmeia)* and wonders *(terata)*." Note that the Lord enabled the apostles[10] to do these signs and wonders (obviously evidencing the miraculous gifts of the Spirit) in order to confirm both the gospel they were bringing and themselves as properly accredited messengers of that gospel.

To the Corinthians Paul writes: "The things that mark an apostle [or, the signs of a true apostle, RSV]—signs *(sēmeiois)*, wonders *(terasin)* and miracles *(dynamesin)*—were done among you with great perseverance" (2 Cor. 12:12). In this passage Paul is vindicating his apostleship over against men who claimed to be apostles but were not. You people at Corinth, Paul is saying, should certainly know that I am a true apostle, since the signs of an apostle were demonstrated in your midst in great abundance. We may be reasonably certain that these "signs, wonders and miracles" included the miraculous gifts of the Spirit which were so prominently in evidence in Corinth (see 1 Cor. 12 to 14). Is not Paul telling us here that the miraculous gifts which he was able not only to perform but also to transmit to others in Corinth served the purpose of authenticating his apostleship?

---

10. Barnabas is also called an apostle in v. 14.

In the Epistle to the Romans Paul makes a summarizing statement about his mission to the Gentiles, in which he again refers to the function of these miraculous gifts: "I will not venture to speak of anything except what Christ has accomplished through me in leading the Gentiles to obey God by what I have said and done—by the power of signs *(sēmeiōn)* and miracles *(teratōn)*, through the power of the Spirit" (15:18-19). Is it not clear from these words that the signs and wonders Paul was permitted to perform were means whereby Christ enabled him to bring the Gentiles to obedience, and were thus inseparably connected with his ministry as the apostle to the Gentiles? It is particularly significant that in the list of gifts which Paul urges the church at Rome to use in 12:6-8 miraculous gifts of the Spirit like healing and tongue-speaking are not mentioned. In chapter 15 Paul recognizes that these miraculous gifts had been manifested when he brought the gospel, thus implying that their proper function was to authenticate the gospel message. But he is not insisting that these signs and wonders must continue to occur every time believers meet together. The upbuilding of the church is served best, Paul is saying in this book, by the cultivation of such nonmiraculous gifts of the Spirit as teaching, giving, ruling, and showing mercy.

Very clear light is shed on the purpose of the miraculous gifts by Hebrews 2:3-4: "How shall we escape if we ignore such a great salvation? This salvation, which was first announced by the Lord, was confirmed to us by those who heard him. God also testified to it by signs *(sēmeiois)*, wonders *(terasin)* and various miracles *(dynamesin)*, and gifts of the Holy Spirit distributed according to his will." According to this passage the word of salvation was first announced by the Lord Jesus Christ. It was then confirmed to both the writer and the readers of this epistle by those who heard the Lord—that is, by the apostles. God testified *(synepimartyrountos)* to the genuineness of that salvation by those gifts of the Holy Spirit which are here called "signs, wonders and miracles." The purpose of the miraculous gifts of the Spirit, therefore, as described in this text, was to authenticate the message of salvation to these second-generation-after-Christ readers.

From the passages just examined we learn that the miraculous gifts of the Spirit were "signs of an apostle," intended to authenticate the apostles as true messengers from God, and the gospel which they brought as the word of God's grace. Since the work and witness of the apostles was foundational (see Eph. 2:20) and therefore unrepeatable, the miraculous gifts which authenticated the apostles are no longer needed today.

(2) We have no instruction in the New Testament telling us that the church must continue to manifest the miraculous gifts of the Spirit. There are no further references to these miraculous gifts outside of 1 Corinthians 12–14. Neither in the other Pauline epistles nor in the Catholic epistles is

there the slightest allusion to the gift of tongues or to "gifts of healings." The only apparent exception to this is found in James 5:14-15; this passage, however, does not describe a gift of healing but rather prayer for the sick by the elders of the church. Such prayer for the sick is definitely enjoined, but "gifts of healings" are not here endorsed.[11]

Lists of gifts of the Spirit found in New Testament passages other than 1 Corinthians 12 do not mention the miraculous ones just discussed. Earlier I referred to the list found in Romans 12:6-8; the gifts there enumerated are prophecy, ministry, teaching, exhorting, giving, ruling, and showing mercy. Tongue-speaking and "gifts of healings" are not mentioned. The only gift on the list which could in some sense be thought of as miraculous is prophecy. This seems to have been a gift whereby a person was given a specific revelation from God, or enabled to explain the plan of salvation; occasionally a prophet would predict future events. In 1 Corinthians 14, however, Paul expresses a decided preference for prophecy over against speaking with tongues (see vv. 1-5, 12, 18-19); what he stresses about prophecy in verse 3, in fact, is this: "Everyone who prophesies speaks to men for their strengthening, encouragement, and comfort." In mentioning this gift in Romans 12, therefore, Paul is obviously emphasizing, not its value as a spectacular manifestation of the power of the Spirit, but its usefulness for the edification and instruction of the church.[12]

There is also a brief listing of gifts in 1 Peter 4:10-11; only two gifts are mentioned here: speaking *(lalei)* and serving *(diakonei)*. No miraculous gifts are alluded to.

In the Pastoral Epistles Paul enumerates the qualifications for officebearers in the church. But neither in 1 Timothy 3:1-13 nor in Titus 1:5-9, where these qualifications are listed, does Paul breathe a word about tongue-speaking or "gifts of healings." On the other hand, the *charismata* that are prominently mentioned here are the gifts of teaching and ruling (1 Tim. 3:2, 4, 12; Tit. 1:6, 9; cf. also 1 Tim. 5:17; 2 Tim. 2:24). What Paul stresses as necessary for the continued welfare and growth of the church are such nonmiraculous gifts as the ability to teach and the ability to rule.[13]

---

11. "They [gifts of healing] . . . do not in Paul's epistles receive a permanent place in the continuing life of the church and in its upbuilding . . ." (Herman Ridderbos, *Paul*, p. 464). See also Don W. Hillis, *Tongues, Healing, and You* (Grand Rapids: Baker, 1969).

12. On the gift of prophecy, see Wayne A. Grudem, *The Gift of Prophecy in 1 Corinthians* (Washington, D.C.: University Press of America, 1983).

13. On the question of the continuation of the miraculous gifts of the Spirit in the church today, see also Benjamin B. Warfield, *Miracles Yesterday and Today* (Grand Rapids: Eerdmans, 1953; earlier title, *Counterfeit Miracles*); Anthony Hoekema, *What About Tongue-Speaking?* (Grand Rapids: Eerdmans, 1966), pp. 103-13; and *Holy Spirit Baptism* (Grand Rapids: Eerdmans, 1972), pp. 55-71; Richard B. Gaffin, Jr., *Perspectives on Pentecost* (Phillipsburg, NJ: Presbyterian and Reformed, 1979); Colin Brown, *That You May Believe* (Grand Rapids: Eerdmans, 1986), pp. 179-221.

THE HEALING MINISTRY OF THE CHURCH

It would appear, therefore, on the basis of the double line of argumentation just conducted, that the miraculous gifts of the Spirit, including gifts
of healing, are no longer to be looked for in the church today. It must be
admitted that this argumentation is not unanswerable. The conclusion just
mentioned is not one specifically stated by New Testament writers, but is
an inference from the New Testament data.

It cannot be denied, however, that God still answers the prayers of
his people, at times in miraculous ways. Most pastors can tell of marvelous
answers to prayer within their congregations—answers which have sometimes occurred after doctors have given up.

In recent years there has been a new emphasis among evangelical
Christians on the church's ministry of healing. Missionaries have told me
that when new churches are being planted in such countries as Nigeria,
Sri Lanka, and China dramatic healings have occurred in answer to
prayer: sick people have recovered, diseased eyes have been healed, persons have been cured of snake bites, and the like. Dr. C. Peter Wagner,
Professor of Church Growth at Fuller Theological Seminary, affirms that
the phenomenal growth of the church in Latin America is found chiefly
in the Pentecostal churches, where there are many healings in answer to
prayer (which he calls "signs and wonders"). He states that "we do not
see much church growth where there are no accompanying signs and
wonders."[14]

In the past two decades there has also been a revival of the ministry
of healing in the United States and in Europe. Not only Pentecostal
churches and charismatic groups but also Anglican, Episcopal, Lutheran,
Presbyterian, and Reformed churches have begun to hold healing services
or to invite worshipers to come forward for healing at the close of regular
services. There is now a growing literature on the ministry of healing in
the church.[15]

What does the Bible teach about healing? Physical healing was an essential aspect of the ministry of Jesus. Note, for example, Matthew 9:35,
"Jesus went through all the towns and villages, teaching in their
synagogues, preaching the good news of the kingdom and healing every

14. From an address given at the 1986 Oak Brook Conference on Ministry in Oak
Brook, IL, on October 14, 1986. See also his *What Are We Missing?* (Carol Stream, IL: Creation
House, 1978).
15. See, e.g., Morton T. Kelsey, *Healing and Christianity* (New York: Harper and Row,
1973); Francis MacNutt, *Healing* (Notre Dame, IN: Ave Maria Press, 1974); J. Sidlow Baxter,
Divine Healing of the Body; Roy Lawrence, *Christian Healing Rediscovered* (Downers Grove:
InterVarsity, 1980); John Wimber, *Power Evangelism* (San Francisco: Harper and Row, 1986).
Cf. also the *Acts of Synod of the Christian Reformed Church,* 1973, pp. 453-55.

disease and sickness." Further, Jesus gave his disciples authority to heal diseases, both the twelve (Matt. 10:1) and the seventy (Luke 10:1, 9). These healings by Christ, however, were signs of his messianic identity (Matt. 11:4-6; John 10:25-26, 38; Acts 2:22). As we saw earlier in this chapter, the miraculous healings brought about by Jesus' apostles served both to confirm the gospel they were bringing and to identify them as properly accredited messengers of that gospel (Acts 14:3; Rom. 15:18-19; Heb. 2:3-4). In fact, in 2 Corinthians 12:12 these miraculous healings are called the "signs of a true apostle" (RSV). The fact that Jesus and the apostles (who laid the foundation of the church) were able to perform supernatural healings, therefore, does not necessarily imply that we who are Jesus' followers can still bring about such miraculous healings today.

Yet the Bible calls God our healer (Exod. 15:26, RSV) and teaches that God heals our diseases (Ps. 103:3). Then, too, the Scriptures teach us to pray when we are ill or in other kinds of trouble, and promise that our prayers will be answered (though not always in the way in which we expect them to be answered). The following promises that God will hear and answer our prayers certainly do not exclude prayers for the healing of our illnesses: Psalm 91:15; Mark 11:24; Luke 11:9-10; John 15:7; 1 John 5:14-15. The Bible also gives us the following examples of healings in answer to prayer: Isaiah 38:2-5 (Hezekiah); Matthew 15:21-28 (the Canaanite woman); John 4:46-53 (the royal official).

When we think about biblical teaching on healing, James 5:14-16, a well-known and oft-quoted passage, immediately springs to mind:

> (14) Is any one of you sick? He should call the elders of the church to pray over him and anoint him with oil in the name of the Lord. (15) And the prayer offered in faith will make the sick person well; the Lord will raise him up. If he has sinned, he will be forgiven. (16) Therefore, confess your sins to each other and pray for each other so that you may be healed. The prayer of a righteous man is powerful and effective.

The main theme of the passage is not the efficacy of anointing with oil but the power of prayer—see the concluding sentence and note the example of Elijah in verses 17-18. The situation James here describes is that of a person who is obviously "too sick to go to church"; hence he is invited to ask the elders to come to his house. The "elders of the church" were probably older men who had governing and sometimes teaching authority in these early congregations (James is commonly thought to have been written before A.D. 50).

What were these elders asked to do? Literally translated, "let them pray over him, having rubbed him with oil in the name of the Lord." The words rendered "anoint him with oil" in the New International Version (and in most other English versions) are a translation of *aleipsantes elaiō*.

There are two New Testament words commonly translated "anoint": *aleiphō* (the present tense of the verb just mentioned) and *chriō* (the verb from which the English term "Christ" [the Anointed One] is derived). *Chriō* is the more sacred or religious term; it is applied to the anointing of Christ with the Holy Spirit (Luke 4:18; Acts 4:27; 10:38; Heb. 1:9), and to the anointing of Christians by God (2 Cor. 1:21). *Aleiphō*, however, is the more mundane or secular term. It is used of the application of spices to the dead body of Jesus (Mark 16:1) and of the rubbing of ointment on Jesus' feet (Luke 7:38, 46; John 11:2; 12:3). In the passage under discussion, therefore, the expression means "rubbing with oil," not "anointing with oil."[16]

In ancient times people used olive oil in this way; rubbing or massaging the body with oil was a common medicinal practice. It will be recalled that in the Parable of the Good Samaritan the Samaritan is said to have applied oil and wine to the injured man's wounds (Luke 10:34). Still today in the Middle East sick people are often rubbed with oil.

The grammatical structure of the sentence suggests the possibility that the elders first rubbed the sick person with oil (presumably olive oil) and then prayed over him (or her). The application of the oil, however, was for medicinal purposes.[17] James is saying, in other words, that the church's ministry to the sick should include the best medical help that can be found.

The expression which follows in verse 14, "in the name of the Lord," applies to both the praying and the rubbing with oil. These words imply that when the elders thus ministered to the sick, they were doing so as representatives of the Lord, asking the Lord to bless both the medicinal treatment and the prayer. Since, however, the name of the Lord also means his revelation, we must say a bit more about it. According to John 14:14 Jesus told his disciples, "You may ask me for anything in my name, and I will do it." Prayer in Christ's name is prayer which is in harmony with what Christ has revealed about himself; it therefore implies "not my will but your will be done." The prayer for healing which James here recommends must therefore always ask, "Grant this healing, Lord, if it be your will."

16. Note that in the only other New Testament passage where the word "anointing" is associated with healing it is *aleiphō* that is used: "They [the twelve] drove out many demons and anointed many sick people with oil and healed them" (Mark 6:13).

17. On the question of the function of the oil, see R. C. Trench, *Synonyms of the New Testament* (1880; Grand Rapids: Eerdmans, 1948), pp. 136-37; R. C. H. Lenski, *Hebrews and James* (Columbus: Wartburg, 1946), pp. 660-61; Spiros Zodhiates, *The Patience of Hope* (Grand Rapids: Eerdmans, 1960), pp. 122-31; John Wilkinson, "Healing in the Epistle of James," *Scottish Journal of Theology*, Vol. 24, No. 3 (August 1971), pp. 338-40. Other interpreters, however, view the anointing with oil here as an act of consecration.

James goes on to say in verse 15, "and the prayer offered in faith [literally, the prayer of faith] will make the sick person well; the Lord will raise him up." James here stresses the importance of faith—the faith of the person being prayed for as well as that of the elders who are praying. Earlier in his epistle James had warned that a "double-minded" person who does not believe but doubts will not receive anything from the Lord (1:6-8). But there is more to be said. One of the problems involved in the interpretation of this verse is the absoluteness of the statement, "the Lord will raise him up"—it seems to leave no room for instances where healing does not occur. Verse 15, however, must be seen in the light of what James said in 4:13-17. There he counsels his readers against presumptuously saying, "tomorrow I will do this or that"; rather, he cautions, you should say, "if it is the Lord's will, we will live and do this or that" (4:15). Surely the same qualification must apply to the prayer for the sick he recommends in chapter 5. The "prayer offered in faith" does not try to dictate to God—"God, you *must* heal this person." Rather, the person praying submits himself to God's sovereignty: "Lord, heal this sick friend if such healing be your will." Praying in this way does not impose limitations on our petitions; rather, it takes away limitations—those occasioned by our imperfect knowledge of what is best for the sick person. After all, the purpose of prayer is not to try to make God agree with us, but to bring us into harmony with his will.[18]

The last sentence of verse 15, translated literally, reads, "If he has been committing sin, it will be forgiven him." The tense of the first verb indicates continued and persistent sinning. The passage suggests a possible connection between persistent sin and illness; in 1 Corinthians 11:30, it may be recalled, Paul indicates that in some instances there could be such a connection: "That [your sinful behavior when the Lord's Supper is celebrated] is why many among you are weak and sick." But the story of Job and Jesus' words about the man born blind (John 9:3) show that often illnesses are not related to or caused by specific previous sins. It is of course true that all sick people are also sinners, and that their need to have their sins forgiven is even more crucial than their need to be healed of physical illness. Perhaps James's point here is simply this: in answer to believing prayer, there will be healing in the area of forgiveness as well as physical healing, if it be God's will.

In verse 16 James says, "Therefore, confess your sins to each other and

18. I do not therefore agree with people who say, as some do, that "a prayer for healing should never be accompanied by the words, 'if it be thy will' " (Lawrence, *Christian Healing*, p. 113). Prayer for healing must always be accompanied, either verbally or nonverbally, by the addition, "if it be your will."

pray for each other so that you may be healed." Though nothing is said here about sickness, the word "healed" *(iathēte)* suggests that James is still thinking about sick people (though "healing" may refer to other areas than just the physical). At this point in the passage James goes beyond prayer by the elders. Here he tells us that all the members of the congregation can take part in its healing ministry. We should all confess our sins to each other and pray for each other, so that God may grant us healing of the spirit as well as healing of the body. Here, incidentally, rubbing with oil is not mentioned.

The concluding sentence of verse 16 underscores the importance of prayer—the main point of the entire passage: "The prayer of a righteous man is powerful and effective."

A few observations are now in order. James writes about healing in answer to prayer; neither the elders who are asked to pray nor the other members of the congregation whom he mentions in verse 16 are said to be people who possess "gifts of healing." Note, further, that the praying James here specifies occurs in the sick person's home. Though this injunction does not rule out praying for the sick during meetings of the congregation, such "healing services" are not specifically recommended. Moreover, the passage says nothing about the laying on of hands. Again, this does not mean that such laying on of hands is wrong; the only conclusion we can draw is that it is not essential to the ministry of healing. It should also be observed that James prescribes a combination of medical means and prayer. And we need both. Doctors and nurses are indeed engaged in a healing ministry, and we praise God for them. Surely sick people need the best of medical attention. But we also need to pray for their healing.

Some *cautions* should be uttered. First, we cannot expect that physical healing will occur every time we pray for the sick. This was true even in New Testament times. The Apostle Paul was able to exercise the gift of healing, but even he either could not or did not heal every illness with which he came into contact. To Timothy he wrote, "I left Trophimus sick in Miletus" (2 Tim. 4:20). To the Philippians Paul mentioned an almost fatal illness which he either could not or did not prevent: that of Epaphroditus, who "was ill, and almost died" (Phil. 2:27). Further, Paul himself lived with a painful "thorn in the flesh" (very likely some kind of physical ailment) which he repeatedly asked the Lord to remove, but which God did not take way (2 Cor. 12:7-10).

When we pray for the healing of physical illnesses, therefore, we must always remember that it may not be the Lord's will to grant such a request. Sometimes, as in the case of Paul's thorn, God may desire to use an illness or a disability to enrich the spiritual life of the person involved (see Rom.

5:3; Heb. 12:4-11).[19] One thinks, for example, of Joni Eareckson Tada who, despite her crippling disability, has been marvelously used by God in a ministry of love to thousands of handicapped people.

A second caution: When a person who has been prayed for is not physically healed, we must never say, "He (or she) did not have enough faith." Such a statement is cruel and judgmental; it is an attempt to read someone else's heart—something only God can do. Further, such a statement may be totally false. Certainly no one can say that the reason Paul's thorn was not removed was that he lacked faith. Genuine faith is ready to submit to the Lord's will, and in a specific instance it may not be the Lord's will to heal. By way of illustration, note the following letter from Professor Carl A. Clark which appeared in *Christianity Today:*

> This year I celebrate (?) the 60th anniversary of the accident that left me a paraplegic. Yet I have served the Lord as pastor, denominational administrator, and theological seminary professor. I did not have to be healed to experience the presence and power of the Holy Spirit. I have not known any Christian seriously ill or injured who did not pray for healing. Is Wimber [John Wimber, who was featured in an earlier issue of the magazine] saying that neither I nor any of the hundreds who prayed for my healing had "enough" faith?[20]

A final—and probably most important—caution is this: we must never allow physical healing to become the primary aspect of worship or of the work of the church. The primary goal of preaching and prayer must always remain the salvation of sinners and the equipment of God's people for kingdom service. I therefore have a problem with what is said about the work of John Wimber, pastor of Vineyard Christian Fellowship in California, in the August 8, 1986, issue of *Christianity Today:*

> Traditionally, the church has emphasized the power of God in the proclamation of the gospel and in the moral improvement of Christian lives. Wimber says this is deficient; he scorns the practice of claiming the Spirit's presence purely by faith. When the Holy Spirit moves in power, he says, you know without a doubt something supernatural has occurred.[21]

If Wimber has been quoted correctly here, I must register my dissent. The power of the Holy Spirit, both in New Testament times and today, is primarily revealed in the life-changing dynamic of regeneration and

---

19. Colin Brown puts it well: "There is no specific, unqualified promise of health and healing in the New Testament to those who have faith. But there are promises of forgiveness and grace to those who repent and believe. . . . If God heals, it is an uncovenanted mercy. But when he forgives, it is a covenanted mercy" (*That You May Believe*, pp. 202-203).

20. *Christianity Today*, Vol. 30, No. 14 (October 3, 1986), p. 8.

21. Tim Stafford, "Testing the Wine from John Wimber's Vineyard," *Christianity Today*, Vol. 30, No. 11 (August 8, 1986), p. 18.

sanctification — the kind of dynamic that changed church-persecuting
Saul into missionary Paul. "Signs and wonders," including miraculous
healings, must never be allowed to upstage the bringing of lost sons back
to the Father's home.

Elaborating a bit further on this point, I should like to call attention to
some of the more prominent usages of the word "power" *(dynamis)* in the
New Testament. According to Acts 1:8 the power which Jesus says the
apostles will receive when the Holy Spirit has been poured out is power
for witnessing. Paul tells us in Romans 1:16 that he is not ashamed of the
gospel since it is "the power of God for salvation to everyone who has faith"
(RSV). We learn from 1 Corinthians 1:18 that to us who are being saved the
power of God is revealed in the word or message of the cross. And in the
next chapter of 1 Corinthians Paul ties in his preaching with the power of
the Spirit: "My message and my preaching were not with wise and per-
suasive words, but with a demonstration of the Spirit's power, so that your
faith might not rest on men's wisdom, but on God's power" (1 Cor. 2:4-5).

According to Ephesians 1:19-20, Paul prays that the Ephesians may
know "what is the immeasurable greatness of his [God's] power *(dynamis)*
towards us who believe, according to the energy *(energeia)* of the strength
(kratos) of his might *(ischys)* which he exerted in Christ when he raised him
from the dead" [my own translation]. Paul here piles up four different
words for power, suggesting that he needs to stretch the language to its
limits to indicate the amazing divine strength available for believers—a
power as great as that which raised Christ from the dead. But the emphasis
here is not on miraculous healings or other spectacular phenomena but
on the power to live a new life for God, which will reveal itself in the doing
of good works to the praise of his name (2:10).

Three words for power are also used in Colossians 1:11, where Paul
prays that the Colossian believers may live a life worthy of the Lord,
"being strengthened with all power according to his glorious might so that
[they] may have great endurance and patience." Here the purpose of the
endowment with power is the growth of steadfastness and patience in the
midst of difficulties.

Earlier we looked briefly at the "thorn in the flesh" passage, 2 Corinthians 12:7-10. Assuming that this thorn was some kind of physical infir-
mity, we may see this incident as a possible divine response to a prayer
for healing. Three times Paul asked the Lord to take this thorn away, but
God's answer was, "My grace is sufficient for you, for my power is made
perfect in weakness" (v. 9). Paul then utters these remarkable words,
"Therefore I will boast all the more gladly about my weaknesses, so that
Christ's power may rest on me." Since the word translated "rest" is
episkēnōsē, derived from the Greek word for tent *(skēnē)*, Paul is really

saying, "so that the power of Christ may pitch its tent upon me." Paul has experienced a remarkable divine power, revealed not in the healing of his affliction but in the enduring of that affliction. He startles us when he says that through his continuing to bear the thorn he had asked God to remove, the power of Christ now permanently rests upon him. And he concludes, "For when I am weak, then I am strong" (v. 10). Here, then, is a power of God manifested not in the healing of a physical affliction but rather in the ability to live with such an affliction to the glory of God's name. This aspect of God's power we must never lose sight of.

To what conclusions may we come? First, that healing should be part of the normal concern of the church. By healing I mean healing in answer to prayer. Whether the church should minister to the sick in their homes, in hospitals, or in church services is relatively immaterial. But, it must be emphasized, the prayers of the Christian community—important as they are—do not guarantee physical healing.

Second, this ministry of healing does not exclude but includes the services of the medical professions. To refuse to use medical services, as some so-called "faith healers" suggest we should do, is to neglect what God in his providence has provided for the relief of illness, and thus to reveal disobedience to God.

Third, the healing for which the Christian community must pray is wider than physical healing. It must include spiritual and emotional healing, the removal of anxieties, healings of disruptive family relationships, and the like. People who ask for the prayers of fellow Christians ought to be encouraged to come with various types of need: the removal of deep-seated guilt feelings, the healing of secret sorrows, the acceptance of personal limitations, as well as recovery from physical illness. The goal of the church's healing ministry must be nothing less than the healing of the whole person. Roy Lawrence puts it well: "Christian healing is concerned not so much with cures as with wholeness; with that harmony with God which helps a person to be more of a person than he [or she] was before, spiritually, mentally, physically."[22]

THE FRUIT OF THE SPIRIT

As was said above, there is an important relationship between the gifts of the Spirit and the fruit of the Spirit, since the Spirit's gifts should never be exercised apart from the Spirit's fruit. We go on now to see what the Bible teaches about the fruit of the Spirit.

22. *Christian Healing*, pp. 24-25. See also John Wilkinson, "Healing in the Epistle of James," p. 344.

Paul describes the fruit of the Spirit in Galatians 5. After having shown that those who have been justified by faith in Christ should no longer be entangled in a yoke of slavery, but should now exercise their Christian liberty, Paul goes on in this chapter to point out that the key to the believer's newfound freedom is the Holy Spirit. The Christian life is now to be lived, not first of all in obedience to a set of rules (though the rules of God are still important guidelines for Christians), but in the strength of the Holy Spirit. "So I say, live by the Spirit, and you will not gratify the desires of the sinful nature [or, of the flesh, RSV]" (Gal. 5:16). After sketching the antithesis between the flesh *(sarx)* and the Spirit *(pneuma)*, Paul lists a number of "works of the flesh" (RSV) in verses 19-21. Then, by way of contrast, follows the description of the fruit of the Spirit: "But the fruit of the Spirit is love, joy, peace, patience, kindness, goodness, faithfulness, gentleness and self-control" (vv. 22-23).

The first thing that strikes us as we look at this description is that the fruit of the Spirit is one. Though we often tend to speak about the "fruits" of the Spirit, in Galatians 5:22 the word for fruit is in the singular *(karpos)*. The obvious contrast is with the works of the flesh: whereas the works *(erga)* are many, the fruit *(karpos)* is one. Perhaps Paul is suggesting that, though a life of fleshly indulgence lacks unity and integration, there is harmony and unified purpose in a life lived in the Spirit.

We may note another, though related, contrast here. Though there are, as we saw, many gifts of the Spirit, there is only one fruit. Both in 1 Corinthians 12 and in Romans 12 the word for gifts *(charismata)* is in the plural, and the clear teaching of these chapters is that not everyone has all the gifts. What Paul teaches us in Galatians 5, however, is that every true believer should bear the entire fruit of the Spirit. When I say this, I do not intend to disparage the gifts of the Spirit; we must all "eagerly desire the greater gifts" (1 Cor. 12:31). But, though no one has all the gifts, each of us should reveal the fruit. We can be saved without many of the Spirit's gifts, but we cannot be saved without the Spirit's fruit.

The fact that the Spirit's fruit is one, moreover, has another implication. It implies that growth in spiritual maturity is not a matter of practicing now this virtue and then that one, in piecemeal fashion. It is not a matter of saying to oneself: this week I'll practice love, next week I'll cultivate joy, and the week after that I'll work on peace. Spiritual growth means yielding ourselves habitually and totally to the Holy Spirit, being led by the Spirit, walking and living in the Spirit day by day and hour by hour. When we do so, we shall be growing in all these virtues together.

This leads to a second observation about the fruit of the Spirit: the fact that it is called fruit suggests the thought of growth. When fruit first appears on, say, an apple, pear, or peach tree, it is quite small; it takes a full season to bring the fruit to its full size and mature flavor. By way of analogy, we do not expect to see the Spirit's fruit in mature form in a young child or in a new convert; there must be time for ripening and maturing. Producing the fruit of the Spirit must, therefore, not be thought of as a single, climactic, datable happening, or as a kind of "second blessing" experience, but rather as a continuing process of spiritual growth. This growth, further, is not a process in which we remain passive; it involves a lifelong discipline of prayer, trust, and spiritual warfare.

A third observation about the fruit of the Spirit is that it is a multiple fruit. It is a single fruit with many facets. These facets are nine in number — nine Christian virtues, which we may conveniently divide into three groupings: virtues involving basic dispositions, virtues relating to others, and virtues relating to ourselves.

The first three virtues mentioned involve basic dispositions toward both God and man: love, joy, and peace. *Love*, the most important virtue, elsewhere called the fulfillment of the law (Rom. 13:10), is mentioned first. Since no object is specified, we may assume that love for both God and man is meant. We must love God above all, and others as ourselves. The Greek word *agapē* used here implies that self-giving love is meant: a love which does not ask, What is there in it for me? but which seeks to give itself unselfishly to others. It will be recalled that Paul also stresses the priority of love over all the other virtues in 1 Corinthians 13—a chapter which occurs in the midst of his discussion of spiritual gifts. The most brilliant of the gifts of the Spirit, Paul is there saying, is worse than useless without love.

When Paul next mentions *joy*, this must mean first of all the joy involved in being in Christ—"an inexpressible and glorious joy," to quote Peter's words (1 Pet. 1:8). Such joy in God should spill over into our fellowship with others. It is a sad commentary on the anemic state of our Christian faith that we have so many joyless Christians—believers who seem to think that the highest mark of Christian piety is a gloomy face and a doleful voice. If we are truly living and walking in the Spirit, our lives will radiate Christian joy—a joy so deep and genuine that nothing can ever take it away. And that joy will be our strength (Neh. 8:10)!

The third virtue is *peace*. Obviously, peace with God is meant—the peace which flows from the knowledge that we have been reconciled to God in Christ, that all our sins have been forgiven, that we can now call God Father, and that we are now heirs of everlasting life. This is a lasting peace, a peace which "transcends all understanding" (Phil. 4:7). Such peace with God is bound to affect our total life-style. It means contentment instead of complaint, trust instead of worry, serenity instead of constant anxiety.

The next three virtues involve our relationship to others. *Patience* (or longsuffering, KJV, ASV) means being slow to anger, patient with others, ready to forgive those who wrong us, ready to bear with those who annoy us. It includes a willingness to accept others just as they are, despite their faults and shortcomings, since God has accepted us just as we are.

Kindness involves courtesy, friendliness, and concern for the other person's feelings. It is the virtue Jesus revealed when he was always ready to help penitent sinners. The opposite of harshness, kindness means graciousness, sensitiveness in dealing with others, a loving approach toward people. In his rendering of a similar term in 1 Corinthians 13:4, J. B. Phillips has beautifully captured the thrust of this word: "it [love] looks for a way of being constructive."

The next virtue, commonly translated *goodness,* is harder to describe. "Beneficence" might be a better rendering of the word: a readiness always to do good to others. In our day, beneficence should reveal itself in social concern. Any so-called religious revival which is concerned only with our individual "happiness in the Lord" but is not concerned about the physical and spiritual needs of others is a fraud. We must be willing to become involved in the effort to solve the agonizing problems of twentieth-century life: poverty, racism, drug abuse, crime, abortion, environmental pollution, and the like.

The last three virtues involve our relationship to ourselves. *Faithfulness* means conscientiousness in performing the tasks God has given us. It also includes reliability. The faithful person is true to his or her word; he does not go back on a promise.

Gentleness, the next virtue mentioned, is the opposite of arrogance, rebellion, and violence. It flows out of humility, and involves a willingness to submit to others when such submission is not contrary to God's will. The gentle person does not always insist on his or her own way, but is willing to do all he or she can to cooperate with others.

The last-mentioned virtue, *self-control,* means literally "power within." It describes the art of ruling ourselves. It means not being at the mercy of our appetites, impulses, or moods, but being able to control ourselves. It is to be understood, of course, that this virtue, like the others just described, cannot be attained or maintained in our own strength but only in the strength of the Spirit.

All nine of these virtues, then, comprise the fruit of the Spirit. As we yield ourselves more fully to the Holy Spirit, we shall be growing not just in some but in all of them. Such yielding to the Spirit is the best antidote to self-centered living. For this is God's promise: "Walk by the Spirit, and you will not carry out the desire of the flesh" (Gal. 5:16, NASB).

In summary, we need both the gifts and the fruit of the Spirit. But we should never seek the gifts apart from the fruit. Teaching is a most valuable gift, but those whose teaching has its roots in conceit and causes strife, malicious talk, and evil suspicions are condemned in no uncertain terms (1 Tim. 6:3-5). Ruling is a gift by which the church can be greatly enriched, but a Diotrephes who abuses his ruling office for his own selfish purposes is sharply rebuked by the Apostle John (3 John 9-10). Exercising the gifts of the Spirit while at the same time revealing the fruit of the Spirit, however, is bound to bring great blessings.

Let us not neglect the Spirit's gifts. But, above all, let us seek the Spirit's fruit. For where the Spirit is yielded to, there the fruit will abound.

BAPTISM WITH THE SPIRIT

There is a further dimension to the work of the Spirit in the process of our salvation, to which we now turn. I refer to two topics which are often linked together: baptism with the Spirit and the fullness of the Spirit.

We look first at the biblical teaching on baptism with the Spirit (or, in shortened form, Spirit-baptism). Pentecostals and Neo-Pentecostals maintain that "baptism with the Holy Spirit" is an experience distinct from and subsequent to regeneration. This baptism is said to be something which every believer should seek.[23] When a believer has had this experience, Pentecostals say, he or she is endowed with power for life and service; also with "an overflowing fullness of the Spirit, a deepened reverence for God, an intensified consecration to God and dedication to his work, and a more active love for Christ, for his Word, and for the lost."[24]

It is my conviction that there is no biblical basis for the Pentecostal doctrine of baptism with the Holy Spirit as just described. Though the expression "baptism with the Spirit" does not occur in the New Testament, there are seven instances in which the verb "to baptize" is used in connection with the Holy Spirit. The expression "to baptize with" or "to be baptized with the Holy Spirit" is found six times in the New Testament: four times in the Gospels, and twice in Acts. (Though Pentecostals commonly speak of baptism "in" the Spirit, the KJV, RSV, and NIV all render the Greek preposition *en* in these texts by "with.")

In the four instances in which the expression "to baptize with the Holy Spirit" occurs in the Gospels (Matt. 3:11; Mark 1:8; Luke 3:16; and John 1:33), it describes the future historical event of the outpouring of the

23. Article 7 of the "Statement of Fundamental Truths" of the Assemblies of God, in *The Constitution and Bylaws of the Assemblies of God* (Springfield, MO: Gospel Publishing House, 1985), p. 107.
24. Ibid.

Spirit on the Day of Pentecost. So, for example, in Mark 1:8 John the Baptist is quoted as saying: "I baptize you with water, but he [Christ] will baptize you with the Holy Spirit." In the first of the Acts references, Acts 1:5, the expression, now in the passive voice, also refers to this event: "In a few days you will be baptized with the Holy Spirit." In these five instances, therefore, "baptism with the Holy Spirit" does not mean an experience which believers must go through after conversion, but a historic event which occurred on Pentecost Day: the bestowal of the Holy Spirit on the church in his fullness—an event which, like the resurrection of Christ, is not repeatable.

What does the expression mean in Acts 11:16, the second Acts reference? Peter is in Jerusalem, telling the Christians in Judea what had happened at the house of Cornelius in Caesarea a few days before. What happened in Caesarea was indeed a "baptism with the Spirit," but it was not an experience distinct from and subsequent to conversion; it was simultaneous with conversion. What Cornelius's Spirit-baptism meant is described in verse 18: "So then, God has granted even the Gentiles repentance unto life." It meant the bestowal of the Spirit for salvation on people who had not been Christian believers before this bestowal. In other words, it was the sovereign act of the Holy Spirit whereby Cornelius and his household were made one with Christ, and thus became members of Christ's body.

The one other New Testament passage which mentions Spirit-baptism is 1 Corinthians 12:13. In the preceding verse Paul has just told us that all Christian believers are one in Christ: "The body is a unit, though it is made up of many parts; and though all its parts are many, they form one body." Verse 13, which follows, gives the reason why this statement is true: "For we were all baptized with one Spirit into one body — whether Jews or Greeks, slave or free—and we were all given the one Spirit to drink." In quoting this passage from the New International Version, I have opted for "with one Spirit" (one of the alternative translations given in the margin) instead of "by one Spirit."

The reason I prefer "with" to "by" is twofold. (1) *Similarity in terminology* to the other six passages which speak of Spirit-baptism: In all the other six texts the preposition introducing the words "the Holy Spirit" is the Greek word *en*, which the NIV translates as "with." In 1 Corinthians 12:13 the Greek word introducing "one Spirit" is also *en*. Why not continue to render it "with"? (2) *Similarity in thought:*

> In every kind of baptism . . . there are four parts. To begin with, there are the
> subject and the object, namely the baptizer and the baptized. Thirdly, there

is the element with or in *(en)* which, and fourthly, there is the purpose for *(eis)* which the baptism takes place.[25]

In John the Baptist's baptism (see Matt. 3:11), the subject of the baptism is John, the object is John's disciples, the element into or with *(en)* which they are baptized is water, and the purpose of the baptism is "for *(eis)* repentance." In the case of the baptism with the Spirit which is predicted in Matthew 3:11, Christ is the baptizer, Christ's disciples are the object of the baptism, the Holy Spirit is the "element" into or with *(en)* which (really whom) the baptism takes place,[26] and the purpose of the baptism is here left unsaid. In the passage we are now considering, 1 Corinthians 12:13, all believers are said to be the object of the baptism, the Holy Spirit is the "element" into or with *(en)* which (really whom) they are baptized, and the purpose of the baptism is that they might form one body *(eis hen sōma)*. The baptizer is not mentioned, but we may assume from what was said about baptism with the Spirit in the other New Testament passage that he is none other than Jesus Christ.[27]

Does Paul in 1 Corinthians 12:13 agree with Pentecostal teaching that Spirit-baptism is an experience distinct from and subsequent to regeneration which should be sought by all Christians? Nothing could be further from the truth. To prove that the body of Christ is one, Paul here affirms: "we were all baptized with one Spirit into one body." What this means is plain as daylight: *all* Christians have been Spirit-baptized. Being baptized with the Spirit is here described as identical with regeneration—with the sovereign act of God whereby we are made one with Christ and incorporated into his body. You don't need to seek a Spirit-baptism as a post-regeneration experience, Paul is saying to the Corinthians and to us; if you are in Christ, you have already been baptized with the Spirit!

THE FULLNESS OF THE SPIRIT

The fact, however, that all Christians have been baptized with the Spirit does not mean that they are always fully yielded to the Spirit or are always filled

25. John R. W. Stott, *Baptism and Fullness* (Downers Grove: InterVarsity, 1976), p. 40. For the argumentation which follows, I am also indebted to Mr. Stott.

26. In both Matthew 3:11 and Luke 3:16 it is added that Christ will baptize his disciples "with fire"; these additional words, however, are not found in the other references to Spirit-baptism.

27. The distinction commonly made by Pentecostals and Neo-Pentecostals between a baptism *in* or *with* the Spirit in the passages from the Gospels and Acts, and a baptism *by* the Spirit in the Corinthians text, is therefore without compelling exegetical foundation. In all the passages involved, Christ is the one who baptizes with the Spirit.

with the Spirit. In Romans 8:9 Paul describes believers as people in whom the Spirit of God is living; yet in the same chapter he tells his readers— presumably believers—that by the Spirit they must put to death the misdeeds of the body (v. 13). Though in 1 Corinthians 12:13 Paul affirms that all Christians, including all the Corinthian believers, have been baptized with the Spirit, in 3:1 and 3 he calls these same Corinthians "worldly" (or "carnal," KJV, ASV), since he finds much jealousy and strife among them.

The fact that, though Christians receive the Holy Spirit at the time of regeneration, they do not necessarily remain filled with the Spirit is confirmed by our experience. Believers may drift away from God, may grieve the Spirit, may become proud, quarrelsome, loveless, or self-indulgent. It may well be true of many of us that though we have all of the Spirit, the Spirit does not have all of us. What believers need, therefore, is not to seek a postregeneration or postconversion "baptism with the Spirit," but rather to be more completely filled with the Spirit.

What, now, does the New Testament teach on the question of being filled with the Spirit? The expression "to be filled with the Spirit" occurs in three different ways in the New Testament:

(1) Sometimes being filled with the Spirit is a momentary experience which qualifies one for a specific task. In these instances the verb "to fill" is used in the aorist tense in the original Greek—a tense which describes momentary or snapshot action. So, for example, in Acts 4:8 we read, "Then Peter, filled (*plēstheis,* from *pimplēmi*) with the Holy Spirit, said to them . . ."; what now follows is Peter's speech to the Sanhedrin after the healing of the lame man. It seems clear that the filling with the Spirit spoken of there was a specific bestowal of the power of the Spirit on Peter, enabling him to speak boldly about the Christ in whose name this man had been healed. Other passages where this type of expression, pointing to a momentary filling with the Spirit, is found are Acts 4:31 and 13:9.

(2) Sometimes we find the expression "full of the Spirit" or "full of the Holy Spirit" (in these instances an adjective is used instead of a verb) employed as a description of certain types of persons. So, for example, it is said of Jesus that he was "full of the Holy Spirit (*plērēs pneumatos hagiou*)" when he returned from the Jordan (Luke 4:1). This type of expression is also used of the seven men who were chosen by the twelve to help in the daily distribution of food (Acts 6:3), of Stephen in particular (Acts 6:5; 7:55), and of Barnabas (Acts 11:24). In these passages being full of the Spirit is not just a momentary endowment for a specific purpose, but a permanent characteristic of a person's life.

(3) There are two places in the New Testament where a different verb is used for "filling" than the one referred to previously, and where the tenses of the verb describe continuation rather than a momentary filling.

The first of these is found in Acts 13:52. Here we read, "And the disciples were filled (*eplērounto*, from *plēroō*) with joy and with the Holy Spirit." Here the tense of the Greek verb is imperfect, implying that these disciples continued to be filled with the Spirit. The other passage, Ephesians 5:18, is the only one in which the expression "be filled with the Spirit" occurs in the epistles: "Do not get drunk on wine, which leads to debauchery. Instead, be filled with the Spirit *(plērousthe en pneumati)*." Here the tense of the verb, again a form of *plēroō*, is present, meaning that we must be continually filled with the Spirit.

Summing up, we may say that New Testament teaching on being filled with the Spirit involves the following three types of experiences: (1) a believer may at times ask for a specific filling of the Spirit to qualify him or her for a specific task. (2) Our goal ought to be so to conduct ourselves that those who observe our lives may feel free to describe us as men and women who are full of the Holy Spirit. (3) We must all continually and growingly be filled with the Spirit.

Since Ephesians 5:18 is an apostolic injunction which is still normative for us today, let us look at it more closely. This passage, along with the next three verses, reads as follows:

> Do not get drunk on wine, which leads to debauchery. Instead, be filled with the Spirit. Speak to one another with psalms, hymns, and spiritual songs. Sing and make music in your heart to the Lord, always giving thanks to God the Father for everything, in the name of our Lord Jesus Christ. Submit to one another out of reverence for Christ.

What is the evidence of being filled with the Spirit? It is not excessive emotionalism or spectacular phenomena (note that nothing is said here about either speaking with tongues or gifts of healing), but rather the following types of behavior: (1) worshiping God together and thus edifying one another; (2) making music in our hearts to the Lord—a joyful inner disposition; (3) always giving thanks to God for everything; and (4) submitting ourselves to fellow Christians out of reverence for Christ.

John R. W. Stott has summarized the evidence of being filled with the Spirit according to Ephesians 5:18-21 in these words:

> The wholesome results of the fullness of the Spirit are now laid bare. The two chief spheres in which this fullness is manifest are worship and fellowship. If we are filled with the Spirit, we shall be praising Christ and thanking our Father, and we shall be speaking and submitting to one another. The Holy Spirit puts us in a right relationship with both God and man. It is in these spiritual qualities and activities, not in supernatural phenomena, that we should look for primary evidence of the Holy Spirit's fullness.[28]

28. *Baptism and Fullness*, pp. 59-60.

We are struck by the prohibition with which verse 18 begins: "Do not get drunk on wine, which leads to debauchery." We see a number of contrasts here. "Do not get drunk on wine" suggests a life of dissipation in contrast with a life of useful service to God and man. The expression further suggests the degrading pleasures of intoxication in contrast with the higher pleasures given by the Holy Spirit. These words also portray the folly of escapism—of running away from problems by taking to drink (and if Paul were writing today, he would undoubtedly have said something about addiction to drugs), in contrast with the wisdom of honestly facing problems and solving them in the strength of the Spirit.

The positive injunction of verse 18 reads, "Be filled with the Spirit." We now note four things about this command:[29]

(1) The verb "be filled *(plērousthe)*" is in the imperative mood. What is said here is not just a hint or a helpful suggestion, but a command—one that comes to us from Christ, through one of his apostles. Being filled with the Spirit, therefore, is not just one option out of many, not simply a desirable but nonessential aspect of our Christian life. It is a command which every Christian must obey.

(2) The verb "be filled" is plural in number. "Let all of you be filled with the Spirit," Paul is saying. This is not a privilege reserved for the few; it is not an experience only exceptional Christians can have; it is not an unreachable ideal. All believers should be filled with the Spirit.

(3) The verb "be filled" is in the present tense. Since the present tense in Greek describes continuing action, these words could be rendered, "keep on being filled with the Spirit," or "be continually filled with the Spirit."

Those addressed in this epistle are said to have been previously sealed with the Spirit (1:13; 4:30). In each of these texts the verb translated "sealed" is in the aorist tense in Greek *(esphragisthēte)*—a tense which describes momentary or snapshot action. When we compare Ephesians 1:13 and 4:30 with 5:18, we learn that, though every believer has been sealed with the Spirit, not every believer remains filled with the Spirit. Spirit-sealed believers (and Spirit-baptized believers) must still be exhorted to be continually filled with the Spirit.

The present imperative teaches us that one may never claim to have received this filling once and for all. Being continually filled with the Spirit is, in fact, the challenge of a lifetime, and the challenge of every new day. Nothing but continued prayerfulness, continued spiritual discipline, and constant watchfulness will enable us to keep on being filled with the Spirit. Being filled with the Spirit, in other words, is not like receiving your M.D.

29. Cf. ibid., pp. 60-61.

from medical school—an experience you can have only once. It is rather like continuing to study the medical journals after you have received your M.D., and continuing to keep abreast of new medical developments in order to keep up with your field. It is not like being born; it is more like breathing.

(4) The verb "be filled" is in the passive voice. The thought is: let the Holy Spirit fill us. How? Since the Holy Spirit is a Person, the only way we can continue to be filled with him is to continue to yield ourselves fully to him. We must take away the obstacles that stand between us and full commitment to God; we must be willing to listen to the Spirit's voice and to follow the Spirit's leading.

A few New Testament passages describe being filled with the Spirit as consisting of walking or living by the Spirit (Rom. 8:4; Gal. 5:16, 25). What does it mean to live or walk by the Spirit? I would suggest two things: living by the Spirit's guidance and living in the Spirit's strength.

Living by the Spirit's guidance means waiting on the Spirit, asking what the Spirit would have us to do, and where the Spirit would have us go. This entails daily study of the Bible, since the Spirit does not lead us apart from the Word. The better we know the Scriptures, the better we shall know how to live by the Spirit. Negatively, living by the Spirit's guidance means to silence the clamor of fleshly voices, to quell the energy of fleshly haste, to restrain every impulse until it has been proved to be of God. Positively, it means to be guided by him, to listen to him as he reveals himself in his Word, and to yield to him continually.

Living by the Spirit's strength means leaning on him for the necessary spiritual power. It means *believing* that the Spirit can give us strength adequate for every need, *asking* for that power in prayer whenever we need it, and *using* that power by faith in meeting our daily problems. The only way we can live by the Spirit's strength is to keep in constant touch with him. The difference between a battery-operated radio and a plug-in radio is that the latter must always be plugged in to the source of power in order to operate. The Spirit gives us strength, not on the battery principle, but on the plug-in principle: we need him every hour.

CHAPTER 4

Union with Christ

"UNION WITH CHRIST," JOHN MURRAY ONCE WROTE, "IS . . . THE CENtral truth of the whole doctrine of salvation. . . . It is not simply a phase of the application of redemption; it underlies every aspect of redemption. . . ."[1] In the words of Lewis Smedes, union with Christ "is at once the center and circumference of authentic human existence"[2]—that is, authentic Christian existence.

We take up this topic next, therefore, because it underlies all of soteriology. John Calvin put it this way: "We must understand that as long as Christ remains outside of us, and we are separated from him, all that he has suffered and done for the salvation of the human race remains useless and of no value for us. . . . All that he [Christ] possesses is nothing to us until we grow into one body with him."[3]

The interrelatedness between union with Christ and the role of the Holy Spirit in our salvation (discussed in the previous chapter) is obvious. Only through the Spirit can we become one with Christ and can Christ live in our hearts. It will be important for us now to look at the biblical teaching on union with Christ. The reasons for this importance will become clear as these teachings are unfolded. We are not saved until we have been made one with Christ, and we remain saved only as we remain in union with Christ.

The New Testament describes this amazing truth—that we can become one with Christ—in two ways. Sometimes New Testament authors teach that as believers *we are in Christ*. The well-known text about our being new creatures here comes to mind: "Therefore, if anyone is in Christ, he is a new creation; the old has gone, the new has come" (2 Cor. 5:17). Other passages which contain this thought include John 15:4, 5, 7; 1 Corinthians 15:22; 2 Corinthians 12:2; Galatians 3:28; Ephesians 1:4, 2:10; Philip-

---

1. *Redemption — Accomplished and Applied* (Grand Rapids: Eerdmans, 1955), pp. 201, 205.

2. *Union with Christ* (Grand Rapids: Eerdmans, 1983), p. xii.

3. *Inst.*, III.i.1.

pians 3:9; 1 Thessalonians 4:16; and 1 John 4:13. To single out just one from this list, note that it was Paul's consuming passion to be in Christ: "I consider [all things] rubbish, that I may gain Christ and be found in him" (Phil. 3:8-9).

At other times, however, the writers of the New Testament tell us that Christ is in us. In Galatians 2:20, for example, Paul writes, "I have been crucified with Christ and I no longer live, but Christ lives in me." Elsewhere Paul celebrates the fact that "God has chosen to make known among the Gentiles the glorious riches of this mystery, which is Christ in you, the hope of glory" (Col. 1:27). This thought is also found in Romans 8:10; 2 Corinthians 13:5; and Ephesians 3:17.

There are, in fact, at least three passages, all in John's writings, where these two concepts (that we are in Christ and that Christ is in us) are combined: John 6:56 ("Whoever eats my flesh and drinks my blood remains in me, and I in him"); John 15:4 ("Remain in me, and I will remain in you"); and 1 John 4:13 ("We know that we live in him and he in us, because he has given us of his Spirit"). It would seem, therefore, that these two types of expression are interchangeable. When we are in Christ, Christ is also in us. Our living in him and his living in us are as inseparable as finger and thumb.

As we think about the scope and the breadth of union with Christ, we should see this union as extending all the way from eternity to eternity. Union with Christ begins with God's pretemporal decision to save his people in and through Jesus Christ. This union, further, is based on the redemptive work for his people which Christ did in history. Finally, this union is actually established with God's people after they have been born, continues throughout their lives, and has as its goal their eternal glorification in the life to come. We go on, then, to see union with Christ as having its roots in divine election, its basis in the redemptive work of Christ, and its actual establishment with God's people in time.[4]

---

4. In organizing the material in this way, I take leave to differ from my respected former teacher at Calvin Theological Seminary, Professor Louis Berkhof. He describes union with Christ as having four phases: (1) the federal union of Christ and those whom the Father has given him in the counsel of redemption (a pretemporal agreement between God the Father and God the Son); (2) the union of life ideally established in the counsel of redemption; (3) the union of life objectively realized in Christ; and (4) the union of life subjectively realized by the operation of the Holy Spirit (*Systematic Theology*, pp. 448-49). My difficulty with Berkhof's presentation is that the first three phases of union with Christ as he lists them are descriptions of a projected union which has not yet taken place. Actual union with Christ can only take place with actual people.

For this reason I prefer to designate Berkhof's earlier "phases" of this union as comprising its roots and its basis, and to reserve the expression "union with Christ" for the union which is actually put into effect between Christ and existing human beings.

THE ROOTS OF UNION WITH CHRIST

Union with Christ has its roots in divine election. The passage which springs to mind is Ephesians 1:3-4,

> Praise be to the God and Father of our Lord Jesus Christ, who has blessed us in the heavenly realms with every spiritual blessing in Christ. For he chose us in him before the creation of the world to be holy and blameless in his sight.

These words tell us that our thinking about union with Christ must begin with God's gracious decision, made before the creation of the world, to save his people in Christ.

God has blessed us, so Paul begins, with every spiritual blessing in Christ, not on the ground of our worthiness, but because *(kathōs)* God chose us in him (Christ) before the creation of the world. From the expression translated "before the creation of the world" *(pro katabolēs kosmou)* we learn that God's choosing of his people must be understood as having taken place before the universe *(kosmos)* was called into existence. This expression is found in two other places in the New Testament: John 17:24 ("You [the Father] loved me [Christ] before the creation of the world"); and 1 Peter 1:20 ("He [Christ] was chosen before the creation of the world, but was revealed in these last times for your sake"). Just as the Father loved and chose Christ before the foundation of the universe, so we who are Christ's people were chosen by the Father before the world was created and before any of us existed. The very thought boggles the mind! We shall never be able to understand it; we can only bow our heads in wonder.

God chose us "to be holy and blameless in his sight." These words not only show the purpose God had in mind in choosing us; they also take away all ground for pride. As Calvin says about this text, "If he [God] chose us that we should be holy, he did not choose us because he foresaw that we would be so."[5]

For our present discussion the most important words in the passage are "in him" *(en autō)*. From verse 3 we learn that they refer to Christ. "In him" again underscores the gracious mode of our salvation: God the Father chose us to be saved not because of any merit he foresaw in us but only on the basis of our predetermined oneness with Christ.

"He chose us in him" further implies that our election (that is, our being chosen by God to be saved) should never be thought of apart from Christ. Union between Christ and his people was planned already in eternity, in the sovereign pretemporal decision whereby God the Father

5. *Inst.*, III.xxii.3.

selected us as his own. Christ himself was chosen to be our Savior before the creation of the world (1 Pet. 1:20); Ephesians 1:4 teaches us that when the Father chose Christ, he also chose us. He decreed that Christ would have a people who belonged to him from eternity to eternity. Those chosen to be saved, in other words, were never contemplated by the Father apart from Christ or apart from the work Christ was to do for them—they were chosen *in Christ*. God did not decide first to save his people from their sins, and then later to bring in Christ as the executor of that salvation.[6] Union with Christ is not something "tacked on" to our salvation; it is there from the outset, even in the plan of God. As Herman Bavinck used to say, Christ must never be thought of apart from his people, nor his people apart from Christ.

The fact that we have been chosen in Christ from eternity is basic to the whole of soteriology. It is only because of our preassigned union with Christ from before the creation of the world that all the blessings of salvation eventually come to us. Here at the very beginning all human merit is excluded. To God be all the praise!

THE BASIS FOR UNION WITH CHRIST

Union with Christ has its basis in Christ's redemptive work. Since God the Father had presented to his Son a people to redeem from sin, Christ came to earth to carry out this redemptive work *for his people*. We must therefore never think of Christ's work of redemption apart from the union between Christ and his people which had been planned and decreed from eternity. We remember what the angel said to Joseph before Jesus was born: "You are to give him the name Jesus, because he will save his people from their sins" (Matt. 1:21).

In the tenth chapter of John's Gospel Jesus himself tells us that he came to earth to redeem a particular people. In verse 11 of that chapter we read, "I am the good shepherd. The good shepherd lays down his life for the sheep *(hyper tōn probatōn)."* *Hyper* with the genitive case means "for the sake of." These words tie in with what we learned from Ephesians 1:4 —there is a group of people who were chosen in Christ before the creation of the world; for this group, here called his sheep, Christ will lay down his life.

According to verse 26 Jesus goes on to say to the unbelieving Jews

---

6. It is therefore better to say that Christ is the *foundation* rather than the executor of our election. Cf. Lewis B. Smedes, *All Things Made New* (Grand Rapids: Eerdmans, 1970), pp. 124-25. See also G. C. Berkouwer, "Election in Christ," in *Divine Election*, trans. Hugo Bekker (Grand Rapids: Eerdmans, 1960), pp. 132-71.

who were surrounding him, "But you do not believe because you are not my sheep." The fact that these Jews do not believe on Jesus is here cited as evidence that they do not belong to Christ's sheep. This does not necessarily mean that it is impossible that any of them may later come to believe. At the moment, however, they do not believe, and thus reveal that they do not belong, at least at present, to Christ's sheep. If we put together verse 11 and verse 26, we conclude that the sheep for whom Christ was ready to lay down his life do not include everybody, since Christ specifically excludes from the number of his sheep those who refuse to believe on him.

If we now look ahead at verses 27 and 28, we note that the eternal security of Christ's sheep is tied in with the fact that Christ does his redemptive work for his people: "My sheep listen to my voice; I know them, and they follow me. I give them eternal life, and they shall never perish; no one can snatch them out of my hand." It is the sheep for whom Christ will lay down his life who enjoy this security, not those who reject him and thus reveal that they do not belong to his sheep. The conclusion is inescapable: Christ did his saving work specifically for his sheep, his people.

John's Gospel surprises us in another way. John tells us that Jesus sometimes refers to a group of people whom the Father had given to him. For example, according to John 6:39, Jesus said, "And this is the will of him who sent me, that I shall lose none of all that he has given me, but raise them up at the last day." In his so-called High-Priestly Prayer, recorded in John 17, Jesus said to the Father, "You granted him [the Son] authority over all people that he might give eternal life to all those you have given him" (v. 2), and also "I have revealed you to those whom you gave me out of the world" (v. 6). Later in the prayer Jesus petitioned, "Father, I want those you have given me to be with me where I am, and to see my glory" (v. 24). These passages clearly echo Ephesians 1:4, which speaks of the Father's choosing us in Christ before the creation of the world. The Father, in a way we shall never be able to fathom, in a way which is the afterglow of his indescribable love, gave to his Son before the universe was founded a people to redeem.

One may, of course, speak of the infinite value and worth of the death of Christ, as do the Canons of Dort.[7] One may say, as is often done, that Christ's redemptive work was *sufficient* for all, though *efficient* only for God's elect. But the fact remains that the redeeming work Christ did while he was on earth was done for a distinct group—for the church ("Christ

7. "This death of God's Son is the only and entirely complete sacrifice and satisfaction for sins; it is of infinite value and worth, more than sufficient to atone for the sins of the whole world." Canons of Dort, II,3 (1986 trans.).

loved the church and gave himself up for her," Eph. 5:25), or for a people of his own ("Who [Christ] gave himself for us to redeem us from all wickedness and to purify for himself a people that are his very own, eager to do what is good," Tit. 2:14).

The saving work of Christ, therefore, was done for his people — a people of his own possession, a people who belong to him for time and eternity. This work we must see as the meritorious basis for union with Christ. It is only because our Savior did all these things for his people that actual union between Christ and his own has become possible.

ACTUAL UNION WITH CHRIST

Having looked at the roots of and the basis for union with Christ, we now go on to see what the Bible has to say about the actual union established between Christ and his people in the course of history. This union underlies and makes possible the entire process of salvation. From beginning to end, we are saved only in Christ.

(1) *We are initially united with Christ in regeneration.* By regeneration, also called the new birth, is meant that act of the Holy Spirit whereby he initially brings a person into living union with Christ, so that he or she who was spiritually dead now becomes spiritually alive. Later this topic will be discussed in greater detail. At this time our concern is to see that it is at the moment of regeneration that actual union with Christ begins.

Ephesians 2:4-5 reads as follows: "Because of his great love for us, God, who is rich in mercy, made us alive with Christ even when we were dead in transgressions." I take it that "made us alive" refers to spiritual life, and therefore describes our regeneration, particularly since these words are contrasted with "when we were dead in transgressions." The passage, in other words, describes the transition from spiritual death to spiritual life. In the Greek this act of God's mercy is described as follows: *synezōopoiēsen tō Christō:* "made [us] alive together with Christ." The point Paul is making is that this "making alive" takes place in union with Christ. Though in ourselves, by nature, we were spiritually dead in sin, at a certain point in time God caused us to share the life of Christ, and thus to become spiritually alive. In other words, regeneration occurs when we are for the first time savingly united with Christ.

A few verses farther down we come across verse 10: "For we are God's workmanship, created in Christ Jesus to do good works, which God prepared in advance for us to do." Note particularly the phrase *ktisthentes en Christō Iēsou* ("created in Christ Jesus"). The word "created" pictures God's sovereignly calling into existence something that did not exist before. Here the term refers, not to the origin of the universe as in Genesis

1:1, but to the origin of new spiritual life in those who were spiritually dead before. We have been made a new spiritual creation, Paul is saying. The concept describes an entirely new kind of life—a life filled with good works, sparkling with love, and devoted to God's glory. But this new life begins in regeneration. Once again we see that we have been created anew (or regenerated) only in Christ Jesus. Not only did God choose us in Christ; he also re-created us in Christ.

It is therefore at the moment of regeneration that union between Christ and his people is actually established. This union is not only the beginning of our salvation; it sustains, fills, and perfects the entire process of salvation.

(2) *We appropriate and continue to live out of this union through faith.* It is important to remember that the only way in which we can appropriate union with Christ is by faith. Though, as we saw, it is the Spirit who brings us into this living union, we can only grasp and continue to enjoy this union by faith. By nature we are "old selves," enslaved to sin and alienated from God, but as we exercise our faith Christ can and does live in us. Through faith we actualize and experience our having been made new creatures in Christ.

In Galatians 2:20 Paul writes, "I have been crucified with Christ and I no longer live, but Christ lives in me. The life I live in the body, I live by faith in the Son of God, who loved me and gave himself for me." So strongly does Paul here express the truth of union with Christ that he affirms that there is a sense in which he is no longer living, but Christ is living in him. Yet in another sense he does still live: "The life I live in the body, I live by faith." He no longer lives as one who is a slave to sin; he now lives as a person in whom Christ dwells. But he can only become aware of and draw power from that indwelling of Christ through faith. Faith means living daily in the joyful awareness that Christ lives in us.

In Ephesians 3:16-17 Paul says, "I pray that out of his glorious riches he [the Father] may strengthen you with power through his Spirit in your inner being, so that Christ may dwell in your hearts through faith." The Greek verb here translated "dwell," *katoikeō*, is used in the New Testament to describe permanent residents of a town or village, in distinction from people whom we today would call "transients" (see Heb. 11:9).[8] Paul prays that Christ may live or dwell permanently in the hearts of his readers by faith. According to this passage, therefore, faith is the means whereby we continue to experience Christ's indwelling and whereby we are enabled to reveal that we are genuinely one with Christ.

---

8. The word *paroikeō* is here used to describe "a stranger in a foreign country." Cf. Moulton and Milligan, VGT, pp. 338, 495.

(3) *We are justified in union with Christ.* By justification is meant that act of God by which he imputes (or credits to the account of) believers the perfect satisfaction and righteousness of Christ in such a way that all their sins are forgiven and they are considered perfectly righteous in the sight of God.

It is important to see our justification as inseparable from union with Christ. James S. Stewart puts it well: "It is certain that such an idea as justification, for instance, can only be gravely misleading, when it is not seen in the light of a union with Christ in which the sinner identifies himself with Christ in his attitude to sin."[9] Sometimes we are tempted to understand Christ's work for us as "having paid for our sins" on the cross in a totally impersonal way; we then think of ourselves as accepting this payment also in an impersonal way, apart from fellowship with Christ. An analogy would be my having run up a bill at a clothing store, and my learning that some kind friend had paid the bill for me; I could accept such a payment without ever seeing my friend or having any kind of fellowship with him (except for a formal thank-you note). So-called "commercial" theories of the atonement tend to fall into the same erroneous understanding. But such views are quite wrong. The Bible teaches that we can appropriate the saving work of Christ for us, and thus be justified, only in a personal way, through living union with him.

1 Corinthians 1:30 illustrates this point: "It is because of him [God] that you are in Christ Jesus, who has become for us wisdom from God— that is, our righteousness, holiness and redemption." We are saved because we are in Christ, who has become for us our righteousness. Not only does Christ *bring* us righteousness; he *is* our righteousness. And we are righteous (or justified) only because we are in him.

Paul often comes back to this thought. In his second epistle to the Corinthians he says, "God made him [Christ] who had no sin to be sin for us, so that in him we might become the righteousness of God" (2 Cor. 5:21). Whereas in 1 Corinthians 1 Paul said that Christ became our righteousness, here he affirms that we can become the righteousness of God. The language again is striking. We don't just receive, or "share" (Today's English Version), but we become, become identified with, God's righteousness. This, however, happens only *in him.* When we are in Christ, God sees us, not as we are in our sin, but as we are in Christ—impeccably righteous.

In Philippians 3 Paul enumerates a number of things which he formerly considered gains—some based on the circumstances of his birth, some based on his own achievements. Though formerly he rested on these

9. *A Man in Christ* (New York: Harper and Brothers, [1935]), p. 152.

supposed gains, thinking that he had earned his salvation through his own merits, he now has learned to consider all these things loss for the sake of Christ:

> What is more, I consider everything a loss compared to the surpassing greatness of knowing Christ Jesus my Lord, for whose sake I have lost all things. I consider them rubbish, that I may gain Christ and be found in him, not having a righteousness of my own that comes from the law, but that which is through faith in Christ—the righteousness that comes from God and is by faith (vv. 8-9).

Paul no longer wants to be found "in himself"—to have God judge him solely on the basis of his own accomplishments. He knows that he can never be justified or saved in that way. He now wants "to be found in Christ," and in this way to possess "the righteousness that comes from God." No clearer passage could be adduced to show that we are justified only in union with Christ.

(4) *We are sanctified through union with Christ.* Sanctification in the progressive sense may be defined as that work of God by which the Holy Spirit progressively renews the life of the believer and enables him or her to live to the praise of God. This aspect of our salvation, too, can only be experienced in union with Christ.

Looking once again at 1 Corinthians 1:30, we note that Christ is there said to have become for us not only our righteousness but also our holiness (or sanctification, KJV, ASV, NASB, RSV; Gk. *hagiasmos*). If Christ is indeed our sanctification, we can only be sanctified through being one with him.

In John 15 Jesus, using the figure of the vine, describes the sanctified life as a life of fruitbearing:

> No branch can bear fruit by itself; it must remain in the vine. Neither can you bear fruit unless you remain in me. I am the vine; you are the branches. If a man remains in me and I in him, he will bear much fruit; apart from me you can do nothing (vv. 4-5).

Only as we continue to remain in Christ can we live the life of consecration to which God has called us.

Paul pictures the development of Christian maturity as a growing up of the believer into Christ, who is our Head (Eph. 4:15). We can only grow and mature in love, knowledge, and unity as we identify ourselves more and more with Christ. This thought is summed up in a masterful way in 2 Corinthians 5:17, "Therefore, if anyone is in Christ, he is a new creation; the old has gone, the new has come!"

Sanctification through union with Christ, however, does not mean that we lose our individuality. Rather, it means that our gifts and abilities are progressively honed, developed, and purified so that we become our best selves. James Stewart puts it this way, "Union with Christ, so far from obliterating the believer's personal qualities and characteristics, throws these into greater relief."[10] Lewis Smedes makes the point even more vividly: "Christ communicates Himself in a way that changes us without diminishing us, transforms us without deifying us, Christianizes us without making us Christs."[11]

(5) *We persevere in the life of faith in union with Christ.* The Bible teaches that true believers are so preserved by God that they are enabled to persevere in the life of faith to the end. This blessing of perseverance, however, can only be experienced in union with Christ. Jesus plainly teaches this in John 10:27-28, "My sheep listen to my voice; I know them, and they follow me. I give them eternal life, and they shall never perish; no one can snatch them out of my hand." If we are truly in Christ, in other words, we shall always be in him.

The same thought is conveyed in one of the most comforting passages in Paul's epistles:

> For I am convinced that neither death nor life, neither angels nor demons, neither the present nor the future, nor any powers, neither height nor depth, nor anything else in all creation, will be able to separate us from the love of God that is in Christ Jesus our Lord (Rom. 8:38-39).

Note that the love of God from which we cannot be separated is the love of God *in Christ*. Only in Christ is this love revealed, and therefore only in union with Christ can this love be experienced. If we are in Christ we shall persevere to the end, since no created power and no possible future happening ("neither the present nor the future") will in any way be able to separate us from Christ and from the love of God which is in Christ.

(6) *We are even said to die in Christ.* From Romans 14:8 we learn, "If we live, we live to the Lord; and if we die, we die to the Lord. So, whether we live or die, we belong to the Lord." Not only does Paul say here that we die to or in the Lord; he says that we continue to be the Lord's even after we die. This thought is strikingly expressed in the Heidelberg Catechism:

> Q. What is your only comfort in life and in death?
>
> A. That I am not my own, but belong—body and soul, in life and in death— to my faithful Savior Jesus Christ.[12]

It is therefore not surprising that in 1 Thessalonians 4:16 Paul describes

---

10. Ibid., p. 166.
11. *All Things Made New*, p. 188.
12. Heidelberg Catechism, Q. and A. 1 (1975 trans.).

believers who have died as "the dead in Christ." And this thought is echoed in Revelation 14:13, "Blessed are the dead who die in the Lord *(en kyriō)* from now on." Even when we die we die in Christ.

(7) *We shall be raised with Christ.* In one sense, of course, believers have already been raised with Christ (Col. 3:1). Already in this life, as James S. Stewart so aptly writes, the believer "has begun to live daily in the romance and wonder and thrilling stimulus of Jesus' fellowship."[13] But there remains a resurrection still to come—that of the body at the time of Christ's return. This resurrection of the body, however, will also be a resurrection in Christ. We learn this from 1 Corinthians 15:22, "For as in Adam all die, so in Christ all will be made alive." Paul is not here discussing the resurrection of unbelievers; his only concern here is with the resurrection of believers—of those who belong to Christ (see v. 23). Since Christ, who is our Head, was raised from the dead, we who belong to him will also be raised in the physical sense. But we shall be resurrected *in Christ*—in fellowship, in union with him.

(8) *We shall be eternally glorified with Christ.* "When Christ, who is your life, appears," writes Paul in Colossians 3:4, "then you also will appear with him in glory." The future glorification of God's people, that is to say, will be a sharing of the final glorification of Christ. 1 Thessalonians 4:16-17 describes what will happen when Christ again returns to earth: The dead in Christ will rise first; then we who are still alive and are left "will be caught up together with them in the clouds to meet the Lord in the air. And so we will be with the Lord forever." Future glory, in other words, will be nothing other than a continued unfolding of the riches of union with Christ. Much of what the future holds in store for us is left undescribed in the Bible. But of one thing we can be sure: we shall be eternally in Christ and with Christ, sharing his glory.

Summing up, we could say that union with Christ has its source in our election in Christ before the creation of the world and its goal in our glorification with Christ throughout eternity. Union with Christ was planned from eternity, and is destined to continue eternally. This union, therefore, is what makes our life as Christians significant, happy, and victorious. We are pilgrims and strangers on this earth, but Christ lives in us forever.

THE SIGNIFICANCE OF UNION WITH CHRIST

Once you have had your eyes opened to this concept of union with Christ, you will find it almost everywhere in the New Testament. This thought is

13. *A Man in Christ,* p. 192.

especially prominent in the letters of Paul. Though we usually think of John as a writer who stresses our union with Christ, it would be a great mistake to think of this emphasis as lacking in Paul. As a matter of fact, the expression "in Christ" *(en Christō)* does not occur in John's writings, whereas this expression, together with cognate expressions such as "in the Lord" *(en Kyriō)* or "in him" *(en autō)*, occurs 164 times in Paul's epistles.[14] (It should be added, however, that "in me" *[en emoi]*, referring to Christ, does occur frequently in John's Gospel, and that "in him" *[en autō]* is often found in John's epistles.)

The person who made this discovery about the phrase "in Christ" *(en Christō)* was G. Adolf Deissmann who, in 1892, wrote his *Die Neutes-tamentliche Formel "in Christo Jesu"* (The New Testament Formula "in Christ Jesus"). He had made a study of the use of "in" *(en)* with the personal dative in Greek literature, and had concluded that Paul was the originator of the formula as a technical religious expression.[15] He found that, whereas the Synoptic Gospels use the word "with" *(meta)* to indicate fellowship with Jesus, Paul consistently uses "in" *(en)* for this. The expression "in Christ," Deissmann concluded, is one of the most characteristic phrases in Paul's epistles.

So conspicuous is the teaching of union with Christ in Paul's writings that one author even finds in this doctrine the key to Paul's theology. I refer to James S. Stewart, whose book, *A Man in Christ*, is a classic treatment of the subject. From the preface I quote the following: "The conviction has grown steadily upon me that union with Christ, rather than justification or election or eschatology, or indeed any of the other great apostolic themes, is the real clue to an understanding of Paul's thought and experience...."[16] For Paul, Stewart says, Christianity was not just a speculative system but a new quality of life: a life in Christ! Paul describes that new quality in such words as these: "I no longer live, but Christ lives in me" (Gal. 2:20); and "To me to live is Christ" (Phil. 1:21).

Stewart goes on to say, "We can regard the doctrine of union with Christ, not only as the mainstay of Paul's religion, but also as *the sheet-anchor of his ethics*."[17] He develops this thought by showing that, for Paul, to be united with Christ means to be identified with Christ's attitude toward sin,[18] to be possessed by an ethical motive of the first order,[19] to

14. G. Adolf Deissmann, *Die Neutestamentliche Formel "in Christo Jesu"* (Marburg: N. G. Elwert, 1892), p. 3.
15. Ibid., p. 70.
16. *A Man in Christ*, p. vii.
17. Ibid., p. 194.
18. Ibid., p. 196.
19. Ibid., p. 197.

have available a source of power,[20] and to be engaged in a lifelong struggle with sin.[21] Stewart summarizes this section of his book as follows:

> Paul would have said that a Christian is a man who strives, every day he lives, to make more and more real and actual and visible and convincing that which he is ideally and potentially by his union with Jesus Christ. . . . His relationship to Christ constrains him. It is a fact, but it is also a duty. It is a present reality, but also a beckoning ideal. . . . "Are you in Christ?" says Paul to the believer. "Then *be* a man in Christ indeed!"[22]

Union with Christ, however, should not be understood only in an individualistic sense. Though it does bring about the renewal of individuals, it does much more than this. Ultimately it involves the renewal and re-creation of the entire universe. Lewis Smedes has said it well:

> The familiar text about being "new creatures in Christ" should not be waved too easily as a slogan for what happens "in me" when I am convinced. The design of Christ's new creation is far too grand, too inclusive to be restricted to what happens inside my soul. No nook or cranny of history is too small for its purpose, no cultural potential too large for its embrace. Being in Christ, we are part of a new movement by His grace, a movement rolling on toward the new heaven and new earth where all things are made right and where He is all in all.[23]

One of the ways in which the doctrine of union with Christ is helpful is in enabling us to preserve a proper balance between two major aspects of the work of Christ: what we might call the *legal* and the *vital* aspects. The Western branch of the Christian church, represented by such theologians as Tertullian and Anselm, tended to emphasize the "legal" side of Christ's work. The aspect of sin these theologians were inclined to stress was guilt, which Christ took away through his atonement, by which he made satisfaction for us and thus paid our debt; the outstanding soteriological blessing was seen as justification; and the most important day on the ecclesiastical calendar was thought to be Good Friday. The Eastern wing of the church, however, represented by such theologians as Irenaeus and Athanasius, was more inclined to stress the "vital" or "life-sharing" side of Christ's work. The aspect of sin these theologians tended to emphasize was pollution, which Christ took away by joining us to himself through his incarnation; the outstanding soteriological blessing was seen as sanctification; and the most important feast day for the church was Easter. For the Western church, the central boon of the Christian life was

20. Ibid.
21. Ibid., p. 198.
22. Ibid., p. 199.
23. *Union with Christ*, p. 92.

deemed to be forgiveness, whereas for the Eastern church it was everlasting life. The Western church tended to accent the Christ who is *for us;* the Eastern church, on the other hand, was more inclined to celebrate the Christ who is *in us.*

We must always keep these two aspects of Christ's work together: the legal and the vital, Christ for us and Christ in us. Standing as we do in the Western tradition, we are probably inclined to overstress the legal aspect of our Savior's work and to understress the vital or life-sharing aspect. The doctrine of union with Christ can help us to keep these two facets in proper balance. Christ came to earth not just to pay the price for our salvation, as one might pay an overdue bill, but also to bring us into and keep us always in living union with himself. Through union with Christ we receive every spiritual blessing. Christ not only died for us on Calvary's cross many years ago; he also lives in our hearts, now and forever.

CHAPTER 5

The Gospel Call

THE CALL OF THE GOSPEL MUST BE BROUGHT TO ALL PEOPLE. THE BIBLE leaves us in no doubt about this. In his Great Commission Jesus said to his disciples and to the church of all ages, "Go and make disciples of all nations." Though the churches of Reformed persuasion have always maintained the doctrines of unconditional election (that God has graciously chosen his people from before the creation of the world) and definite atonement (that Christ atoned for the sins of those who had been chosen as his people), these churches have also—though with occasional exceptions—affirmed that the offer of the gospel should be brought to all hearers of the word.

The Scriptures clearly teach that the gospel must be preached to all. Whether we can square this with particular election is another question. But the rule for our preaching must always be the revealed will of God. In the last analysis, it is God's business to bring into harmony the predetermined outcome of the preaching of the gospel with the general offer of salvation. We are bound to the means God has prescribed for bringing people to salvation. And the most important of these means is the preaching of the gospel.

The gospel call can be defined as follows: The offering of salvation in Christ to people, together with an invitation to accept Christ in repentance and faith, in order that they may receive the forgiveness of sins and eternal life.[1] We may therefore distinguish the following three elements:

(1) *A presentation of the facts of the gospel and of the way of salvation.* The work Christ has done for our salvation must be clearly and carefully set forth. This should be done in language which is understandable to people today, and in a way that is relevant to present-day needs and problems. Important as it is to be relevant, however, the preacher must first of all be faithful to the Scriptures. There is a sense in which the message of the crucified Christ will always seem irrelevant and offensive. It is not pleasant to be told that we are sinners, by nature objects of God's wrath,

1. Adapted from Berkhof, ST, p. 459.

unable in our own strength to work our way out of this predicament. Paul found this to be so; yet he continued to preach the gospel which gave some people offense: "We preach Christ crucified: a stumbling block to Jews and foolishness to Gentiles, but to those whom God has called, both Jews and Greeks, Christ the power of God and the wisdom of God" (1 Cor. 1:23-24).

(2) *An invitation to come to Christ in repentance and faith.* The gospel call must be more than a presentation; it must include an earnest invitation. Jesus himself invites people to come to him in repentance and faith: "Come to me, all you who are weary and burdened, and I will give you rest" (Matt. 11:28). The preacher should not minimize the seriousness of sin, but should stress the importance of genuine repentance. It should be made clear that faith is not just intellectual assent to certain truths, but an acceptance of Christ with the total person, including commitment to his service.

The gospel invitation is, however, at the same time a command, like a summons which comes from a king. Note how Jesus expresses this point in the Parable of the Great Banquet: "And the master said to the servant, 'Go out to the highways and hedges, and compel people to come in, that my house may be filled' " (Luke 14:23). The gospel invitation is not one a person may feel free to accept or decline, as one might with an invitation to go bowling, but it is an order from the sovereign Lord of all creation to come to him for salvation—an order that can be ignored only at the cost of one's eternal perdition.

It is a serious mistake to think that pastors who preach to the members of established churches do not need to issue an invitation to accept Christ for salvation. Herman Bavinck conducts a significant discussion about extremes to be avoided in preaching.[2] Well-balanced preaching, he says, should combine the covenantal and the evangelistic emphases. In sermons addressed to people who have not heard the gospel previously, the preacher must not merely invite his hearers to believe and repent; he must also build them up in the faith. In sermons addressed to members of established churches, on the other hand, the preacher may not rest content with building up believers in the faith, or with merely drawing out the implications of the faith which is assumed to be in them. There must always be, even in the preaching that is addressed to church members, an earnest summons to faith and repentance. No preacher may blandly assume that everyone in church is saved. There will always be children and young people who have not yet committed their lives to Christ, and there

2. *Roeping en Wedergeboorte* (Kampen: Zalsman, 1903), pp. 157-87. For an English summary of this discussion see "Two Types of Preaching," *Reformed Journal*, Vol. 5, No. 5 (May 1955), pp. 5-7.

will usually be adults who have not made a clear-cut decision for the Lord. These too must be addressed and urged to come to Christ.

(3) *A promise of forgiveness and salvation.* The gospel call must also include the promise that those who respond properly to this call will receive the forgiveness of sins and eternal life in fellowship with Christ. This promise is, however, conditional: you will receive forgiveness and salvation if you repent and believe. In later chapters repentance and faith will be discussed more fully. When I call the promise included in the gospel call conditional, I do not mean that this is a condition which human beings can fulfill in their own strength. God alone can enable the hearer of the gospel call to repent and believe. The hearer must therefore pray that God will empower him or her to do so, and must give God the praise when he does so. But the condition must be fulfilled if the blessing is to be received —this the preacher must make clear.

THE GOSPEL CALL INVITES ALL HEARERS

What are the characteristics of the gospel call? First, it is general or universal, involving an invitation which comes to everyone who hears the gospel. This is clear from the Parables of the Wedding Banquet (Matt. 22:1-14) and the Great Banquet (Luke 14:16-24). Each of these parables pictures the gospel call. Though there are points of difference between the two parables, the basic thrust of both is the same: someone (in Matthew's parable, a king; in Luke's, simply "a certain man"), having invited many guests to a banquet, sends his servants (or, as in Luke, his servant) out to bid the invited guests to come. When these refuse to come, the host sends his servant or servants into the streets and alleys of the town and into the roads and country lanes to bring others besides the originally invited guests into the banquet hall, so that his house may be filled.

In each parable a form of the word *kaleō* is used to describe the summoning of the guests who had been invited to the banquet (Matt. 22:3; Luke 14:17). In the Matthew passage, in fact, there is a combination of two forms of the verb: the king sent his servants *kalesai tous keklēmenous,* "to call those who had been called." The call to attend the banquet, therefore, has come and comes again to all the originally invited guests. Yet these guests all refuse to come, though others invited later do come. In both parables there were people who had been called or invited to come, but who did not come. Jesus puts it succinctly in Matthew 22:14, "For many are called, but few are chosen" (RSV).

It seems clear that these parables must be interpreted as referring to the gospel call. The first group of invited guests stands for the Jews, God's ancient covenant people, who had been previously called through prophets, priests, and God-fearing kings, and who are now being called again by Christ and his disciples. In both parables those first invited refuse to come. The second group of invited guests, both in Matthew and in Luke (people who live within the town), seem to stand for Jews other than those previously called—tax collectors, sinners, and the like. The people in this second group are willing to come to the banquet. The third group of guests, mentioned only by Luke (people in the "roads and country lanes," and therefore outside of the town), may stand for the Gentiles to whom the gospel would come later as the church would fulfill Christ's Great Commission (Matt. 28:19-20). In both Matthew 22 and Luke 14, therefore, Jesus teaches that many are called to accept the gospel invitation who refuse to do so—that, in other words, there is a general call which comes to all to whom the gospel is preached.

In this connection we take note also of Matthew 11:28, "Come to me, all you who are weary and burdened, and I will give you rest." Though only those who recognize their sinful state will come to Christ, the call is addressed to all who "labor and are heavy laden," whether they realize their condition or not.

Acts 17:30 speaks of the general or universal call in terms of a command: "In the past God overlooked such ignorance, but now he commands all people everywhere to repent." The last chapter of the Bible, in fact, contains an urgent general call: "The Spirit and the bride say, 'Come!' And let him who hears say, 'Come!' " (Rev. 22:17). The New Testament clearly teaches, therefore, that the call or summons of the gospel comes to all to whom the word is preached or taught.

When a preacher or missionary brings the gospel he cannot, of course, restrict himself to those whom the Bible calls "the elect" (those whom God has chosen to be saved); he does not know who they are. The preacher addresses everybody; he invites every listener to be saved. Needless to say, the preacher or missionary earnestly or fervently desires that all to whom the gospel call comes will be saved. But now the question arises, Is there also such a desire on God's part? Does God earnestly desire that all those who hear the gospel should repent, believe, and be saved?

On this question there has been and still is a difference of opinion among Reformed theologians here in the United States, in the Netherlands, and in England.[3] Restricting myself to the American phase of this controversy, I observe that the late Herman Hoeksema and the Protestant

3. On the denial of the so-called well-meant gospel offer by Reformed theologians, see Herman Hoeksema, *The Protestant Reformed Church in America*, 2nd ed. (Grand Rapids, 1947), pp. 317-53; *Reformed Dogmatics* (Grand Rapids: Reformed Free Publishing Association, 1966), pp. 465-68; "*Whosoever Will*" (Grand Rapids: Eerdmans, 1945). Cf. also Klaas Schilder, *Heidelbergsche Catechismus*, Vol. 2 (Goes: Oosterbaan and LeCointre, 1949); Peter Toon, *The*

Reformed Church in the United States and in Canada of which he was the
founder teach that God does not seriously desire the salvation of all those
to whom the gospel comes. The Christian Reformed Church, however, in
opposition to Hoeksema, and in agreement with the majority of Reformed
theologians, affirms that God does seriously desire the salvation of all to
whom the gospel comes. This leads us to a consideration of the second
characteristic of the gospel call.

THE GOSPEL CALL IS SERIOUSLY MEANT

So that we may understand this controversy, we first look at the position
of Herman Hoeksema on this point. According to Hoeksema, the gospel
call is never an offer. For if it were an offer, it would imply that all those
to whom the gospel comes are able to accept this offer in their own
strength. This, however, is not true. Only the elect (those whom God chose
from eternity to be saved) are given the ability to accept the gospel call.
This gospel call is therefore not a universal offer of grace and salvation,
but it is an odor of life to life and an odor of death to death, in accordance
with the express purpose of God.[4]

It must be remembered that Hoeksema's theology is dominated by
the overruling causality of the double decree of election and reprobation.[5]
He contends that it is impossible to maintain the decrees of election and
reprobation and still speak of a well-meant offer of the gospel to all to
whom the gospel comes. For to speak of such an offer implies that God
desires that all who hear the gospel should be saved, and that God therefore has a favorable attitude toward all such hearers. But if this is so,
counters Hoeksema, how can one explain Scripture passages which teach
that God intends to harden the hearts of some to whom the gospel comes?
How can God have an attitude of favor toward the reprobate? As a matter of fact, this author contends, God never grants the reprobate any token
of grace. Everything God does to or for the reprobate in this life is
deliberately designed to prepare him or her for eternal damnation.[6]

Emergence of Hyper-Calvinism in English Nonconformity, 1689-1765 (London: The Olive Tree,
1967).

For a summary and critique of the views of Hoeksema and Schilder on this point, see
A. C. De Jong, *The Well-Meant Gospel Offer: The Views of H. Hoeksema and K. Schilder*
(Franeker: T. Wever, 1954).

4. De Jong, *The Well-Meant Gospel Offer*, pp. 42-43.

5. By election is meant God's choice from before the creation of the world of a certain
number of human beings to be saved. By reprobation is meant God's decision, also from
before the creation of the world, to pass by some human beings in the distribution of his
grace and to condemn them for their sins.

6. De Jong, *Well-Meant Offer*, pp. 43-45.

Hoeksema also sees an inconsistency between the teaching of the well-meant offer of the gospel and the doctrine of limited atonement.[7] "They [people who accept the well-meant offer] profess to believe that atonement is limited, and that Christ died only for the elect; yet, on the other hand, they also insist that God sincerely and well-meaningly offers salvation to all men."[8] Hoeksema does not think it possible to combine these two doctrines; they simply contradict each other.

For Hoeksema, the doctrines of election and reprobation make it impossible to speak of gospel preaching as an offer of grace to the reprobate. If preaching, then, is not an offer, what is it? It consists of a universal proclamation joined to a particular promise. This proclamation includes a number of statements concerning the truth revealed in the gospel. It is a declaration that God will save his elect in the way of faith, and that he will condemn the reprobates who refuse to accept the gospel.[9]

According to Hoeksema, the promise of the gospel does not come to everyone who hears it; it comes only to the elect. This promise is never universal but always particular. Preaching is never grace for the reprobate. Preaching by itself is neither a blessing nor a curse. It is a neutral presentation, which always turns into a curse for the reprobate and into a blessing for the elect.[10]

Summing up, then, according to Hoeksema God does not desire the salvation of all to whom the gospel comes; he desires the salvation only of the elect. Therefore we cannot say that the gospel is a well-meant offer of salvation to all who hear it.

Taking issue with Hoeksema on this point, the Christian Reformed Church of North America maintains, in agreement with the majority of Reformed theologians, that the preaching of the gospel is a well-meant offer of salvation, not just on the part of the preacher, but on God's part as well, to all who hear it, and that God seriously and earnestly desires the salvation of all to whom the gospel call comes.

What is the Scriptural basis for the well-meant gospel call? We look first of all at two passages from Ezekiel. Ezekiel 18:23 is in the form of a question: "Do I take any pleasure in the death of the wicked? declares the Sovereign LORD. Rather, am I not pleased when they turn from their ways and live?" Ezekiel 33:11 gives the answer to this question: "As surely as I

---

7. This doctrine, generally taught by Reformed theologians, and often called the doctrine of "definite atonement," holds that the purpose of the atonement was to secure the salvation of the elect only and that Christ therefore did his saving work specifically for his people.

8. Hoeksema, *"Whosoever Will,"* p. 148.

9. De Jong, *Well-Meant Offer,* pp. 47-48.

10. Ibid., p. 49.

live, declares the Sovereign LORD, I take no pleasure in the death of the wicked, but rather that they turn from their ways and live. Turn! Turn from your evil ways! Why will you die, O house of Israel?"

Ezekiel prophesied to the exiles from the Southern Kingdom, who had been carried into Babylonian captivity because of their shameful unfaithfulness to God. The prophet is pleading with his countrymen to repent of their sins — particularly of the sins of idolatry and covenant-breaking—and to return to God. In these two passages he states emphatically that God takes no pleasure in the death of impenitent sinners, but that he desires that they should turn from their evil ways and live. Though these words were addressed to the Israelites, there is no reason whatever to assume that they are addressed only to "the elect" among Israel. Surely to suggest that all the Israelites in Babylon were elect in the sense defined above is to go contrary to Paul's words in Romans 9:6 ("For they are not all Israel, that are of Israel," ASV), and to the teachings of Scripture in general. In fact, we are given the distinct impression that most of the Jews who were carried away into captivity were covenant breakers who had sunk very far into idolatry and disobedience. So when the prophet here exclaims that God has no pleasure in the death of the wicked, there is no justification for limiting these "wicked" to the elect wicked. The point is crystal clear: God does not delight in *(chāphēts)* the death of the impenitent hearers of the gospel, but he delights in their turning to him in repentance so that they may be saved. This is God's revealed will toward all who hear the gospel call, including the call to repentance trumpeted by the Old Testament prophets.

Calvin has some significant words to say about the passage from Ezekiel 18:23:

> We hold, then, that God wills not the death of a sinner, since he calls all equally to repentance, and promises himself prepared to receive them if they only seriously repent. If anyone should object—then there is no election of God, by which he has predestinated a fixed number to salvation, the answer is at hand: the Prophet does not here speak of God's secret counsel, but only recalls miserable men from despair, that they may apprehend the hope of pardon, and repent and embrace the offered salvation.[11]

We turn next to a New Testament passage, Matthew 23:37, "O Jerusalem, Jerusalem, you who kill the prophets and stone those sent to you, how often I have longed to gather your children together, as a hen gathers her chicks under her wings, but you were not willing" (cf. the parallel passage, Luke 13:34). Here Jesus, sobbing out his grief, tells Jerusalem

11. John Calvin, *Commentary on Ezekiel*, trans. Thomas Myers (Grand Rapids: Eerdmans, 1948), 2:247.

how often he has longed to have her citizens come to him to be saved, and how grieved he is at their refusal to do so. He uses the figure of the hen gathering her chicks under her wings to protect her brood from impending danger. The danger of which Jesus is speaking is that of the coming judgment. In the very next verse Jesus tells Jerusalem that her house will be left desolate—a reference to the coming destruction of the city. But in Jesus' final discourses the destruction of Jerusalem is usually a type of the end of the world.[12] Those who are not in Christ when he comes again at the end of the world will be eternally lost. So what Jesus here specifically warns against is the unspeakable tragedy of everlasting perdition.

"But you were not willing!" There is a sharp contrast here between what Jesus wanted and what the inhabitants of Jerusalem wanted: "I longed . . . but you were not willing." Most interpreters understand this cry of Jesus as a lament. Christ emphatically declares that though he yearned for the conversion and salvation of the people of Jerusalem, they were not willing to believe on him so that they might be saved.

Since Jesus speaks here as the Messiah, the God-man, the revealer of the Father, we must understand his words as disclosing the attitude of God the Father toward Jerusalem, as well as that of Christ. For Jesus said on another occasion, "Anyone who has seen me has seen the Father" (John 14:9); he also affirmed, "My teaching is not my own. It comes from him who sent me" (John 7:16). Surely it would never do to think of Christ as feeling one way about the salvation of the children of Jerusalem, and of the Father as feeling a different way. Surely there can be no diversity of attitude within the Holy Trinity!

No one would care to contend that every person in Jerusalem was among the number of God's elect. We have, then, in this passage a clear indication that God does seriously and earnestly desire the salvation of all those to whom the gospel comes, including those who do not belong to his elect.

In 2 Peter 3:4 the writer speaks of scoffers who say, "Where is the promise of his [Christ's] coming?" (RSV). It seems that already in Peter's day people were wondering why Jesus had not yet returned. The answer is given in verse 9: "The Lord is not slow in keeping his promise, as some understand slowness. He is patient with you, not wanting anyone to perish, but everyone to come to repentance."

The word rendered "patient" is *makrothymei*, literally, "is of long spirit," or "is longsuffering" (KJV) toward you. The apparent delay of Christ's Second Coming, Peter says, does not mean that the Lord is slow or forgetful of his promise, but rather that he is longsuffering toward us,

---

12. See my *The Bible and the Future* (Grand Rapids: Eerdmans, 1979), pp. 148-49.

"not wanting anyone to perish, but [wanting] everyone to come to repentance." So the alleged "delay" is actually an evidence of divine grace. The Lord wishes to give human beings living on this earth full opportunity to repent and be saved; hence he has not yet returned.

But now note particularly the words, "not wanting anyone to perish." One might conceivably read into this phrase the meaning, "not wanting any of the elect to perish." But this is not what Peter says; to introduce this thought is to smuggle into the text something which is not there. The negative form of the statement leaves no room for the possibility of excluding anyone: The Lord does not wish that *any* should perish. According to this passage it is clearly the Lord's desire that all those who hear the gospel should come to repentance and be saved.

Again Calvin's comment on this text is helpful:

> It could be asked here, if God does not want any to perish, why do so many in fact perish? My reply is that no mention is made here of the secret decree of God by which the wicked are doomed to their own ruin, but only of His loving-kindness as it is made known to us in the Gospel. There God stretches out His hand to all alike, but He only grasps those (in such a way as to lead to Himself) whom He has chosen before the foundation of the world.[13]

The word translated "wanting" in 2 Peter 3:9 is *boulomenos*. As we reflect on the passages we have been looking at, we find a clear parallel between *mē boulomenos* ("not wanting") in this verse, *posakis ēthelēsa* ("how often I have longed") in Matthew 23:37, and *'im-'echpōts* ("I take no pleasure") in Ezekiel 33:11. God does not *want* anyone to perish, he *takes no pleasure* in the death of the wicked, and Jesus *often longed* to gather the children of Jerusalem to the place of safety. These divinely inspired statements describe God's revealed will that all those who hear the gospel should come and be saved.

Perhaps the clearest New Testament passage on this point is 2 Corinthians 5:20, "We are therefore Christ's ambassadors, as though God were making his appeal through us. We implore you on Christ's behalf: Be reconciled to God." An ambassador does not present his own sentiments or opinions about a matter, but only those of his sender. Paul here calls himself and his fellow apostles ambassadors, implying that when he and others urge people to be reconciled to God, they are uttering not simply their own wishes but the wishes of the God who sent them. The genitive absolute construction, *hōs tou theou parakalountos di' hēmōn*, expands the thought of "we are ambassadors," and further explains what this ambassadorship involves: "so that actually God is making his appeal through

13. John Calvin, *Commentary on the First and Second Epistles of Peter*, trans. William B. Johnston (Grand Rapids: Eerdmans, 1963), p. 364.

us."[14] The appeal is this: "be reconciled to God." Obviously, then, the desire that his readers or hearers be reconciled to God is not just Paul's wish, but God's desire as transmitted by Paul. Applying what this passage teaches about preaching in general, we are certainly justified in saying that the desire that people be reconciled to God which comes to expression in preaching is not just a desire on the part of the preacher or missionary, but on the part of the God for whom the preacher speaks and of whom he is an ambassador.[15]

THE CANONS OF DORT ON THE WELL-MEANT OFFER

Do the Reformed Confessions have anything to say on this matter? In the Canons of Dort[16] there are two articles which have particular bearing on this point. The first is found in Chapter II, Article 5:

> It is the promise of the gospel that whoever believes in Christ crucified shall not perish but have eternal life. This promise, together with the command to repent and believe, ought to be announced and declared without differentiation or discrimination to all nations and people, to whom God in his good pleasure sends the gospel.

The other article, III-IV, 8, is even more significant:

> All who are called through the gospel are called seriously (*serio vocantur*). For seriously and most genuinely (*serio et verissime*) God makes known in his Word what is pleasing to him: that those who are called should come to him. Seriously (*serio*) he also promises rest for their souls and eternal life to all who come to him and believe.

By way of background, we should note that the expression *serio vocantur* ("are called seriously") was chosen deliberately. For this expression had been used by the Remonstrants or Arminians at the Synod of Dort when they voiced their objections to the teachings of the Calvinists.[17] In reply to a request from the officers of the synod asking the Arminians to

14. Cf. on this point Philip E. Hughes, *Paul's Second Epistle to the Corinthians* (Grand Rapids: Eerdmans, 1962), p. 210 and n. 50.

15. On the question of the well-meant gospel offer, see also John Murray and Ned Stonehouse, *The Free Offer of the Gospel* (Phillipsburg, NJ: Lewis J. Grotenhuis, [1948]).

16. Statements of doctrine adopted by the Synod of Dort which met in Dordrecht, The Netherlands, in 1618-19. This confession is still accepted by the Christian Reformed Church and by the Reformed Church in America. The translation from the Latin text is one that was adopted by the Christian Reformed Synod of 1986.

17. The Synod of Dort had been called to settle a controversy in the Reformed churches of the Netherlands occasioned by the rise of Arminianism—a theological system initiated by Jacob Arminius, a professor of theology at the University of Leiden. A number of followers of Arminius, called Arminians or Remonstrants, were present at the synod; their views were rejected.

state their views more fully than they had done before, the Arminians who were present at the synod handed in a document called "The Opinions of the Remonstrants" *(Sententiae Remonstrantium).* In this document they made the following statements about the well-meant gospel offer: "Whomever God calls to salvation he calls seriously *(serio vocat):* that is, with a sincere and completely unhypocritical intention and will to save."[18] The Arminians were here saying to the Calvinists: "One of the problems we have with your position is that, granted your doctrines of election and limited atonement, you cannot possibly believe in a well-meant gospel call—you cannot maintain that God seriously calls *(serio vocat)* all to whom the gospel comes."[19]

Against this background the fact that the Canons of Dort not only affirmed the well-meant gospel call, but did so in exactly the same words used by the Arminians, is all the more significant. In reply to what the Arminians had said, the theologians at Dort stated: "We quite agree with you that God seriously, earnestly, unhypocritically, and most genuinely calls to salvation all to whom the gospel comes. In stating this, we even use the very same words you used in your document: *serio vocantur* ('are seriously called'). But we insist that we can hold to this well-meant gospel call while at the same time maintaining the doctrines of election and limited or definite atonement. We do not feel the need for rejecting the doctrine of election and repudiating the teaching of definite atonement in order to affirm the well-meant gospel call."

AVOIDING A RATIONALISTIC SOLUTION

Peter Toon, in his *The Emergence of Hyper-Calvinism in English Nonconformity,* points out that among the English nonconformists of the late seventeenth and middle eighteenth centuries there emerged a type of Hyper-Calvinism which, like that of Herman Hoeksema and the Protestant Reformed Churches, denied the well-meant gospel call.[20] One of the reasons why this type of theology developed, according to Toon, was an overly rationalistic understanding of God's dealings with human beings.[21]

---

18. *Sententiae Remonstrantium,* III-IV, 8 [trans. mine]. The text can be found in J. N. Bakhuizen Van Den Brink, *De Nederlandsche Belijdenisgeschriften* (Amsterdam: Holland, 1940), pp. 282-87.

19. Interestingly enough, this was precisely the difficulty Herman Hoeksema had with the well-meant gospel call, though he stood at the opposite end of the theological spectrum from the Arminians.

20. Among the hyper-Calvinists mentioned by Toon are Joseph Hussey (1660-1726) and John Gill (1697-1771).

21. *The Emergence of Hyper-Calvinism,* p. 147.

The same comment can be made, I believe, about the position of Herman Hoeksema and his followers on the gospel call—it is based on an overly rationalistic understanding of God's dealings with his human creatures. Here is the crux of the matter. The Bible teaches, as we saw above, that God seriously desires that all who hear the gospel should believe in Christ and be saved. The same Bible also teaches that God has chosen or elected his own people in Christ from before the creation of the world. To our finite minds it seems impossible that both of these teachings could be true. A kind of rational solution of the problem could go into either of two directions: (1) To say that God wants all who hear the gospel to be saved; that therefore he gives to all who hear sufficient grace to be saved if they so desire; this grace is, however, always resistible; many do resist and thus frustrate God's design. This is the Arminian solution, which leaves us with a God who is not sovereign, and which thus denies a truth clearly taught in Scripture. (2) The other type of rational solution is that of Hoeksema and the Hyper-Calvinists: Since the Bible teaches election and reprobation, it simply cannot be true that God desires the salvation of all to whom the gospel comes. Therefore we must say that God desires the salvation only of the elect among the hearers of the gospel. This kind of solution may seem to satisfy our minds, but it completely fails to do justice to Scripture passages like Ezekiel 33:11, Matthew 23:37, 2 Corinthians 5:20, and 2 Peter 3:9.

We must refuse to go into either of these two rationalistic directions. Since the Scriptures teach both eternal election and the well-meant gospel call, we must continue to hold on to both, even though we cannot reconcile these two teachings with our finite minds. We should remember that we cannot lock God up in the prison of human logic. Our theology must maintain the Scriptural paradox.[22] With Calvin, our theological concern must be not to build a rationally coherent system, but to be faithful to all the teachings of the Bible.

The well-meant gospel call has tremendous significance for missions. The missionary or evangelist must bring the gospel message with this confidence: "Not only do I desire each of you to turn from your sins to God so that you may be saved, but this is God's desire as well. God has no pleasure in the death of anyone who is not living in harmony with his will; God wants you to turn from your ways and live. God is therefore making his appeal through me, as I say to you, 'Be reconciled to God!' " With this confidence we must bring the gospel to everyone, trusting that God will bless the word and will bring about the results which he has decreed.

---

22. See above, pp. 5-7.

CHAPTER 6

Effectual Calling

HAVING LOOKED AT THE GOSPEL CALL, WE TURN NEXT TO THE QUESTION of the response to this call. Not all who hear the gospel call accept it and come to salvation—some do, but some do not. How do we account for this?

Various answers have been given to this question. Some (Semi-Pelagians[1] and Arminians[2]) have said that the acceptance of the gospel call is dependent ultimately and exclusively on the human will. According to this view, all who hear the gospel have the ability to accept it—either by the natural capability of the will to respond (Semi-Pelagians), or because of a sufficient enabling grace given to all whereby inherited depravity can be overcome (Arminians). God does not in any way determine or control the outcome of the gospel call—this outcome is dependent on the human will alone. Here, therefore, is a point in God's universe where God is not in complete control; he chooses to step back, wait, and see what people will do with the gospel call. The sovereignty of God, so clearly taught in Scripture, is here denied.

Augustine (354-430), however, and those who followed the Augustinian tradition in theology, maintained that the reason why those who accept the gospel call do so must ultimately be sought, not in the human will (though they would admit that the human will is active in this acceptance) but in the sovereign grace of God. This Augustinian tradition has been maintained by Calvinistic[3] or Reformed theologians. According to Reformed theology human beings are by nature unable to respond to the gospel call with repentance and faith. The reason for this is that they are all born in a sinful state and condition known as "original sin," consisting

---

1. Semi-Pelagians were fifth- and sixth-century theologians who tried to steer between the views of Augustine and Pelagius with regard to the priority of divine grace (Augustine) or the human will (Pelagius) in the initial work of salvation. See "Semi-Pelagianism," EDT, pp. 1000-1001.

2. Arminians opposed the doctrine of predestination as taught by John Calvin. They maintained that the human will must cooperate with divine grace before new spiritual life can be received. See "Arminianism," EDT, pp. 79-81.

3. John Calvin lived from 1509 to 1564. Though born in France, he did most of his work in Geneva, Switzerland.

in "pervasive depravity" and "spiritual inability."[4] Because of his or her spiritual inability the unregenerate person is unable, apart from the special working of the Holy Spirit, to change the basic direction of his life from sinful self-love to love for God. Unless God by his Spirit opens the heart of the hearer, thus enabling him or her to believe, he or she will never accept the gospel call. This opening of the heart happens in what Reformed theologians describe as "internal" or "effectual" calling. We shall be looking at the biblical basis for this doctrine in a moment.

First of all, however, something must be said about terminology. Some Reformed theologians use the term "internal calling" to describe the kind of call I am now discussing. This terminology implies that the gospel call should be thought of as an "external call." But that suggests that the call of the gospel never really gets inside the person who rejects it, since it only touches him or her on the outside—since it only reaches the ear, as we sometimes say, but not the heart. This is, however, not necessarily so. In the Parable of the Sower Jesus describes the "wayside" hearer as one who has heard the word but in whose case the evil one comes and "snatches away what was sown in his heart" (Matt. 13:19). The gospel may be rejected by someone not just on the basis of a superficial hearing of it, but despite a thorough understanding of it, despite a receiving of that word in her "heart"—in the inner core of her being.

The expression "internal calling" also has its difficulties. It suggests that the difference between these two ways of looking at calling lies simply in the aspect of the human being to which each calling appeals: the outside or the inside. But surely this is quite inadequate. For these reasons I prefer to designate the calling which refers to God's opening of the heart to enable a person to believe as "effectual calling."

THE BIBLICAL BASIS FOR EFFECTUAL CALLING

At this point we must step back and reflect on what the Bible teaches about what fallen human beings are by nature. Are they by nature—that is, apart from a special working of the Holy Spirit—able to respond to the gospel call in faith and repentance?

The Bible clearly teaches that they are not. We turn first of all to 1 Corinthians 2:14, "The man without the Spirit [or "unspiritual man," RSV; "natural man," KJV; Gk. *psychikos*] does not accept the things that come from the Spirit of God, for they are foolishness to him, and he cannot understand them, because they are spiritually discerned." Paul refers here to man as he is by nature, to unregenerate man. Such people not only cannot understand the things that come from God's Spirit; even worse,

4. On original sin, see my *Created in God's Image* (Grand Rapids: Eerdmans, 1986), pp. 143-54.

these things are foolishness to them. Paul makes a similar point in Romans
8:7, "The sinful mind [or "the carnal mind," KJV; "the mind of the flesh,"
ASV; Gk. *to phronēma tēs sarkos*] is hostile to God. It does not submit to
God's law, nor can it do so." The "sinful mind" is the mind of the human
being by nature; if that mind is hostile to God (or "enmity against God,"
KJV) and is not able to submit to divine law, how can it respond favorably
to God's summons to repent and believe? The condition of human beings
by nature is described in the most devastating words by Ephesians 2:1-2:
"As for you, you were dead in your transgressions and sins, in which you
used to live when you followed the ways of this world." Our condition
by nature, Paul is here saying, is not just one of spiritual sickness—a sickness which could perhaps be healed by some efforts on our part. No, our
condition is one of spiritual death. And how can spiritually dead people
respond favorably to the gospel call?

That we are not able by nature to accept the call of the gospel was
clearly taught by Jesus when he said to Nicodemus, "I tell you the truth,
no one can see the kingdom of God unless he is born again [literally, "born
from above"; Gk. *gennēthē anōthen*]. . . . No one can enter the kingdom of
God unless he is born of water and the Spirit" (John 3:3, 5). Not only can
we not enter God's kingdom; we cannot even see it unless we have
received new life from above. Note also what Jesus said to the Jews, "No
one can come to me unless the Father who sent me draws him" (John 6:44).
Because we are by nature spiritually dead we need to be made spiritually alive before we can respond affirmatively to God's overtures of grace:
"Because of his great love for us, God, who is rich in mercy, made us alive
with Christ even when we were dead in transgressions" (Eph. 2:4-5).

If our condition by nature is as described in the passages just quoted,
it is obvious that we cannot in our own strength accept the gospel call. To
ask people who are by nature spiritually dead, hostile to God, unable to
understand the things of God's Spirit, and unable to submit to God's law,
to respond favorably to his invitation to repent of sin and believe in Christ
is like asking a totally deaf woman to answer your question or a totally
blind man to read a note you have written. It is like standing on top of a
roof and asking a man on the sidewalk below to fly up to join you.

Does the Bible teach that there is such a thing as an effectual call—
one in which God efficaciously enables us to respond to the gospel call
with a Yes? Indeed it does. It will be helpful to turn first of all to 1 Corinthians 1:22-24,

> Jews demand miraculous signs and Greeks look for wisdom, but we preach
> Christ crucified: a stumbling block to Jews and foolishness to Gentiles, but to
> those whom God has called [literally, "to the called ones"; Gk. *autois de tois
> klētois*], both Jews and Greeks, Christ the power of God and the wisdom of
> God.

When Paul preached he found that some of his hearers accepted and some rejected his message. The only way he could have found out that the crucified Christ whom he preached was a stumbling block to certain Jews and foolishness to certain Greeks was by preaching to them and noting their responses. Even those to whom the preached Christ became a stumbling block or foolishness, however, would have received the gospel call. When Paul adds, "to those whom God has called, both Jews and Greeks, Christ the power of God and the wisdom of God," he can mean nothing else than "to those whom God has effectually called"—called in such a way that they responded favorably to the gospel. So the word *klētois* as used in this passage must refer to the effectual call.

To prove that effectual calling is described here, ask yourself whether those for whom the crucified Christ is a stumbling block or foolishness have been called. If Paul had been thinking only of the gospel call, he would have had to say Yes to this question. But here Paul particularly excludes these unbelieving hearers from the number of those who have been called; only those for whom the gospel is the power of God and the wisdom of God are here designated as the *klētoi*, those who have been called. And in this sense, the sense of having been effectually called, the former class of people were not called.

To highlight the difference between these two types of calling once again, compare this passage with Luke 14:24, "I tell you, not one of those men who were invited [literally, "those called," *tōn keklēmenōn*] will get a taste of my banquet." In the Luke passage none of the called are saved; but in the passage from 1 Corinthians only the called are saved.

The distinction, therefore, between these two types of calling is not just a "Calvinistic fiction," as some Arminians allege,[5] but is clearly based on Scripture.

We look next at Romans 8:28-30. We begin with verse 28: "We know that all things work together for good to those who love God, who have been called according to his purpose."[6] Who are the people for whom all things work together for good (or for whose good God works in all things)? They are described in two ways: "those who love God," and those "who have been called according to his purpose." The first of these two expressions describes what these people do: they "love God." The second expression describes what God has done for them: they are people "who have been called according to his [God's] purpose" *(tois kata prothesin*

5. See Richard Watson, *Theological Institutes* (New York: Carlton and Porter, 1857), 2:353.
6. For the first half of the text I am following the NIV margin. Some ancient manuscripts insert *ho theos* ("God") after *synergei* ("work together"). On the basis of this reading the passage could be rendered, "in all things God works for the good of those who love him" (NIV text). Actually, the basic meaning is the same in both readings.

klētois). Surely much more is meant here by *klētois* (those "who have been called") than having been summoned by the call of the gospel. To be sure, the gospel call is a call according to God's purpose. But can it be said that all things work together for good for all those who have been called by the gospel, regardless of whether they believe or not? Can it be said that all those who receive the gospel call are people who love God? Obviously not. It is quite clear, therefore, that here, as in 1 Corinthians 1:24, the word *klētois* (those "who have been called") refers to effectual calling: those in whom God by his Holy Spirit has effectually brought about new life, thus enabling these hearers to respond believingly to the gospel call. This calling is "according to his purpose" to bring them to salvation—a purpose rooted in his having chosen them in Christ before the creation of the world (Eph. 1:4).

The verses which follow, 29-30, give the reason for the statement made in verse 28:

> (29) For those God foreknew he also predestined to be conformed to the likeness of his Son, that he might be the firstborn among many brothers. (30) And those he predestined, he also called (*ekalesen,* from *kaleō*); those he called (*ekalesen*), he also justified; those he justified, he also glorified.

"Called" in verse 30 must also be understood as referring to effectual calling, for two reasons: (1) "Called" is only expressing in the form of a verb (*ekalesen*) what was previously expressed in verse 28 in the form of a substantive: "[those] who have been called" *(klētois).* The persons designated "those he called" in verse 30 are the same persons described as "[those] who have been called according to his purpose" in verse 28. For, as was noted, verses 29 and 30 give the ground or reason for what was said in verse 28. (2) All those said to have been "called" in verse 30 are also said to be justified: "those he called, he also justified." One cannot say that all those who have received the gospel call, regardless of their response to it, are justified. But one can say that all those who have been effectually called are justified—and will eventually be glorified. "Called," therefore, both in verse 28 and verse 30, must mean effectually called.[7]

Another passage where the word for calling is used in the sense of ef-

---

7. It is interesting to observe how one Arminian theologian, Richard Watson, explains Romans 8:30. Contending that "calling" in the Bible always means the gospel call which can be refused, and rejecting the concept of effectual calling, he interprets the passage as follows: "They [those described in the text] are therefore CALLED, invited by it [the gospel] to this state and benefit: the calling being obeyed, they are JUSTIFIED; and being justified, and continuing in that state of grace, they are GLORIFIED.... The apostle supposes those whom he speaks of in the text as 'called,' to have been obedient ..." (*Theological Institutes,* 2:359-60). Note that this author adds to the text: "those whom he called, *and who obeyed the call,* he justified." But what Paul wrote was this: "those he called, he also justified." Watson can maintain his interpretation only by reading into the text words which are not there.

fectual calling is 1 Corinthians 1:9, "God is faithful, by whom you were called (*eklēthēte,* from *kaleō*) into the fellowship of his Son, Jesus Christ our Lord" (RSV). The fellowship of God's Son means union and communion with Christ—a fellowship which implies that Christ will sustain to the end the believers Paul is addressing (v. 8). "Called" in this passage, therefore, cannot mean simply the gospel call which can be either rejected or accepted; it must mean the effectual call whereby these Christian friends have been brought into a living relationship with Christ.

Paul, in fact, usually uses the word "call" in the sense of effectual calling. See, for example, also Romans 1:7; 9:23-24; 1 Corinthians 1:26; Galatians 1:15; and Ephesians 4:1, 4. But this use of the word "calling" is not limited to Paul; we find the word used in this sense also by other New Testament writers.

Peter uses the word in this way in 1 Peter 2:9, "But you are a chosen people, a royal priesthood, a holy nation, a people belonging to God, that you may declare the praises of him who called you (*kalesantos,* from *kaleō*) out of darkness into his wonderful light." Since Peter here addresses his readers as "a chosen people" and "a people belonging to God," it is clear that "called" means more than the gospel call which could be refused. You are no longer in the darkness, but you are now in the light, Peter is saying, because of God's effectual call.

We should look also at 2 Peter 1:10, "Therefore, my brothers, be all the more eager to make your calling and election sure." In this passage calling is not only mentioned in the same breath with election; it is treated as inseparably united with our election. There is only one definite article *(tēn)* before the two nouns, *klēsin* (calling) and *eklogēn* (election). This means that these two are treated as one unit and are to be thought of as such: not your calling as somehow separate from your election, but your calling and election together.[8]

Obviously, therefore, "calling" *(klēsin)* here cannot refer to the gospel call alone, for two reasons: (1) It is linked with "election" *(eklogēn)* by a single definite article, and "election" can only refer to God's choosing of his own from eternity. A calling which is of one piece with election can only be effectual calling. (2) There is no particular point in telling someone to make sure or to confirm his or her gospel call; once having heard the gospel or once having read the gospel message, she has been called in that sense. "Making your calling sure" must therefore mean: make sure that you have been effectually called—that is, that you have been elected

8. Cf. A. T. Robertson, *Grammar of the Greek New Testament in the Light of Historical Research* (Nashville: Broadman, 1934), p. 787: "Sometimes groups more or less distinct are treated as one for the purpose in hand, and hence use only one article. Cf . . . 2 Pet. 1:10." See also F. Blass and A. Debrunner, *A Greek Grammar of the New Testament,* trans. R. W. Funk (Chicago: University of Chicago Press, 1961), sec. 276 (3).

to eternal life in Christ. You can make sure of this, Peter explains, by "making every effort to add to your faith goodness; and to goodness, knowledge; and to knowledge, self-control," and so on (vv. 5-7). By observing the fruits of effectual calling in your lives, Peter is saying, you can make sure that you have been effectually called.

A similar use of the word "calling" can be found in the first verse of the Epistle of Jude: "Jude, a servant of Jesus Christ and a brother of James, to those who have been called *(klētois)*, who are loved by God the Father and kept by Jesus Christ." Surely not all who have received the gospel call are loved by the Father and kept by Christ, but only those who have been effectually brought into the fellowship of the Triune God. There is also a passage in the Book of Revelation in which the word "called" is used to describe the "chosen and faithful followers" of Christ: "They [the ten kings who are associates of the beast] will make war against the Lamb, but the Lamb will overcome them because he is Lord of lords and King of kings— and with him will be his called *(klētoi)*, chosen and faithful followers" (Rev. 17:14). We conclude that the New Testament does indeed teach that there is an effectual calling by God which is not the same as the gospel call.[9]

How, now, shall we define effectual calling? Briefly, the effectual call is the gospel call made effective to salvation in the hearts and lives of God's people. The gospel call was described in the previous chapter. But unless God supernaturally changes the heart of the hearer, he or she will not respond in faith. This changing of the heart occurs in effectual calling.[10] A more complete definition of effectual calling, therefore, might be: that sovereign action of God through his Holy Spirit whereby he enables the hearer of the gospel call to respond to his summons with repentance, faith, and obedience.

THE GOALS OF EFFECTUAL CALLING

The last word, obedience, suggests another aspect of effectual calling, namely, that it is directed toward certain goals. This is implied in the concept of calling: we are called to something, to some end or goal. The New Testament indicates in a number of ways to what goals God's effectual calling summons us.

---

9. The doctrine of effectual calling is rejected by the following Arminian theologians: Adam Clarke, *The New Testament of our Lord and Saviour Jesus Christ* (New York: Mason and Lane, 1837), 2:101; Richard Watson, *Theological Institutes*, 2:352-61; William B. Pope, *A Compendium of Christian Theology* (New York: Hunt and Eaton, 1889), 2:344-45; H. Orton Wiley, *Christian Theology* (Kansas City: Beacon Hill, 1958), 2:343-44.

10. At this point the question might be raised: Does not the changing of the heart occur in regeneration? It does indeed. The relation between effectual calling and regeneration will be taken up in Chapter 7.

We are called into fellowship with Jesus Christ (1 Cor. 1:9). We are called to eternal life (1 Tim. 6:12), to God's kingdom and glory (1 Thess. 2:12), and to a holy life (1 Thess. 4:7; see 2 Tim. 1:9). We are called to follow Christ as an example of godly suffering (1 Pet. 2:21). We are called to Christian freedom (Gal. 5:13) and to peace (Col. 3:15). We are called to win the prize: "I press on toward the goal to win the prize for which God has called me heavenward in Christ Jesus" (Phil. 3:14).

The effectual call, therefore, summons us to a distinctive kind of life, a life that is different, that separates us morally and spiritually from this present evil world. To use the language of Ephesians 4:1, those who have been effectually called must live lives worthy of the calling to which they have been called.

But living such lives requires our own diligent involvement. Though the effectual call is a fruit of God's sovereign grace, it brings into play our full responsibility. As John Murray puts it, "The sovereignty and efficacy of the call [that is, the effectual call] do not relax human responsibility but rather ground and confirm that responsibility. The magnitude of the grace enhances the obligation."[11]

EFFECTUAL CALLING IN REFORMED THEOLOGY

As was mentioned, the doctrine of effectual calling has been and still is a significant aspect of Reformed theology. We find a reference to this type of calling already in Augustine:

> When, therefore, the gospel is preached, some believe, some believe not; but they who believe at the voice of the preacher from without, hear of the Father from within, and learn; while they who do not believe, hear outwardly but inwardly do not hear nor learn;—that is to say, to the former it is given to believe; to the latter it is not given. Because "No man," says He, "cometh to me except the Father which sent me draw him" (John 6:44).[12]

John Calvin also taught the effectual call, designating it "the inward calling":

> . . . Only when God shines in us by the light of His Spirit is there any profit from the Word. Thus the inward calling, which alone is effectual and peculiar to the elect, is distinguished from the outward voice of men.[13]

---

11. *Redemption—Accomplished and Applied* (Grand Rapids: Eerdmans, 1955), p. 113.

12. *On the Predestination of the Saints,* Chapter 15, in *Nicene and Post-Nicene Fathers,* ed. Philip Schaff, First Series (Grand Rapids: Eerdmans, 1956), 5:506. See also, by the same author, *On the Grace of Christ,* 24, 25.

13. Calvin, *Commentary on Romans and Thessalonians,* trans. Ross MacKenzie (Grand Rapids: Eerdmans, 1979), on Romans 10:16, p. 232. Cf. *Inst.,* III.xxiv.8; IV.i.2.

Other Reformed theologians who teach the doctrine of effectual calling include:

The Canons of Dort speak of effectual calling. When they do so, they generally qualify the word "calling" by some such word as "effectual." Note, for example, the following statement: "This elect number [those whom God has chosen from eternity], though by nature neither better nor more deserving than others, but with them involved in one common misery, God has decreed to give to Christ to be saved by Him, and effectually to call *(efficaciter vocare)* and draw them to His communion by his Word and Spirit."[14] Elsewhere in the Canons both the gospel call and the effectual call are mentioned in the same paragraph:

> But that others who are called by the gospel *(per ministerium evangelii vocati)* obey the call and are converted is not to be ascribed to the proper exercise of free will, . . . but it must be wholly ascribed to God, who, as He has chosen His own from eternity in Christ, so He calls them effectually *(efficaciter vocat)* in time.[15]

The Westminster Confession similarly teaches the effectual call: "All those whom God hath predestinated unto life, and those only, he is pleased, in his appointed and accepted time, effectually to call, by his word and Spirit, out of that state of sin and death in which they are by nature, to grace and salvation by Jesus Christ. . . ."[16]

How is effectual calling related to the gospel call? As we have seen, these two callings are not the same. Not all those who are summoned by the gospel call respond to it in repentance and faith; "for many are called, but few are chosen" (Matt. 22:14, RSV). On the other hand, all those who have been called effectually do turn to God in faith and repentance.

It is important, however, to keep these two types of calling together. Reformed theologians often speak of the gospel call and the effectual call as two aspects or sides of one calling.[17] Ordinarily God calls effectually where the word is being preached or taught. The powerful working of the

---

Charles Hodge, *Systematic Theology*, Vol. 2 (1871; Grand Rapids: Eerdmans, 1940), pp. 675-710; Robert L. Dabney, *Lectures in Systematic Theology* (1878; Grand Rapids: Zondervan, 1972), pp. 553-55; Abraham Kuyper, *The Work of the Holy Spirit*, trans. Henri De Vries (New York: Funk and Wagnalls, 1900), pp. 318, 343-48; William G. T. Shedd, *Dogmatic Theology*, Vol. 2 (1888; Grand Rapids: Zondervan, n.d.), pp. 490-91; A. H. Strong, *Systematic Theology*, Vol. 3 (Philadelphia: Griffith and Rowland, 1907-1909), pp. 791-93; Bavinck, *Dogmatiek*, 4:11-15; also by Bavinck, *Our Reasonable Faith*, trans. Henry Zylstra (1909; Grand Rapids: Eerdmans, 1956), pp. 419-23; Berkhof, ST, pp. 469-72; John Murray, *Redemption*, pp. 109-15; Herman Hoeksema, *Reformed Dogmatics* (Grand Rapids: Reformed Free Publishing Association, 1966), pp. 456-78.

14. Canons of Dort, I,7 (text from Schaff, *Creeds of Christendom* [New York: Harper, 1877]), 3:582.

15. Ibid., III-IV,10 (Schaff, *Creeds*, 3:589-90). Note that in the 1986 translation of the Canons "calls them effectually" has been changed to "effectively calls."

16. Westminster Confession, X,1. See also the Shorter Catechism, Q. 31.

17. Herman Bavinck, *Roeping en Wedergeboorte* (Kampen: Zalsman, 1903), p. 215; Berkhof, ST, p. 469.

Spirit then unites itself with the presentation of the word by the preacher or the teacher. How does the Spirit then work? By (1) opening the heart and thus enabling the hearer to respond (Acts 16:14), (2) enlightening the mind so that the hearer can understand the gospel message (1 Cor. 2:12-13; cf. 2 Cor. 4:6), and (3) bestowing spiritual life so that the hearer can turn to God in faith (Eph. 2:5). One could say, therefore, that the word which is heard in the gospel call is made effective in the effectual call. Herman Bavinck puts it this way: "It is one and the same word which God allows to be proclaimed through the external [or gospel] call and which he writes on the hearts of the hearers through the Holy Spirit in the internal [or effectual] call."[18]

SOME OBJECTIONS CONSIDERED

At this point it may be helpful to consider certain objections which have been raised against the doctrine of effectual calling. One is this: this doctrine takes away every incentive for evangelism and missions. For if only those who have been effectually called are able to respond to the gospel call in faith, why should we preach to people? Why should we not simply wait for God to call his elect with the effectual call? Does not this doctrine make missionary preaching and teaching useless?

The answer is a decisive No. For the preaching and teaching of the gospel are the divinely ordained means whereby people are brought to faith. Note Paul's words: "And how, then, can they call on the one they have not believed in? And how can they believe in the one of whom they have not heard? And how can they hear without someone preaching to them?" (Rom. 10:14).

Another way of meeting this objection is to point out that, though only God's elect (those chosen by him from the creation of the world) will be effectually called and will therefore come to salvation, we do not know who they are. Bavinck again is helpful here: "The gospel is proclaimed to human beings, not as elect or reprobate, but as sinners who are all in need of redemption."[19] It is our task to preach the gospel to all; we must trust God to enable those whom he has chosen in Christ to respond with saving faith. The doctrine of effectual calling, therefore, far from being a deterrent to evangelism and missions, is rather an incentive and a source of encouragement: we are confident that God will bring his own to salvation through the preaching and teaching of his word.

A second objection is this: Does not the doctrine of effectual calling put into the hands of unbelievers a tool whereby they can excuse them-

18. *Roeping en Wedergeboorte*, p. 215 [trans. mine].
19. *Dogmatiek*, 4:5 [trans. mine].

selves for not accepting the gospel? In the light of this teaching, can't they defend themselves for not believing by pointing out that they have not been called with the right kind of calling, and can they then not blame God for their unbelief?

By way of reply, we may say that the Bible clearly teaches that a person who rejects the gospel call has only himself or herself to blame. Jesus said to the unbelieving Jews in Jerusalem: "You diligently study the Scriptures because you think that by them you possess eternal life. These are the Scriptures that testify about me, yet you refuse to come to me to have life" (John 5:39-40). On another occasion Jesus wept over Jerusalem, saying, "How often I have longed to gather your children together, as a hen gathers her chicks under her wings, but you were not willing" (Matt. 23:37). And when Paul was in Pisidian Antioch he said to the Jews who were abusing and insulting him, "We had to speak the word of God to you first. Since you reject it . . . we now turn to the Gentiles" (Acts 13:46). The Bible never says that a person who rejects the gospel does so because God did not call him or her effectually; the rejection of the gospel is always ascribed to human refusal to believe. The Canons of Dort put it this way: "The cause or guilt of this unbelief [that is, refusal to believe the gospel], as well as of all other sins, is in no wise in God, but in man himself; whereas faith in Jesus Christ and salvation through Him is the free gift of God. . . ."[20]

A final objection which could be raised is that the doctrine of effectual calling violates the paradox of divine sovereignty and human responsibility that was discussed earlier.[21] I there pointed out that since human beings are both creatures and persons, they are at the same time both totally dependent on God and able to make responsible decisions. This means that God does not deal with us as robots but as persons. This also means that both God and believers are involved in the process of salvation; in faith, repentance, sanctification, and perseverance both God works and we work. If this is so, the objector affirms, why do you say that effectual calling is exclusively the work of God and not in any way the work of man? If the human being is both a creature and a person, why is not effectual calling a work in which both God and man are active? Does not effectual calling as you have defined it mean that God is now treating us as robots rather than as persons?[22]

So much for the objection. What shall we say in reply? The answer to this objection depends on one's anthropology—one's view of the natural

20. Canons of Dort, I,5 (Schaff, *Creeds*, 3:581).
21. See above, pp. 4-7.
22. The same objection can be raised against the doctrine of regeneration as a work of God alone, and not a work in which God and man are both involved. The answer given here should meet that objection as well.

state of man after the Fall. If you believe that the natural state of human beings today is that of moral and spiritual neutrality, so that they can do good or bad as they please (the Pelagian view), you will not even feel the need for an effectual call or for regeneration. If you believe that our natural state is one of spiritual and moral sickness, but that we all still have the ability to respond favorably to the gospel call (the Semi-Pelagian view), you will not need an effectual call. If you believe that, though we are partially or totally depraved, God gives to all a sufficient enabling grace so that everyone who hears the gospel call is able to accept it by cooperating with this sufficient grace (the Arminian view), you will not feel the need for an effectual call. But if you believe that we are by nature totally dead in sin, and therefore unable to respond favorably to the gospel call unless God in his sovereign grace changes our hearts so that we become spiritually alive (the Reformed view), you will realize how desperately you need God's effectual call. The view last described, I believe, most faithfully reflects biblical teaching.[23]

Let me use an illustration. Let us suppose that you are drowning within earshot of friends on the shore. You cannot swim. Wishing to respect your integrity as a person, and wanting to enable you to help yourself as much as possible, one of your friends standing on the shore, an excellent swimmer, shouts to you that you should start swimming to shore. The advice, though well-meant, is worse than useless, since you can't swim. What you need, and need desperately, is for your friend to jump in and tow you to shore with powerful strokes, so that your life may be saved. What you need at the moment is not just advice, good advice, even gracious advice—you need to be rescued!

This, now, is our situation by nature. We are lost sinners. We are dead in sin. Being dead in sin, we cannot make ourselves alive. Since we are dead in sin, our ears are deaf to the gospel call and our eyes are blind to the gospel light. We need a miracle. This miracle occurs when God in his amazing grace calls us effectually through his Spirit from spiritual death to spiritual life, from spiritual darkness into his marvelous light. After we have been made spiritually alive, we can once again become actively involved in the process of our salvation—in repentance, faith, sanctification, and perseverance. But at the very beginning of the process, at the point where, being spiritually dead, we need to become spiritually alive, we need nothing less than a miraculous rescue from the murky waters of sin in which, if left alone, we would drown. This is what happens in the effectual call.

So let us praise God for the marvel of effectual calling!

23. See my *Created in God's Image*, pp. 143-54. For the Pelagian view, see ibid., pp. 154-56.

I sought the Lord, and afterward I knew
    He moved my soul to seek Him, seeking me;
It was not I that found, O Savior true;
    No, I was found of Thee.[24]

24. No. 498 in the 1987 *Psalter Hymnal* of the Christian Reformed Church (Grand Rapids: CRC Publications, 1987). Author unknown.

CHAPTER 7

Regeneration

CHRISTIANS ARE NOT JUST "NICE PEOPLE"; THEY ARE, OR ARE SUPPOSED to be, new people. C. S. Lewis in his *Mere Christianity,* borrowing two Greek words, distinguishes between two kinds of life: *Bios* and *Zōē. Bios* is the kind of life every person has—biological life, which is kept going by food, air, and water, but which eventually ends in death. *Zōē,* on the other hand, is spiritual life, the kind of life God gives us when we are born again—life that lasts forever.[1] These two kinds of life, Lewis goes on to say, are not only different; they are actually opposed to each other. *Bios* is basically self-centered, whereas *Zōē* is God-centered and other-centered.[2]

This leads us to a consideration of our next topic: regeneration, or the new birth—God's bestowal of what Lewis calls *Zōē.* This is a most important topic, since it deals with the very beginning of the process of salvation.

REGENERATION IN THREE SENSES

The Bible speaks of regeneration in three different but related senses: (1) as the beginning of new spiritual life, implanted in us by the Holy Spirit, enabling us to repent and believe (John 3:3, 5); (2) as the first manifestation of the implanted new life (Jas. 1:18; 1 Pet. 1:23); and (3) as the restoration of the entire creation to its final perfection (Matt. 19:28, KJV, ASV, NASB). In the last-named passage the word *palingenesia,* translated "regeneration" in the versions mentioned, and found in only one other New Testament passage (Titus 3:5), is used to describe the renewal of the entire universe—the "new heaven and new earth" of 2 Peter 3:13 and Revelation 21:1-4.

In this chapter I will deal only with the first two senses described above. It should be noted that in earlier Reformed theology regeneration was viewed in a wider sense than it often is today. Calvin, for example, used the term to describe our total renewal, including conversion and

1. *Mere Christianity* (New York: Macmillan, 1960), pp. 139-40.
2. Ibid., p. 154.

sanctification.[3] The Belgic Confession of 1561 also identifies regeneration with the Christian's entire new life.[4] Many seventeenth-century theologians equated regeneration with conversion.[5] More recently, however, Reformed theologians have felt the need to distinguish between regeneration in the narrower sense (meaning [1] above) and the broader sense (meaning [2] above)—that is, between the implanting of new life by the Spirit and the first manifestations of that new life in conversion.

I plan now to deal with regeneration primarily in its narrower sense. In this sense regeneration may be defined as that work of the Holy Spirit whereby he initially brings persons into living union with Christ, changing their hearts so that they who were spiritually dead become spiritually alive, now able and willing to repent of sin, believe the gospel, and serve the Lord.[6]

BIBLICAL TEACHING ON HUMAN DEPRAVITY

As has often been said, one's doctrine of man is determinative for his or her doctrine of salvation. Nowhere is this more true than in the consideration of regeneration. For our understanding of regeneration hinges on our conception of human depravity. If human beings today are not depraved at all, regeneration or new spiritual life is not really necessary. If human depravity is thought of as being only partial—that is, if fallen man is conceived of as still having the ability to turn to God in faith apart from a special working of the Holy Spirit—regeneration will be understood in a way quite different than if "natural" (or unregenerate) human nature be thought of as totally depraved. If, however, human beings are seen as being totally or pervasively depraved—that is, as totally unable to turn to God in faith apart from a special working of the Spirit—one's understanding of the nature of regeneration will be different still.

The Bible clearly teaches that human beings are indeed totally or pervasively depraved. We note briefly some of the passages which teach this. According to Jeremiah 17:9, "The heart is deceitful above all things and beyond cure. Who can understand it?" As little as the Ethiopian can change his skin, or the leopard can change its spots, so little can the people of Israel do good, who are accustomed to doing evil (Jer. 13:23).

The New Testament teaches the pervasive depravity of fallen human

3. *Inst.*, Book III, Chapter 3.
4. "We believe that this true faith, produced in man by the hearing of God's Word and by the work of the Holy Spirit, regenerates him and makes him a 'new man'" (Belgic Confession, Art. 24, 1985 trans.).
5. See, e.g., the Canons of Dort, III-IV,11 and 12.
6. The broader sense (sense [2] above) will be discussed later in the chapter.

nature in unmistakable terms. In Romans 7:18 Paul, describing his unregenerate state, says, "I know that nothing good lives in me, that is, in my sinful nature. For I have the desire to do what is good, but cannot carry it out." In the next chapter his description is even more vivid: "The sinful mind [the mind of man or woman by nature] is hostile to God. It does not submit to God's law, nor can it do so. Those controlled by the sinful nature cannot please God" (Rom. 8:7-8). "The man without the Spirit [unregenerate man] does not accept the things that come from the Spirit of God, for they are foolishness to him, and he cannot understand them, because they are spiritually discerned" (1 Cor. 2:14).

Jesus had already said to the unbelieving Jews who were listening to him, "No one can come to me unless the Father who sent me draws him" (John 6:44). Not willing to grant that we are only sick or half alive spiritually by nature, Paul tells the Ephesians, "As for you, you were dead in your transgressions and sins" (Eph. 2:1). A few verses later, however, he goes on to affirm, "But because of his great love for us, God, who is rich in mercy, made us alive with Christ even when we were dead in transgressions" (vv. 4-5).[7]

Since this is our condition by nature, it is abundantly clear that we can no more give ourselves or help give ourselves spiritual life than a corpse can give itself biological life. In the light of the biblical description of fallen human nature, regeneration must be understood, not as an act in which God and man work together, but as the work of God alone.

BIBLICAL TEACHING ON REGENERATION

What does the Bible teach about regeneration? Already in the Old Testament we are taught that only God can bring about the radical change which is necessary to enable fallen human beings again to do what is pleasing in his sight. In Deuteronomy 30:6 we find our spiritual renewal figuratively described as a circumcision of the heart: "The LORD your God will circumcise your hearts and the hearts of your descendants, so that you may love him with all your heart and with all your soul, and live." Since the heart is the inner core of the person, the passage teaches that God must cleanse us within before we can truly love him. What we would call regeneration is described by Jeremiah in these words: "I will put my law

7. A fuller discussion of the biblical evidence for pervasive depravity, together with the reason why the word "pervasive" is preferred to the word "total," can be found on pp. 150-54 of my *Created in God's Image* (Grand Rapids: Eerdmans, 1986). See also Berkhof, ST, pp. 246-50. Creedal statements of this doctrine can be found in the Westminster Confession, Chapter 6; the Heidelberg Catechism, Qq. 5-8; the Canons of Dort, III-IV,1-4; and the Belgic Confession, Arts. 14 and 15.

in their minds and write it on their hearts" (31:33). Ezekiel uses a figure to describe regeneration which, though reflecting Old Testament modes of thought, we still often use today: "I will give you a new heart and put a new spirit in you; I will remove from you your heart of stone and give you a heart of flesh" (36:26; cf. 11:19). Here God, through Ezekiel, promises the Babylonian exiles that in the future he will renew them within.

The New Testament provides us with fuller and richer teaching on regeneration than does the Old. In the Synoptic Gospels the word "regeneration" is not used in the sense of "new birth." The thought is, however, present. When Jesus says, "Every good tree bears good fruit, but a bad tree bears bad fruit" (Matt. 7:17), he implies that the tree must be made good before it can bear good fruit. When he affirms, "Every plant that my heavenly Father has not planted will be pulled up by the roots" (Matt. 15:13), he implies that those plants which his heavenly Father has planted will not be uprooted. Statements such as these clearly suggest the necessity of regeneration.

No New Testament writer refers more frequently to regeneration or the new birth than does the Apostle John. We look first at John 1:12-13:

> (12) To all who received him, to those who believed in his name, he gave the right to become children of God—(13) children born not of natural descent, nor of human decision or a husband's will, but born of God.

Arminian theologians often quote verse 12 to prove that faith must precede regeneration: "To those who believed in his name he gave the right to become children of God." But we must not separate verse 12 from verse 13. The latter verse tells us that being children of God is not the result of natural descent or human decision, but of divine activity alone. It is, of course, true that those who believed in Christ did receive the right to become children of God—but behind their faith was the miraculous deed of God whereby they were spiritually reborn. They were born not of man but of God.

Perhaps no New Testament chapter teaches the sovereignty of God's activity in regeneration as clearly as does the third chapter of John's Gospel. Nicodemus, a Pharisee, a ruler of the Jews, came to Jesus by night. His introductory statement evidenced high regard for Jesus as a teacher but a lack of understanding of Christ's real mission: "Rabbi, we know you are a teacher who has come from God. For no one could perform the miraculous signs you are doing if God were not with him" (John 3:2). Jesus' reply (in v. 3) sounds the keynote of the entire discussion: "I tell you the truth, no one can see the kingdom of God unless he is born again" (or "from above," mg.; Gk. *gennēthē anōthen*). *Gennēthē* is an aorist passive form of *gennaō*, which may mean either "to beget" or "to be born." The versions commonly render the verb here in the second sense, "be born"; verse 4 indicates that this is the sense that was here intended. *Anōthen* literally means "from above"; it may also mean "again" or "anew." In John's Gospel the word *anōthen* is used three times in chapter 3 (in vv. 3, 7, and 31); it is also used in 19:11 and 19:23. In the last three instances it unquestionably means "from above." I conclude that here in verse 3, as well as in verse 7, Jesus' words should be translated, "born from above." The expression would then include the thought that one must be born again, but would point specifically to the fact that this new birth is a birth from above.

Jesus is here telling Nicodemus that he cannot even begin to see the Kingdom of God which the former is ushering in, and the spiritual realities of that kingdom, unless he has been born from above. The aorist form of the verb, *gennēthē*, indicates that this new birth is a single occurrence, happening once for all. The passive voice of the verb tells us that this is an occurrence in which human beings are wholly passive. In fact, the very verb used, even apart from the passive voice, tells us the same thing. We did not choose to be born; we had nothing to do with our being born. We were completely passive in our natural birth. So it is also with our spiritual birth. The adverb *anōthen* tells us further that this new birth is a birth from above: a birth from heaven, in distinction from an ordinary birth which is from the earth.

Summing up, from verse 3 we learn that regeneration is absolutely necessary if one is to see the Kingdom of God, and that it is a change in which human beings are completely passive—as passive as they are in their natural birth. We also learn from verse 3 that this new birth is from above—that it must therefore be brought about by a supernatural and superhuman agency.

After Nicodemus had expressed his amazement, and had asked his question about the possibility of entering a second time into his mother's womb, Jesus replied, "I tell you the truth, no one can enter the kingdom of God unless he is born of water and the Spirit" (v. 5). Though some interpreters see in the word "water" a reference to baptism, it seems more likely that water should here be understood as a symbol of inner purification, as it often was in the Old Testament.[8] The expression "born of . . . the Spirit" designates the divine agent of this new birth: the Holy Spirit. Though previously Jesus had only said that this was a birth "from above," here he specifically identifies the divine author. In this new birth

---

8. Cf. Ezekiel 36:25, "I will sprinkle clean water on you, and you will be clean." On this point, see John Murray, *Redemption— Accomplished and Applied* (Grand Rapids: Eerdmans, 1955), pp. 121-22; and Bavinck, *Dogmatiek,* 4:21.

we are therefore utterly dependent on the sovereign activity of the Spirit of God.

When we come to verse 6 we must resist the temptation to interpret the word "flesh" *(sarx)* in the usual Pauline sense, as meaning human nature totally enslaved by sin. For John the word "flesh" often means "the physical weakness inseparable from human existence,"[9] and that is what it seems to mean here. So when Jesus affirms, "That which is born of the flesh is flesh, and that which is born of the Spirit is spirit" (v. 6, RSV), he is saying that what is merely born physically continues to be unregenerate human nature and nothing more, whereas what is born of the Holy Spirit is spiritual in its essence. One can pass from the lower level to the higher only through a supernatural new birth. Regeneration, in other words, brings about a radical change in our nature.

"You should not be surprised at my saying, 'You must be born again' " (v. 7). These words are often understood as meaning that we must do something in our own strength in order to be born again. But this is not what Jesus meant. He was telling Nicodemus here that he and all others (the second "you" is in the plural) need to be born from above *(anōthen)* in order to see and enter into his kingdom.[10]

In verse 8 Jesus describes both the sovereignty and the mystery of the action of the Spirit in regeneration: "The wind blows wherever it pleases. You hear its sound, but you cannot tell where it comes from or where it is going. So it is with everyone born of the Spirit." The action of the Spirit in regenerating people is as sovereign as the wind which blows wherever it pleases. But this action is also deeply mysterious, as are the movements of the wind. Yet, Jesus goes on to say, "you hear its sound"—did Jesus and Nicodemus perhaps hear a gust of wind at this point? You don't understand the movements of the wind, but you can hear its sound. Similarly, you don't understand the mysteries of the new birth, but you can tell from certain outward signs whether you have been born again. What these outward signs are we shall learn when we look at John's first epistle.

Summing up again, from verses 5 to 8 we have learned that the divine agent of regeneration is the Holy Spirit, that the new life received in this new birth is radically different from mere biological life, and that, though regeneration is a mysterious happening, we can know that it has occurred through observing its fruits.

What does Paul teach about regeneration? In Paul's writings the word "regeneration" *(palingenesia)* occurs only once, in Titus 3:5, "He saved us

---

9. Leon Morris, *The Gospel According to John* (Grand Rapids: Eerdmans, 1971), p. 219, n. 37. Cf. TDNT, 7:138-39.

10. Cf. Peter Toon, *Born Again* (Grand Rapids: Baker, 1987), p. 28.

... by the washing of regeneration and renewal in the Holy Spirit" (RSV). In John 3 regeneration was pictured as a new birth or a birth from above; here we have a similar figure: *palingenesia,* from *palin,* meaning "again," and *genesia,* meaning "genesis" or "birth." The word points to a new beginning. The expression "the washing of regeneration" is probably an allusion to baptism, pointing to the spiritual reality for which baptism stands.[11] The words "renewal in the Holy Spirit" tell us that regeneration involves not only purification from sin but also a spiritual renewal which is wrought in us by the Spirit and which continues in the process of sanctification.

Though this is the only place where Paul uses the word "regeneration," allusions to regeneration in his letters are frequent. In Ephesians 2:5 Paul affirms that when we were dead in transgressions, God made us alive together with Christ. In Ephesians 2:10 and 2 Corinthians 5:17 Paul uses a new figure for regeneration: it is such a startlingly different kind of existence that it can only be compared to a new creation: "For we are God's workmanship, created in Christ Jesus"; "Therefore, if anyone is in Christ, he is a new creation." From these Pauline statements we learn that regeneration is the fruit of the Spirit's purifying and renewing activity, that it is equivalent to making dead persons alive, that it takes place in union with Christ, and that it means that we now become part of God's wondrous new creation.

Peter also deals with regeneration in his first epistle. He uses the word *anagennaō,* which could mean either "to beget again" or "to cause to be born again": "In his great mercy he has given us new birth into a living hope through the resurrection of Jesus Christ from the dead" (1 Pet. 1:3). Peter here ties in regeneration both with Christ's resurrection and with our hope. We were made to be born again, he says, through the resurrection of Jesus Christ from the dead. Christ's resurrection is indeed the source of our new spiritual life; since God made us alive together with Christ, our new life is a sharing of Christ's resurrection life. Through this wondrous event we have been born again into a living hope—a hope that we shall someday enter into an inheritance that can never perish, spoil, or fade (v. 4). Peter thus sees regeneration in an eschatological perspective: the beginning of our new life in Christ opens up a glorious vista of our eternal inheritance.[12]

John makes a number of references to regeneration in his first epistle.

11. Note that in Q. 73 of the Heidelberg Catechism this expression is interpreted as referring to baptism.
12. 1 Peter 1:23, which also deals with regeneration, will be discussed later in this chapter.

These passages all stress that regeneration is bound to reveal itself in certain specific types of behavior. From 1 John 2:29 we learn that the regenerate person is one who keeps on doing right things: "If you know that he is righteous, you know that everyone who does what is right has been born of him." The verb translated "has been born" is in the perfect tense *(gegennētai)*, indicating that this person has been regenerated in the past and continues to show evidence of that regeneration in the present.[13]

From 1 John 3:9 we gather that one who has been regenerated does not continually live in sin: "No one who is born of God will continue to sin, because God's seed remains in him; he cannot go on sinning, because he has been born of God." "Continue to sin" translates *hamartian ou poiei;* the present tense of the verb describes continued action. The meaning is: does not keep on doing and enjoying sin, with complete abandon. "Cannot go on sinning" is a rendering of *ou dynatai hamartanein;* the verb for "sinning" is again in the present tense. What John means is: he or she is not able to keep on sinning with enjoyment, to keep on living in sin. "The believer may fall into sin, but he will not walk in it."[14]

1 John 4:7 tells us that one who has been regenerated loves his or her fellow believer: "Dear friends, let us love one another, for love comes from God. Everyone who loves has been born of God and knows God." The word for "love" used here, *agapaō,* points to a self-giving love, the kind of love exemplified by Christ. Someone who has been born again, John is saying here, keeps on loving fellow believers unselfishly.

In 1 John 5:1 we read that the regenerated person is one who has faith: "Everyone who believes that Jesus is the Christ is born of God [literally, has been born of God]." In opposition to the views of those who claim that faith must precede regeneration, this passage tells us that faith is the outward evidence of regeneration.

From 1 John 5:4 we learn that one who has been regenerated overcomes the world: "For everyone born of God overcomes the world." "World" here, as often in John's epistles, means the world at enmity with God, as the source of temptation and sin. In 2:15 John warns his readers: "Do not love the world or anything in the world." In the passage before us, however, John assures us that those who have been born again will not be defeated by the world's temptations but will win the victory.

John affirms in 1 John 5:18 that the regenerate person is so guarded by Christ that he or she does not fall away from the faith: "We know that anyone born of God does not continue to sin *(ouch hamartanei;* the verb is

13. The perfect tense in Greek means past action with abiding result. In each of the other passages in 1 John that we are looking at, the verb describing the new birth of believers is similarly in the perfect tense.

14. John R. W. Stott, *The Epistles of John* (Grand Rapids: Eerdmans, 1964), p. 136.

again in the present tense); the one who was born of God keeps him safe, and the evil one cannot harm him." As in 3:9 John here tells us again that the born-again person does not continue to live in sin. By "the one who was born of God" John means Christ, who was the Son of God in a unique way. Christ guards the regenerate person so that the devil cannot harm him or her—cannot administer a deadly wound (Calvin). A person who has been born from above, in other words, will not fall away from grace, since he or she is kept from doing so by Christ.

From John's first epistle we have learned that the regenerate person is someone whose outward life is marked by the following characteristics: he or she does what is right, does not continue to live in sin, loves his or her fellow believer, believes that Jesus is the Christ, and keeps on overcoming the world. If, therefore, someone should ask, How can I know whether I have been regenerated? the person should be told to look for these evidences, since John tells us that these are the marks of a person who has been born again.[15]

We sum up now what we have learned from our biblical study of regeneration: regeneration is a radical change from spiritual death to spiritual life, brought about in us by the Holy Spirit—a change in which we are completely passive. This change involves an inner renewal of our nature, is a fruit of God's sovereign grace, and takes place in union with Christ.

On the basis of this exegetical study, we must affirm strongly that regeneration in the sense in which we have been discussing it (as the implanting of new spiritual life) is not an act in which human beings cooperate with God, but an act of which God is the sole author. Regeneration, in other words, is "monergistic,"[16] the work of God alone, not "synergistic,"[17] something which is accomplished by God and man working together. We saw that regeneration is described in John's Gospel and first epistle by means of verbs in the passive voice: *gennēthē, gennēthēnai, gegennētai, gegennēmenos.* We have noted the striking figure found in Ephesians 2:5, "God . . . made us alive with Christ even when we were dead in transgressions." How, now, could dead people make themselves alive? How could dead people cooperate with God in making themselves alive? Regeneration, the Bible teaches, is a work of God in which human beings are passive. From these biblical teachings about regeneration we

---

15. The possibility that regeneration could remain inactive in a person for many years before it would lead to repentance and faith ("dormant regeneration"), taught, for example, by Abraham Kuyper (see E. Smilde, *Een Eeuw van Strijd over Verbond en Doop* [Kampen: Kok, 1946], pp. 105-106), would seem to be ruled out by these passages from John's epistles.

16. From two Greek words meaning "working alone."

17. From two Greek words meaning "working together."

learn God's total sovereignty in soteriology: our salvation is God's work from the very beginning. Therefore to him be all the praise!

THE ESSENTIAL NATURE OF REGENERATION

Regeneration is deeply mysterious—first, because it is by definition a supernatural work of God; second, because we can never observe or experience regeneration; we can only observe its effects. Understanding regeneration in the narrower sense, as the implanting of new life, we can never be certain when it occurs; we can only deduce from certain evidences with greater or lesser certainty (greater with respect to ourselves, lesser with respect to others) that it has occurred.

I should like to make three comments about the essential nature of regeneration:

(1) *Regeneration is an instantaneous change.* It is not a gradual process, like progressive sanctification. How can it be, if it is the change from spiritual death to spiritual life? We think again of Ephesians 2:5, where regeneration is described as the making alive of dead sinners; the verb there translated "made us alive with Christ," *synezōopoiēsen,* is in the aorist tense, signifying momentary or snapshot action. In Acts 16:14 we read about the conversion of Lydia: "The Lord opened her heart to respond to Paul's message." The opening of the heart obviously describes regeneration. The verb rendered "opened" *(diēnoixen)* is also in the aorist tense. Though we cannot be sure when regeneration occurs, it must be instantaneous, since there is no middle position between death and life.

(2) *Regeneration is a supernatural change.* The Arminians (then called Remonstrants) at the Synod of Dort contended that regeneration was a change brought about by moral persuasion. The synod rejected this position as being Pelagian and unbiblical:

> The Synod rejects the errors of those . . . who teach that the grace by which we are converted to God [here the word "conversion" is used as a synonym for "regeneration"] is nothing but a gentle persuasion, or (as others explain it) that the way of God's acting in man's conversion that is most noble and suited to human nature is that which happens by persuasion. . . .[18]

18. Canons of Dort, III-IV, Rejection of Errors, Par. 7 (1986 trans.). For more recent Arminian teachings on regeneration, see A. M. Hills, *Fundamental Christian Theology* (1931; Salem, OH: Schmul, 1980), 2:200-213; also H. Orton Wiley, *Christian Theology* (Kansas City: Beacon Hill, 1958), 2:403-28. Note particularly the following statement by Wiley: "Arminians . . . regard regeneration as conditionally bestowed upon graciously aided penitents through the instrumentality of faith" (op. cit., p. 421). "Graciously aided" means aided by the "prevenient grace" of God extended to all, which enables people who cooperate with the Spirit to respond to the gospel call in faith and repentance, but which can be resisted (ibid., pp. 344-47). Cf. also Toon, *Born Again,* pp. 118-20, 162-65, 171-73, 177-80.

The way in which the theologians of Dort answered the Arminians and set forth what they deemed to be the Scriptural view of regeneration is worth quoting:

> This is the regeneration, the new creation, the raising from the dead and the making alive so clearly proclaimed in the Scriptures, which God works in us without our help. But this certainly does not happen only by outward teaching, by moral persuasion, or by such a way of working that, after God has done his work, it remains in man's power whether or not to be reborn or converted. Rather, it is an entirely supernatural work, one that is at the same time most powerful and most pleasing, a marvelous, hidden, and inexpressible work, which is not lesser than or inferior in power to that of creation or of raising the dead, as Scripture . . . teaches.[19]

(3) *Regeneration is a radical change.* Since the term "radical" comes from the Latin word for "root" *(radix),* this means that regeneration is a change at the very root of our nature.

(a) *Regeneration means the giving or "implanting" of new spiritual life.* As we saw earlier, human beings are by nature spiritually dead (Eph. 2:1, 5; Col. 2:13; Rom. 8:7-8). It is at the moment of regeneration that the dead sinner becomes spiritually alive, that resistance to God is changed to nonresistance, and that hatred for God is changed to love. Regeneration means that the person who was outside of Christ is now in Christ. Hence this is a radical, not just a superficial change.

(b) *Regeneration is a change which affects the whole person.* Most Reformed theologians opposed the view of John Cameron (1579-1625), a French theologian, that the Holy Spirit in regenerating a person merely illumines the mind or intellect in such a way that the will inevitably follows the guidance of the intellect in moral and spiritual matters. Not only does this view represent an erroneous type of faculty psychology; it is also quite unrealistic. I may be thoroughly convinced in my mind that a certain course of action is proper, but if I am still "dead in transgressions and sins," I will never follow that right course of action. The Arminians at the Synod of Dort also had an inadequate view of the role of the will in regeneration when they insisted that man's will was not at all affected by sin, so that all that was necessary was the removal of certain hindrances to the proper functioning of the will: "the darkness of the mind and the unruliness of the emotions."[20]

19. Canons of Dort, III-IV, Art. 12. See also Art. 11. For further references to regeneration in the Reformed creeds, see the Heidelberg Catechism, Q. 8; the Belgic Confession, Art. 24 (the broader view). The Westminster Confession does not generally use the term "regeneration"; it employs the expression "effectual calling" instead: see Chapter X; also Q. 31 in the Shorter Catechism.

20. Canons of Dort, III-IV, Rejection of Errors, Par. 3.

Over against these inadequate conceptions, Reformed theologians insisted that regeneration is a total change—a change which involves the
whole person. In Scriptural terms, regeneration means the giving of a new
heart. And the heart in Scripture stands for the inner core of the person,
the center of all activities, the fountain out of which all the streams of men-
tal and spiritual experiences flow: thinking, feeling, willing, believing,
praying, praising, and so on. It is this fountain which is renewed in
regeneration. It should be added, however, that this does not mean the
removal of all sinful tendencies. Though regenerated persons are new,
they are not yet perfect.[21]

(c) *Regeneration is a change which takes place below consciousness.* This is
evident, first, from the way the Scriptures describe our natural state. If we
are, as the Bible says, by nature dead in sin, corrupt, not subject to God's
law, not able to accept the things that come from the Spirit of God, we cannot consciously decide to change ourselves into the opposite of our natural
state. We must be changed at the very root of our being, in a supernatural
way. Hence this must be a change in what psychologists would call the
subconscious—a change which, however, is bound to reveal itself in our
conscious life.

Further, that this change takes place below consciousness is also evident from the terms used in the Bible to describe regeneration: "I will give
you a new heart"; "unless he is born from above"; "that which is born of
the flesh is flesh, and that which is born of the Spirit is spirit"; "made us
alive with Christ." Expressions of this sort denote a transformation so radical that it must be a change in the subconscious roots of our being. In
regeneration in the narrower sense, therefore, we are not active but passive.

"Irresistible Grace"

It is commonly said that Calvinists believe in "irresistible grace." This expression is, in fact, part of the "TULIP" acronym, which stands for the so-
called "Five Points of Calvinism": Total depravity, Unconditional election,
Limited atonement, Irresistible grace, and Perseverance of the saints.[22]
The term "irresistible grace" conveys an important biblical truth. As we
saw, regeneration is monergistic and not synergistic. It is not a work in
which God and man cooperate, but it is the work of God alone. All that

21. The question of the relationship between our regeneration and the sinful tenden-
cies that still remain in us will be taken up in Chapter 12.
22. For helpful discussions of these five points, together with Scriptural proof, see
Edwin H. Palmer, *The Five Points of Calvinism* (Grand Rapids: Baker, 1972); also David
N. Steele and Curtis C. Thomas, *The Five Points of Calvinism* (Philadelphia: Presbyterian and
Reformed, 1965).

was said about the natural state of fallen human beings, about effectual calling, and about the way in which God regenerates his people supports the affirmation that the grace which regenerates us is indeed irresistible.

Objections, however, have been raised against the use of the expression "irresistible grace." The first objection is that this term suggests a kind of overpowering domination on God's part, giving the impression that God violates our wills and deals with us as if we were things instead of persons. A second objection is the contention that God's grace may indeed sometimes be resisted—does not the Bible speak of those who resisted the Holy Spirit (Acts 7:51)?

These objections, however, can be answered. I dealt with the first objection earlier, in connection with effectual calling.[23] In reply to the contention that God violates our wills in regeneration, we may say that since we are by nature dead in sin, our wills need to be renewed so that we may again serve God as we should. God's action in regenerating us, therefore, is no more a violation of our wills than is the artificial respiration applied to a person whose breathing has stopped. Herman Bavinck has put it well: God's [effectual] calling "is so powerful that it cannot be conquered, and yet so loving that it excludes all force."[24] Or listen to C. S. Lewis: "The hardness of God is kinder than the softness of men, and His compulsion is our liberation."[25]

In connection with the second objection, it should be noted that the expression "irresistible grace" did not originate with the Calvinists. It was the Remonstrants (or Arminians) at the Synod of Dort (1618-19) who used this expression, which they had gotten from the Jesuits, to characterize the Reformed position on regeneration.[26] Bavinck goes on to say that Reformed theologians did not wish to deny that God's grace was often resisted. Therefore they preferred to speak of "invincible" or "unconquerable" grace, or to say that God's saving grace was "finally irresistible."[27] The grace of God may indeed be resisted, but it will not be successfully resisted by those whom God has chosen in Christ to salvation from before the creation of the world. As Cornelius Plantinga aptly says, "Nobody can finally hold out against God's grace. Nobody can outlast Him. Every elect person comes . . . to 'give in and admit that God is God.' "[28]

23. See above, pp. 89-91.
24. *Roeping en Wedergeboorte* (Kampen: Zalsman, 1903), p. 224.
25. *Surprised by Joy* (London: Collins, Fontana Books, 1960), p. 183.
26. Bavinck, *Dogmatiek*, 4:65.
27. Ibid., pp. 65-66.
28. Cornelius Plantinga, Jr., *A Place to Stand* (Grand Rapids: CRC Publications, 1979), p. 151.

REGENERATION RELATED TO OTHER DOCTRINES

(1) *The relation between regeneration and effectual calling.* Some Reformed
theologians wish to distinguish between regeneration and effectual calling. Louis Berkhof, for example, prefers to say that effectual calling follows regeneration in the narrower sense.[29] John Murray, however, thinks
that it is best to say that effectual calling precedes regeneration.[30]

I prefer to think of regeneration (in the narrower sense) and effectual
calling as identical. There is precedent for this view. Seventeenth-century
theology generally identified the two.[31] More recently the same position
was taken by Augustus Hopkins Strong[32] and Herman Bavinck.[33] Since
effectual calling is the sovereign work of God whereby he enables the
hearer of the gospel call to respond in repentance and faith, it is not different from regeneration. These two expressions describe the change from
spiritual death to spiritual life by means of different figures: the bestowal
of new life (regeneration) or the bestowal of the ability to respond to the
gospel call in faith (effectual calling).

We may note that these two are parallel in that both are new begin-
nings which lead to continuing spiritual growth. Regeneration issues in
conversion and leads to a life of obedience and consecration. Effectual calling, as we saw above, summons us to a distinctive kind of life: a life of fellowship with Christ, holiness, freedom, and peace.[34]

(2) *The relation between regeneration and conversion.* Regeneration, in the
narrower sense in which we have been discussing it, must not be identified with conversion but distinguished from it. Regeneration leads to
and issues in conversion (that is, in faith and repentance). Putting it the
other way, conversion is the outward evidence that regeneration has taken
place.

By way of illustration, we look again at Acts 16:14:

> One of those listening (*ēkouen*, imperfect) was a woman named Lydia, a
> dealer in purple cloth from the city of Thyatira, who was a worshiper of God.
> The Lord opened (*diēnoixen*, aorist) her heart to respond (*prosechein*, present)
> to Paul's message.

Since the heart stands for the inner core of the person, we may assume
that the opening of the heart describes regeneration. This led Lydia to
respond believingly to what Paul was saying—to accept it, to embrace it,

29. Berkhof, ST, p. 471.
30. *Redemption*, pp. 115, 119-20.
31. Berkhof, ST, p. 470.
32. *Systematic Theology* (Philadelphia: Griffith and Rowland, 1907), 3:793.
33. *Dogmatiek*, 4:59.
34. See above, pp. 86-87.

and to act upon it. This type of response is what we call conversion. Note the tenses used by Luke: while Lydia was listening to Paul (continuing action), the Lord in a moment of time opened her heart (snapshot action), so that she now began to give heed (continuing action) to what Paul was saying.

Regeneration and conversion, as in Lydia's case, occur simultaneously. But *causally* regeneration must be "prior" to conversion. One can only respond in repentance and faith after God has given new life. The situation can be compared to what happens when we turn on the faucet and the water starts running: the turning on of the faucet and the running of the water are simultaneous, but, in causal terms, the faucet must be turned on before the water starts running.

Regeneration, therefore, as we learned from the first epistle of John, will make itself felt in the new direction of our lives. This new life will result in "new views of God, of Christ, of sin, of holiness, of the world, of the gospel, and of the life to come."[35]

(3) *The relation between regeneration and sanctification.* In one sense the two are identical. As I hope to show later,[36] there is a sense in which sanctification is *definitive*. Definitive sanctification occurs at a point in time rather than along a time line; it means that at a certain moment we die to sin and are raised with Christ. It does not mean being able to live in sinless perfection, but it does mean that those who are in Christ have made a decisive and irreversible break with sin as the sphere in which they live, and are now enabled to serve God in the newness of the Holy Spirit. When sanctification is thus understood, it is identical with regeneration.

More commonly, however, sanctification is thought of as a lifelong process. When sanctification is seen in this way, regeneration must be understood to be the beginning of sanctification.[37] Regeneration is not a process but is instantaneous; however, it leads to a life of growth in holiness and obedience. Such growth is one of the blessings of sanctification. In this sense, then, regeneration is the first step in progressive sanctification. The two are related to each other as initial newness and progressive newness.

We should not fail to note here that regeneration has a social aspect. We often think of being "born again" as referring primarily to "personal salvation" in an individualistic sense. But we must remember that regeneration makes us members of the body of Christ.[38] It therefore has

35. Charles Hodge, *Systematic Theology* (1871; Grand Rapids: Eerdmans, 1940), 3:34.
36. See below, Chapter 12.
37. Cf., e.g., G. C. Berkouwer's chapter on regeneration in his *Faith and Sanctification*, trans. John Vriend (Grand Rapids: Eerdmans, 1952), entitled "The Genesis of Sanctification."
38. See the discussion of 1 Corinthians 12:13 on pp. 48-50 above.

social implications. It means that we owe love to one another as fellow members of Christ. Peter ties this in with our regeneration: "Love one another deeply, from the heart. For you have been born again" (1 Pet. 1:22-23). And Paul extends this obligation of love to all whom our lives may touch: "Therefore, as we have opportunity, let us do good to all people, especially to those who belong to the family of believers" (Gal. 6:10).

(4) *The relation between regeneration and baptism.* The New Testament often associates baptism with new spiritual life. Paul does so in Romans 6:3-4: "Don't you know that all of us who were baptized into Christ Jesus were baptized into his death? We were therefore buried with him through baptism into death in order that, just as Christ was raised from the dead through the glory of the Father, we too may live a new life." He also does so in Colossians 2:11-12, "In him [Christ] you were also circumcised, in the putting off of the sinful nature, . . . having been buried with him in baptism." Peter, in fact, affirms that the water of the flood "symbolizes baptism that now saves you also"—presumably, from sin (1 Pet. 3:21).

Some churches, indeed, teach baptismal regeneration. This, for example, is the official teaching of the Roman Catholic Church: "Other effects of Baptism are the remission of original and actual sin and of the punishment due to them (Denzinger, 1316) and regeneration in Christ or adopted sonship."[39] Lutherans also teach baptismal regeneration. This is how one Lutheran systematic theologian explains this teaching:

> Baptism is a means imparting the remission of sins. . . . Baptism . . . is a means to awaken and strengthen faith and therefore also a washing of regeneration and renewing of the Holy Ghost (Tit. 3:5). . . . Observe also that even as the remission of sin and regeneration are bestowed through Baptism as a means, . . . so also the implantation into the body of Christ . . . is wrought, and not merely portrayed, by the Holy Ghost through Baptism.[40]

Both Roman Catholics and Lutherans, however, teach that the regeneration received in baptism may again be lost.

The Reformed view of the sacraments, however, is that they are "holy signs and seals for us to see. They were instituted by God so that by our use of them he might make us understand more clearly the promise of the gospel, and might put his seal on that promise."[41] In Reformed theology baptism is not considered a means whereby regeneration is bestowed, but rather a sign and seal of our regeneration: "Baptism is a sacrament of the New Testament . . . to be unto him [the person baptized] a sign and seal

---

39. T. M. De Ferrari, "Baptism (Theology of)," in *The New Catholic Encyclopedia* (New York: McGraw-Hill, 1967), 2:65.

40. Francis Pieper, *Christian Dogmatics,* Vol. 3 (St. Louis: Concordia, 1953), pp. 264, 269-70.

41. Heidelberg Catechism, Q. 66 (1975 trans.).

of the covenant of grace, of his ingrafting into Christ, of regeneration, of remission of sins, and of his giving up unto God, through Jesus Christ, to walk in newness of life. . . ."[42]

Baptism, therefore, does not automatically bring about regeneration, but it pictures (its function as a sign) and confirms (its function as a seal) that blessing. For those baptized as adults, it confirms the blessing as these adults continue to accept by faith God's promise of new life in Christ presented in the gospel. For those baptized as infants, the sacrament confirms the blessing as they later on accept by faith what their baptism stood for.[43]

REGENERATION AND THE PREACHER

We now face a problem. If regeneration, as has been shown, is totally the work of God and not in any sense the work of man, what can the preacher do about it? He may tell his hearers that they must be born again (John 3:7). But he cannot urge them to regenerate themselves, since they cannot do this. Neither can he urge them to become regenerated, since only the Holy Spirit can bestow regeneration. How, then, must the preacher handle the doctrine of regeneration?

By way of reply, I would like at this point to discuss *the relation between regeneration and the word.* Regeneration usually occurs during the preaching, teaching, or reading of the Bible. From Acts 16:14 we have learned that Lydia's regeneration took place as she was listening to Paul's gospel message.

We look next at James 1:18, "He [God] chose to give us birth *(apekyēsen)* through the word of truth, that we might be a kind of firstfruits of all he created." The verb here used, *apokyein,* does not mean "to beget" but "to give birth to." It is used earlier in verse 15 of this chapter, where James says that sin, when it is full-grown, gives birth to death. God the Father, however, who is the source of every good and perfect gift (v. 17), has shown us his unfathomable mercy by giving us new birth—a birth which is the evidence of our having received new spiritual life. The new birth as James here describes it is not regeneration in the narrower sense

42. Westminster Confession, XXVIII, 1.
43. Attention is called at this point to Abraham Kuyper's view of presupposed prebaptismal regeneration as a ground for the baptism of the infants of believing parents. It is to be presupposed, so he taught, that such children have usually been regenerated already before they are baptized, and that therefore their baptism is the seal of a grace presumed to be already present (see Smilde, *Eeuw van Strijd,* pp. 107, 114, 116-17). This understanding, however, was not accepted by most Reformed theologians. The common Reformed position is that the infants of believing parents should be baptized because they are members of the covenant of grace (see on this point Berkhof, ST, pp. 639-40).

—the implanting of new life—but in the broader sense, namely, the first manifestation of the new life in conversion.[44] Regeneration in this broader sense, James is here saying, is produced in us through the word of truth, through the Bible.

Peter makes a similar point:

> Now that you have purified yourselves by obeying the truth so that you have sincere love for your brothers, love one another deeply, from the heart. For you have been born again *(anagegennēmenoi)*, not of perishable seed, but of imperishable, through the living and enduring work of God (1 Pet. 1:22-23).

The verb *anagennaō* means either "to beget again" or "to cause to be born again." In this passage, as well as in the third verse of this chapter, it is commonly understood in the second sense, and it is so translated in the New International Version. You have been born again, Peter tells his readers, "through the living and enduring word of God"; from verse 25 it is evident that Peter is referring to the preached word. We note again that regeneration in the broader sense is brought about through the preaching of the Bible. The gospel is, in fact, called "the seed of regeneration" in the Canons of Dort.[45]

We conclude, therefore, that though God by his Holy Spirit works regeneration in the narrower sense in us immediately, directly, and invincibly, the first manifestations of that new spiritual life come into existence through the word — whether it be preached, taught, or read.[46] New spiritual life, in other words, is bestowed immediately by God; but the new birth is produced mediately, through the word.

What, then, is the preacher's duty as far as regeneration is concerned? He must preach the gospel. Such preaching and teaching is essential: "How, then, can they call on the one they have not believed in? And how can they believe in the one of whom they have not heard? And how can they hear without someone preaching to them?" (Rom. 10:14). The preacher cannot demand regeneration from his hearers, but he can and should call them to faith in the gospel and repentance from sin.

This is precisely what Jesus did. After having told Nicodemus about the need for regeneration (John 3:3, 5), Jesus went on to say, "For God so

44. See above, pp. 93-94.
45. Canons of Dort, III-IV, Art. 17.
46. There are, however, exceptions to this rule. Infants of believers who die in infancy, and are therefore unable to respond to the word, can be regenerated apart from the word. Note Westminster Confession, X,3: "Elect infants, dying in infancy, are regenerated and saved by Christ through the Spirit, who worketh when, and where, and how he pleaseth. So also are all other elect persons who are incapable of being outwardly called by the ministry of the Word." Cf. also Canons of Dort, I,17.

loved the world that he gave his one and only Son, that whoever believes in him shall not perish but have eternal life" (v. 16). This is also what Peter did on the Day of Pentecost: "Repent and be baptized, every one of you" (Acts 2:38). This, too, is what Paul did. When the Philippian jailer asked, "What must I do to be saved?" Paul replied, "Believe in the Lord Jesus, and you will be saved" (Acts 16:30-31). When Nicodemus and the jailer believed the gospel message, they came to realize that God had given them new life in regeneration. They became aware of their regeneration through its results.

But, you may say, how can I ask a person to do something he or she cannot do in his or her own strength? We must trust that God will give the hearer the ability to repent and believe. A good illustration is Jesus' healing of the paralytic. Jesus said to this man, "Get up, take your mat and go home" (Matt. 9:6). But the poor man was not able to get up; he was paralyzed. Yet Jesus told him to get up. As Jesus did so, he bestowed on the man strength enabling him to get up. So the preacher must trust that God will enable the hearers of the gospel to respond in faith. And the hearer must trust that God will give him or her strength to accept the preached word with a believing heart.

With respect to his believing hearers, the preacher's duty and privilege is to remind them of the amazing dimensions of the miraculous new birth they have experienced. We often fail to recognize these dimensions. There is often little appreciation for the newness we have in Christ. Our lives often fail to glow with the radiance of God.

The preacher should set forth the full biblical teaching on regeneration, thus helping his hearers to be more and more what in Christ they already are. Regeneration means *new life.* After the apostles had been imprisoned, an angel of the Lord opened the doors of the jail and said to them, "Go . . . and tell the people the full message of this new life" (Acts 5:20). Paul tells us that we have been made one with Christ so that "as Christ was raised from the dead by the glory of the Father, we too might walk in newness of life" (Rom. 6:4, RSV). And in Romans 7:6 he reminds us that we now serve "in the new way of the Spirit, and not in the old way of the written code."

As regenerated people we now live and walk *in the light.* "Whoever lives by the truth comes into the light" (John 3:21). We who claim to have fellowship with God "walk in the light, as he [God] is in the light" (1 John 1:7). As those who have been born again, we must "put aside the deeds of darkness and put on the armor of light" (Rom. 13:12).

Born-again people are part of God's *new creation.* We have been created anew in Christ (Eph. 2:10). "Neither circumcision nor uncircumcision means anything; what counts is a new creation" (Gal. 6:15). And this is what we are. Listen to Paul's exhilarating trumpet call: "Therefore, if anyone is in Christ, he is a new creation; the old has gone, the new has come!" (2 Cor. 5:17).

Let the people of God, then, see themselves in this light. This is what it means to be born again. It does not mean sinless perfection, but it does mean newness. Those who are in Christ are genuinely new, though not yet totally new.[47]

47. On the doctrine of regeneration, see also W. E. Best, *Regeneration and Conversion* (Grand Rapids: Baker, 1975); Helmut Burkhardt, *The Biblical Doctrine of Regeneration*, trans. O. R. Johnston (Downers Grove: InterVarsity, 1978); Stephen Charnock, *The Doctrine of Regeneration* (1840; Grand Rapids: Baker, 1980); Johnnie C. Godwin, *What It Means to be Born Again* (Nashville: Broadman Press, 1977); Herman A. Hoyt, *Expository Messages on the New Birth* (Grand Rapids: Baker, 1961); Arthur W. Pink, *Regeneration or the New Birth* (Swengel, PA: Bible Truth Depot, n.d.).

CHAPTER 8

Conversion

CHARLES SPURGEON WAS ON HIS WAY TO CHURCH ONE SUNDAY MORN-
ing. It was snowing. The snow was so heavy that he trudged down a side
street and came to a little Primitive Methodist Chapel. A thin-looking man
—a shoemaker, or tailor, or something of that sort—went into the pulpit
to preach. The preacher announced his text: "Look unto me, and be ye
saved, all the ends of the earth" (Isa. 45:22). Though grammar and diction
left much to be desired, he spoke earnestly and directly to his audience of
twelve. Finally the preacher looked at Spurgeon, who was sitting under
the gallery, and said, "Young man, you look very miserable . . . and you
will always be miserable if you don't obey my text. Look to Jesus Christ!
You have nothin' to do but to look and live!" Spurgeon looked to Christ
in faith, and the darkness of his soul rolled away. He had found salvation.[1]

This account of Spurgeon's conversion leads us to our next topic.
Conversion, as was pointed out earlier, is the outward evidence of
regeneration. When we speak of conversion, we are looking at the Christian life from the viewpoint of its new direction: away from sin and toward
God. Commonly conversion is thought of as consisting in repentance and
faith; these two aspects will be discussed in detail in the next chapters. In
this chapter I wish to make some comments about conversion as a whole.

CONVERSION DEFINED

Briefly, conversion may be defined as the conscious act of a regenerate person in which he or she turns to God in repentance and faith. It involves a
twofold turning: away from sin and toward the service of God. In its
richest sense, conversion should include the following elements: (1) il-
lumination of the mind, whereby sin comes to be known in its true sense,
as behavior which is displeasing to God; (2) genuine sorrow for sin, not

---

1. Condensed from the account found in *The Autobiography of Charles H. Spurgeon,*
reproduced in Hugh T. Kerr and John M. Mulder, eds., *Conversions* (Grand Rapids:
Eerdmans, 1983), pp. 129-32.

just remorse because of its bitter results; (3) humble confession of sin, both to God and to others who were hurt by our sin; (4) hatred of sin, including a deliberate resolve to flee from it; (5) a return to God as our gracious Father in Christ, in faith that he can and will forgive our sins; (6) a wholehearted joy in God through Christ; (7) genuine love for God and others, together with delight in God's service.[2]

CONVERSION THE WORK OF GOD AND MAN

Conversion is first of all the work of God. Though conversion is the outward evidence of regeneration, the new life implanted in regeneration continues to exist only in dependence on God. We cannot maintain that new life in our own strength. We need to continue to be strengthened with power through God's Spirit in our inner being (Eph. 3:16).

Old Testament believers wanting to be converted to God but lacking the strength to do so realized that only God could enable them to turn back to himself: "Restore us to yourself, O LORD, that we may return; renew our days as of old" (Lam. 5:21; cf. Jer. 31:18). The New Testament similarly underlines this point. Jesus taught that the new life received in regeneration can only reveal itself as we remain in union with him: "I am the vine; you are the branches. If a man remains in me and I in him, he will bear much fruit; apart from me you can do nothing" (John 15:5). In a startling statement which spans our entire history from the moment of the new birth to the appearance of our Lord upon the clouds of heaven, Paul tells us that he is confident "that he who began a good work in you will carry it on to completion until the day of Christ Jesus" (Phil. 1:6). Surely this sovereign work of God includes our conversion. As will be shown, both repentance and faith, which are aspects of conversion, are gifts of God.

We could say, therefore, that God is the cause of our conversion.

> But "cause" is a cold word which suggests mechanically forcing somebody to do something he does not want to do. The real situation is infinitely more complex, mysterious, existential. People, as they later see, are moved, drawn, lured by God. They are "chased down by the hound of heaven." But while they are going through the process of conversion, God's movements may be largely hidden in events that seem quite "natural." An old friend turns up; you come upon a book; a disappointing job obliges you to reexamine your goals; you discover that earning more money does not satisfy you.[3]

In distinction from regeneration in the narrower sense, however, conversion is also a work of man. In fact, both in the Old and New Testaments,

2. Bavinck, *Dogmatiek*, 4:152.
3. Cornelius Plantinga, Jr., *A Place to Stand*, Teacher's Manual (Grand Rapids: CRC Publications, 1979), pp. 114-15.

conversion is pictured more often as a work of man than as a work of God. Abraham Kuyper points out that the Old Testament word *shūbh*, meaning "to turn back," occurs 74 times as a description of man's turning to God, but only five times as a designation of conversion as a deed of God; he also observes that in the New Testament the words for conversion are used 26 times to describe conversion as a human activity, but only two or three times to depict conversion as a work of God.[4]

From the Old Testament we may recall the passage whereby the old shoemaker brought about Spurgeon's conversion: "Look unto me, and be ye saved, all the ends of the earth" (Isa. 45:22, KJV; cf. also 55:7). Or we may think of Ezekiel 33:11, "Turn! Turn from your evil ways! Why will you die, O house of Israel?" New Testament passages describing conversion as a requirement for human beings include Peter's summons on the Day of Pentecost: "Repent and be baptized, every one of you, in the name of Jesus Christ so that your sins may be forgiven" (Acts 2:38). Paul's words to the Philippian jailer also come to mind: "Believe in the Lord Jesus, and you will be saved—you and your household" (Acts 16:31). As Paul unfolds the precious truth of salvation by grace, he again calls for the exercise of personal faith: "If you confess with your mouth, 'Jesus is Lord,' and believe in your heart that God raised him from the dead, you will be saved" (Rom. 10:9). And in 2 Corinthians he trumpets forth the marching orders for preachers of the gospel: "We are therefore Christ's ambassadors, as though God were making his appeal through us. We implore you on Christ's behalf: Be reconciled to God" (2 Cor. 5:20).

In all these passages, and many more, God calls on us to be converted, to turn to him, to repent and believe, to be reconciled to him. In the doctrine of conversion, therefore, we see an example of the paradox we discussed earlier:[5] conversion is both the work of God and the work of man. God must convert us, and yet we must turn to him; both are true. We should not jettison either side of the paradox. The preacher therefore must earnestly and fervently urge his hearers to be converted, trusting that God will enable them to do so. And when conversion does occur, he as well as his hearers must give God all the praise.

VARIOUS TYPES OF CONVERSIONS

We may distinguish various types of conversions. *True conversion*, as defined above, can occur only once in a person's life. The Bible gives many examples: Naaman (2 Kings 5:15), Manasseh (2 Chron. 33:12-13), Zacchaeus (Luke 19:8-9), the three thousand on the Day of Pentecost (Acts

---

4. *Dictaten Dogmatiek*, 2nd ed. (Kampen: Kok, 1910), Vol. 4, *Locus de Salute*, p. 94.
5. See above, pp. 5-7.

2:41), Saul (Acts 9:1-19), Cornelius (Acts 10:44-48), Lydia (Acts 16:14), the Philippian jailer (Acts 16:29-34).

The Bible occasionally speaks of so-called *national conversions:* times when an entire nation returned to the Lord. One such national conversion occurred under Joshua, when the people of Israel pledged to serve the LORD and to obey him (Josh. 24:14-27). Other national conversions occurred under Hezekiah (2 Chron. 29:10-36) and Josiah (2 Kings 23:1-3). We also recall the conversion of the people of Nineveh in response to Jonah's preaching (Jonah 3:1-10). These "national conversions," however, were all short-lived. They certainly did not bring about the true conversion of every member of the nation. In the case of Israel, after the godly ruler had been succeeded by an evil one, the people went back to their sinful ways.

We note that there may be *temporary conversions*—conversions which are not genuine but only apparent. Jesus speaks about such a conversion in the Parable of the Sower—the person who received the seed that fell in rocky places. This kind of sowing describes the man who "hears the word and at once receives it with joy. But since he has no root, he lasts only a short time. When trouble or persecution comes because of the word, he quickly falls away" (Matt. 13:20-21). People, in other words, may sometimes seem to have been converted, but the appearance is deceiving.

The New Testament gives some actual examples: Hymenaeus and Alexander (1 Tim. 1:19-20), Philetus (2 Tim. 2:17-18), and Demas, who "loved this present world" (2 Tim. 4:10). The Apostle John, in fact, penned sad words about those who

> went out from us, but . . . did not really belong to us. For if they had belonged to us, they would have remained with us; but their going showed that none of them belonged to us (1 John 2:19).

There can also be *second conversions.* Whereas true conversion cannot be repeated, it is possible for a believer to drift so far away from God that he must return to God again. Though David was indeed a converted man, having been called "a man after God's own heart" (1 Sam. 13:14), he fell into outrageous sin. Psalm 51, however, written after David's fall, records his "second conversion":

> Cleanse me with hyssop, and I will be clean;
>   wash me, and I will be whiter than snow. . . .
> Hide your face from my sins
>   and blot out all my iniquity,
> Create in me a pure heart, O God,
>   and renew a stedfast spirit within me. . . .
> Restore to me the joy of your salvation
>   and grant me a willing spirit (Ps. 51:7, 9-10, 12).

A second conversion was also necessary in the life of Peter. Before his shameful denial of his Lord, Jesus had said to him, "Simon, Simon, Satan has asked to sift you as wheat. But I have prayed for you, Simon, that your faith may not fail. And when you have turned back, strengthen your brothers" (Luke 22:31-32). This "turning back" cannot mean Peter's first conversion, since he had earlier made his great confession, "You are the Christ, the Son of the living God" (Matt. 16:16), and since Jesus here said, "that your faith may not fail." What Jesus here predicted was a returning to the Lord after Peter's disgraceful sin.

The letters to the seven churches of Asia Minor found in the Book of Revelation also enjoin some readers to second conversions. To the church in Ephesus Jesus writes: "Repent and do the things you did at first" (Rev. 2:5). Similar summons are found in Revelation 2:16; 2:22; 3:3; and 3:19. The people here addressed had turned to Christ, but had drifted into sexual immorality, idolatry, merely nominal Christianity, and spiritual luke-warmness. From these sins they had to turn away.

Second conversions of this sort are not always necessary in the lives of believers. But they may become so. When they do, they do not mean a turning away from sin in its totality, as in true conversion, but from some particular sin into which a Christian has fallen.

It is interesting to note that the Canons of Dort, in the very chapter in which they affirm the perseverance of the saints, recognize the type of situation we are now discussing. After having said that believers must constantly watch and pray so that they may not be led into temptation, the Canons go on to say,

> When they [believers] fail to do this, not only *can* they be carried away by the flesh, the world, and Satan into sins, even serious and outrageous ones, but also by God's just permission they sometimes *are* so carried away—witness the sad cases, described in Scripture, of David, Peter, and other saints falling into sins.[6]

The Canons then go on to describe what I have called second conversion: "God, who is rich in mercy, according to his unchangeable purpose of election does not take his Holy Spirit from his own completely, even when they fall grievously. . . . By his Word and Spirit he certainly and effectively renews them to repentance."[7]

VARIATIONS IN THE PATTERN OF CONVERSION

Though true conversion can occur only once, there can be many variations

---

6. Canons of Dort, V,4 (1986 trans.).
7. Ibid., V,6 and 7.

in its pattern. Herman Bavinck points out some interesting differences between the conversions of the great Reformers:

> Luther's conversion was a transition from deep feelings of guilt to the joyful awareness of God's forgiving grace in Christ. Zwingli experienced conversion particularly as a being set free from the bondage of the law into the happiness of knowing himself to be a child of God. Calvin's conversion, however, was a deliverance from error into truth, from doubt to certainty.[8]

The pattern of conversion may also vary in other ways. Although the entire person is always involved, a conversion may be predominantly intellectual, volitional, or emotional. An example of a primarily intellectual conversion would be that of C. S. Lewis, who in his spiritual autobiography *Surprised by Joy* indicates that he wrestled with intellectual problems and hindrances until finally, after he had met those difficulties and had surrendered himself to God, God dragged him, kicking and screaming, into the Kingdom, "the most dejected and reluctant convert in all England."[9] An example of a predominantly volitional conversion would be that of Augustine who, after years of fruitless struggling against his sins, finally, upon reading Romans 13:14 ("Put on the Lord Jesus Christ, and make no provision for the flesh, to fulfil the lusts thereof"), found in Christ the strength to overcome.[10] An example of a conversion which was chiefly emotional in nature would be that of John Bunyan who, after years of emotional upheavals caused by fear that he had committed the unpardonable sin, finally found peace of soul by resting in Christ.[11]

The most common variation in the pattern of conversion is that between gradual and sudden or crisis conversions. The outstanding biblical example of a crisis conversion is, of course, that of the Apostle Paul. One can hardly imagine a more dramatic occurrence: fire-breathing Saul, on his way to Damascus to persecute Christians, was suddenly, through a blinding light and a voice from heaven, turned into missionary Paul (Acts 9:1-19; see also 22:3-14 and 26:9-18). The conversions of Lydia (Acts 16:13-14) and of the Philippian jailer (Acts 16:25-34) were also of the crisis type. It seems likely that most of the Gentiles who were brought to Christ by Paul and the other apostles experienced crisis conversions, since conversion for them meant not just a recognition of Jesus as the Christ, but also a sharp break with a former life of sin (see 1 Cor. 6:11; Eph. 2:11-13).

Since the New Testament describes the establishment of the church by missionaries, it does not give us specific examples of gradual conversions, that is, conversions which take place over a period of time. We may

8. Bavinck, *Dogmatiek*, 4:159 [trans. mine].
9. See Kerr and Mulder, *Conversions*, pp. 199-204.
10. Ibid., pp. 11-14.
11. Ibid., pp. 48-53. Many other fascinating conversion accounts are found in this book. They reveal great variety in the pattern of conversion.

think of Timothy, whose grandmother Lois and mother Eunice are said to have been believers (2 Tim. 1:5), and who is said to have known the Scriptures from infancy (2 Tim. 3:15). Yet even Timothy probably embraced the Christian faith, in distinction from the Jewish faith in which he had been brought up, at a certain time—when he met Paul in Lystra (Acts 16:1). The exhortation, however, to bring up children "in the training and instruction of the Lord" (Eph. 6:4) strongly suggests that the conversions of the children of Christian parents are usually of the gradual rather than of the crisis type.[12]

This brings up the question: Do covenant children—that is, the children of Christian parents—need to be converted? If children have been brought up in the Christian faith from infancy, we would not ordinarily expect to see the dramatic change in their lives that is associated with a crisis conversion. We would rather expect to see a gradual growth into a mature Christian faith and a dedicated Christian life. But this does not mean that covenant children do not need to be converted. Every covenant child must make a personal commitment to Christ. There must be a personal realization of sin, a deepening of faith, an appropriation of the blessings of salvation, and a dedication to the service of the Lord.

The conversions of covenant children will, therefore, ordinarily be of the gradual type. But, since no two people are alike, there may also be many differences in their conversions.

> Much variation is possible in the way in which those born of Christian parents later come to conversion. Some are led gently, with no earthshaking upheavals, growing steadily from childhood to young manhood, and from young manhood to full maturity as fathers in Christ. Others, however, who for a time openly lived sinful lives, or became alienated from their Christian upbringing, are suddenly brought to conversion, through some gripping word or arresting circumstance, often by means of a violent emotional struggle.[13]

As was said earlier,[14] there is a tendency in covenant communities simply to assume that all children of believers are "automatically" saved because they have been brought up in Christian homes. As a result, preaching in covenantal churches often fails to include a summons to the unsaved to turn to Christ in faith and repentance. But this is a serious deficiency. Children of believing parents, as well as children whose parents are not believers, must personally and consciously give their hearts to Christ and their lives to his service, and they should be summoned from the pulpit to do so. Let us listen to Bavinck once again:

---

12. See G. W. Bromiley, "Conversion," ISBE, 1:768-70.
13. Bavinck, *Dogmatiek*, 4:158 [trans. mine].
14. See above, p. 69.

In preaching addressed to the church the earnest summons to faith and conversion ought never to be lacking. Preaching on the basis of the covenant of grace does not excuse the preacher from such a summons but, on the contrary, obligates him to do so. . . . For no matter how great are the blessings God gives us in that covenant—that we have been included in the covenant of grace from birth, that we have been born into a Christian church and of Christian parents, that we have been baptized and brought up in a Christian family — all these blessings are still not enough. Ultimately everything depends on personal, saving faith; only he who believes in the Son has everlasting life. Even within the church, therefore, everyone must examine himself and prove himself, to see whether he is in the faith.[15]

Conversion is a necessary step in or aspect of the process of salvation. But not all of God's people experience conversion in the same way. We may not therefore set up one pattern of conversion for everybody. Pietists and those who are mystically inclined maintain that people must go through a violent and agonizing soul-struggle, must first have hung for a while on the very edge of despair, before they can consider themselves to have been soundly converted. Although it is true that one must have genuine sorrow for sin, we cannot and may not expect everyone to have the same kind of emotional experience in his or her conversion. Others insist that every Christian should know the day or the hour of his conversion. This insistence usually goes along with the understanding that only a crisis conversion is authentic.

But this is not necessary. To set up the same pattern for everyone is highly dangerous and contrary to Scripture. What is most important about a conversion is not the way in which it occurs, or even the time at which it occurs, but its genuineness. If one is going in the wrong direction, it is immaterial whether he or she now makes a U-turn or goes around several blocks; the thing that matters is whether in the end he or she is going in the right direction.[16]

15. Herman Bavinck, *Roeping en Wedergeboorte* (Kampen: Zalsman, 1903), pp. 184-85 [trans. mine].

16. Other recent studies of conversion include W. E. Best, *Regeneration and Conversion* (Grand Rapids: Baker, 1975); Bernhard Citron, *The New Birth: A Study of the Evangelical Doctrine of Conversion in the Protestant Fathers* (Edinburgh: University Press, 1951); Hans Kasdorf, *Christian Conversion in Context* (Scottdale: Herald Press, 1980); Eric Routley, *The Gift of Conversion* (London: Lutterworth, 1957).

A specific type of conversion occurs when a former cult member becomes a true Christian. See, e.g., William J. Schnell, *Thirty Years a Watchtower Slave* (Grand Rapids: Baker, 1956); James R. Adair and Ted Miller, eds., *We Found Our Way Out* (Grand Rapids: Baker, 1964); Edmund C. Gruss, *We Left Jehovah's Witnesses* (Philadelphia: Presbyterian and Reformed, 1974).

CHAPTER 9

Repentance

MATTHEW'S GOSPEL TELLS THE STORY OF TWO MEN WHO EVIDENCED sorrow for their sins. The first is Peter, who shamefully denied his Lord. Afterward "he went outside and wept bitterly" (Matt. 26:75). Some days later Jesus restored him to his discipleship, telling him to feed his sheep (John 21:15-17).

The other is Judas, who betrayed his Master for 30 pieces of silver. When he saw that Jesus had been condemned, he "repented himself" (KJV), saying, "I have sinned, for I have betrayed innocent blood" (Matt. 27:3). After having hurled the pieces of silver into the temple, Judas went away and hanged himself.

There was a world of difference between these two. Peter's repentance, resulting as it did in forgiveness and restoration, was genuine. Judas's was not. Though Judas realized that he had done wrong, there is no evidence that he confessed his sin to Jesus and begged him for forgiveness. The word rendered "repented himself" in the King James Version is a form of the Greek verb *metamelomai*, literally, "to care for afterward"; the New International Version here translates it, "he was seized with remorse." Judas's subsequent suicide ends one of the saddest chapters in the Bible. It brings to mind Jesus' solemn words, "Woe to that man who betrays the Son of Man! It would be better for him if he had not been born" (Matt. 26:24).

It is important, therefore, to know what true repentance is. Conversion, as was said earlier, is commonly thought of as involving two aspects, repentance and faith. We now take up these two aspects in turn, beginning with repentance.

THE IMPORTANCE OF REPENTANCE

It is exciting to observe that the New Testament both begins (Matt. 3:2) and ends (Rev. 3:19) with a summons to repentance. This fact leads William D. Chamberlain, in his excellent study *The Meaning of Repentance*, to write,

The important fact for our purpose is that the first note and the last note struck in the New Testament is repentance. It is the most universal note in the New Testament, even more so than the Resurrection. This is especially noteworthy in light of the fact that it was belief in the Resurrection that made Christian preaching possible. Repentance gave Christian preaching its objective.[1]

To illustrate this importance, let us look at a few representative passages. Both John the Baptist and Jesus begin their public ministries by preaching, "Repent, for the kingdom of heaven is near" (Matt. 3:2; 4:17). The entire thrust of the Sermon on the Mount is that in order to enter the kingdom of heaven people must repent of their sinful practices, completely change their thought processes, and seek to follow what Jesus commands. When, after his resurrection, Jesus appeared to his disciples, he opened their minds so that they could understand the Scriptures, telling them, "This is what is written: The Christ will suffer and rise from the dead on the third day, and repentance and forgiveness of sins will be preached in his name to all nations, beginning at Jerusalem" (Luke 24:46-47). The preaching of repentance, then, is the purpose of Jesus' suffering and resurrection.

What was the purpose of Paul's ministry? He explains this in his speech before King Agrippa. When Jesus appeared to Paul on the road to Damascus, he said,

> I will rescue you from your own people and from the Gentiles. I am sending you to them to open their eyes and turn them from darkness to light, and from the power of Satan to God (Acts 26:17-18).

Paul's ministry, therefore, was to bring people to repentance. In this light we can understand his words to his hearers in Athens: "Therefore since we are God's offspring, we should not think that the divine being is like gold or silver or stone. . . . In the past God overlooked such ignorance, but now he commands all people everywhere to repent" (Acts 17:30-31). Note also Paul's universal appeal in Romans 2:4, "Do you show contempt for the riches of his [God's] kindness, tolerance and patience, not realizing that God's kindness leads you toward repentance?"

In the last book of the Bible the exalted Lord, speaking to the church in Laodicea, repeats his urgent summons to repentance: "Those whom I love I rebuke and discipline. So be earnest and repent" (Rev. 3:19). And Peter tells us that the reason Christ has not yet returned to earth is that he wishes people everywhere to repent and be saved: "The Lord is not slow in keeping his promise, as some understand slowness. He is patient with

---

1. *The Meaning of Repentance* (Philadelphia: Westminster, 1943), p. 80.

you, not wanting anyone to perish, but everyone to come to repentance" (2 Pet. 3:9).

THE RELATION BETWEEN REPENTANCE AND FAITH

Sometimes the question is discussed: Which is prior, repentance or faith? Some theologians hold that repentance should precede faith: "Repentance leads immediately to saving faith, which is at once the condition and the instrument of justification."[2] Others, however, maintain that repentance follows faith. Calvin, for example, states the point strongly:

> Now it ought to be a fact beyond controversy that repentance not only constantly follows faith but is also born of faith. . . . Such persons have never known the power of repentance. . . .[3]

Actually, we ought not to speak of the priority of either. Though repentance can and should be distinguished from faith, these two should never be separated. Both follow from regeneration and are aspects of conversion. John Murray puts it well:

> The faith that is unto salvation is a penitent faith and the repentance that is unto life is a believing repentance. . . . Faith is faith in Christ for salvation from sin. But if faith is directed to salvation from sin, there must be hatred of sin and the desire to be saved from it. Such hatred of sin involves repentance. . . . Again, if we remember that repentance is turning from sin unto God, the turning to God implies faith in the mercy of God as revealed in Christ. It is impossible to disentangle faith and repentance. Saving faith is permeated with repentance and repentance is permeated with faith.[4]

WORD STUDY

The Old Testament words for repentance are *nicham* and *shūbh. Nicham,* the niphal form of *nācham,* means to be sorry, to be moved to pity, or to repent of wrongdoings. It is often used of God to indicate a change or possible change in his plans: Genesis 6:6-7; Exodus 32:12, 14; Deuteronomy 32:36; Judges 2:18. But this word is also used to describe sorrow for sin in human beings: Judges 21:6, 15; Job 42:6; Jeremiah 8:6; 31:19. The passage from Job illustrates the second usage: "Therefore I despise myself and repent in dust and ashes."

Much more commonly used for repentance is the other Old Testament word, *shūbh.* This word means to turn back, to go in the opposite

---

2. H. Orton Wiley, *Christian Theology* (1940; Kansas City: Beacon Hill, 1958), 2:364.
3. *Inst.,* III.iii.1.
4. *Redemption—Accomplished and Applied* (Grand Rapids: Eerdmans, 1955), p. 140.

direction. It highlights the fact that repentance means a change of direction, from the wrong way to the right way. It means a turning away from
sin (1 Kings 8:35), from iniquity (Job 36:10, ASV), from transgression (Isa.
59:20, ASV), from wickedness (Ezek. 3:19), and from evil ways (Neh. 9:35).
Positively, *shūbh* means turning to the Lord: Psalm 51:13; Isaiah 10:21;
Jeremiah 4:1; Hosea 14:1; Amos 4:8; Malachi 3:7. The second half of the
last-named verse reads: "Return to me, and I will return to you, says the
LORD Almighty."

Rich promises are attached to such returning to the LORD. When
God's people do this, God will hear from heaven, forgive their sin, and
heal their land (2 Chron. 7:14); the LORD will have mercy on them and
abundantly pardon (Isa. 55:11); and the LORD will prevent their death
(Ezek. 33:11). But the prophets insist that such a turning to the LORD must
be a matter of the heart:

> "Even now," declares the LORD, "return to me with all your heart, with fast-
> ing and weeping and mourning." Rend your heart and not your garments.
> Return to the LORD your God, for he is gracious and compassionate, slow to
> anger and abounding in love (Joel 2:12-13).

The two chief New Testament words for repentance are *metanoia* and
epistrephō. The verb corresponding to *metanoia* is *metanoeō*; it is the common Septuagint rendering of *nicham*. *Epistrephō*, however, is the common
Septuagint translation of *shūbh*. Though one cannot draw hard and fast
lines, generally *metanoia* seems to emphasize the inner change involved in
repentance, whereas *epistrephō* stresses the change in one's outward life
which implements and gives expression to the inward change.

We look next at the meaning of *metanoia* and *metanoeō*. At this point I
must issue an important corrective. We usually tend to think of repentance, as described by the New Testament word *metanoia*, primarily in
negative terms. We are inclined to think of it as an emotional crisis consisting of sorrow for sin and fear of punishment, involving regret, remorse,
and much introspection. Popular understandings of repentance tend to
turn the Christian's gaze backward instead of forward, and inward rather
than outward. The traditional view seems to rivet a person's attention
upon himself or herself rather than on others, and to lead to a gloomy instead of a joyful piety.

One of the reasons for this misunderstanding can be found in the standard translations of the verb *metanoeō*. The Latin Vulgate rendered this
verb with the phrase *poenitentiam agite* (literally, "do penance"), suggesting an external understanding of repentance, as if it consisted only in the
doing of certain works of satisfaction. The so-called Douai Bible, a Roman
Catholic English version, the New Testament part of which appeared in

1582, perpetuated this error by rendering *metanoeō* with "do penance." Luther's German Bible followed the Vulgate tradition, translating the verb in question by *thut Busse*, "do penance." Even some modern German versions still use this expression. The older French Bibles rendered *metanoeō* by *repentez-vous*, which stresses remorse, regret, and compunction. A similar comment can be made about the older Spanish translation, *arrepentios*. Our English versions generally render *metanoeō* with "repent" — a word which lays undue stress on the emotional side of the change involved, emphasizing sorrow for past sin. Chamberlain summarizes the effect of these renderings in the following words: "These infelicitous translations have caused much of European and American Christianity to chant its faith in the wrong key: regret, remorse, and morbid introspection have been regarded as characteristics of true piety."[5]

Metanoeō and *metanoia* have a much richer meaning than these translations suggest. The noun is a combination of *meta* and *nous*. *Meta* means with, after, or beyond; in this case it points to a change in what follows. *Nous* means mind, attitude, way of thinking, disposition, character, or moral consciousness. Literally, therefore, *metanoia* means a change of mind or heart. It involves much more than sorrow for sin (though this is included), more also than just an intellectual change. It involves a change in the entire person, and in his or her outlook on life. You could say that it means a change of thinking, feeling, and willing. J. B. Phillips has caught the meaning of the verb *metanoeō* very well: "You must change your hearts and minds—for the kingdom of heaven has arrived" (Matt. 4:17).

Arndt and Gingrich define *metanoia* as follows: "A change of mind, repentance, turning about, conversion. . . . Mostly of the positive side of repentance, as the beginning of a new religious and moral life."[6] *Metanoia* therefore means not just a turning away from evil deeds, but also a turning in a new direction.[7] For example, in Matthew 3:8 John the Baptist is reported as saying, "Produce fruit in keeping with repentance" (*karpon axion tēs metanoias*). Acts 11:18 speaks of "repentance unto life" (*metanoian eis zōēn*). In 2 Corinthians 7:10 we read about a "repentance that leads to salvation" (*metanoian eis sōtērian*), and in 2 Timothy 2:25 of a "repentance leading . . . to a knowledge of the truth" (*metanoian eis epignōsin alētheias*).

It is exciting to see how William Chamberlain develops the rich biblical meaning of repentance. Repentance, he says, looks ahead in hope and

5. *Meaning of Repentance*, p. 29.

6. William F. Arndt and F. Wilbur Gingrich, *A Greek-English Lexicon of the New Testament*, 4th ed. (Chicago: University of Chicago Press, 1957), pp. 513-14.

7. Cf. the definition of *metanoeō* found in VGT: "Its meaning deepens with Christianity, and in the New Testament it is more than 'repent,' and indicates a complete change of attitude, spiritual and moral, towards God" (p. 404).

anticipation, whereas regret or remorse only looks backward in shame.[8] Repentance not only means a change of conduct but deals primarily with the springs of our action, and with the source of our motives.[9] The New Testament doctrine of repentance calls men's minds to be patterned after God's mind, in order that their conduct may be in keeping with his will, and that they may participate in his reign.[10] On the Day of Pentecost Peter's summons to repentance called for a reversal of his hearers' judgment of Jesus.[11] Paul, speaking to the Athenians, told them that repentance meant completely changing their ideas about God, and turning to him "in whom we live and move and have our being."[12]

Repentance in the biblical sense, Chamberlain concludes, means the making of a new man: "It is the change of the life design: the whole life pattern is changed; the goal of life is different; the aspirations are different."[13] In short, repentance is a pilgrimage from the mind of the flesh to the mind of Christ.[14] No more dramatic illustration of what repentance means can be found than in the amazing transformation that changed Saul the Jesus-hater into a man in Christ: "Paul is the greatest example in Christian history of what repentance does to a man."[15]

The other common New Testament word for repentance is *epistrephō*. The noun form of this verb, *epistrophē*, is used only once, in Acts 15:3, "reporting the conversion of the Gentiles" (RSV). The verb form, however, is used frequently. The basic meaning of the verb (*epi*, meaning "toward"; plus *strephō*, meaning "to turn") is "to turn about" or "to turn toward." In the New Testament it is used particularly to describe a turning from sin to God. One finds it in such expressions as "turning to God" (*epi ton theon*, Acts 15:19; *pros ton theon*, 1 Thess. 1:9), and "you have returned to the Shepherd and Overseer of your souls" (1 Pet. 2:25). Perhaps the most striking usage of *epistrephō* is found in Acts 26:18. Paul here tells King Agrippa that the Lord sent him to the Gentiles "to open their eyes and turn them from darkness to light, and from the power of Satan to God, so that they may receive forgiveness of sins and a place among those who are sanctified by faith in me."

Epistrephō, therefore, describes a total change in behavior, a reversal of one's life-style, a complete turnaround. Negatively, the word means a turning from wicked ways (Acts 3:26, though here *apostrephō* is used), or

8. *Meaning of Repentance*, p. 47.
9. Ibid., p. 41.
10. Ibid., p. 55.
11. Ibid., p. 63.
12. Ibid., p. 68.
13. Ibid., p. 38.
14. Ibid., p. 47.
15. Ibid., p. 67.

from the error of one's way (James 5:20). Positively, it describes a turning to the Lord (Luke 1:16; Acts 9:35; 11:21; 2 Cor. 3:16), or a turning of the hearts of the fathers to their children and the disobedient to the wisdom of the righteous (Luke 1:17). Sometimes, however, *epistrephō* includes both the negative and the positive side: it may mean a turning from worthless things to God (Acts 14:15), from idols to serve the living God (1 Thess. 1:9), or from darkness to light (Acts 26:18).

It is interesting to note that sometimes the New Testament uses only one of these two words to describe repentance, whereas at other times it uses both words. In Acts 15:3 only *epistrophē* is used. In Acts 11:18 only *metanoia* is used: "So then, God has granted even the Gentiles repentance unto life." Sometimes the two words are used together, as in Acts 3:19, where Peter is reported as saying to a crowd gathered in Solomon's portico, "Repent *(metanoēsate)*, then, and turn *(epistrepsate)* to God, so that your sins may be wiped out, that times of refreshing may come from the Lord." Both words are also used together in Acts 26:20, where Paul tells Agrippa that he has preached, both to Jews and Gentiles, "that they should repent *(metanoein)* and turn *(epistrephein)* to God." The meanings of these two words, therefore, overlap.

THE CONCEPT OF REPENTANCE

Repentance may be defined as the conscious turning of the regenerate person away from sin and toward God in a complete change of living, which reveals itself in a new way of thinking, feeling, and willing.

Repentance is a unitary experience, not to be divided into parts. The following aspects of repentance, however, may be distinguished, though they should never be separated.

(1) *An intellectual aspect.* True repentance involves, first, a knowledge of the holiness and majesty of God. It was Isaiah's vision of the holiness of God that led him to say, "Woe to me! I am ruined! For I am a man of unclean lips" (Isa. 6:5). Repentance must include a recognition of our own sin and guilt, as a transgression of God's law and a violation of his will for our lives. There must also be an understanding of the mercy of God and of his readiness to forgive, since apart from such an understanding knowledge of sin would only lead to fear and despair.

(2) *An emotional aspect.* There must be a heartfelt sorrow for sin itself, not just for the results of sin. This is what Paul means by "godly sorrow." Godly sorrow is not identical with repentance but "brings repentance that leads to salvation" (2 Cor. 7:10). This type of sorrow is contrasted with "worldly sorrow"—regret and remorse about the sad consequences of sin and the disillusionment that follows—which brings death. Judas's

sorrow, which we looked at earlier, was of this sort; it led only to his suicide. The roots of godly sorrow must lie in love for God: we are sorry that we have sinned because we love God and are grieved to have displeased him. The deepest sorrow for sin, therefore, is felt at the foot of the cross.

In addition to grief for our sin, however, there must also be joy: joy in God's forgiveness, in the doing of God's will, and in fellowship with others. As Chamberlain reminds us, when joy is missing, our repentance is incomplete.

(3) *A volitional aspect.* There must be an inward turning from sin and a seeking of forgiveness, but also a change of purpose and motivation. The inward change must reveal itself outwardly. We must turn back to God in grateful obedience; we must bring forth the fruits of repentance. Repentance must issue in a changed life.

Jesus made it quite clear that true repentance involves nothing less than total commitment: "Anyone who loves his father or mother more than me is not worthy of me; anyone who loves his son or daughter more than me is not worthy of me; and anyone who does not take his cross and follow me is not worthy of me. Whoever finds his life will lose it, and whoever loses his life for my sake will find it" (Matt. 10:37-39). "If anyone would come after me, he must deny himself and take up his cross and follow me" (Matt. 16:24). "Any of you who does not give up everything he has cannot be my disciple" (Luke 14:33).

Another way of describing true repentance is to call it, as the Heidelberg Catechism does, "the dying-away of the old self, and the coming-to-life of the new."[16] The dying away of the old self is described as follows: "It is to be genuinely sorry for sin, to hate it more and more, and to run away from it."[17] Calvin, who describes repentance as "mortification of the flesh and vivification of the spirit," expands on this thought:

> For from "mortification" we infer that we are not conformed to the fear of God and do not learn the rudiments of piety, unless we are violently slain by the sword of the Spirit and brought to nought. As if God had declared that for us to be reckoned among his children our common nature must die![18]

The Catechism describes the coming to life of the new self in these words: "It is wholehearted joy in God through Christ and a delight to do every kind of good as God wants us to."[19] Calvin ties this in with our oneness with Christ in his resurrection:

16. Heidelberg Catechism, Q. 88 (1975 trans.).
17. Ibid., Q. 89.
18. *Inst.*, III.iii.8.
19. Heidelberg Catechism, Q. 90 (1975 trans.).

If we share in his [Christ's] resurrection, through it we are raised up into newness of life to correspond with the righteousness of God. Therefore, in a word, I interpret repentance as regeneration, whose sole end is to restore in us the image of God that had been disfigured and all but obliterated through Adam's transgression.[20]

REPENTANCE THE WORK OF GOD AND MAN

The Bible speaks of repentance as both the work of God and the work of man. We have already looked at a number of biblical passages where repentance is described as a work of man—where, in fact, people are urged to repent and return to God (Isa. 55:7; Ezek. 33:11; Matt. 4:17; Acts 3:19; 17:30; 26:18; 26:20). In Acts 11:18, however, repentance is clearly pictured as a work of God—or, rather, as a work which God enables human beings to do: "So then, God has granted even the Gentiles repentance unto life." To the same effect is 2 Timothy 2:25, where Paul urges Timothy to correct his opponents with gentleness "in the hope that God will grant them repentance leading them to a knowledge of the truth." Sinners must repent, to be sure, but God must enable them to do so.

What is man's responsibility in repentance? The Scriptures clearly teach that human beings must repent. All the usages of *epistrephō* in the New Testament describe repentance as something we must do. *Metanoeō* and *metanoia* are also mostly used to stress human responsibility.

It is instructive to see how the Canons of Dort express the activity of human beings in their repentance. After describing the supernatural way in which God brings about regeneration, the Canons go on to say, "And then the will, now renewed, is not only activated and motivated by God but in being activated by God is also itself active. For this reason, man himself, by that grace which he has received, is also rightly said to believe and to repent."[21]

What is the preacher's responsibility in repentance? The New Testament teaches that preachers must urgently call their hearers to repentance. For example, in the Great Commission Jesus instructs his disciples (and, through them, the church of all time) to "make disciples of all nations" (Matt. 28:19). Paul says, "We are therefore Christ's ambassadors, as though God were making his appeal through us. We implore you on Christ's behalf: Be reconciled to God" (2 Cor. 5:20). In 1 Corinthians 9:22, in fact, Paul puts it as strongly as this: "I have become all things to all men so that by all possible means I might save some." And James says, "Whoever turns

---

20. *Inst.*, III.iii.9. Note that Calvin here uses the word "regeneration" to describe our total renewal, not just the beginning of it.

21. Canons of Dort, III-IV,12 (1986 trans.).

a sinner from the error of his way will save him from death and cover over a multitude of sins" (James 5:20).

Yet Jesus himself said, according to John 6:65, "No one can come to me unless the Father has enabled him." And Paul affirmed, in 1 Corinthians 3:6, "I planted the seed, Apollos watered it, but God made it grow." It was therefore neither Paul nor Apollos but only God who enables people to repent and believe.

We see here again the paradox. The preacher must call people to repentance and conversion; yet only God can empower them to repent. We must always keep both aspects of the truth in mind: (1) it is the preacher's solemn duty to urge people to repent; (2) it is God who sovereignly bestows on people the gift of repentance, enabling them to turn to him.

REPENTANCE MUST CONTINUE THROUGHOUT LIFE

The first of Luther's Ninety-five Theses reads as follows: "Our Lord and Master Jesus Christ, when he said, *Poenitentiam agite,* willed that the whole life of believers should be repentance."[22] These words underscore a most important point about repentance. Calvin, the other great Reformer, makes a similar point:

> Indeed, this restoration [of the image of God] does not take place in one moment or one day or one year; but through continual and sometimes even slow advances God wipes out in his elect the corruptions of the flesh, cleanses them of guilt, consecrates them to himself as temples, renewing all their minds to true purity, that they may practice repentance throughout their lives and know that this warfare will end only at death.[23]
>
> Therefore, I think he has profited greatly who has learned to be very much displeased with himself, not so as to stick fast in this mire and progress no farther, but rather to hasten to God and yearn for him in order that, having been engrafted into the life and death of Christ, he may give attention to continual repentance.[24]

Jesus' demand that we deny ourselves, take up our cross, and follow him describes what we must do throughout life. When Paul asks his readers not to be conformed to the pattern of this world but to be transformed by the renewing of their minds (Rom. 12:2), he is holding before them a lifelong challenge. When the Heidelberg Catechism describes repentance as the dying of the old self and the coming to life

22. *The Works of Martin Luther,* Philadelphia Edition (Philadelphia: Muhlenberg Press, 1943), 1:29.
23. *Inst.,* III.iii.9.
24. *Inst.,* III.iii.20.

of the new self, it is referring to an activity that does not end until our lives are over.

The fact that repentance is a lifelong activity has some important implications. First, it suggests that we must distinguish between an initial repentance at the beginning of the Christian life and a repentance which continues throughout that life. There is indeed a turning from sin to God that begins a person's Christian pilgrimage, but there is also one that characterizes the entire journey. We should not therefore simply think of repentance as a single step in the process of salvation (as in the older concept of an *ordo salutis*[25]), but, at least in one sense, we must think of repentance as an aspect of the entire process. The Christian life in its totality is a life of repentance.

Second, we should observe that repentance in the lifelong sense is not basically different from sanctification, though it embodies the sanctifying process from a unique angle. All the points that have been made about repentance apply to sanctification as well: that it is a turning from sin to God, a change of life pattern, a pilgrimage from the mind of the flesh to the mind of Christ, a putting off of the old self and a putting on of the new. In other words, the terms the Bible uses to describe the process of salvation overlap in meaning. Salvation is not many things but one thing, though it may be looked at from different points of view.

Third, it should be remembered that repentance in its full biblical sense is never perfectly exercised by us. When indeed do we totally turn from sin to God, and from the mind of the flesh to the mind of Christ? Do we ever perfectly hate sin? When are we completely free from impulses that spring from the old nature, and when do we spotlessly exemplify the new self to which we have been raised with Christ? Certainly never in this present life. As the Heidelberg Catechism soberly admits, "In this life even the holiest have only a small beginning of this obedience."[26] Daily we should ask God's forgiveness, not only for our sins, but also for the imperfection of our repentance. Repentance as described in the Bible is a high ideal; we must continue to try to reveal it, but we shall never fully do so in this life.

But, praise God, we are not saved by the perfection of our repentance. We are saved not by our meritorious acts but only by the merits of Jesus Christ: "By grace you have been saved through faith . . . not by works, so that no one can boast" (Eph. 2:8). Repentance is indeed necessary for salvation, but it does not need to be perfect repentance. If it did, who could be saved?

25. See above, Chapter 2.
26. Heidelberg Catechism, Q. 114 (1975 trans.).

CHAPTER 10

Faith

A MISSIONARY WAS SITTING AT HIS DESK, LOOKING DESPERATELY FOR a word. He was translating the Gospel of John into the language of the African tribe with which he was working, but he didn't know their word for "faith." While he was pondering, a member of the tribe came into the missionary's hut, threw himself into a chair, and uttered an expression which meant, "I'm leaning all my weight on this chair." At once the missionary leaped up, dancing with joy, exclaiming, "I've got my word! Faith is leaning all your weight on Christ!" More can be said about faith than this, but surely this is at the heart of it.

THE IMPORTANCE OF FAITH

It is hard to overemphasize the importance of faith in the process of salvation. Both the noun and the verb commonly used for faith in the New Testament (*pistis* and *pisteuein*) occur approximately 240 times. Faith is an essential aspect of conversion, along with repentance; both repentance and faith are necessary for salvation.

Without faith, the author of Hebrews tells us, it is impossible to please God (Heb. 11:6). Faith is the outstanding "work" which God requires of us (John 6:29); believing in Christ is that which God commands us to do (1 John 3:23). The purpose of the writing of the Gospels, so John tells us, is "that you may believe that Jesus is the Christ, the Son of God, and that by believing you may have life in his name" (John 20:31).

Faith is the means whereby we are saved (Rom. 10:9), and the way to an assured hope (Heb. 11:1). Until the time of our resurrection we are guarded by God's power through faith (1 Pet. 1:5). In the Christian life the only thing that counts, Paul tells us, is faith working through love (Gal. 5:6). Luke further underscores the importance of faith by using a single word to describe Christians: "believers" (Acts 2:44).

WORD STUDY

Before we look at the Old Testament words, we may note, as B. B. Warfield points out, that the attitude of faith and trust is seldom called "faith" in the Old Testament, though it is there often implied and frequently paraphrased.[1]

The three most common Old Testament words for faith, however, are *he'emīn, bātach,* and *chāsāh. He'emīn* is the hiphil form of *'āman.* According to the Brown-Driver-Briggs Hebrew lexicon, the basic meaning of this verb in the Qal is "to confirm or support." The hiphil form then means "to cause to support" or "to cause to be firm"; applied to persons this would mean "to cause someone to support you"—hence, "to believe or trust in someone." The verb is used in the well-known Genesis passage, "Abram believed the LORD, and he credited it to him as righteousness" (15:6). See also Isaiah 7:9; Habakkuk 2:4; Psalm 78:22.

Another Old Testament word for faith is *bātach.* This word means "to confide in, to lean upon, to trust." An example of its use can be found in Psalm 25:2, "In you I trust, O my God. Do not let me be put to shame." See also Psalms 13:5; 84:12; Proverbs 16:20; Isaiah 26:3-4.

A third Old Testament word occasionally used for faith is *chāsāh,* meaning "to seek refuge." As an example, we may cite Psalm 57:1, "I will take refuge in the shadow of your wings until the disaster has passed." See also Psalms 2:12, 25:20, 31:1, and 91:4.

When we turn to the New Testament, it is interesting to note that Paul at one point describes the New Testament era as one in which "faith has come" (Gal. 3:25). He is not trying to say that there was no faith before this time, but rather that the chief object of our faith, Jesus Christ, has now appeared on the scene.

The words used most frequently for faith in the New Testament are the noun *pistis* and the verb *pisteuein. Pistis* may be used, first, in the sense of "the faith by which we believe" *(fides qua creditur),* to denote a conviction of the truth of anything. With reference to God, it is the conviction that God exists, that he is the creator and ruler of all, and the provider of salvation through Christ. With reference to Christ, it means the belief that Jesus is the Messiah through whom we obtain salvation. This is the most common usage of the word—see, for example, Acts 11:24, Romans 3:28, and Ephesians 2:8. Occasionally, however, *pistis* may describe "the faith which is believed" *(fides quae creditur)* — that is, the content of what is

1. Benjamin B. Warfield, "Faith," in *Biblical and Theological Studies,* ed. Samuel Craig (Philadelphia: Presbyterian and Reformed, 1952), pp. 410-11.

believed. It is so used in Jude 3: "Contend for the faith that was once for all entrusted to the saints." See also Galatians 1:23 and 1 Timothy 4:1.

The verb *pisteuein* may mean (1) to think to be true (Matt. 24:23), or (2) to accept the message given by God's messengers (Acts 24:14). Most characteristically, however, it means (3) to accept Jesus as the Messiah, the divinely appointed author of eternal salvation (John 3:16). In this sense faith includes more than just believing a message to be true; it also involves trusting in Christ, resting on him, and leaning on him.

Summing up, it may be said that faith in the New Testament sense involves both the acceptance of a body of truth on the basis of the testimony of the apostles or of others who transmitted that testimony, and a personal trust in Christ as Savior.

Pisteuein appears in the New Testament in various constructions. It may be used with a pronoun in the dative case (Matt. 21:25), with *hoti* followed by a noun clause (Rom. 10:9), with *en* (Eph. 1:13), with *epi* and the dative (Rom. 9:33), and with *epi* and the accusative (Rom. 4:5). The most common construction, however, is with *eis* and the accusative (John 3:16, 36).

FAITH AS DESCRIBED BY VARIOUS BIBLE WRITERS

Faith was central in the lives of the people of God in Old Testament as well as in New Testament times. If we take as our starting point the Mother Promise of Genesis 3:15, we note at once that this first revelation of the covenant of grace called for a response of faith on the part of God's people. Abel, we are told in the Book of Hebrews, offered God a better sacrifice by faith (Heb. 11:4); by faith Enoch walked with God (v. 5); and by faith Noah became an heir of righteousness (v. 7).

As we move on to the patriarchal period, Abraham appears as the outstanding Old Testament example of faith, so much so that he has become known as "the father of believers." Paul teaches that Abraham was justified by faith (Rom. 4:1-3), and that all who believe are children of Abraham (Gal. 3:7). Sarah, Isaac, and Jacob—all these likewise lived by faith.

There are some who claim that the period of Israel's history after the exodus from Egypt was an era of law rather than grace. This, however, is not true. Paul tells us in Galatians 3:17, "The law, introduced 430 years later [after the time of the patriarchs], does not set aside the covenant previously established by God and thus do away with the promise." The point is this: the giving of the law at Sinai did not overthrow the promises made to Abraham, Isaac, and Jacob. The heart of these promises was the coming of the Redeemer through faith in whom Abraham had been justified. So faith in God—a faith that looked forward to Christ—was still required during and after the Mosaic period.

In the Book of Psalms faith is depicted in many ways: as trusting in God, finding refuge in him, committing ourselves to him, fleeing to him, and the like. The prophets repeatedly call their hearers back to faith in the God of Israel—a faith which should reveal itself in genuine repentance, turning from idolatry, concern for justice, love for people in need, and rededication to God's service. According to the eleventh chapter of the Book of Hebrews, the spiritual giants of Old Testament times should be looked upon as heroes of faith.

If faith in the Old Testament is saying Amen to God, faith in the New Testament is saying Amen to the gospel. In the Synoptic Gospels Jesus asks for faith in himself, in his person. Often this is done in connection with miracles, but faith in the Synoptics is not limited to miraculous faith. According to Mark 1:15 Jesus said, "Repent and believe the good news!" Later Jesus said to Peter, "I have prayed for you, Simon, that your faith may not fail" (Luke 22:32). At another time our Lord is reported to have said, "Come to me, all you who are weary and burdened, and I will give you rest" (Matt. 11:28). Though the word "faith" is not used in this passage, Jesus here clearly teaches the necessity of personal faith in him.

In John's Gospel *pisteuein* occurs almost a hundred times; it is therefore one of John's key words. Here the stress is less on miraculous faith and more on saving faith. Probably the best-known verse in the Bible is John 3:16, "For God so loved the world that he gave his one and only Son, that whoever believes in him shall not perish but have eternal life." For similar uses of the word, see John 3:18, 36; 6:47; 7:38; and 11:25-26. *Pisteuein* in John's Gospel means acknowledging Christ as the Savior whom the Father sent into the world, cleaving to him, and trusting in him. Through such faith one obtains eternal life, not just as a future hope but also as a present possession.

In the Book of Acts faith involves at least two things: (1) acceptance of the apostolic testimony about Christ, and (2) personal trust in Christ for salvation. Both in Peter's Pentecost sermon and in Paul's addresses, there is first a presentation of the facts of the gospel, and then an exhortation to believe in Christ, repent of sin, and be saved.

Paul was combating the rabbinical conception of faith as a meritorious good work. Hence we find in him the following emphases: (1) we are justified by faith alone, apart from the works of the law (Rom. 3:28); (2) our union with Christ is experienced and maintained through faith (Eph. 3:17); (3) faith must express itself in love and godly living (Gal. 5:6). In other words, as there must be fruit worthy of repentance (Matt.

3:8), so there must also be fruit that grows out of faith. We see here a Pauline emphasis which is parallel to that of James.

The danger warned against by the author of Hebrews is particularly that of shrinking back (Heb. 10:38-39), of falling away, of slipping back into legalism or unbelief. Hence he points to past heroes of faith (chap. 11) as incentives for the life of faith today. Spurred on by their examples, we must keep on running with perseverance *(hypomonē)* the race marked out for us (12:1). In Hebrews, therefore, faith is pictured as the dynamic of the Christian life, whereby believers are empowered to persevere to the end.

Opposing the notion that faith is a mere intellectual assent to the truth, James insists that faith without deeds is dead (2:26). His blunt words shake us out of our complacency: "What good is it, my brothers, if a man claims to have faith but has no deeds? Can such faith save him?" (2:14).

The first epistle of Peter ties in faith with hope; it was written "so that your faith and hope might be in God" (1:21, ASV). Through faith we are "shielded by God's power until the coming of the salvation that is ready to be revealed in the last time" (1:5). This final salvation is, in fact, the goal of our faith (1:9).

Over against an incipient Gnosticism, which elevated knowledge far above simple faith, John in his epistles emphasizes that true faith brings knowledge with it: "I write these things to you who believe in the name of the Son of God so that you may know that you have eternal life" (1 John 5:13).

We find, therefore, a rich diversity in the way various Bible writers describe faith. Yet amidst this diversity there is a basic unity. Though in Old Testament times faith looked forward to the Redeemer who was to come, and in New Testament times faith looked back to the Savior who had come, in both eras salvation was obtained only through a living faith in Christ.

OTHER NEW TESTAMENT DESCRIPTIONS OF FAITH

The closest thing to a definition of faith in the New Testament is found in Hebrews 11:1, "Now faith is the assurance of things hoped for, the conviction of things not seen" (RSV). The word translated "assurance" is *hypostasis*, the noun form of the verb *hyphistamai*, which means "to stand under as a support."[2] In this passage *hypostasis* means "reality"—the reality of that which is hoped for.[3] In the papyri of the early Christian centuries this

2. Helmut Köster, *"hypostasis,"* TDNT, 8:572.
3. Ibid., pp. 585-87.

word is often used to designate a document which constitutes proof of ownership, like a deed to a house. Moulton and Milligan, in fact, suggest the following translation of the first half of the verse, "Faith is the *title-deed* of things hoped for."[4] Faith as here described, therefore, gives believers a guarantee that they will someday possess the transcendental realities for which they hope.

The word "conviction" in the second half of the verse translates the Greek word *elenchos*, which may mean either "proof" or "conviction."[5] If we combine these two meanings, the word can be rendered "convincing evidence." Ordinarily we are convinced of the existence of things by the testimony of our senses. But faith is here pictured as the evidence whereby we are convinced of the existence of things not seen—the spiritual and future realities that are the objects of our faith. The rest of the chapter indicates that faith of this sort was the driving power of the heroes there described, enabling them to persevere against all odds.

Faith is described in the New Testament by means of a number of striking figures. It is called a *coming to Christ:* "All that the Father gives me will come to me, and whoever comes to me I will never drive away" (John 6:37). Faith, seen in this light, is a going away from ourselves to Christ, no longer trusting in self but trusting only in him. It means finding in Christ our hope of salvation, our deepest joy, and our purpose in life.

Faith is further portrayed as an *eating of Christ:* "I am the living bread that came down from heaven. If anyone eats of this bread, he will live forever" (John 6:51). Here faith is depicted as the appropriation of Christ. As the bread we eat becomes part of us, so the Christ we accept by faith also becomes part of us. Faith, then, is born out of a felt need; through faith we receive spiritual nourishment.

Faith is also pictured as a *drinking of Christ:* "Whoever drinks the water I give him will never thirst. Indeed, the water I give him will become in him a spring of water welling up to eternal life" (John 4:14). As a man dying of thirst desperately needs water, so we urgently need to find life in Christ. Again we see that faith in Christ satisfies life's deepest needs. When once we have imbibed this water of life, our spiritual thirst is permanently quenched.

Once again, faith is depicted as an *abiding in Christ:* "He who abides in me, and I in him, he it is that bears much fruit, for apart from me you can do nothing" (John 15:5, RSV). As the fruitbearing branch must remain in the vine, so we must remain in Christ. Faith means resting in Christ,

4. VGT, p. 660.
5. William F. Arndt and F. Wilbur Gingrich, *A Greek-English Lexicon of the New Testament*, 4th ed. (Chicago: University of Chicago Press, 1957), p. 248.

leaning on him, drawing strength from him moment by moment, and living in constant fellowship with him. Faith is not just believing that Christ did something important for us many years ago; it includes the recognition that Christ is now living in us and that we are now living in him. Faith grasps not just a Christ for us, but also a Christ in us.[6]

These figures are very rich. Each one has something unique to contribute to our understanding of faith. Yet they all agree in one respect: faith is a leaning on, a trusting in, a resting on God in Christ instead of on ourselves. It is quite clear that faith is more than just a momentary decision. It is also clear that faith is more than the acceptance of intellectual propositions. Faith involves not only the whole person but also the whole of life.

THE SCHOLASTIC VIEW OF FAITH

Scholasticism is the name given to the theology and philosophy taught in the medieval schools of Europe from the eleventh to the fourteenth centuries. The teachings of the scholastic theologians were summarized in the Canons and Decrees of the Council of Trent (1563). The view of faith set forth in these Canons can be expressed in the following statements:

(1) Faith is always a deed of the intellect. Though it is brought into existence by the will, it has its seat in the intellect. Faith is assent to all those things which God has proposed to be believed. Its object is not so much the person of Christ as certain truths which must be intellectually apprehended.

(2) In thus assenting to God's truth, human beings, cooperating with God's grace, (do a meritorious deed which calls for a reward, and thus) prepare themselves for justification. [Note: what has been placed between parentheses is affirmed by some, but denied by other, scholastic theologians.]

(3) Yet this faith in itself, as *fides informis* (not "informed faith" but "unformed faith") is insufficient for justification. It does not include a personal relationship to God or to Christ, since it is only an intellectual assent to revealed truths, and is fully retained even in mortal sin.

(4) To faith love must be added: *fides informis* must become *fides formata caritate* ("faith formed by love"). It is through the sacrament of baptism that a person receives this love, and that he or she receives this fully formed faith—which is the only kind of faith that justifies. It is therefore really the sacrament that justifies rather than faith.

(5) Since the ordinary believer cannot understand all the articles of

6. For a fuller development of this point, see Chapter 4 above.

belief proposed by the church, he or she does not need to embrace all of them with explicit faith, but may accept much if not most of the truth with a *fides implicita* ("implicit faith"): that is, with mere assent to what the church teaches.

(6) The believer can never attain to absolute certainty about personal salvation; all he or she can have is a kind of conjectural certainty, which does not exclude the possible loss of salvation.

CALVIN'S TEACHING ON FAITH

John Calvin vigorously opposed the scholastic view of faith. He rejects the idea that faith must be thought of as mere assent,[7] and that we may think of it as mere "implicit faith," meaning unquestioning submission to the church's teachings without really understanding them. He calls this kind of "faith" ignorance rather than knowledge and says that this conception has not only buried true faith but utterly destroyed it.[8] He also repudiates the distinction between *fides informis* and *fides caritate formata*. *Fides informis*, he affirms, is not true faith at all, because by it someone who has no fear of God and no sense of piety is still said to be able to believe whatever is necessary for salvation.[9] Calvin calls such "unformed faith" just a shadow or image of faith, but not real faith.[10]

True faith, he goes on to say, consists in knowledge of God, particularly of his mercy. At this point he gives his well-known definition of faith: "A firm and certain knowledge of God's benevolence towards us, founded upon the truth of the freely given promise in Christ, both revealed to our minds and sealed upon our hearts through the Holy Spirit."[11] When Calvin here refers to the heart in distinction from the mind, he means by the former the will and the emotions.

Though this definition of faith sounds intellectualistic, Calvin does not mean to say that faith is mere intellectual knowledge. Like Luther, he holds that trust belongs to the essence of faith. In his commentary on Romans 10:10 Calvin asserts that faith is not just intellectual knowledge but a "firm and effectual confidence." In the *Institutes* he adds,

> It will not be enough for the mind to be illumined by the Spirit of God unless the heart is also strengthened and supported by his power. In this matter the Schoolman [the Scholastics] go completely astray, who in considering faith

7. *Inst.*, III.ii.1.
8. *Inst.*, III.ii.2-3.
9. *Inst.*, III.ii.8.
10. *Inst.*, III.ii.10.
11. *Inst.*, III.ii.7.

identify it with a bare and simple assent arising out of knowledge, and leave out confidence and assurance of heart.[12]

On another page he says, "It [the knowledge of Christ] is a doctrine not of the tongue but of life. It is not apprehended by the understanding and memory alone, as other disciplines are, but it is received only when it possesses the whole soul, and finds a seat and resting place in the inmost affection of the heart."[13]

Summarizing the differences between Calvin and the Scholastics on faith, we may say that for Calvin faith is (1) a personal relationship to God and to Christ; (2) a sure knowledge of the love and mercy of God in Christ, not a bare assent to truths which are either not understood at all or only half understood; and (3) a firm confidence or trust which is opposed to doubt. We should also note that (4) Calvin rejects every suggestion that there is anything meritorious about faith.

THE CONCEPT OF FAITH

Saving faith may be defined as a response to God's call by the acceptance of Christ with the total person—that is, with assured conviction of the truth of the gospel, and with trustful reliance on God in Christ for salvation, together with genuine commitment to Christ and to his service.

The following aspects of faith, though never to be separated, may be distinguished: (1) *Knowledge*. It is obvious that we cannot have faith in someone of whom we know nothing, or about whom we know the wrong things. An illiterate Australian aborigine might say, "I have faith in Christ," without knowing anything about him. Would this be true faith? A Jehovah's Witness might say, "I have faith in Christ," but the Christ in whom he claims to have faith is not divine but only a creature. Is this true faith? We must surely have enough knowledge to know in whom we believe, and what Christ has done for us.

The Bible clearly teaches that without knowledge there can be no true faith. When Jesus appeared to his disciples after his resurrection, he explained to them why he had had to suffer and rise from the dead: "Then he opened their minds so they could understand the Scriptures" (Luke 24:45). When Paul preached in Athens, he reminded his hearers of the altar he had found in their city containing the inscription, "To an Unknown God." After saying, "Now what you worship as something unknown I am going to proclaim to you" (Acts 17:23), he proceeded to tell them who the true God is, what he had done, and what kind of repentance he required

12. *Inst.*, III.ii.33.
13. *Inst.*, III.vi.4.

of them. And in his epistle to the Romans Paul underscores the importance of knowledge in saving faith:

> Everyone who calls on the name of the Lord will be saved. How, then, can they call on the one they have not believed in? And how can they believe in the one of whom they have not heard? And how can they hear without someone preaching to them? . . . Consequently, faith comes from hearing the message, and the message is heard through the word of Christ (Rom. 10:13-14, 17).

Since God is the infinite one, and since faith embraces God and his saving work for us, the knowledge involved in faith does not mean total comprehension. It is significant that the first section of the chapter on the doctrine of God in Bavinck's *Dogmatics* is entitled "The Incomprehensibility of God." This author goes on to say, "The truth which God has revealed about himself in nature and in the Bible far transcends human understanding."[14] Calvin recognizes this point as well:

> When we call faith "knowledge" we do not mean comprehension of the sort that is commonly concerned with those things which fall under human sense perception. . . . He [Paul, when he talks about the love of Christ which surpasses knowledge] means that what our mind embraces by faith is in every way infinite, and that this kind of knowledge is far more lofty than all understanding. . . . From this we conclude that the knowledge of faith consists in assurance rather than in comprehension.[15]

The character of the knowledge of faith is different from knowledge in science or mathematics. It is what Emil Brunner calls *I-Thou* truth, not *I-it* truth.[16] It is knowledge which involves what God has done for me, for my brothers and sisters in Christ, and for those who are not yet brothers or sisters in Christ. One could even say that it is a knowledge which includes love, just as, conversely, when God is said to know us, it means that he loves us. When, therefore, Calvin says that faith is "a firm and certain knowledge of God's benevolence toward us," and when the Heidelberg Catechism affirms that true faith is "a knowledge and conviction that everything God reveals in his Word is true,"[17] it is this type of knowledge they are describing.

At this point we may ask, How much knowledge is necessary? Faith, as we saw, must embrace the truth of the gospel and of Christ's redemptive work for us. But how much of the gospel must one know to be saved?

---

14. Bavinck, *Dogmatiek,* 2:1 [trans. mine].

15. *Inst.,* III.ii.14.

16. *The Christian Doctrine of the Church, Faith, and the Consummation,* trans. D. Cairns (Philadelphia: Westminster, 1960), p. 259.

17. Heidelberg Catechism, Q. 21 (1975 trans.).

This is not easy to say. We must have enough knowledge to realize that we are sinners who need redemption, that we cannot save ourselves but that only Christ can redeem us from sin and from the wrath of God, and that Christ died and arose for us. Our knowledge may be as slender as that of the thief on the cross (Luke 23:42); yet he had enough faith to be saved.

Does growth in knowledge mean spiritual growth? The answer depends on what one means by knowledge. If it is mere abstract, intellectual knowledge, mere rote-memory knowledge, mere "Bible Trivia" knowledge, not necessarily. Paul, in fact, talks about a type of knowledge that "puffs up," but does not build up (1 Cor. 8:1). But if growth in knowledge means growth in understanding what Christ has done for us, what the Spirit is doing in us, and what God wants us to do for him and to be for him, then growth in knowledge is bound to bring spiritual growth. This is the type of knowledge Peter has in mind when he enjoins his readers, in 2 Peter 3:18, "But grow in the grace and knowledge of our Lord and Savior Jesus Christ."

Another aspect of faith is (2) *assent*. By assent I mean that activity by which we firmly accept the teachings of God's Word as true. Such assent must involve the total person: with our whole selves we accept as true what the Bible teaches us about sin, Christ, salvation, and God's purpose for our lives. If the knowledge involved in our faith does not include assent, our faith is not genuine.

A third aspect of faith is (3) *trust*. This is the crowning aspect of faith. That true faith includes trust is evident from the words used for faith in Scripture, from the figures the Bible uses to describe faith, and from the very nature of the activity involved in faith. Faith is looking away from self, and leaning wholly on Christ for salvation. It is the personal appropriation of Christ and his merits. It means resting on Christ's finished work, and accepting what he has done as having been done for us. In the words of the Heidelberg Catechism, faith is "a deep-rooted assurance, created in me by the Holy Spirit through the gospel, that . . . not only others, but I too, have had my sins forgiven, have been made forever right with God, and have been granted salvation."[18]

It should be added that trust also includes obedience. This is clear from Hebrews 3:18-19, where those who did not enter the Land of Canaan because of their unbelief are said to have been disobedient. In sharp contrast, "By faith Abraham, when called to go to a place he would later receive as his inheritance, obeyed and went, even though he did not know where he was going" (Heb. 11:8). In Romans 1:5, in fact, Paul even speaks

18. Ibid.

about "the obedience of faith" (RSV). Faith, therefore, must lead to obedient service in Christ's kingdom, since, as James puts it, faith without works is dead.

Though it is often said that faith is passive (since we are saved by receiving what Christ has done for us), there is also a sense in which faith is active. Faith is active in obedience.

These three aspects of faith cannot be separated, though sometimes one aspect is more prominent than another. For a person like C. S. Lewis the knowledge-aspect of faith would probably stand out, whereas for someone like John Bunyan the trust-aspect would predominate. But it is important to remember that faith involves the whole person. Nothing, in fact, is more determinative of the quality of our lives than our faith.

THE CENTRAL MYSTERY OF FAITH

By the central mystery of faith I mean the fact that faith is both the gift of God and the task of man. We are here reminded again of the paradox of God's sovereignty and human responsibility.

(1) *Faith as the Gift of God.* It is hard to find specific biblical texts teaching that faith is the gift of God. The fact that we are completely dependent on God for our salvation as well as for everything else certainly implies that we cannot have true faith unless God enables us to do so. A number of Scripture passages point us in this direction.

Faith is the fruit of divine election. Paul and Barnabas were at Pisidian Antioch. After the Jews had rejected the gospel, the speakers turned to the Gentiles who were present, about whom we read, "And when the Gentiles heard this [that the Servant of the Lord was to be a light for the Gentiles], they were glad and glorified the word of God; and as many as were ordained to eternal life believed" (Acts 13:48, RSV). F. F. Bruce's comment on this passage is significant:

> We cannot agree with those who attempt to tone down the predestinarian note of this phrase by rendering "as many as were disposed to eternal life" (so Alford, *ad loc.*). The Greek participle is *tetagmenoi* from *tassō*, and there is papyrus evidence for this verb in the sense of "inscribe" or "enroll." . . .[19]

I conclude that our English versions correctly render this verb "ordained" (KJV, ASV, RSV), "chosen" (Today's English Version), "destined" (Phillips, JB), "marked out" (NEB), or "appointed" (NASB, NIV) for eternal life. If this is so, the faith of those Gentiles who believed was a fruit of divine election and therefore clearly a gift of God.

19. *Commentary on the Book of Acts* (Grand Rapids: Eerdmans, 1955), p. 283, n. 72.

Faith is the result of regeneration. The Apostle John tells us, "Whoever believes that Jesus is the Christ has been begotten by God" (1 John 5:1, JB). The word rendered "has been begotten" *(gegennētai)* is in the perfect tense in the Greek, a tense which describes past action with abiding result. Everyone who has faith, John is therefore saying, reveals that he or she has been begotten or born of God and is still in that regenerate state. Since God is the sole author of regeneration, and since only regenerated persons can believe, we see again that faith is a gift of God.

Faith is the fruit of the operation of the Spirit. At the beginning of a discussion about spiritual gifts Paul says, "I tell you that no one who is speaking by the Spirit of God says, 'Jesus be cursed,' and no one can say, 'Jesus is Lord,' except by the Holy Spirit" (1 Cor. 12:3). Since the statement, "Jesus is Lord," is obviously an utterance of faith, we conclude that no one is able to believe in Christ apart from the power of the Holy Spirit.

The Father enables us to come to Jesus. As we saw earlier, coming to Jesus is a biblical figure for faith. According to John 6:65, Jesus said to his disciples, "No one can come to me unless the Father has enabled him." That is, the ability to believe in Christ must be given by the Father; unless this ability is given, no one can believe.

Jesus is the author of our faith. In Hebrews 12:2 Jesus is described as being both "the author and perfecter of our faith." The word rendered "author" translates *archēgon,* which in this context means "originator" or "founder."

God is said to bestow faith. Two passages come up for consideration here. The first is Philippians 1:29, "For it has been granted to you on behalf of Christ not only to believe on him, but also to suffer for him." Two things are here said to have been granted or given freely *(echaristhē)* to the readers of this epistle: believing in Christ and suffering for his sake. Faith is described as something which is granted or freely bestowed on us by God.

The other passage is Ephesians 2:8, "For it is by grace you have been saved, through faith—and this not from yourselves, it is the gift of God." The last part of the text reads as follows in the Greek: *kai touto ouk ex hymōn, theou to dōron. Kai touto* is translated "and this." The question now is, To what does *kai touto* refer? Some say, To faith. Sometimes this interpretation is defended by the following argumentation: previous to this point Paul has already said that salvation is God's free gift. But now he brings up something new: faith. "And this also," he continues (namely, this faith through which you are saved), "is not your own doing but is the gift of God."

There are, however, two difficulties with this interpretation: (1) *touto* is neuter, whereas *pistis,* the Greek word for faith, is feminine; (2) the expression *kai touto* is an emphatic adverbial construction which heightens the force of the preceding clause;[20] it could be translated "and this, mind you." What Paul is then affirming here can be paraphrased as follows: By grace you have been saved through faith; and all of this (namely, your being saved by grace through faith) is not your own doing but is the gift of God. Since faith is included, one could say that this passage teaches indirectly that faith is the gift of God.[21]

(2) *Faith as the Task of Man.* All one has to do to learn that faith is also depicted as a task of man is to look up the word "faith" or "believe" in any biblical concordance, and to note that most commonly faith is described as something human beings must do in response to the gospel. For example, faith is so described in John 3:16, "For God so loved the world that he gave his one and only Son, that whoever believes in him shall not perish but have eternal life." Or think of Paul's words in Romans 3:28, "For we maintain that a man is justified by faith apart from observing the law." John tells us in his first epistle, "This is the victory that has overcome the world, even our faith" (1 John 5:4).

Highlighting the responsibility of the preacher, the missionary, and the individual Christian witness is the fact that faith is brought about by means of the Word—preached, taught, or read. After referring to many miraculous signs which have not been recorded in his Gospel, John goes on to say, "But these are written that you may believe that Jesus is the Christ, the Son of God" (John 20:31). And Paul teaches that "faith comes from hearing the message, and the message is heard through the word of Christ" (Rom. 10:17). Hence the Heidelberg Catechism, in answer to the question of where faith comes from, replies, "The Holy Spirit produces it in our hearts by the preaching of the holy gospel. . . ."[22]

Yet, though it is our responsibility to believe the gospel, our faith is not in any way meritorious. Our being saved by grace through faith, as we learned from Ephesians 2:8-9, is not through ourselves, but "it is the gift of God—not by works, so that no one can boast." B. B. Warfield makes the point vividly:

> It is not, strictly speaking, even faith in Christ that saves, but Christ that saves through faith. The saving power resides exclusively, not in the act of

---

20. Cf. Arndt and Gingrich, *Greek-English Lexicon*, p. 601 under g; also A. T. Robertson, *A Grammar of the Greek New Testament in the Light of Historical Research* (Nashville: Broadman Press, 1934), p. 1182: "See in particular Eph. 2:8, *kai touto ouk ex hymōn*, where *touto* refers to the whole conception, not to *chariti*."

21. Herman Ridderbos raises some objections to the interpretations of Philippians 1:29 and Ephesians 2:8 just given, in his *Paul: An Outline of His Theology*, trans. J. R. De Witt (Grand Rapids: Eerdmans, 1975), p. 234, n. 57.

22. Heidelberg Catechism, Q. 65 (1975 trans.).

faith or the attitude of faith or the nature of faith, but in the object of faith; . . .
so that we could not more radically misconceive it than by transferring to
faith even the smallest fraction of that saving energy which is attributed in
the Scriptures solely to Christ himself.[23]

THE ASSURANCE OF SALVATION

The Roman Catholic Church officially denies that a believer can have assurance of his or her salvation, unless a person should have received a
special revelation to that effect. Note the following statements from the
Canons and Decrees of the Council of Trent:

> No one can know with a certainty of faith, which can not be subject to error,
> that he has obtained the grace of God.[24]
>
> No one, moreover, so long as he is in this mortal life, ought so far to
> presume as regards the secret mystery of divine predestination, as to deter-
> mine for certain that he is assuredly in the number of the predestinate . . . for
> except by special revelation, it cannot be known whom God hath chosen
> unto himself.[25]
>
> If anyone saith, that a man, who is born again and justified, is bound of
> faith to believe that he is assuredly in the number of the predestinate: let him
> be anathema.[26]

Though the Council of Trent was held in the sixteenth century, the
teaching of the church on this point has not basically changed. As
evidence, I quote the following from a recent Roman Catholic dictionary
of theology:

> CERTAINTY OF SALVATION: a concept of Protestant theology which sig-
> nifies a belief in justification so firm that this belief is inconsistent with any
> doubt of a man's ultimate salvation. Such a certainty of salvation—which
> Catholic theology describes as *absolute*—was repudiated by the Council of
> Trent, because whereas the Christian is absolutely forbidden to doubt what
> God has done in Jesus Christ or to doubt his universal salvific will, this does
> not exclude all possible doubt of one's own eternal salvation.[27]

We see here one of the deepest and most basic differences between
the Roman Catholic and the Protestant conceptions of soteriology. G. C.

---

23. "Faith," p. 425. Cf. also J. Gresham Machen, *What Is Faith?* (Grand Rapids:
Eerdmans, 1946), pp. 174, 180.

24. Canons and Decrees of the Council of Trent, Chap. 9 (Denzinger, *Enchiridion Sym-
bolorum* [36th ed.], 1534); translation from Philip Schaff, *Creeds of Christendom* (New York:
Harper, 1877), 2:99.

25. Ibid., Chap. 12 (Denzinger, 1540), translation from Schaff, *Creeds*, 2:103.

26. Ibid., Canon 15 on Justification (Denzinger, 1565); translation from Schaff, *Creeds*,
2:113.

27. Karl Rahner and Herbert Vorgrimler, *Dictionary of Theology*, 2nd ed. (New York:
Crossroad, 1981), p. 63.

Berkouwer has some significant things to say about this question in his *Conflict with Rome.*[28] He points out that on the matter of assurance of salvation Roman Catholics do an abrupt about-face. On the doctrine of the church they assert that we Protestants can have no certainty, since we do not have the true apostolic succession, and since we do not recognize the infallible authority of the one true church. On the question of assurance of salvation, however, they accuse us of having too much certainty—since, according to them, one can never be certain of his or her salvation, apart from a special revelation. For Roman Catholics, in other words, one can be certain of the teachings of the church, but one cannot be certain that he or she is saved.

Berkouwer goes on to show that Rome's denial of the assurance of salvation is consistent with its conception of the nature of salvation. It is precisely because the Roman Catholic Church conceives of salvation as a joint effort by man and God, and as a blessing which can only be maintained through the doing of good works, that it must say to the believer: you can never be absolutely sure of your salvation.[29] For if one's "assurance" of salvation must be based on one's performance of good works, the most he or she can attain is the kind of conjectural certainty which Rome teaches. This point is vividly stated in Article 24 of the Belgic Confession:

> Moreover, although we do good works, we do not base our salvation on them; for we cannot do any work that is not defiled by our flesh and also worthy of punishment.... So we would always be in doubt, tossed back and forth without any certainty, and our poor consciences would be tormented constantly if they did not rest on the merit of the suffering and death of our Savior.[30]

Because Rome's denial of the possibility of assurance touched upon the very heart of the gospel, the Reformers sharply attacked Roman Catholic teaching on this matter. The basic question involved here is whether one is saved by grace alone or whether one's salvation depends in part on his or her meritorious good works.[31] If the latter is true, one can never be sure of salvation. If, however, the former is true — as the Reformers taught—then one can be sure of salvation, even though he or she may not always be in full possession of that assurance.

28. *Conflict with Rome,* trans. David H. Freeman (Grand Rapids: Baker, 1958), Chap. 5, "The Problem of the Assurance of Salvation," pp. 113-51.

29. Ibid., pp. 118-20.

30. Belgic Confession, Art. 24 (1985 trans.).

31. That present-day Roman Catholic theologians still maintain that our good works can be meritorious is evident from the following statement: "Through meritorious works there comes about a growth in grace...; our merits 'earn' an increase of grace" (Rahner and Vorgrimler, *Dictionary of Theology,* p. 305).

What was Calvin's position on the assurance of salvation? Calvin teaches that assurance of salvation is not only possible but belongs to the essence of faith, and is not something additional to faith. In his comment on Romans 8:14 he says, "All who are led by the Spirit of God are the sons of God; all the sons of God are heirs of eternal life; and therefore all who are led by the Spirit of God ought to feel assured of eternal life."[32] In the *Institutes* Calvin puts it as strongly as this:

> He alone is truly a believer who, convinced by a firm conviction that God is a kindly and well-disposed Father toward him, promises himself all things on the basis of his generosity; who, relying upon the promises of divine benevolence toward him, lays hold on an undoubted expectation of salvation. . . . No man is a believer, I say, except him who, leaning upon the assurance of his salvation, confidently triumphs over the devil and death.[33]

Anthony Lane summarizes Calvin's views on this point as follows: "Calvin taught that assurance, far from being impossible, is an essential ingredient of salvation. . . . It is clear that Calvin allowed no dichotomy between saving faith and the assurance or confidence that one is forgiven. . . . To separate faith and confidence is like separating the sun from its light and heat."[34]

Calvin, however, does not deny that believers may often lack full assurance of salvation: "Surely, while we teach that faith ought to be certain and assured, we cannot imagine any certainty that is not tinged with doubt, or any assurance that is not assailed by some anxiety. On the other hand, we say that believers are in perpetual conflict with their own unbelief."[35] He does not agree with Rome that the believer cannot have assurance except by means of a special revelation. He insists that every believer ought to rest in the security of his or her salvation. But he adds that not every believer always exercises her faith in this complete or, if you will, ideal way. A believer may certainly wrestle with doubts but—and here the difference between Calvin and Rome comes out clearly—he or she ought not to be content to remain in this doubtful frame of mind, or even to glory in it as an evidence of proper Scriptural humility, but to fight against these doubts and try to attain greater certainty.

32. *Romans and Thessalonians*, trans. Ross Mackenzie (Grand Rapids: Eerdmans, 1973), p. 167.
33. *Inst.*, III.ii.16.
34. "Calvin's Doctrine of Assurance," *Vox Evangelica*, Vol. 11 (1979), p. 32. Lane believes that according to the Westminster Confession of Faith assurance is not of the essence of faith but is something extra (ibid., pp. 47-48). John Murray agrees ("The Assurance of Faith," *Collected Writings of John Murray* [Carlisle, PA: Banner of Truth, 1977], 2:265). Louis Berkhof, however, disputes this judgment (ST, p. 508).
35. *Inst.*, III.ii.17.

Turning now to what the Bible teaches on the question of assurance, we look at three types of passages:

(1) *Passages showing that ideally faith should carry assurance with it:*
Hebrews 11:1, "Now faith is the assurance of things hoped for, the conviction of things not seen" (RSV). According to this text, which we discussed earlier, faith, when it is what it ought to be, carries with it certainty about spiritual realities, definite assurance and conviction about the salvation which is hoped for.

1 John 5:13, "I write these things to you who believe in the name of the Son of God so that you may know that you have eternal life." Anyone who denies that a believer can have assurance of salvation will have a difficult time getting around this text. Over against the incipient Gnosticism which held that knowledge was far superior to simple faith, John insists that those who have faith in Christ also have knowledge—the knowledge that they have eternal life. Not just an elite group among believers, not just those who have received some special revelation, but all true believers may and should *know* that they have eternal life.

(2) *Passages indicating that true believers may at times lack assurance:* Jesus often rebuked his disciples in words like these: "O you of little faith" (Matt. 6:30; 8:26; 14:31; 16:8; Luke 12:28). According to Luke 17:5, the disciples once pleaded with Jesus, "Increase our faith!" Mark 9:24 records the oft-quoted words of the man who said to Jesus, "I do believe; help me overcome my unbelief!" And the author of Hebrews warns his readers, "See to it, brothers, that none of you has a sinful, unbelieving heart that turns away from the living God" (Heb. 3:12). From these passages and others like them we learn that believers may not possess full assurance of salvation at once, and that they may be deprived of that assurance after having enjoyed it for a while.

(3) *Passages indicating the need for cultivating greater assurance of salvation:* Peter writes, "Therefore, my brothers, be all the more eager to make your calling and election sure" (2 Pet. 1:10). He here urges his readers to strengthen their assurance that they have been effectually called and chosen by God to salvation. Assurance of salvation must therefore be both possible and desirable.

Another passage of this sort is Romans 8:16, "The Spirit himself testifies with our spirit that we are God's children." *Symmartyrei,* the word rendered "testifies with," is in the present tense, indicating that this is a continuing witness. The testimony of the Spirit here described is a joint witness with that of our own spirits. The Holy Spirit, in other words, confirms the witness of our own spirits that we are children of God. But note that this confirming testimony of the Spirit is not something that comes only once, in some sudden, dramatic moment, or in some ecstatic emotional experience. The tense is present, describing continuing action. The Spirit *continually testifies* with our spirits that we are children of God. This is a witness which continues throughout life, which works through the Word, which comes through various types of experiences and trials.

In summary, the Scriptures teach that, ideally, faith should carry with it full assurance of salvation but also that believers may for a time lack such assurance. This being the case, we must try to cultivate greater assurance of salvation and pray that we may discern with increasing clarity the confirming testimony of the Spirit that we are children of God.

What do our Reformed creeds say about this matter of assurance? The Heidelberg Catechism, as we saw, describes saving faith in terms of assurance (Q. 21). Though the Belgic Confession does not give a definition of faith, its treatment of faith in Article 22 implies that true faith includes assurance: "Those who possess Jesus Christ through faith have complete salvation in him." The Canons of Dort treat this question more fully than do the other two creeds mentioned. They first assert that believers can have assurance of their salvation:

> Concerning this preservation of those chosen to salvation and concerning the perseverance of true believers in faith, believers themselves can and do become assured in accordance with the measure of their faith, by which they firmly believe that they are and always will remain true and living members of the church, and that they have the forgiveness of sins and eternal life.[36]

The Canons go on to indicate the way in which one can obtain such assurance:

> This assurance does not derive from some private revelation beyond or outside the Word, but from faith in the promises of God which he has very plentifully revealed in his Word for our comfort, from the testimony of the Holy Spirit testifying with our spirit that we are God's children and heirs (Rom. 8:16-17), and finally from a serious and holy pursuit of a clear conscience and of good works.[37]

They sound a realistic note when they further state that believers do not always feel this full assurance:

> Meanwhile, Scripture testifies that believers have to contend in this life with various fleshly doubts and that under severe temptation they do not always experience this full assurance of faith and certainty of perseverance. But God, the Father of all comfort, does not let them be tempted beyond what

36. Canons of Dort, V,9 (1986 trans.).
37. Ibid., V,10.

they can bear, but with the temptation also provides a way out (1 Cor. 10:13), and by the Holy Spirit revives in them the assurance of their perseverance.[38]

J. Gresham Machen once said, "Our salvation does not depend upon the strength of our faith."[39] How true this is! Neither the weakness of our faith nor our sense of unworthiness needs to shake our assurance of salvation. The ground for that assurance is not anything in us, but is found completely in Christ and in his saving work for us.[40]

38. Ibid., V,11.
39. *What is Faith?*, p. 251.
40. On the question of assurance, cf. also Herman Bavinck, *The Certainty of Faith*, trans. Harry der Nederlanden (1901; St. Catharines: Paideia Press, 1980); Louis Berkhof, *The Assurance of Faith* (Grand Rapids: Smitter, 1928); G. C. Berkouwer, "Election and the Certainty of Salvation," in *Divine Election*, trans. Hugo Bekker (Grand Rapids: Eerdmans, 1960), pp. 278-306; C. Graafland, *De Zekerheid van het Geloof* (Wageningen: Veenman, 1961); John Murray, "The Assurance of Faith," *Collected Writings*, 2:264-74.

CHAPTER 11

Justification

MARTIN LUTHER HAD TRIED EVERYTHING: SLEEPING ON HARD FLOORS, going without food, even climbing a staircase in Rome on his hands and knees—but to no avail. His teachers at the monastery told him that he was doing enough to have peace of soul. But he had no peace. His sense of sin was too deep.

He had been studying the Psalms. They often mentioned "the righteousness of God." But this term bothered him. He thought it meant God's punitive righteousness, whereby he punishes sinners. And Luther knew that he was a sinner. So when he saw the word *righteousness* in the Bible, he saw red.

One day he opened his Bible to the Book of Romans. There he read about the gospel of Christ which is the power of God for salvation (1:16). This was good news! But the next verse said, "For therein is the righteousness of God revealed"—there was that bad word *righteousness* again! And Luther's depression returned. It got worse when he went on to read about the wrath of God revealed from heaven against all the unrighteousness of men (v. 18).

So Luther turned again to verse 17. How could Paul have written such terrible words? Had he, Luther, perhaps misunderstood them? "For therein is the righteousness of God revealed from faith to faith: as it is written, The just shall live by faith" (KJV). Suddenly the light dawned on him. The "righteousness of God" Paul here had in mind was not God's punitive justice which leads him to punish sinners, but rather a righteousness which God *gives* to the needy sinner, and which that sinner accepts by *faith*. This was a spotless and perfect righteousness, earned by Christ, which God graciously bestows on all who believe. No longer did Luther need to seek the basis for peace of soul in himself, in his own good works. Now he could look away from himself to Christ, and live by faith instead of groveling in fear.

At that moment the Protestant Reformation was born. Bells began to ring in Luther's soul. Peace and joy now flooded his being. Romans 1:17 now became for him the very "gate of Paradise"—the key which unlocked the Bible.

152

It does not surprise us, therefore, that Luther called the doctrine of justification by faith "the article of a standing or falling church." Implied is the thought that if the church is right on this doctrine it will be basically right on all other teachings, but if it is wrong on this doctrine it will be wrong on every other teaching as well. In similar vein, Calvin says that the doctrine of justification is "the main hinge on which religion turns,"[1] and John Murray affirms that there is no more important or ultimate question than the one that is answered by the doctrine of justification.[2] James Packer sums up the significance of justification in a comprehensive way:

> As understood by the Reformers and their followers, and by Paul as I read him, this theme [justification] is theological, declaring a work of amazing grace; anthropological, demonstrating that we cannot save ourselves; Christological, resting on incarnation and atonement; pneumatological, rooted in Spirit-wrought faith-union with Jesus; ecclesiological, determining both the definition and the health of the church; eschatological, proclaiming God's truly final verdict on believers here and now; evangelistic, inviting troubled souls into everlasting peace; pastoral, making our identity as forgiven sinners basic to our fellowship; and liturgical, being decisive for interpreting the sacraments and shaping sacramental services. No other biblical doctrine holds together so much that is precious and enlivening.[3]

In today's world there is little emphasis on the biblical doctrine of sin. In 1973, in fact, psychiatrist Karl Menninger felt compelled to produce a book entitled *Whatever Became of Sin?*[4] But a person with a shallow sense of sin and of the wrath of God against our sin will neither feel the need for nor understand the biblical doctrine of justification. James Buchanan put it this way: "The best preparation for the study of this doctrine [justification] is—neither great intellectual ability, nor much scholastic learning,—but a conscience impressed with a sense of our actual condition as sinners in the sight of God."[5] Luther's words about the qualifications of a theologian come to mind here: "A theologian is made, not by thinking or reading or speculating, but by living and dying and being damned" (from his lecture on the fifth Psalm).

WORD STUDY

The Old Testament word usually rendered "justify" is *hitsdiq*, the hiphil form of *tsadaq*. The Hebrew-English lexicon of Brown, Driver, and Briggs

1. *Inst.*, III.xi.1.
2. "Justification," *Collected Writings of John Murray* (Carlisle, PA: Banner of Truth, 1977), 2:203.
3. James Packer et al., *Here We Stand* (London: Hodder and Stoughton, 1986), p. 5.
4. New York: Hawthorn Books, 1973.
5. *The Doctrine of Justification* (1867; Grand Rapids: Baker, 1955), p. 222.

lists only one instance where this word in the hiphil may mean "to make righteous" or "to turn to righteousness"—Daniel 12:3, "Those who lead many to righteousness [will shine] like the stars for ever and ever." Otherwise this word is always used in a forensic or legal sense, as meaning, not "to make just or righteous," but "to declare judicially that one is in harmony with the law." Note, for example, Deuteronomy 25:1, "If there be a controversy between men, and they come into judgment, and *the judges* judge them; then they shall justify *(hitsdiqu)* the righteous, and condemn the wicked" (ASV). Here *hitsdiq* is contrasted with a word which means "to condemn"; thus the legal sense is intended. In Proverbs 17:15 we read, "He who justifies *(matsdiq)* the wicked and he who condemns the righteous are both alike an abomination to the LORD" (RSV). "Justifies" here cannot mean "to make righteous." For certainly a person who made the wicked righteous would not be an abomination to the LORD. Clearly the forensic sense is meant: "pronounces or declares righteous."[6]

The New Testament verb translated "to justify" is *dikaioō;* it is used 39 times. It is employed in the sense of "declaring someone righteous" in Luke 18:14, "This man . . . went home justified before God." In his speech in Pisidian Antioch Paul is recorded as having said, "Through him [Jesus] everyone who believes is justified from everything you could not be justified from by the law of Moses" (Acts 13:39). The reference in the previous verse to the forgiveness of sins implies that "justified from" means freedom from condemnation because of sin.

In Paul's writings the word *dikaioō* is clearly used in a forensic or legal sense, as the declaring of a sinner to be righteous. It means the opposite of "condemnation" in Romans 8:33-34, "Who will bring any charge against those whom God has chosen? It is God who justifies. Who is he that condemns?" The opposite of condemnation, however, is not "making righteous" but "declaring righteous." The forensic sense of *dikaioō* is brought out very clearly in Romans 4:5, "To the man who does not work but trusts God who justifies *(dikaiounta)* the wicked, his faith is credited as righteousness." The word rendered "credited" *(logizetai)* is a legal term. *Dikaioō* here does not mean "to make righteous" but "to declare righteous"; the faith of this person is credited to his account as righteousness. By *dikaioō* Paul means the legal imputation[7] of the righteousness of Christ to the believing sinner.[8]

Moulton and Milligan, in their *Vocabulary of the Greek Testament Il-*

6. For other examples of the forensic use of *hitsdiq,* see Job 32:2; 33:32; Exodus 23:7; 1 Kings 8:32; and Isaiah 53:11.
7. The concept of imputation will be discussed later in this chapter.
8. For other examples of the forensic use of *dikaioō,* see Romans 3:20, 24, 26, 28; 5:1, 9; 8:30; 1 Corinthians 6:11; Galatians 2:16; 3:24; Titus 3:7.

lustrated from the Papyri,[9] give a number of usages of *dikaioō* which come close to Paul's employment of the word. For example, the word is used in a papyrus dating from the middle of the first century to refer to the awarding of a verdict in the courts[10]—a striking parallel to the Pauline usage of the term. With one exception, where the word is used in a special way in connection with the mystery religions, *dikaioō* in the papyri of the early Christian centuries can never mean anything like "an infusion of grace"; it always has a legal or forensic meaning.

Gottlob Schrenk says:

> In Paul the legal usage [of *dikaioō*] is plain and indisputable. . . . For Paul the word *dikaioun* does not suggest the infusion of moral qualities, . . . [or] the creation of right conduct. It implies the justification of the ungodly who believe, on the basis of the justifying action of God in the death and resurrection of Christ.[11]

SCRIPTURAL TEACHINGS ON JUSTIFICATION

We look first at the Old Testament. The outstanding Old Testament passage dealing with justification is Genesis 15:6. God has just told Abram that a son coming from his own body will be his heir, and that his descendants will be as numerous as the stars in the sky. The author of Genesis then goes on to say, "Abram believed the LORD, and he credited [a form of the verb *chashabh*] it to him as righteousness." Since the promise of numerous seed must have included the promise of the birth of the one in whom all peoples on earth would be blessed (Gen. 12:3), we infer that Abram's faith included belief in the Messiah who was to come (though the full details of his coming and work had not yet been revealed).[12] This faith in the divine promise God credited to Abram as righteousness—that is to say, by this faith Abram was justified. Paul quotes Genesis 15:6 in Romans 4:3 and 22 and in Galatians 3:6 to show that Abraham, the father of believers, was justified by faith and not by works. James also alludes to Genesis 15:6 (James 2:23) as a reference to Abraham's justification, though James's purpose in quoting it differs from Paul's.

That God forgives our sins is clearly taught elsewhere in the Old Testament. Though the word "justification" is not used in Psalm 103:8-12, the assurance given in these verses that God will not treat us as our sins

9. Grand Rapids: Eerdmans, 1957; orig. pub. 1930.
10. P. 162. The papyrus is P Ryl II 119[14].
11. *"Dikaioō,"* TDNT, 2:215.
12. It may well be that Jesus was referring to Genesis 12:3 when he said to the Jews, "Your father Abraham rejoiced at the thought of seeing my day; he saw it and was glad" (John 8:56).

deserve nor repay us according to our iniquities, and that he has removed our sins from us as far as the east is removed from the west, certainly embodies the blessing conveyed to us through justification: the total forgiveness of our sins. The same comforting message is brought by the stirring words with which Micah closes his prophecy (7:18-19). When Isaiah says that the LORD has laid on the suffering servant who is to come the iniquity of us all (53:6) and that by his knowledge that righteous servant will justify (a form of *hitsdiq*) many (53:11), he is similarly proclaiming, in prophetic language, with a vision which parts the curtains of the future, the doctrine of justification by faith.

We move on to examine New Testament teachings on justification. The outstanding expositor of this doctrine is the Apostle Paul—probably because he had undergone such an abrupt about-face in his own understanding of the way we can attain true righteousness before God. We look first at Romans 3:21-28.

Though the Epistle to the Romans is more than a treatise on justification by faith, it does set forth that doctrine with great clarity and precision. Paul begins the letter by asserting that the wrath of God against sin is being revealed from heaven against all the godlessness and wickedness of men. After thundering against the sins of the Gentiles, he goes on to discuss the sinfulness of the Jews. He sums up his indictment in 3:9 by stating that Jews and Gentiles alike are all under sin, and by adding (in 3:20) that no human being will be justified or declared righteous in God's sight by observing the law (literally, "by works of law"), since through the law comes knowledge of sin.

We turn now to verse 21: "But now a righteousness from God (*dikaiosynē theou*), apart from law, has been made known, to which the Law and the Prophets testify." What is meant by *dikaiosynē theou*? That attribute of God whereby he judges us wholly according to our works, and condemns us when we fail to keep his law? No, for Paul has just said that through the law comes knowledge of sin, and that the righteousness he is now describing has been made known apart from law. Moreover, this righteousness is not one attained through the keeping of the law. It is, on the contrary, as we learn from verse 22, a righteousness obtained through faith in Jesus Christ. For this reason the New International Version correctly translates *dikaiosynē theou* as "a righteousness *from* God." This righteousness from God, therefore, must be a righteousness which God provides, and which is declarative and forensic. In other words, this passage deals directly with justification by faith.

From this passage we learn a number of things about justification:

(1) We learn that this doctrine *has its roots in the Old Testament*: "to which the Law and the Prophets testify" (v. 21). By "the Law and the

Prophets" Paul means the Old Testament Scriptures.[13] Over against Judaizing opponents who contended that Paul's doctrine of justification by faith was an innovation, Paul maintains that this doctrine is witnessed to by the Old Testament. He gives proof for this in chapter 4.

(2) We learn next that this justification is *appropriated by faith*: "This righteousness from God comes through faith in Jesus Christ to all who believe" (v. 22). This, then, is a righteousness apart from the keeping of the law, which is a gift from God, and which is received by faith.

(3) The *necessity* for this justification is affirmed in the last part of verse 22 and in verse 23: "There is no difference, for all have sinned and fall short of the glory of God." The first verb, "have sinned" *(hēmarton)*, is in the aorist tense, and should probably be understood as a summary aorist. When Paul looks at human beings, he concludes that all without exception have sinned. The second verb, "fall short of" *(hysterountai)*, is in the present tense, which describes continuing action. We could therefore paraphrase as follows: "continually fall short of the glory of God." Though interpretations of this last expression (which is found nowhere else in the New Testament) differ, the view which deserves preference is that it means falling short of glorifying God by imperfectly doing his will.[14] In other words, though people differ in many ways, all are alike in this: they are sinners, desperately in need of this justification.

(4) The *basis* for this justification is the atoning work of Jesus Christ. Two words particularly come up for consideration here: *apolytrōsis* and *hilastērion*. *Apolytrōsis* is the word translated "redemption" in verse 24, "through the redemption that came by Christ Jesus." Originally the word described the process of buying back a slave and giving him his freedom through the payment of a ransom. This figure is here applied to the work of Christ: he redeemed us by ransoming us, by paying a price—the price of his own precious blood.[15]

The other word is *hilastērion*, translated "propitiation" in the King James and American Standard Versions, "expiation" in the Revised Standard Version, and "sacrifice of atonement" in the New International Version: "God presented him [Christ] as a sacrifice of atonement, through faith in his blood" (v. 25). The NIV margin explains "sacrifice of atone-

13. Though the full designation of the Old Testament Scriptures was "The Law, the Prophets, and the Writings," Paul here uses only the first two to indicate the entire Old Testament. For parallels, see Matthew 5:17; 7:12.
14. For parallel expressions, see 1 Corinthians 6:20 (RSV); 10:31; Ephesians 1:12; Philippians 1:11.
15. Cf. 1 Peter 1:18-19, "For you know that it was not with perishable things such as silver or gold that you were redeemed *(elytrōthēte,* a verb derived from *lytron)* from the empty way of life handed down to you from your forefathers, but with the precious blood of Christ, a lamb without blemish or defect."

ment" as meaning "the one who would turn aside his [God's] wrath, taking away sin." *Hilastērion* is used in the Septuagint (the Greek version of the Old Testament) as a translation of *kappōreth,* the lid of the ark found in the tabernacle (the so-called mercy seat), which was sprinkled with blood on the Day of Atonement. The Day of Atonement was the high point of Old Testament worship; the sacrifices offered on that day for the sins of the people were uniquely prefigurative of Christ. The blood of the goat of the sin-offering was sprinkled on the mercy seat in order to take away the sins of the people. When Paul says that God presented Christ as a *hilastērion,* he means that through the substitutionary sacrifice of Christ on the cross God's wrath against our sin has been averted and our guilt has been removed.

The word used to translate *hilastērion* in the Revised Standard Version, "expiation," means simply "the cancellation of sin." But this rendering, which was championed by C. H. Dodd,[16] does not do full justice to the Greek term. The word "expiation" fails to recognize the presence of the wrath of God against our sin. That God is wrathful against sin is clearly taught, both in the Old Testament and in the New. Paul himself speaks of God's wrath in Romans 1:18, 24, 26, and 28; in Ephesians 2:3 he affirms that we are all by nature "objects of wrath"; and in 1 Thessalonians 1:10 he describes Jesus as the one "who delivers us from the wrath to come." Since God is holy, our sin must evoke his wrath. But God has so richly shown his love to us that he gave his Son for us, so that through the shedding of Christ's blood the Father's wrath against our sin could be removed.[17]

We must therefore never say that Christ by his sacrifice had to change a hating God into a loving God. Paul tells us here that God *presented* Christ as a sacrifice of atonement for us. In other words, God himself provided the propitiatory sacrifice. Behind the work of Christ is the love of God. Think of 1 John 4:10, "This is love: not that we loved God, but that he loved us and sent his Son as an atoning sacrifice for our sins." Eternity will be too short for us adequately to praise both the Father and the Son for the amazing love by which we have been redeemed!

(5) We also learn from this passage the *rightness* of our justification. Although justification is a work of God's grace ("[they] are justified free-

---

16. *The Bible and the Greeks* (London: Hodder and Stoughton, 1935), pp. 82-95.

17. That Christ made propitiation for our sins is taught by other Bible writers as well. See Hebrews 2:17; 1 John 2:2 and 4:10, where words are used which are cognates of *hilastērion.* On the question of the proper translation of *hilastērion,* see Roger Nicole, "C. H. Dodd and the Doctrine of Propitiation," *Westminster Theological Journal,* Vol. 17, No. 2, pp. 117-57; Leon Morris, *The Apostolic Preaching of the Cross* (Grand Rapids: Eerdmans, 1956), pp. 125-85; Leon Morris, "Propitiation," EDT, p. 888.

ly by his grace," v. 24), it is nevertheless not at the expense of his justice—understanding by justice God's rectitude, that attribute by means of which he does all things justly and rightly. There is no conflict in our justification between God's justice and his grace, since both meet at the cross of Christ. God provides the sacrifice (by grace) and Christ bears the penalty for our sins (satisfying God's justice).

We have here *first* a reference to the sins of Old Testament saints: "He did this to demonstrate his justice, because in his forbearance he had left the sins committed beforehand unpunished" (v. 25). The sins of Old Testament believers could justly be left unpunished, with a view to the sacrifice of Christ which was to be brought later. *Secondly,* Paul speaks of God's justice in forgiving the sins of believers today: "he did it to demonstrate his justice at the present time, so as to be just and the one who justifies those who have faith in Jesus" (v. 26). Today God can *justly* justify the sinner, since Christ has fully satisfied for his people the claims of divine justice.

The conclusion of the whole matter is stated in verse 28: "For we maintain that a man is justified by faith apart from observing the law." Justification is therefore not obtained by works but only by faith.

Another important Pauline passage is Galatians 2:16. The occasion for this reference to justification by faith was Peter's inconsistent action at Antioch. Paul had there opposed Peter to his face because the latter's action (going over to eat with the Jewish Christians who still observed the Jewish food laws, after first having eaten with the Gentile Christians) jeopardized the teaching that we are justified by faith alone. What Peter did could be interpreted as giving support to Judaizers who taught that people are justified partly by their works.

In Galatians 2:15 Paul refers to himself and the other apostles as "Jews by birth and not Gentile sinners." The point of the allusion to Jews is this: Even we, who as Jews were taught respect for the law, now have come to realize that we are justified by faith alone.

We look now at verse 16: "[We] know that a man is not justified by works of the law but through faith in Jesus Christ, even we have believed in Christ Jesus, in order to be justified by faith in Christ *(ek pisteōs Christou),* and not by works of the law *(ex ergōn nomou),* because by works of the law shall no one be justified" (RSV). Note the contrast here between "by faith" and "by works." Justification is by faith in Christ and not by works.

Probably the most dramatic statement of the doctrine of justification in Paul is that found in Philippians 3:8b-9. Though the Judaizers do not seem to have constituted the threat in Philippi which they did in Galatia, nevertheless Paul takes note of them in 3:2, where he warns his readers against "those mutilators of the flesh." He insists that we who are believers should glory in Christ Jesus, and should put no confidence in the flesh (v. 3). Paul goes on to say that if any man might think that he has reasons for putting confidence in the flesh, he certainly would have them. He enumerates seven such possible grounds of confidence: four based on birth (v. 5a), and three based on his presumed moral achievements (vv. 5b-6). The crowning "achievement" of all is the one mentioned last: "as for legalistic righteousness, faultless."

However, Paul continues in verse 7, "But whatever was to my profit I now consider loss for the sake of Christ." That is, I have gladly renounced every particle of trust in these advantages and apparent achievements, which once meant so much to me. At this very moment, in fact, I consider these former gains "rubbish" (v. 8).

What follows, the rest of verse 8 and verse 9, is the reason why Paul was willing to count all his former gains as loss: "that I may gain Christ and be found in him, not having a righteousness of my own that comes from the law, but that which is through faith in Christ—the righteousness that comes from God and is by faith." The words "be found in him," as we saw in an earlier chapter, tie in justification with union with Christ. Observe again the clear contrast between a righteousness which Paul earned himself by trying to keep the law, and one which he received by faith. An additional but related contrast is that between "a righteousness of my own" and "the righteousness that comes from God."

Most incontrovertibly, therefore, this passage sets forth the truth that we are justified, not on the basis of any works which we do ourselves, but solely on the basis of what Christ has done for us. The righteousness of God thus obtained through faith is a treasure of such incomparable worth that in comparison with it we too should count every other gain but loss.

What about James's teaching on justification? When we compare what James says in 2:14-26 with Paul's teaching on justification, there seems to be a real contradiction between the two. Paul says, in Galatians 2:16, "A man is not justified by works of the law" (RSV);[18] but James says, in 2:21, "Was not Abraham our Father justified by works, when he offered his son Isaac upon the altar?" Paul says, in Romans 3:28, "For we hold that a man is justified by faith apart from works of law"; whereas James says, in 2:24, "You see that a man is justified by works and not by faith alone."

Three types of solution to this problem have been suggested: (1) James is combating Paul's teachings; (2) James is combating an antinomian misconception of Paul's teachings about justification; (3) Paul

18. I use the RSV throughout this discussion of James, since its rendering of *ex ergōn*, "by works," is more literal than that of the NIV, "by what he does."

and James deal with different problems, and therefore do not contradict each other.

Those who adopt the first solution, who see a contradiction between Paul and James, may simply accept the possibility of having contradictory teachings in Scripture (as does Karl Barth, who mentions this very difference between Paul and James as an example),[19] or they may be inclined to reject James as not belonging to the canon of Scripture. Neither of these assertions, however, is acceptable.

Since, as is generally accepted, James was probably written before Romans, both the first and the second solutions are unlikely. This leaves the third as the most satisfactory: Paul and James are dealing with different problems. The problem Paul faced was that of opposing people who trusted in their keeping of the law for salvation (as he had himself once done during his Pharisaic period); hence he teaches that a person is justified by faith apart from works of law—that is, works done as a means of earning salvation. James, however, was combating people who were inclined to think that a mere intellectual belief in the truths of Christianity was sufficient for salvation. Note 2:14, "What does it profit, my brethren, if a man says he has faith but has not works? Can his faith [or such faith, NIV] save him?" James replies to people of this sort by saying, "Faith apart from works is dead" (v. 26).

It should be noted, however, that the works about which James writes are not the same as the works Paul has in mind. Paul in this connection always uses the expression "works of the law" or "works of law" (*erga nomou*), when he says that we are justified apart from works (Rom. 3:20, 28; Gal. 2:16). When James speaks of works, on the other hand, he never calls them "works of the law," but simply "works" (*erga*). Luther gives us the key to this distinction when he says,

> He [Paul] calls those deeds works of the law which one does apart from faith and grace and which the law impels either by the fear of punishment or by the alluring promise of temporal rewards. But works of faith he calls deeds which are done in the spirit of liberty and only from the love of God. These can be done only by people who have been justified by faith. The works of the law, however, do not contribute anything to the justification of anyone; indeed, they are a great hindrance because they keep one from seeing himself as unrighteous and in need of justification.[20]

When James says that one cannot be justified by a faith which is without the works of faith, he is not saying anything different from Paul,

19. *Church Dogmatics* (Edinburgh: T. and T. Clark, 1956), I/2, p. 509.
20. *Lectures on Romans*, Vol. 15 of the *Library of Christian Classics*, trans. and ed. by Wilhelm Pauck (Philadelphia: Westminster, 1961), p. 101.

who expresses the same thought in many places. To cite just one, there is Galatians 5:6, "For in Christ Jesus neither circumcision nor uncircumcision is of any avail, but faith working through love" (or "expressing itself through love," NIV).

There remains, however, the question of what James means when he says that a man is justified by works (2:21, 24). Is he contradicting Paul here? Not if we correctly understand James's use of the word "justify" (*dikaioō*). When James says that Abraham was justified by works when he offered his son Isaac upon the altar (v. 21), he is not denying that Abraham was actually justified long before this incident occurred—when, according to Genesis 15:6, "Abraham believed God, and it was reckoned to him as righteousness" (v. 23). The point James is making is that "faith was completed (*eteleiōthē*, 'brought to its goal') by works" (v. 22); that, in other words, the deed of offering up Isaac revealed that the faith by which Abraham had been justified was a living faith. This deed showed that Abraham's justification was genuine. I suggest, therefore, that we understand *dikaioō* in James to mean: "to be revealed as justified." James Packer puts it this way:

> In James 2:21, 24-25 its reference [that of *dikaioō*] is to the proof of a man's acceptance with God that is given when his actions show that he has the kind of living, working faith to which God imputes righteousness. . . . The justification which concerns James is not the believer's original acceptance by God, but the subsequent vindication of his profession of faith by his life. It is in terminology, not thought, that James differs from Paul.[21]

Verse 24 could then be rendered, "You see that a man is revealed as justified by works, and not by faith alone." That is, a person will not be justified by a faith which remains alone, but only by a faith which reveals its genuineness in works of grateful obedience.

Thus, despite apparent contradiction between Paul and James, there is a deep, underlying unity. Paul would agree with James that only a living faith justifies. Both Paul and James would agree with Calvin's dictum: "It is therefore faith alone which justifies, and yet the faith which justifies is not alone."[22]

---

21. "Justification," EDT, p. 594. For similar understandings of *dikaioō* in James, see Calvin, *Commentary on James*, trans. A. W. Morrison (Grand Rapids: Eerdmans, 1980), p. 285; James Buchanan, *The Doctrine of Justification* (Grand Rapids: Baker, 1955), p. 247; R. V. G. Tasker, "James, Epistle of," *The New Bible Dictionary*, ed. J. D. Douglas (Grand Rapids: Eerdmans, 1962), p. 598.

22. Calvin, "Antidote to the Canons of the Council of Trent," in *Tracts and Treatises in Defense of the Reformed Faith*, trans. Henry Beveridge (1851; Grand Rapids: Eerdmans, 1958), 3:152.

THE ROMAN CATHOLIC VIEW OF JUSTIFICATION

The sixteenth-century Roman Catholic Church sharply opposed Protestant teachings on justification as they had been developed by Luther and Calvin. It expressed this opposition particularly in the Canons and Decrees of the sixth session of the Council of Trent. This sixth session was held from June 21, 1546, to January 13, 1547. Later in 1547 John Calvin published his *Acts of the Council of Trent with the Antidote*,[23] in which he sharply attacked the position of Rome on the doctrine of justification. The reason for Calvin's opposition will become clear as we examine, in brief summary, the view of justification which the Council of Trent set forth in its sixth session.

(1) *In Roman Catholic theology according to Trent, justification is thought of primarily as an infusion of grace which results in a change in man's spiritual and moral nature, rather than as a declarative act, in which God imputes the righteousness of Christ to the believer.* For proof of this observation, note the following quotation from Chapter 7 of Session 6: "Whence in the very act of being justified, at the same time that his sins are remitted, a man receives through Jesus Christ, to whom he is joined, the infused gifts of faith, hope, and charity."[24] Though remission of sins is mentioned here, what is emphasized is the infused gifts of faith, hope, and charity or love. Earlier in Chapter 7 the point is put this way: "Justification is not only the remission of sins. . . , but sanctification and renovation of the interior man through the voluntary reception of grace and gifts, whereby a man becomes just instead of unjust. . . ."[25] Justification is here described as not merely the remission of sins, but also as the sanctification and renewal of the inward man. We observe at this point a confusion between what we Protestants call justification and what we call sanctification. We would include remission of sins under justification and the renewal of the person under sanctification, but in the theology of Trent both remission and renewal are thought of as aspects of justification.

Whereas the decree of justification states the teachings of Trent in positive form, the canons which follow the decree express these teachings in negative form. This is what Canon 11 rejects:

> If anyone says that men are justified either through the imputation of Christ's justice alone, or through the remission of sins alone, excluding grace and charity which is poured forth in their hearts by the Holy Spirit and in-

23. The section dealing with justification can be found in *Tracts and Treatises*, 3:19-162.
24. *The Church Teaches, Documents of the Church in English Translation*, by John F. Clarkson et al. (St. Louis: B. Herder, 1955), p. 234.
25. Ibid., p. 233.

heres in them, or also that the grace which justifies us is only the good will of God: let him be anathema.[26]

Here Trent sharply attacks the Protestant position. Contrary to the clear teaching of Romans 4:5-6, Rome explicitly denies that man is justified through the imputation of Christ's righteousness alone. To the same effect is Canon 9: "If anyone says that a sinful man is justified by faith alone, . . . : let him be anathema."[27] At this point the fathers of Trent repudiate the so-called material principle of the Reformation: that we are justified by faith alone.

We conclude that for Trent the chief thing in justification is the spiritual and moral renewal of man and woman, rather than the forgiveness of sins. Justification is not conceived of forensically or declaratively, but as an infusion of grace which brings about sanctification.

(2) *Faith, therefore, does not have central significance in justification but occupies a subordinate place.* The Scriptures teach that we are justified by faith —for example, in Romans 3:28. While Trent recognizes that there is a sense in which we can be said to be justified by faith, its emphasis falls elsewhere. "We may then be said to be justified through faith, in the sense that 'faith is the beginning of man's salvation,' the foundation and source of all justification . . ." (Chapter 8).[28] This can be affirmed because faith is recognized as the first of the seven preparations for justification (see Chapter 6). At this stage, however (the stage of preparation for justification), faith is only "unformed faith" *(fides informis)*, which is insufficient for justification. It does not become justifying faith, as we saw earlier, until it has become "faith formed by love" *(fides caritate formata)*, which happens only when a person has received infused grace in baptism.[29] In the teaching of Trent what really justifies is not faith but the sacrament of baptism. Whereas Protestants would say that the instrumental cause of justification is faith, Trent says that it is baptism (Chapter 7).[30]

(3) *The grace of justification, once having been received, can again be lost.* Whereas the Bible clearly teaches, in Romans 8:30, that those whom God justifies he will also glorify,[31] Trent, having taken the position it has, must go on to state that justification can be lost. "We must also assert . . . that the grace of justification, once received, is lost not only by unbelief, which

---

26. Ibid., p. 243.
27. Ibid.
28. Ibid., p. 235.
29. See the discussion of "The Scholastic View of Faith" on pp. 138-39 above.
30. *The Church Teaches*, pp. 233-34.
31. Though the tense of *edoxasen* ("he glorified") in this passage is aorist, it should be understood as a proleptic aorist, pointing to the future (cf. John Murray, *The Epistle to the Romans* [Grand Rapids: Eerdmans, 1959], 1:321).

causes the loss of faith, but also by any other mortal sin, even though faith is not lost" (Chapter 15).[32] By "mortal sin" the Roman Catholic Church means a sin in which one breaks God's law in a major way, with full knowledge and with deliberate intent. In committing such a sin one dies as a child of God, since love for God has been extinguished. Note that, though justification is lost when one commits a mortal sin, faith is not lost (unless the sin be that of unbelief). The faith that remains, however, is not sufficient for salvation; it is mere "unformed faith."[33]

(4) *The justice or righteousness received in justification can also be increased.* Here again the difference between Roman Catholicism according to Trent and Protestantism comes out clearly. Whereas we would say that a person is either justified or not justified, and that, if justified, he or she does not need to increase in justification, Trent affirms that believers can increase in justification: "Having, therefore, been thus justified, and made the friends . . . of God, . . . they, through the observance of the commandments of God and of the Church, faith co-operating with good works, increase in that justice which they have received through the grace of Christ, and are still further justified . . ." (Chapter 10).[34] The same point is put negatively in Canon 24: "If anyone says that justice which has been received is not preserved and even increased before God through good words, . . . : let him be anathema."[35] It is plain that Trent conceives of the justice received in justification not as the imputation to us of the perfect righteousness of Christ, but as a subjective quality in us that can be increased or decreased.

(5) *Justification enables believers to merit eternal life.* One of Paul's strongest emphases is that no one can earn eternal life by his or her good deeds. Think, for example, of Ephesians 2:8-9, "For it is by grace you have been saved, through faith—and this not from yourselves, it is the gift of God—not by works, so that no one can boast." Yet the Council of Trent teaches that justified persons can merit eternal life through good works.

This point is made in a negative way in Canon 32:

> If anyone says that the good works of a justified man are gifts of God to such an extent that they are not the good merits of the justified man himself; or that, by the good works he performs through the grace of God and the merits of Jesus Christ (of whom he is a living member), the justified man does not truly merit an increase of grace, life everlasting, and, providing that he dies

---

32. *The Church Teaches*, p. 240.
33. It should be remembered, however, that, according to Roman Catholic teaching, if one confesses to a priest after having committed a mortal sin, justification can again be restored through the sacrament of penance—see Chapter 14 of Session 6.
34. Philip Schaff, *The Creeds of Christendom* (New York: Harper, 1877), 2:99.
35. *The Church Teaches*, p. 245.

in the state of grace, the attainment of that life everlasting, and even an increase of glory: let him be anathema.[36]

Trent here admits that the good works which this justified man does are the gifts of God, and that he can only perform them through the grace of God and the merits of Jesus Christ. But, the Council goes on to say, these good works are at the same time the good merits of the justified man himself. By these good works the justified man now merits an increase of grace, life everlasting, and even an increase of glory.

The idea that one can "merit an increase of grace" would seem to be a contradiction in terms. For if something is of grace, how can it be merited? And if it is merited, how can it still be grace? Further, the teaching that one can merit everlasting life is clearly contrary to Scripture: "He [God] saved us, not because of righteous things we had done, but because of his mercy" (Titus 3:5). Crystal clear are the words of Romans 6:23, "For the wages of sin is death, but the gift of God is eternal life in Christ Jesus our Lord."

It will now be obvious why the Reformers attacked the Roman Catholic conception of justification so vehemently: they were convinced that Rome's teaching on this point obscured and threatened the gracious character of justification, and made it necessary for believers to add to the merits of Christ certain merits of their own. In the teachings of Trent the precious truth that we are saved by grace alone—which is the very heart of the gospel—is not only jeopardized but buried under a mountain of good works.

Karl Barth's questions are very much to the point:

> Is there in Paul anything like a sacramentally infused and therefore inherent righteousness? Could he have described true Christian faith as a mere *initium salutis* ("beginning of salvation") and therefore as something which needs to be filled out in relation to justification? . . . Where did he ever say and how could he possibly have said, that although the Christian ought not to doubt the mercy of God, the merits of Christ and the power of the sacraments, yet . . . even in faith there can be no absolute assurance *de sua gratia* ("concerning his own grace"), in the question of whether there is grace for him? Above all, where did he ever bring the sanctification of a Christian and his justification into the relationship which forms the substance of the positive teaching of the *Tridentinum* [the Council of Trent]: that justification is only completed in sanctification, in the doing of the good and meritorious works provided and made possible and accomplished by the grace of justification. . . ?
>
> How could he possibly speak of an *incrementum* or *augmentum* ("increase") of the grace of justification by the practice of love, by the accomplish-

---

36. Ibid., p. 246.

ment of certain works, which carries with it an augmentation of the glory to be expected in eternity? Or, finally, of a repetition of justification . . . in view of the situation of a fall from grace which constantly arises in practice in the life of every Christian? . . .[37]

What about recent developments in the Roman Catholic Church, particularly since Vatican II? Have they brought about any changes in Rome's doctrinal position? This is not an easy question to answer. We begin by noting Hans Küng's significant book, *Justification: The Doctrine of Karl Barth and a Catholic Reflection*, which first appeared in 1957.[38] Whatever else may be said about it, this book certainly opened up new possibilities for dialogue between Roman Catholics and Protestants. Küng's main thesis — which caused something of a sensation in the theological world — was that Barth's teaching on justification was in fundamental agreement with the teaching of the Roman Catholic Church, particularly that of the Council of Trent, on that doctrine. When one reads this book for the first time, one often feels as if he is reading a Protestant rather than a Roman Catholic study.

For example, Küng admits that the original biblical meaning of *tsadaq* and *dikaioō* is forensic, and that justification in the biblical sense means "declaring just."[39] He has a section on *sola fide* ("by faith alone") in which he admits that a person is justified by God's grace alone, through faith and not through works.[40] He also has a section entitled *Soli Deo Gloria* ("to God alone the glory") in which he asserts that everything a man does comes from God, and that therefore God must receive all the praise.[41] Küng says further that by the term *merit* he means nothing other than the biblical concept of reward, and that therefore we should not argue about a word.[42]

What shall we say to all this? We must certainly be grateful for the new openness between Roman Catholics and Protestants which has come about since Küng published this book, and since the Second Vatican Council (1962-65) was convened. We can only hail with rejoicing the greater emphasis on Bible study by lay members now found in the Roman Catholic Church, and hope that this will lead to a theology that is more biblically based than it was in the past.

Getting back to Küng, however, some serious difficulties remain.

---

37. *Church Dogmatics*, IV/1, p. 625.
37. *Church Dogmatics*, IV/1, p. 625.
38. My references are to the English translation, published in 1964 by Thomas Nelson in New York.
39. Küng, *Justification*, pp. 209-12.
40. Ibid., p. 252.
41. Ibid., p. 265.
42. Ibid., pp. 270-73.

Rudolf J. Ehrlich, after a competent and substantial study of Küng's view, comes to the conclusion that Küng's teaching is not in agreement with Trent.[43] He puts it this way: "Protestants would entirely misunderstand Küng if they thought he was trying to show that the Roman Church, having become aware of the truth of the Reformation teaching on justification . . . , was now willing to incorporate Protestant concepts into its own doctrinal system."[44] John R. W. Stott, in his recent book *The Cross of Christ*, demonstrates that Küng's view of justification is in certain respects not the same as the Protestant view.[45] Stott adds, "More than a quarter of a century has passed since the publication of his [Küng's] book, and one is not conscious of any widespread proclamation in the Roman Catholic Church of the gospel of justification by grace alone through faith alone."[46]

To see whether there has been any basic change in Rome's teaching on justification, let us look at some statements on justification by recent Roman Catholic theologians. Karl Rahner, commonly recognized as representing newer trends in Catholic theology, says this: "Justification, understood as God's deed, transforms man down to the deepest roots of his being; it transfigures and divinises him. For this very reason the justified man is not 'at the same time justified and a sinner.'"[47] It is obvious that this is not the Protestant view of justification; the word "divinises" even suggests the possibility that the boundary between the creature and the Creator is being wiped out. In the *New Catholic People's Encyclopedia* we find the following definition of justification: "Justification means the process by which man is saved from his state of sin and reborn in Christ through sanctifying grace, a process which makes him just or right in the sight of God."[48] In distinction from the Protestant view, justification is here called a process—a process which includes rebirth and sanctification. In Rahner and Vorgrimler's *Dictionary of Theology*, a recent Roman Catholic publication, we find this brief exposition of justification:

> Justification is the event in which God, by a free act of love, brings man . . . into that relationship with him which a holy God demands of man. . . . He does so by giving man a share in the divine nature. This happens when God causes the Holy Spirit . . . to dwell efficaciously in the depths of man's being as the spirit of the adoption of sons, of freedom and of holiness, divinizing

43. *Rome: Opponent or Partner?* (London: Lutterworth, 1965), pp. 189-98.
44. Ibid., p. 104.
45. *The Cross of Christ* (Downers Grove: InterVarsity, 1986), pp. 184-86.
46. Ibid., p. 186.
47. Karl Rahner, "Justified and Sinner at the Same Time," in *Theological Investigations*, trans. K. and B. Kruger (Baltimore: Helicon Press, 1969), 6:222.
48. Published by the Catholic Press in Chicago in 1973. The quotation is from 2:523.

him, and gives him proof of this new creation . . . through the word of faith and the signs of the sacraments. This justice, which is not merely imputed in juridical fashion but makes a man truly just, is at the same time the forgiveness of sins. . . . There can be no reflexive certainty of salvation for any individual. . . . This justice, God-given and received, can also be lost if man rejects divine love by serious sin. . . . Man can both preserve and continually increase it [justification].[49]

As we read this description, we find many echoes of the teachings of Trent.

There is therefore no evidence of an essential change in Roman Catholic teaching on justification. Since that teaching has been shown to be in basic disagreement with the Bible, we must reluctantly continue to oppose Rome on this crucial point of doctrine.[50]

Before we leave this subject, we should face one of the chief criticisms Roman Catholic theologians have advanced against the Protestant view of justification. They argue that the purely forensic or declarative understanding of justification leaves people totally unchanged, and therefore falls short of full salvation from sin. The Reformed or Lutheran doctrine of justification, so they say, is a mere "legal fiction," a "robe thrown over a corpse."

The answer to the objection is this: justification is just one facet of our salvation. The person who has been justified by faith is at the same time one who is being renewed by the Spirit. As was pointed out in an earlier chapter,[51] the process of salvation has many aspects which exist side by side. Being in Christ includes regeneration, conversion, sanctification, and perseverance, as well as justification. One who is in Christ is indeed a new creation, with new motives, new standards, and new goals. Understanding justification as a declarative act of God safeguards the precious teaching that we are saved by grace alone and not by works. But this understanding in no way excludes the renewing and transforming work of the Holy Spirit in the lives of God's people.[52]

49. Karl Rahner and Herbert Vorgrimler, *Dictionary of Theology,* 2nd ed. (New York: Crossroad, 1981), pp. 260-61.

50. Cf. R. G. England, *Justification Today: the Roman Catholic and Anglican Debate* (Oxford: Latimer House, 1979). After having discussed both Küng and Trent at some length, he says, "While the work of leading Roman Catholic scholars has eased the difficulties felt by Anglican Evangelicals with the teaching of Trent, it has not of itself removed certain basic difficulties" (p. 40).

Note also the thoroughly documented article, "U.S. Lutheran–Roman Catholic Dialogue on Justification by Faith," the result of five years of discussion, in *Origins, N.C. Documentary Service,* Vol. 13, No. 17 (October 6, 1983), pp. 279-304. Though the two groups did find a number of points of agreement, and did arrive at a better understanding of each other's positions, basic disagreements remained.

51. See above, Chapter 2, and note the chart on p. 16.

52. On this point, see also G. L. Carey, "Justification and Roman Catholicism," in James Packer et al., *Here We Stand,* p. 124; also John R. W. Stott, *The Cross of Christ,* pp. 187-89.

JUSTIFICATION IN THE REFORMED CONFESSIONS

The church writes confessions or creeds in order to summarize biblical teachings and to give an articulate expression to the Christian faith. The Reformed Confessions of the sixteenth and seventeenth centuries reflect the thinking of the Calvinistic wing of the Protestant Reformation. In examining what these confessions say about justification, we shall see the radical difference between their position on this doctrine and that of the Canons and Decrees of the Council of Trent.

A. *The Heidelberg Catechism* (1563). This catechism, written at the request of Frederick the Third, the Elector of the German Palatinate, by Zacharias Ursinus, a professor at the University of Heidelberg, and Caspar Olevianus, the court preacher, has become known as the most pastoral and personal of the creeds of the Reformation. The description of justification given in Question and Answer 60 is one of the most heart-warming ever written:

Q. How are you right with God?

A. Only by true faith in Jesus Christ.
   Even though my conscience accuses me
      of having grievously sinned against all God's commandments
      and of never having kept any of them,
   and even though I am still inclined toward all evil,
   nevertheless,
      without my deserving it at all,
      out of sheer grace,
   God grants and credits to me
   the perfect satisfaction, righteousness, and holiness of Christ,
      as if I had never sinned nor been a sinner,
      as if I had been as perfectly obedient
         as Christ was obedient for me.
   All I need to do
   is to accept this gift of God with a believing heart.[53]

The following observations about this answer suggest themselves: (1) the acceptance of our justification goes hand in hand with a deep conviction of sin and of our continuing inclination to sin;[54] (2) justification is a totally undeserved gift of God's grace; (3) justification is here defined, not as an infusion of grace, but as the imputation[55] of the perfect satisfaction

---

53. Heidelberg Catechism, Q. 60 (1975 trans.).
54. Luther expressed the same point in his well-known formula: the justified believer is at the same time righteous and a sinner *(simul justus et peccator).*
55. The older translation of the Catechism has "grants and imputes *(schenket und zurechnet)* to me the perfect satisfaction . . . of Christ," whereas the 1975 translation renders "zurechnet" by "credits to me." See the fuller discussion of the term "imputation" later in this chapter.

and righteousness of Christ to the believing sinner; (4) both the negative and the positive aspects of justification are stated: God has forgiven all our sins, and he now looks upon us as if we had been as perfectly obedient as Christ was; (5) we receive this blessing by faith alone.

B. *The Belgic Confession* (1561). This confession was written by Guido de Brès, a preacher in the Reformed churches of Belgium, as a summary of the beliefs of Reformed Christians who were being persecuted by the Roman Catholic government. What is said about justification can be found in two articles. From Article 22 we cull the following:

> And therefore we justly say with Paul that we are justified "by faith alone" or by faith "apart from works" (Romans 3:28). However, we do not mean, properly speaking, that it is faith itself that justifies us—for faith is only the instrument by which we embrace Christ, our righteousness. But Jesus Christ is our righteousness in making available to us all his merits and all the holy works he has done for us and in our place. And faith is the instrument that keeps us together with him in communion with all his benefits. When those benefits are made ours they are more than enough to absolve us of our sins.[56]

The points of interest here are that we are justified by faith alone apart from works, that Christ is our righteousness, that faith is not a meritorious work but only an instrument, and that Christ's benefits are more than adequate to cover all our sins.

From Article 23 we further learn that God grants us a righteousness which is apart from works: "We believe that our blessedness lies in the forgiveness of our sins because of Jesus Christ, and that in it our righteousness before God is contained, as David and Paul teach us when they declare that man blessed to whom God grants righteousness apart from works (Ps. 32:1; Rom. 4:6)."

C. *The Westminster Confession of Faith* (1647). A Puritan Calvinist creed drawn up by 131 pastors and 30 laymen at Westminster Abbey in London, this is the last of the classic Reformed confessions. From the chapters on justification I quote these words:

> Those whom God effectually calleth he also freely justifieth; not by infusing righteousness into them, but by pardoning their sins, and by accounting and accepting their persons as righteous; not for any thing wrought in them, or done by them, but for Christ's sake alone; . . . by imputing the obedience and satisfaction of Christ unto them, they receiving and resting on him and his righteousness by faith; which faith they have not of themselves, it is the gift of God.[57]

Here we note the following points: (1) justification is tied in with ef-

---

56. The text is from the 1985 translation.
57. Westminster Confession, XI,1.

fectual calling (since, as we saw earlier, effectual calling is identical with regeneration,[58] this confession is saying that regeneration and justification can never be separated); (2) justification is understood as meaning, not the infusion of righteousness, but the imputation of Christ's obedience to believers; (3) both the negative and the positive aspects of justification are mentioned: the forgiveness of sins and the accepting of believers as righteous; (4) justification is received and rested upon by faith; and (5) this faith is not a human achievement but the gift of God.

The chapter goes on to say:

> Faith, thus receiving and resting on Christ and his righteousness, is the [only] instrument of justification; yet is it not alone in the person justified, but is ever accompanied with all other saving graces, and is no dead faith, but worketh by love.[59]

Two additional points are here made: (6) faith is the only instrument for receiving justification; (7) yet this faith is never alone, but works through love.

In a later section of the chapter the confession affirms:

> God doth continue to forgive the sins of those that are justified; and although they can never fall from the state of justification, yet they may by their sins fall under God's fatherly displeasure . . . until they humble themselves, confess their sins, beg pardon, and renew their faith and repentance.[60]

Contrary to Trent, the Westminster divines at this point maintain (8) that believers can never fall from the state of justification, (9) but that those justified must continue to confess their sins to God, (10) in the confidence that God will continue to forgive them.

THE CONCEPT OF JUSTIFICATION

Justification may be defined as that gracious and judicial act of God whereby he declares believing sinners righteous on the basis of the righteousness of Christ which is credited to them, forgives all their sins, adopts them as his children, and gives them the right to eternal life.

How, now, must we understand the doctrine of justification? A number of observations follow.

(1) The doctrine of justification presupposes a recognition of *the reality of God's wrath*. The God with whom we have to do is a holy God—one who cannot but be wrathful against our sin: "Your [God's] eyes are too

---

58. See above, p. 106.
59. Westminster Confession, XI,2.
60. Ibid., IX,5.

pure to look on evil; you cannot tolerate wrong" (Hab. 1:13). Unless we realize that God's wrath rests upon the sins we have committed and still do commit, we shall never feel the need to be justified. The Bible, as we saw earlier,[61] clearly teaches that God directs his wrath against our sin. Jesus himself, the supreme revealer of what God is like, solemnly declared that the wrath of God abides on those who reject the Son (John 3:36). Paul tells us that we are all by nature the objects of God's wrath (Eph. 2:3)—a wrath which comes upon those who are disobedient to him (Eph. 5:6). Because of this wrath we are said to be alienated from God on account of our evil behavior (Col. 1:21) and to be under God's curse (Gal. 3:10) until we are redeemed by Christ, who saves us from God's wrath (Rom. 5:9). Just as in a Rembrandt painting a brightly lit subject is framed in darkness, so we must see the doctrine of justification as a gracious message of light against the somber backdrop of the wrath of God.[62]

(2) Justification is a *declarative* or *judicial* act of God and not a process. That this is so has been shown earlier in this chapter, in the word study and in the section dealing with biblical teachings on justification. God declares or pronounces us righteous, not on the basis of what we are in ourselves, not on the ground of our good deeds, but solely on the basis of the righteousness of Christ. This blessing is totally unmerited: "nothing in my hands I bring; simply to thy cross I cling." By means of this declaration we are delivered from God's wrath, and are reconciled to him (Col. 1:22). Because of our justification there is now no condemnation for us who are in Christ (Rom. 8:1). Having been redeemed from the curse, we are now sharers of the blessing of Abraham (Gal. 3:13-14).

Justification is not a process; it takes place once for all when a person accepts Christ by faith. Though this is so, the believer must continue to appropriate his or her justification by a continuing exercise of faith. The blessing of justification, therefore, after it has been received, is a never-ending source of comfort, peace, and joy.

(3) Justification is received *by faith alone*, and is not in any way merited by our own good works (Rom. 3:28). In this connection an important pastoral observation suggests itself. Many believers find it difficult to continue to accept their justification, since their experience of still falling into sin seems to belie it. It will be remembered that according to the Heidelberg Catechism our persistent inclination to sin need not rob us of the assurance of our justification. More to the point, however, is Hendrikus

61. See above, p. 158.
62. On the wrath of God, see also Leon Morris, *Apostolic Preaching*, pp. 161-66; and his *The Cross in the New Testament* (Grand Rapids: Eerdmans, 1965), pp. 189-92; James Packer, "The Wrath of God," in *Knowing God* (Downers Grove: InterVarsity, 1973), pp. 134-42; John Stott, *The Cross of Christ*, pp. 102-10; W. C. Robinson, "Wrath of God," EDT, pp. 1196-97.

Berkhof's observation that our having received justification by faith implies that we do not actually experience it:

> Is justification an event which we consciously experience? . . . The origin [of justification] lies outside us, in Christ. In the Bible and in the interpretation of the church this event comes to us as a "message," a "word." It does not arise out of ourselves. . . . Hence in our faith . . . we step outside the world of our experience. We receive the opposite of what we experience. In the face of an entirely contrary experience, we need to be *told* this ever and again. But where we allow ourselves to be told, it enters our experience as a sense of liberation, joy, release, and security.[63]

(4) Justification is rooted in *union with Christ*. It is only because we are one with Christ that his righteousness can be credited to us, and can therefore become our own. This thought has been more fully developed in a previous chapter.[64]

(5) Justification is based on *the substitutionary work of Christ* for us. It involves Christ's exchanging places with us, and bearing for us the wrath of God against sin which we deserved. This is taught already in Isaiah 53, often called "the gospel in the Old Testament," where we read that "the LORD has laid on him [the suffering servant, who according to Acts 8:35 is Jesus Christ] the iniquity of us all" (v. 6), and that this servant "bore the sin of many" (v. 12). Echoing the words of the prophet, Peter says that Christ bore our sins in his body on the tree (1 Pet. 2:24), and the author of Hebrews affirms that Christ was offered up to take away the sins of many (Heb. 9:28). Christ himself clearly taught that he was to die as our substitute, telling us that the Son of Man came "to give his life as a ransom for (*anti*, meaning 'instead of' or 'in the place of') many" (Matt. 20:28; cf. Mark 10:45). Using a different preposition, Paul expresses a similar thought when he says that Christ died for all (*hyper*, meaning "in behalf of" or "for the sake of," 2 Cor. 5:15), and that Christ was made to be sin for us (v. 21).

That Christ was our substitute is taught with inescapable clarity and force in Galatians 3:13, "Christ redeemed us from the curse of the law by becoming a curse for us *(hyper hēmōn)*." We deserved that curse, since we do not and cannot obey God's law perfectly (vv. 10-11). But Christ bore the curse in our stead, as our substitute, even *becoming* a curse for us, so that we might be delivered from it. Luther has described the meaning of Galatians 3:13 vividly and unforgettably:

> Our most merciful Father, seeing us to be oppressed and overwhelmed with the curse of the law, and so to be holden under the same, that we could never

---

63. Hendrikus Berkhof, *Christian Faith*, trans. Sierd Woudstra, rev. ed. (Grand Rapids: Eerdmans, 1986), pp. 437-38.
64. See above, pp. 61-62.

be delivered from it by our own power, sent his only Son into the world, and laid upon him all the sins of all men, saying, Be thou Peter that denier; Paul that persecutor, blasphemer, and cruel oppressor; David that adulterer; that sinner which did eat the apple in Paradise; that thief which hanged upon the cross; and briefly, be thou the person which hath committed the sins of all men; see therefore that thou pay and satisfy for them.[65]

(6) Justification involves *the imputation of Christ's righteousness to us.* The word "imputation" occurs in many creedal statements about justification, and in older English versions of the Bible. For example, this word is employed eight times in the King James Version to translate the Greek word *logizomai* ("to reckon"). "Imputation" is a legal or judicial term; it means to reckon to the account of another. It is used in three connections in the New Testament: of the imputation of Adam's sin to his posterity (Rom. 5:12-21), of the imputation of the sins of his people to Christ (2 Cor. 5:21), and of the imputation of the righteousness of Christ to his people.[66] Justification involves imputation in this last sense.

It is particularly Paul who develops the thought that the righteousness of Christ is imputed to us in justification. By the righteousness of Christ he means the merit Christ acquired by bearing God's wrath against our sins and by perfectly obeying God's law. In Romans 4:6 and 11 Paul speaks of God's "crediting" or "imputing" *(logizomai)* to believers righteousness apart from works. In verse 3 he quotes Genesis 15:6, "Abraham believed God, and it was credited *(elogisthē,* a form of *logizomai)* to him as righteousness." He then points out that this righteousness was not received by Abraham because of his works but because he trusted God, the one who "justifies the ungodly" (or "acquits the guilty," NEB). For this reason Abraham's faith was credited or imputed to him as righteousness (vv. 4-5).

Paul next finds a reference to imputation in Psalm 32:1-2, particularly in the words, "Blessed is the man to whom the LORD imputes no iniquity" (RSV, quoted from the Septuagint in Rom. 4:8). Paul interprets this blessing in a positive way: David, he says, is here speaking of the blessedness of the man "to whom God credits *(logizetai)* righteousness apart from works" (v. 6). The blessing of the imputation of righteousness is here said to have been received, first by Old Testament believers in David's time

65. Martin Luther, *Commentary on St. Paul's Epistle to the Galatians* (1981; Grand Rapids: Baker, 1979), pp. 274-75. On Christ as our substitute, see also Berkhof, ST, pp. 376-79; Leon Morris, *The Cross in the New Testament,* pp. 173-75, 220-24, 379-81, 404-19; Herman Ridderbos, *Paul,* trans. J. R. De Witt (Grand Rapids: Eerdmans, 1975), pp. 190-93; James I. Packer, "What Did the Cross Achieve? The Logic of Penal Substitution," *Tyndale Bulletin,* Vol. 25 (1974), pp. 3-45; John Stott, *The Cross of Christ,* pp. 141-49; 344-46.
66. Cf. C. W. Hodge, "Imputation," ISBE, 2:812-15.

(vv. 6-8), then by all uncircumcised believers (v. 11), and finally by all those who believe in him who raised Jesus from the dead (vv. 23-24).

In Romans 4 Paul deliberately uses the word *logizomai* to indicate the way we can receive righteousness apart from works, affirming that it is God who does this imputing or crediting. In 1 Corinthians 1:30 Paul indicates that the righteousness we receive in justification is the righteousness of Christ, "who has become for us wisdom from God—that is, our righteousness, holiness and redemption." "Christ has become our righteousness" is simply another way of saying that the perfect righteousness of Christ has been credited to our account. And in 2 Corinthians 5:21, "God made him who had no sin to be sin for us, so that in him we might become the righteousness of God," it is made clear that the imputation of Christ's righteousness is based on our oneness with him. Commenting on this passage, James Packer puts it well:

> God declares them [believers] to be righteous, because he reckons them to be righteous; and he reckons righteousness to them, not because he accounts them to have kept his law personally (which would be a false judgment), but because he accounts them to be united to the one who kept it representatively (and that is a true judgment). For Paul union with Christ is not fancy but fact—the basic fact, indeed, in Christianity; and the doctrine of imputed righteousness is simply Paul's exposition of the forensic aspect of it.[67]

(7) In justification *God's mercy and justice come together*. The Bible often brings together two complementary aspects of God's nature: the prophet reminds us that in wrath God remembers mercy (Hab. 3:2); we are told to note both the kindness and the severity of God (Rom. 11:22), and to observe that, when we confess our sins, God is faithful and righteous in forgiving those sins (1 John 1:9). Both of these aspects meet in our justification. Justification is a marvelous gift of God's grace and mercy; it is totally undeserved. Yet this gift is not at the expense of God's justice. God cannot simply abandon or even relax his justice, since he is a holy God; he cannot forgive our sin unless his righteousness has been satisfied.

The Bible therefore teaches that God can justify us only because his justice has indeed been fully satisfied for us by Christ's atonement, in which God's only Son bore the divine wrath we deserved, and by Christ's perfect obedience to the law — an obedience which we should have rendered but could no longer render. God, so Paul unfolds for us in Romans 3, justifies us "freely by his grace through the redemption that came by Christ Jesus" in order that he might "demonstrate his justice . . . , so as to be just and the one who justifies those who have faith in Jesus" (vv. 24, 26). In the cross of Christ, therefore, "God's justice and love are

67. "Justification," EDT, p. 596.

simultaneously revealed."[68] Similarly, in our justification the kindness and severity of God kiss each other.

(8) Justification has *both a negative and a positive side*. On the negative side, it means the forgiveness of our sins. On the positive side, it includes our adoption as children of God and our reception of the right to eternal life. Later in the chapter these two sides will be treated more fully.

(9) Justification has *eschatological implications*. It means that the verdict which God will pronounce over us on the Day of Judgment has been brought into the present. We therefore do not need to fear the Judgment Day; we who believe in Christ have already crossed over from death to life (John 5:24). Our having been adopted as children of God, one of the fruits of our justification, points forward to the future completion of that blessing (Rom. 8:23), and the right to eternal life which our justification bestows conveys a gift which will never end (John 11:25-26). Justification once received can never be lost.

(10) Though justification *must never be separated from sanctification*, these two blessings *are distinct*. The first thing we should observe here is that justification and sanctification must never be separated. As Paul affirms in 1 Corinthians 1:30, God does not justify anyone whom he does not also sanctify. Both of these blessings are aspects of our union with Christ. Our justification is one of the fruits of our oneness with Christ, but we cannot be in union with Christ without at the same time being involved in the process of sanctification, whereby Christ through his Spirit makes us progressively more like himself. In the chapter on the order of salvation this thought has been more fully developed.[69]

John Calvin has some memorable words on this point:

> Why, then, are we justified by faith? Because by faith we grasp Christ's righteousness, by which alone we are reconciled to God. Yet you could not grasp this without at the same time grasping sanctification also. For he "is given unto us for righteousness, wisdom, sanctification, and redemption" [1 Cor. 1:30]. Therefore Christ justifies no one whom he does not at the same time sanctify. These benefits are joined together by an everlasting and indissoluble bond, so that those whom he illumines by his wisdom he redeems; those whom he redeems, he justifies; those whom he justifies, he sanctifies.[70]

Though justification and sanctification always occur together, however, they must also be carefully distinguished from each other. One of the errors of traditional Roman Catholic teaching on justification, as we saw,

---

68. G. C. Berkouwer, *The Work of Christ*, trans. C. Lambregtse (Grand Rapids: Eerdmans, 1965), p. 277.

69. See above, Chapter 2.

70. There is, however, also a sense in which we may speak of sanctification as definitive, as occurring at a certain point in time. See below, pp. 202-209.

is that justification and sanctification are not kept distinct, since justification is said to include the renewal and transformation of the believer. The problem with this view is that it makes the forgiveness of sins received in justification dependent in some sense on the progress one is making in the sanctified life.

The following differences between justification and sanctification should be recognized:

(a) Justification removes the guilt of sin, whereas sanctification removes the pollution of sin and enables the believer to grow in his or her likeness to Christ.

(b) Justification takes place outside the believer and is a declaration made by God the Father about his or her judicial or legal status. Sanctification, however, takes place within the believer and progressively renews his or her nature.

(c) Justification takes place once for all and is neither a process nor a repeated event. Sanctification, however, as it is usually understood, is a process which continues throughout life and is not completed until after this life is over.[71]

Why is it important to maintain these distinctions? First, to do full justice to biblical teaching on these soteriological blessings. Further, to maintain the truth that justification means the imputation of the righteousness of Christ to the believing sinner wholly apart from that believer's deeds—that, in other words, our justification is based solely on the suffering and obedience of Jesus Christ, and not one whit on our own good works.

THE NEGATIVE AND POSITIVE SIDES OF JUSTIFICATION

By the negative side of justification I mean the blessing of the forgiveness of sins. Expanding on this point, justification means a permanent change in our judicial relation to God whereby we are absolved from the charge of guilt, and whereby God forgives all our sins on the basis of the finished work of Jesus Christ. Apart from Christ, our judicial relation to God is one of condemnation — we stand condemned on account of our sins, both original and actual.[72] When we are justified, our judicial relation to God is changed from one of condemnation to one of acquittal; the negative side of that judicial change is the remission or forgiveness of our sins.

71. See below, p. 202.
72. Original sin is the sinful state in which we were born, involving condemnation because of the sin of Adam, our first head. Actual sins are the sins of act, word, or thought that we ourselves commit. See my *Created in God's Image* (Grand Rapids: Eerdmans, 1986), pp. 143-54, 162-64, 172-73.

This leads us to ask: Which sins are forgiven in justification—past and present sins only (including the guilt of original sin), or future sins as well? Some Reformed theologians have demurred at the thought that all the future sins of a believer are forgiven at the time of his or her justification, fearing that such teaching might lead to moral laxity and to laziness in the battle against sin. For this reason some taught that justification is not a single act, but an act which must be repeated every time a believer confesses his or her sins.

A prominent representative of this position was William à Brakel in his book *Redelijke Godsdienst* ("Reasonable Worship"), originally published in 1700.[73] He distinguishes between reconciliation and justification. The reconciliation of the elect, he says, is complete in Christ and cannot be set aside by any sins committed after they have come to believe. Justification, however, he maintains, is a pronouncement of the acquittal of the sinner; this pronouncement must be repeated after every confession of sin. The believer is thus justified not once but daily—perhaps even oftener. Brakel bases his view on Scripture passages which speak of daily confession of sin, the need to pray for forgiveness, the work of Christ as our Advocate, and on texts which tie in justification with faith.[74] He admits, however, that a believer once justified does not sink into an unreconciled state every time he or she sins, and that the first justification *virtually* implies that God will also forgive the believer's subsequent sins.[75]

This is a point of some importance because of the difficult problem of the relation between justification and our confession of sin. If we are justified once for all, why must we still confess our sins? If, on the other hand, it is necessary to confess daily sins, does this imply that future sins are not included in our justification?

A study of the relevant New Testament passages will reveal that justification takes place in the life of a believer once for all, and not repeatedly. Think of Romans 8:30, "Those he called, he also justified (*edikaiōsen;* the aorist tense implies once-for-all action); those he justified (*edikaiōsen*), he also glorified." Surely Paul was not writing here about a justification which is repeated every day. Think also of Romans 5:1, "Therefore, since we have been justified (*dikaiōthentes*, aorist) through faith, we have peace with God through our Lord Jesus Christ." Here Paul likewise describes justification as happening once for all. The next verse, in fact, confirms this thought: "Through him we have obtained access to this grace in which we stand, and we rejoice in our hope of sharing the glory of God" (5:2,

73. W. à Brakel, *Redelijke Godsdienst*, ed. J. H. Donner (Leiden: D. Donner, 1893), 1:872-82.
74. Ibid., pp. 877-80.
75. Ibid., p. 881.

RSV). Having been justified once for all, we stand in a new relationship to God, that of grace, and we rejoice in a new hope, that of sharing the glory of God (cf. also vv. 9, 10, and 11). The same concept of finality and permanence is conveyed by Romans 8:1, "There is now no condemnation for those who are in Christ Jesus."

But then how about the forgiveness of future sins? In Romans 8:33-34 we read, "Who shall bring any charge against God's elect? It is God who justifies; who is to condemn?" (RSV). Here Paul triumphantly proclaims that no charge can ever be successfully brought against anyone whom God has justified. Satan can never overthrow by his accusations the justification of one of God's elect. From God's point of view, therefore, there can be no objection to saying that when he justifies a person he forgives that person's future sins as well as his or her past sins, since that believer's future life lies before God as an open book.

Shedd puts it this way:

> The justification of a sinner is an all-comprehending act of God. All the sins of a believer, past, present, and future, are pardoned when he is justified. The sum-total of his sin, all of which is before the Divine eye at the instant when God pronounces him a justified person, is blotted out or covered over by one act of God. Consequently, there is no repetition in the Divine mind of the act of justification; as there is no repetition of the atoning death of Christ, upon which it rests.[76]

The Bible teaches, however, that God promises to forgive the sins of believers in the future, after they have presumably been justified. Jesus teaches that if we forgive men when they sin, our heavenly Father will also forgive us (Matt. 6:14); and John affirms that when we confess our sins, God will forgive them (1 John 1:9). And James says about a sick person for whom prayer has been offered in faith, "if he has sinned, he will be forgiven" (5:15). Charles Hodge, discussing the question of whether sins can be forgiven before they are committed, says, "It would perhaps be a more correct statement to say that in justification the believer receives the promise that God will not deal with him according to his transgressions, rather than to say that sins are forgiven before they are committed."[77]

From the believer's point of view, I believe it is better to say that justification means the forgiveness of all past and present sins, and the judicial ground for the forgiveness of future sins. The many small Scriptural injunctions to confess our sins teach us that we must indeed return in

---

76. William G. T. Shedd, *Dogmatic Theology* (1888; Grand Rapids: Zondervan, n.d.), 2:545.

77. *Systematic Theology* (1872; Grand Rapids: Eerdmans, 1949), 3:164.

penitence to God's throne of mercy every day, pleading for pardon. But we then do so on the basis of the merits of Christ applied to us in our justification. Such an experience is then not a renewed justification but rather a renewed application of our justification. When we commit a grave sin, we lose our consciousness of forgiveness; we lose our sense of peace with God. When we confess our sins to God, he again awakens our sense of forgiveness and revives our assurance that we have been justified once for all.

The justified believer, therefore, continues to pray daily for forgiveness; not, however, with the despair of one who thinks herself lost, but in the confidence of a child approaching a loving heavenly Father. Justification occurs once for all; confession of sin and prayer for forgiveness must be repeated.[78]

Justification, however, includes more than the forgiveness of sins; it also embraces, on its positive side, our adoption as children of God and the bestowal of the right to eternal life. In this connection we should look at the two aspects of Christ's work for us, commonly called his *active and passive obedience*. The term "passive obedience" is often misunderstood; many think that it means an obedience in which Christ was "passive" and not active, an "obedience of passivity." But this is not what the adjective "passive" in this expression is intended to convey. The term "passive obedience" originated in the Latin writings of seventeenth-century Lutheran and Reformed theologians. One of these, Johannes Wollebius, used the expression *passiva obedientia* ("passive obedience") as equivalent to *passio* ("suffering," here used of the suffering of Christ).[79] By "passive obedience," therefore, we must understand the sufferings of Christ, culminating in his death on the cross; to avoid misunderstanding, however, I prefer the term "suffering obedience." By "active obedience" we must understand Christ's perfect keeping of God's law; here I prefer the term "law-keeping obedience."

A. A. Hodge summarizes the meaning of these two aspects of Christ's obedience in these words: "In the one aspect, the obedience is called *passive*, to signalize it as penal suffering. In another aspect, the same obedience is called *active*, to signalize it as the doing of that which is commanded."[80] The same author warns us against dividing these two aspects: "The active and passive obedience of Christ, the suffering of the penalty for the remission of sin, and the obeying of the law for life, do not . . . con-

---

78. Cf. Buchanan, *The Doctrine of Justification,* pp. 251-52.
79. From his *Christianae Theologiae Compendium* (Basel, 1626), 81, in Heinrich Heppe, *Reformed Dogmatics,* ed. Ernst Bizer, trans. G. T. Thomson (London: Allen and Unwin, 1950), p. 462.
80. *The Atonement* (Philadelphia: Presbyterian Board of Publication, 1867), p. 254.

stitute two satisfactions, but are one complete and perfect satisfaction of the whole law in all its relations."[81]

We may say, therefore, that through his suffering obedience Christ endured the penalty for our sins and bore the curse for us (Gal. 3:13; compare Rom. 3:24-26 and 5:8-10). He thus merited for us the forgiveness of sins. Through his law-keeping obedience Christ perfectly kept the law for us, earning for us the right to be adopted as children of God and to have eternal life. But we must never forget that the suffering and the law-keeping were two aspects of one obedience.

> It is not even proper to say that the forgiveness of sins is obtained only through his [Christ's] passive obedience and that eternal life is obtained only through his active obedience. For Christ's suffering was not only a bearing of the punishment, but also a fulfillment of the law; and his working was not just a fulfillment of the law, but also a bearing of its punishment. His doing was suffering and his suffering was doing. It was one work which Christ completed.[82]

Earlier I pointed out that the righteousness of Christ which is imputed to us or credited to our account in our justification is the merit he acquired for us through bearing God's wrath against our sin and through perfectly keeping God's law. This righteousness of Christ, therefore, includes two aspects: satisfaction and obedience. The New Testament speaks of Christ as our "second Adam" or "last Adam" (1 Cor. 15:45; cf. Rom. 5:15-21). In order to redeem us Christ had to do a twofold work: he had to suffer the penalty for Adam's sin and for all the sins his people had committed (and would still commit), but he also had to render to God that perfect obedience to God's law which Adam should have rendered but had failed to perform. What is therefore credited to our account in our justification is not only Christ's satisfaction of the penalty for our sins but also his perfect obedience to God's law. Because of the imputation of Christ's law-keeping obedience to us, we who are justified are now looked upon by God as if we "had been as perfectly obedient as Christ was obedient for" us.[83]

Some theologians, however, deny that Christ's active or law-keeping obedience is imputed to us in justification. Among them are Johannes Piscator (1546-1625), a German Reformed theologian, and a number of Arminian theologians: Richard Watson,[84] A. M. Hills,[85] and H. Orton Wiley.[86]

81. Ibid., p. 264.
82. Bavinck, *Dogmatiek,* 3:440 [trans. mine].
83. Heidelberg Catechism, Q. 60 (1975 trans.).
84. *Theological Institutes* (New York: Carlton and Porter, 1857), 2:215-34.
85. *Fundamental Christian Theology* (1931; Salem, Ohio: Schmul, 1980), 2:188-89.
86. *Christian Theology* (Kansas City: Beacon Hill, 1958), 2:396-97.

What arguments are advanced by these theologians against this teaching? (1) It is said that there is no Scriptural basis for this doctrine. Later, however, we shall be looking at the Scriptural evidence for this teaching.

(2) This teaching lessens the sense of obligation for keeping God's law, and tends to lead to carelessness in living.[87] The same objection, however, could be made to the teaching that God forgives us all our sins. One could conceivably twist this doctrine so as to make of it a license to sin. But that possible misuse does not prove that the teaching is wrong.

(3) A third objection is "that it grounds our salvation on the active obedience of Christ instead of conditioning it on his atoning death, and thus leaves no reason for Christ's vicarious suffering."[88] But surely Christ's active obedience and his vicarious suffering are not an either-or. Christ needed to do both.

What is the biblical basis for the teaching that Christ's law-keeping obedience is imputed to us? We look first at Romans 5:18-19,

> (18) Consequently, just as the result of one trespass was condemnation for all men, so also the result of one act of righteousness was justification that brings life for all men. (19) For just as through the disobedience of the one man the many were made sinners, so also through the obedience of the one man the many will be made righteous.

By "one act of righteousness" Paul means the entire obedience of Christ —not just his having suffered the penalty for our sins, but his having perfectly kept God's law. The result of Christ's obedience is "justification that brings life." This justification is received by us because the obedience of Christ, our second Adam and our new head, is imputed to us or credited to our account. Since the "one act of righteousness" is contrasted with "one trespass," the former expression must refer to the law-keeping obedience of Christ.

The contrast between what comes to us through Adam and what comes to us through Christ is continued in verse 19. Through the disobedience of Adam we were made sinners—the Greek word *kathistēmi*, translated "made," here means to "appoint," "constitute," or "place in the status of." Paul is here expressing a forensic or legal idea: because of Adam's disobedience we who are in Adam have been placed in the status of sinners and are therefore under condemnation (see v. 18). From the second half of the verse we learn that through the obedience of Christ we are "constituted" (again a form of *kathistēmi*) righteous. Since the first half of verse 19 describes a legal or forensic concept, by way of analogy the

87. A. M. Hills, *Fundamental Christian Theology*, 2:189.
88. Ibid.

second half must also do so: we who are in Christ are now considered or declared righteous because Christ's active or law-keeping obedience has been imputed to us.

Earlier in this chapter I dealt with Philippians 3:8b-9.[89] Let me just add here that the "righteousness that comes from God" which Paul there mentions is more than the nonimputation of sin. What Paul particularly celebrates in that chapter is that he no longer has a righteousness of his own, one that comes from the law, but he now has a righteousness that comes from God through faith. Similarly, all of us who are found in Christ possess that righteousness—a righteousness from God which is credited to our account in our justification.

In 2 Corinthians 5:21 Paul says, "God made him [Christ] who had no sin to be sin for us, so that in him we might become the righteousness of God." Christ identified himself with our sin, so Paul affirms, in order that in him we might become identified with the righteousness of God. This, again, means more than just having had our sins forgiven. It means that because of Christ's substitutionary work the righteousness of God is now credited to us or imputed to us, with the amazing result that we actually *become* that righteousness. Luther's comment on this passage is worth quoting:

> This is that mystery which is rich in divine grace to sinners, wherein by a wonderful exchange our sins are no longer ours but Christ's, and the righteousness of Christ is not Christ's but ours. He has emptied himself of his righteousness that he might clothe us with it, and fill us with it.[90]

When Paul says in 1 Corinthians 1:30 that Christ has become for us, not only wisdom from God, but also our righteousness, is he not again saying that we are looked upon by God as being perfectly righteous in Christ? Does this language not again convey the thought that the spotless righteousness of Christ—that of his perfect obedience—becomes ours in our justification?

Calvin put it this way:

> It is also evident that we are justified before God solely by the intercession of Christ's righteousness. This is equivalent to saying that man is not righteous in himself but because the righteousness of Christ is communicated to him by imputation. . . . To declare that by him [Christ] alone we are accounted righteous, what else is this but to lodge our righteousness in Christ's obedience, because the obedience of Christ is reckoned to us as if it were our own.[91]

---

89. See above, pp. 159-60. Cf. also pp. 61-62.
90. Martin Luther, *Works*, J. B. Knaske et al., eds. (Weimar edition), 5:608.
91. *Inst.*, III.xi.23.

OUR ADOPTION AS CHILDREN OF GOD

Getting back now to the two positive benefits of justification that we mentioned earlier, we take up first our adoption as children of God. By this I do not mean the spiritual rebirth whereby we become children of God through regeneration, described in Chapter 7. I mean adoption in the legal sense: our being placed in the status of sons and daughters of God, and therefore becoming entitled to all the privileges that go with that status.

The Greek word used in the New Testament to describe this blessing is *huiothesia*. In extrabiblical literature this word meant legal adoption, together with such privileges as heirship and such duties as providing for the adopting parents.[92] In the New Testament the word is used only by Paul and refers to God's placing his people in the legal status of sonship.

The Westminster Shorter Catechism defines adoption as follows: "Adoption is an act of God's free grace, whereby we are received into the number, and have a right to all the privileges, of the sons of God."[93] The Heidelberg Catechism distinguishes between our adoption as God's children and the sonship of Christ: "Christ alone is the eternal, natural Son of God; but we are children of God by adoption, through grace, for his [Christ's] sake."[94] It is God the Father who adopts us as his children when he justifies us. Here I am describing God's redemptive fatherhood, celebrated in Scripture with words like these: "Behold what manner of love the Father hath bestowed upon us, that we should be called children of God" (1 John 3:1, ASV). This is to be distinguished from what we could call the "universal fatherhood of God"—his fatherhood of all people by creation.

What is the Scriptural basis for the doctrine of adoption? In Ephesians 1:5-6 we read, "He [God] predestined us to adoption *(huiothesian)* as sons through Jesus Christ to Himself, according to the kind intention of His will, to the praise of the glory of His grace, which He freely bestowed on us in the Beloved" (NASB). We note that here our being adopted as God's children has its roots in God's eternal decree, and has as its goal the praise of the glory of God's grace.

In Galatians 4:4-7 Paul unfolds in a masterful way the meaning of our adoption:

> When the time had fully come, God sent his Son, born of a woman, born under law, to redeem those under law, that we might receive the full rights

---

92. Eduard Schweizer, "*huiothesia*," TDNT, 8:397-98; cf. also VGT, pp. 648-49.
93. Question 34. Text from Schaff, *Creeds of Christendom*, 3:683.
94. Heidelberg Catechism, Q. 33. From the older translation, found in Schaff, *Creeds*, 3:318.

of sons *(huiothesian)*. Because you are sons, God sent the Spirit of his Son into our hearts, the Spirit who calls out, "*Abba*, Father." So you are no longer a slave, but a son; and since you are a son, God has made you also an heir.

The words "born under law" (that is, under the obligation of keeping the law) point to the active or law-keeping obedience of Christ. Christ, Paul here teaches us, kept the law for us in order to redeem those that were under law (that is, his people) from bondage to a law they could not keep.

This law-keeping obedience of Christ is now tied in with our adoption: "that we might receive the full rights of sons"—that is, that we might be legally adopted by God as his children, thus receiving all the rights involved in that sonship. The reception of this sonship is accompanied by the reception of the Holy Spirit, who applies to our hearts and lives the redemption Christ earned for us. That Spirit not only enables us to accept our sonship by faith, but also to give expression to it by addressing God as our Father. And because we have now been adopted by God as his sons and daughters, we have also become heirs of God, entitled to all the privileges and benefits of that sonship. How inexpressibly rich we are in Christ!

Another eloquent passage describing our adoption, somewhat parallel to the one in Galatians, is Romans 8:15-17:

> You did not receive a spirit that makes you a slave again to fear, but you received the Spirit of sonship *(huiothesias)*. And by him we cry, "*Abba*, Father." The Spirit himself testifies with our spirit that we are God's children. Now if we are children, then we are heirs—heirs of God and co-heirs with Christ, if indeed we share in his sufferings in order that we may also share in his glory.

By "the Spirit of sonship" Paul means the Holy Spirit by whom believers are being led (v. 14). All of us who are in Christ have received that Spirit, through whom we now rejoice to call God our Father. That same Spirit continually testifies (the verb *symmartyrei*, translated "testifies," is in the present tense, signifying action that continues) with our own spirits that we are indeed children of God—a testimony conveyed to us through the Word, through the experiences of life, through daily mercies, hourly strength, and abiding joy. Again Paul makes the point that as sons we are also heirs, but now he adds a new thought: we are co-heirs with Christ. Christ, according to Hebrews 1:2, has been appointed by God to be the "heir of all things"; what is Christ's inheritance by right has become ours by grace. In what does that inheritance consist? It means "sharing in Christ's glory" (v. 17), "the hope of eternal life" (Tit. 3:7), "the kingdom of Christ" (Eph. 5:5)—"an inheritance that can never perish, spoil or fade," kept in heaven for us (1 Pet. 1:4).

But this sonship also has an eschatological dimension. In Romans 8:23 we read that we, who already have the firstfruits of the Spirit, "wait eagerly for our adoption as sons *(huiothesian)*, the redemption of our bodies." Here Paul implies that our sonship is not only something we now have, but also something we do not yet possess. Though we are already sons and daughters of God, we eagerly await the total redemption of our bodies from all the results of sin and from all the limitations under which we now groan, anticipating with delight the time when "we shall be like him, for we shall see him as he is" (1 John 3:2). Our sonship, in other words, looks forward to a future that is too glorious for words!

What benefits follow from our adoption as children of God? (1) We now have the right to approach the throne of grace with confidence (Heb. 4:16; 1 John 5:14). (2) We enjoy the blessing of God's protection and care (Matt. 6:25-34; 1 Pet. 5:7). (3) The adversities we must still undergo are not punishments for our sins but fatherly discipline (Heb. 12:5-11). (4) We are sealed by the Holy Spirit and thus kept by the power of God (2 Cor. 1:22; Eph. 1:13; 4:30).[95]

THE RIGHT TO ETERNAL LIFE

The second positive benefit of our justification, to which we now turn, is our right to eternal life. This, too, is one of the results of our adoption as children of God. From Galatians 4:7 we learn that when we are in Christ we are no longer slaves but sons and daughters of God, and that therefore God also made us heirs. In Titus 3:7 Paul further tells us that our being heirs means the right to eternal life, and that this right is one of the fruits of our justification: God saved us "so that, having been justified by his grace, we might become heirs having the hope of eternal life."

Eternal life is God's gift to all who believe in his Son (John 3:16). But it is also described by John as being given to his people by Jesus Christ: "I give them [my sheep] eternal life, and they shall never perish" (John 10:28; cf. 17:2). In fact, John affirms that leading people to receive eternal life through faith is the main purpose of both his Gospel (John 20:31) and his first epistle (1 John 5:13).

95. On the doctrine of adoption, see also R. A. Webb, *The Reformed Doctrine of Adoption* (Grand Rapids: Eerdmans, 1947); John Murray, "Adoption," in *Redemption — Accomplished and Applied* (Grand Rapids: Eerdmans, 1955), pp. 165-73; James Cook, "The Concept of Adoption in the Theology of Paul," in James Cook, ed., *Saved by Hope* (Grand Rapids: Eerdmans, 1978), pp. 133-40; T. Rees, "Adoption; Sonship," ISBE, 1:53-55; P. H. Davids, "Adoption," EDT, p. 13. A pastorally helpful discussion can be found in James Packer, *Knowing God*, pp. 181-208.

Eternal life *(aiōnios zōē)* is contrasted in the Bible with merely physical life, often described by the Greek word *bios*. So, for example, in Luke 8:14 Jesus describes certain hearers of the gospel as "those who hear, but as they go on their way they are choked by the cares and riches and pleasures of life *(biou)*, and their fruit does not mature" (RSV). Eternal life differs from merely physical life not only in duration but also in quality. Jesus makes this clear when in his so-called High-Priestly Prayer he says, "This is eternal life: that they [Christ's people] may know you, the only true God, and Jesus Christ, whom you have sent" (John 17:3).

Eternal life, therefore, is described in the New Testament as being both a present possession and a future hope. That eternal life is a present possession is clearly stated in John 3:36, "Whoever believes in the Son has eternal life." Paul makes this point the basis for a pastoral injunction: "Take hold of the eternal life to which you were called when you made your good confession" (1 Tim. 6:12).[96]

If this life, however, were only a present blessing that ends when we die, there would be no point in calling it eternal; it is, in fact, also a future hope. Accordingly, Jesus closes his dramatic description of the last judgment by saying, "Then they [the goats] will go away to eternal punishment, but the righteous to eternal life" (Matt. 25:46). And John reports Jesus as saying, "The man who loves his life *(psychēn)* will lose it, while the man who hates his life *(psychēn)* in this world will keep it for eternal life *(zōēn aiōnion)*" (John 12:25).[97]

The right to eternal life, therefore, which has been merited for us by Christ and bestowed on us in our justification, like the blessing of being adopted as children of God, points both to the present and to the future. Qualitatively, we possess eternal life here and now, as we know God in his marvelous grace and experience rich fellowship with him in trust and in service, in prayer and in praise. But we possess it now only as the firstfruits of a greater harvest to come. After the resurrection of the body we shall enjoy eternal life in all its fullness. Then faith will change to sight, death and sorrow will be forgotten, and we will have reached the state of perfect knowledge of God, perfect enjoyment of God, and perfect service of God. And that state, praise God, will never end![98]

---

96. See also John 5:24; 6:40; 6:54; 12:50 (RSV); 17:3; 1 John 5:13.

97. See also Mark 10:29-30; Luke 18:29-30; Galatians 6:8; Titus 1:1-2.

98. On the topic of eternal life, see also R. Bultmann, "The Concept of Life in the New Testament," TDNT, 2:861-72; G. E. Ladd, "Eternal Life," *A Theology of the New Testament* (Grand Rapids: Eerdmans, 1974), pp. 254-59; H. G. Link, "Life," *New International Dictionary of New Testament Theology*, ed. Colin Brown (Exeter: Paternoster, 1976), 2:480-84; J. F. Walvoord, "Eternal Life," EDT, pp. 368-69; R. J. Wallace, "Eternal," ISBE, 2:160-62; E. F. Harrison, "Life," ISBE, 3:129-34.

THE RELATION OF FAITH TO JUSTIFICATION

The New Testament describes this relation by means of three types of expressions: we are said to be justified "through faith" *(ek pisteōs)* or "by faith" *(dia pisteōs* or *pistei)*. Note the following examples: (1) *Ek pisteōs:* Romans 5:1, "Therefore, since we have been justified through faith, we have peace with God through our Lord Jesus Christ." (2) *Dia pisteōs:* Galatians 2:16, "[We] know that a man is not justified by observing the law, but by faith in Jesus Christ." (3) *Pistei:* Romans 3:28, "For we maintain that a man is justified by faith apart from observing the law."

What does each expression stress? *Ek*, meaning "out of" or "through," emphasizes the fact that faith is the "instrument" which appropriates this justification. *Dia pisteōs* and *pistei* (the dative singular of the noun *pistis*) both convey the thought that we are justified by means of faith. It is important to observe that one type of expression never occurs in the New Testament: *dia tēn pistin* ("on account of faith"). Faith is never represented as the meritorious ground for our justification.

How, then, should we express the relation between faith and justification? Various words have been used to describe this relationship. Calvin compares faith to a *vessel:* "We compare faith to a kind of vessel; for unless we come empty and with the mouth of our souls open to seek Christ's grace, we are not capable of receiving Christ."[99] The Belgic Confession calls faith an *instrument:* "Faith is only the instrument by which we embrace Christ, our righteousness."[100] John Murray speaks of faith as an *instrumentality:* "Therefore faith is an indispensable instrumentality in connection with justification."[101] In James Packer's words, faith is "the outstretched *empty hand* which receives righteousness by receiving Christ."[102] Any of these expressions may be used, as long as faith is not described as a meritorious ground for justification.

This point is well expressed in Question 61 of the Heidelberg Catechism:

> Why do you say that you are righteous only by faith?
> Not that I am acceptable to God on account of the worthiness of my faith, but because only the satisfaction, righteousness, and holiness of Christ is my righteousness before God, and I can receive the same and make it my own in no other way than by faith only.[103]

---

99. *Inst.*, III.xi.7.
100. Belgic Confession, Article 22 (1985 trans.).
101. *Redemption*, p. 159.
102. "Justification," EDT, p. 596.
103. Text from Schaff, *Creeds*, 3:327.

A word should be said about the ground for our justification. This ground is not our virtuous deeds, nor "the imperfect obedience of faith."[104] Neither, as we just saw, is it the worthiness of our faith.[105]

At first glance it might seem as though Genesis 15:6, "Abram believed the LORD, and he credited it to him as righteousness," and New Testament quotations of this passage,[106] imply that faith is in some sense the ground for our righteousness. "Credited to him as righteousness" might conceivably be construed as meaning that Abraham's faith was of such worth that it was considered as having merited or earned his righteousness. On the contrary, however, the entire thrust of New Testament teaching rules out such a construction. As we saw in our study of the relevant Scripture passages, nothing that we do can ever be the meritorious basis for God's justifying us. James Packer puts it well:

> When Paul paraphrases this verse [Gen. 15:6] as teaching that Abraham's faith was reckoned for righteousness (Rom. 4:5, 9, 22), all he intends us to understand is that faith — decisive, wholehearted reliance on God's gracious promise (vss. 18ff.)—was the occasion and means of righteousness being imputed to him. There is no suggestion here that faith is the ground of justification.[107]

What, then, is the ground for our justification? Various suggestions have been made. John Stott, for example, states that it is the blood of Christ,[108] stressing Christ's suffering obedience. John Murray affirms that it is the obedience of Christ,[109] thus stressing Christ's law-keeping obedience. It will probably be best to say, with Louis Berkhof, that the ground for our justification is the perfect righteousness of Jesus Christ,[110] by which we mean all that Christ did for us in suffering the punishment which our sins deserved, and in perfectly keeping God's law for us. This perfect righteousness, imputed or credited to us when through faith we become one with Christ, is the totally adequate ground for our justification.

We can now see more clearly why, when Luther rediscovered the doctrine of justification by faith, bells began to ring in his soul. Here is indeed the heart of the gospel. Here is the gateway to Paradise.

---

104. Canons of Dort, II, Rejection of Errors, Par. IV (1986 trans.).
105. Heidelberg Catechism, Q. 61.
106. "Abraham believed God, and it was credited to him as righteousness" (Rom. 4:3); cf. also Romans 4:5, 9, and 22; Galatians 3:6; and James 2:23.
107. "Justification," EDT, p. 596. In this connection I take strong exception to the RSV rendering of the first part of Romans 3:30, "he [God] will justify the circumcised on the ground of their faith." This translation of *ek pisteōs* certainly seems to suggest that faith is in some sense the ground for our justification.
108. *The Cross of Christ*, p. 140.
109. *Redemption*, p. 154.
110. Berkhof, ST, p. 523.

My hope is built on nothing less
  Than Jesus' blood and righteousness;
I dare not trust the sweetest frame,
  But wholly lean on Jesus' name.

On Christ, the solid Rock, I stand—
  All other ground is sinking sand.[111]

---

111. On the doctrine of justification, see also John Owen, *Justification by Faith* (1677; Grand Rapids: Sovereign Grace Publishers, 1959); Berkhof, ST, pp. 510-26; Edward Boehl, *The Reformed Doctrine of Justification*, trans. C. H. Riedesel (1890; Grand Rapids: Eerdmans, 1946); G. C. Berkouwer, *Faith and Justification*, trans. L. B. Smedes (Grand Rapids: Eerdmans, 1954); Markus Barth, *Justification*, trans. A. N. Woodruff III (Grand Rapids: Eerdmans, 1971); J. I. Packer et al., *Here We Stand: Justification by Faith Today* (London: Hodder and Stoughton, 1986).

CHAPTER 12

Sanctification[1]

IN OLD TESTAMENT TIMES GOD TOLD MOSES TO SAY TO THE PEOPLE OF ISRAEL, "Be holy because I, the LORD your God, am holy" (Lev. 19:2). Peter echoes these words in his first epistle: "Just as he who called you is holy, so be holy in all you do; for it is written: 'Be holy, because I am holy' " (1 Pet. 1:15-16). Since God himself is holy, he desires that we, whom he has created in his image, should also be holy. The work of God by which he makes us holy we call *sanctification*.

DEFINITION

We may define sanctification as that gracious operation of the Holy Spirit, involving our responsible participation, by which he delivers us from the pollution of sin, renews our entire nature according to the image of God, and enables us to live lives that are pleasing to him.

Using this definition as a point of departure, I should like to observe, first, that sanctification is concerned with the *pollution* of sin. We commonly distinguish between the guilt and the pollution associated with sin. By *guilt* we mean the state of deserving condemnation or of being liable to punishment because God's law has been violated. In justification, which is a declarative act of God, the guilt of our sin is removed on the basis of the atoning work of Jesus Christ.[2] By *pollution*, however, we mean the corruption of our nature which is the result of sin and which, in turn, produces further sin. As a result of the Fall of our first parents, we are all born in a state of corruption; the sins which we commit are not only products of that corruption but also add to it. In *sanctification* the pollu-

---

1. A revised and expanded version of the chapter "The Reformed Perspective," in *Five Views on Sanctification*, by Melvin E. Dieter, Anthony A. Hoekema, Stanley M. Horton, J. Robertson McQuilkin, and John F. Walvoord. Copyright © 1987 by the Zondervan Corporation. Used by permission.

2. See Chapter 11. Note the differences between justification and sanctification, pp. 177-78.

tion of sin is in the process of being removed (though it will not be total-ly removed until the life to come).

Sanctification, further, effects a renewal of our nature — that is, it brings about a change of direction rather than a change in substance. In sanctifying us, God does not equip us with powers or capacities which are totally different from those we had before; rather, he enables us to use the gifts he gave us in the right way instead of in sinful ways. Sanctification empowers us to think, will, and love in a way that glorifies God: to think God's thoughts after him and to do what is in harmony with his will.

Sanctification also means being enabled to live lives that are pleasing to God. It is commonly said that in sanctifying us God enables us to per-form "good works." These good works must not be thought of as meritorious, and they cannot be done perfectly—that is, without flaw or blemish. Yet they are necessary. In Ephesians 2:10, in fact, good works are described as the fruit of our salvation: "For we are God's workmanship, created in Christ Jesus to do good works, which God prepared in advance for us to do." In other words, we are not saved *by* works but *for* works. Yet, since the expression *good works* might be interpreted somewhat atomistically (as suggesting, say, that we should do so many good works a day), I prefer to say that sanctification enables us to live lives which are pleasing to God.

THE BIBLICAL CONCEPT OF HOLINESS

Since the word *sanctify* means "to make holy" (from two Latin words, *sanctus,* holy; and *facere,* to make), we should look next at what the Bible teaches about holiness in human beings. The chief Old Testament word for *holy* is *qādosh;* from this root both a verb and a noun are derived. The basic meaning of this word seems to be "to separate from other things"— that is, to place something or someone in a realm or category separated from what is common or profane. In the earlier books of the Old Testa-ment, the holiness of God's people is usually defined in ceremonial terms: holiness describes the way in which priests were to be set apart for their special service or by which the people were to purify themselves through certain ritual observances. Later Old Testament books, however, par-ticularly the Psalms and the prophets, describe the holiness of God's people primarily in ethical terms, as involving doing righteousness, speaking the truth, acting justly, loving mercy, and walking humbly with God (Ps. 15:1-2; Mic. 6:8). What is conveyed by the word *qādosh,* therefore, is that God's people are to be set apart for God's service and that they should avoid whatever is displeasing to him.

The chief New Testament word for *holy* is *hagios* and its derivatives.

Though used in various senses, this word often describes the sanctification of believers, as in Ephesians 5:25-26, "Christ loved the church and gave himself up for her, that he might sanctify *(hagiasē)* her" (RSV). In this sense holiness in the New Testament means two things: (1) separation from the sinful practices of this present world, and (2) consecration to God's service. Contrary to popular opinion, therefore, holiness in the biblical sense means more than not doing certain bad things and doing certain good things; rather, it means to be spiritually separated from all that in sinful and to be totally dedicated to God.[3]

We ask next what the Bible teaches about the way in which we are sanctified. We note first that we are sanctified *in union with Christ.* Paul teaches that we are made holy through being united with Christ in his death and resurrection. Certain opponents of Paul had been twisting his teachings about justification by faith so as to make them mean, Let's just go on sinning so that grace may increase (see Rom. 6:1). Paul replies, "By no means! We died to sin; how can we live in it any longer?" (v. 2). He goes on to show that we died to sin in union with Christ, who died for us on the cross: "We were therefore buried with him through baptism into death. . . . Our old self was crucified with him" (vv. 4, 6). Sanctification, therefore, must be understood as a dying to sin in Christ and with Christ, who also died to sin (v. 10).

In the same chapter, however, Paul also tells us that we are one with Christ in his resurrection. For he says,

> We were . . . buried with him . . . into death in order that, just as Christ was raised from the dead through the glory of the Father, we too may live a new life. If we have been united with him like this in his death, we will certainly also be united with him in his resurrection (Rom. 6:4-5).

We are now called to live a new life because we arose with Christ and share his resurrection life with him. Colossians 3:1 mentions the same result: "Since, then, you have been raised with Christ, set your hearts on things above, where Christ is seated at the right hand of God" (see also Eph. 2:4-6). Passages of this sort remind us that we should not only say that Christ died for us and arose for us, but should also confess that we died and arose with Christ—died with him to sin and arose with him to new life.

We are being sanctified through growing into a fuller and richer union with Christ. Paul tells us that God's plan for us is that "speaking the truth

---

3. See in this connection the brief but incisive study of Christian separation by Johannes G. Vos, *The Separated Life: A Study of Basic Principles* (Philadelphia: Great Commission Publications, n.d.). In contrast to Christians who hold that the life of Christian separation means primarily abstinence from certain material things, Vos contends that the Bible requires a spiritual separation from conduct that is sinful in itself.

in love, we will in all things grow up into him who is the Head, that is, Christ" (Eph. 4:15). He goes on to make clear that sanctification involves not simply individuals in isolation from each other but the entire community of God's people: "From him [Christ] the whole body . . . grows and builds itself up in love, as each part does its work" (v. 16). As we grow closer to Christ, we grow closer to each other. We are sanctified through fellowship with those who are in Christ with us.[4]

Our sanctification in union with Christ is masterfully summed up in 1 Corinthians 1:30, "It is because of him that you are in Christ Jesus, who has become for us wisdom from God—that is, our righteousness, holiness and redemption." The word here rendered "holiness" is *hagiasmos*, translated "sanctification" in other versions (KJV, ASV, NASB, RSV). Paul catches us here by surprise. Christ, he says, has not only *brought about* our sanctification; he *is* our sanctification. If we are one with Christ, we are being sanctified; and the only way we can be sanctified is through being one with Christ. Calvin has put it well: "As long as Christ remains outside of us, and we are separated from him, all that he has suffered and done for the salvation of the human race remains useless and of no value for us."[5]

We are also sanctified *by means of the truth*. In his so-called High-Priestly Prayer, Jesus prays for his disciples, "Sanctify them by [or, according to some versions, in] the truth" (John 17:17). Christ, who came to bear witness to the saving truth of God, prays that the Father may keep his disciples in the sphere of this redemptive truth. Once Christ was no longer on the earth this truth would be found in God's Word. He therefore adds, "Your word is truth." We must grow in sanctification through the Bible, which is God's Word. That the Bible is one of the chief means whereby God sanctifies his people is clearly taught in 2 Timothy 3:16-17, "All Scripture is God-breathed and is useful for teaching, rebuking, correcting and training in righteousness, so that the man of God may be thoroughly equipped for every good work." Later in this chapter I will discuss the role of the law of God in our sanctification.

The Bible also teaches that we are sanctified *by faith*. One of the central truths proclaimed in the Protestant Reformation was that we are justified

4. Fellowship with other Christians could, in fact, be thought of as one of the more important means of sanctification. We make progress in Christian living not just by ourselves but as members of the body of Christ. We encourage each other, correct each other, weep and rejoice with each other, and set examples for each other. See in this connection Dietrich Bonhoeffer's little classic, *Life Together*, trans. John W. Doberstein (New York: Harper and Row, 1954); also, Chapters 9 and 12 of my *The Christian Looks at Himself* (Grand Rapids: Eerdmans, 1975).

5. *Inst.*, III.i.1. On the relation between union with Christ and sanctification, see also James S. Stewart, *A Man in Christ* (New York: Harper, 1935), and Lewis B. Smedes, *Union with Christ* (Grand Rapids: Eerdmans, 1983).

by faith. It is equally true, however, that we are sanctified by faith. Paul, recounting Jesus' words spoken to him on the way to Damascus, says that Christ sent him to the Gentiles to "turn them from darkness to light . . . so that they may receive . . . a place among those who are sanctified by faith in me" (Acts 26:18). According to Herman Bavinck, "Faith is the outstanding means of sanctification."[6]

How is faith a means of sanctification? First, by faith we continue to grasp our union with Christ, which is the heart of sanctification. In regeneration, which is totally a work of God, we are made one with Christ and enabled to believe in him, but we continue to live in union with Christ through the exercise of that faith. We learn, for example, from Ephesians 3:17 that Christ dwells in our hearts through faith. Paul expresses this truth graphically in Galatians 2:20, "I have been crucified with Christ and I no longer live, but Christ lives in me. The life I live in the body, I live by faith in the Son of God, who loved me and gave himself for me."

Second, by faith we accept the fact that in Christ sin no longer has the mastery over us. Believers must not only recognize intellectually but embrace in full belief the truth that "our old self was crucified with him [Christ] so that the body of sin might be rendered powerless, that we should no longer be slaves to sin" (Rom. 6:6) and that sin is no longer our master because we are not under law but under grace (v. 14).

Third, by faith we grasp the power of the Holy Spirit, which enables us to overcome sin and live for God. Through faith we must appropriate the encouraging truth that by the Spirit we are able to put to death the misdeeds of the body (Rom. 8:13) and that if we live by the Spirit we will receive strength to cease gratifying the desires of the sinful nature and to bring forth the Spirit's fruit (Gal. 5:16, 22-23). Faith, in fact, is the shield with which we "can extinguish all the flaming arrows of the evil one" (Eph. 6:16).[7]

Finally, faith is not only a receptive organ but also an operative power. True faith by its very nature produces spiritual fruit. "In Christ Jesus," affirms Paul, "neither circumcision nor uncircumcision has any value. The only thing that counts is faith expressing itself [literally, "energizing" itself, from Gk. *energeō*] through love" (Gal. 5:6). Faith produces works (1 Thess. 1:3); the goal of God's command to us is love, "which comes from a pure heart and a good conscience and a sincere faith" (1 Tim. 1:5). In words that are often quoted, James declares, "As the body without the spirit is dead, so faith without deeds is dead" (James 2:26). The Heidel-

---

6. *Dogmatiek*, 4:277.
7. On the work of the Spirit in sanctification, see Chapter 3 above, particularly the sections on "the fruit of the Spirit" and "the fullness of the Spirit."

berg Catechism expresses this truth as follows: "It is impossible for those grafted into Christ by true faith not to produce fruits of gratitude."[8]

We should therefore recognize as Reformational teaching not only justification by faith but also sanctification by faith. The Apostle John sums up the significance of faith: "This is the victory that has overcome the world, even our faith" (1 John 5:4).

THE PATTERN OF SANCTIFICATION

The pattern of sanctification is likeness to God. Since Jesus Christ is the perfect image of God (John 14:8-9; 2 Cor. 4:4; Col. 1:15; Heb. 1:3), we may also say that the pattern of sanctification is likeness to Christ.

God originally created us in his image and likeness (Gen. 1:26-27). Through the Fall into sin, however, the image of God in humankind became perverted. In the process of redemption, particularly in regeneration and sanctification, that image is being renewed.[9]

As we continue to think about sanctification, we now concern ourselves with the third phase of the history of the image of God, namely, with the renewal of the image. Sanctification means that we are being renewed in accordance with the image of God—that, in other words, we are becoming more like God, or more like Christ, who is the perfect image of God. Our renewal in this image, however, may be viewed from two perspectives: as the work of God in us and as a process in which we are actively engaged.

First, then, Scripture teaches that God himself, in sanctifying us, is renewing us in his likeness by making us more like Christ. From Romans 8:29, in fact, we learn that conformity to the image of Christ is the purpose for which God chose us: "For those God foreknew he also predestined to be conformed to the likeness of his Son, that he might be the firstborn among many brothers." God foreknew (in the sense of "foreloved") his chosen people before they came into existence. Those who were so foreknown by him he foreordained, or predestined, to be made like his Son. Since the Son perfectly reflects the Father, "the likeness of his Son" is equivalent to "the likeness of himself." God's goal in election, therefore, is to make us an innumerable company of Christ's brothers and sisters who are fully like his Son and thus fully like himself.

The most vivid description of this aspect of our sanctification is found

8. Heidelberg Catechism, Q. 64 (1975 trans.).

9. On the image of God see G. C. Berkouwer, *Man: The Image of God,* trans. Dirk W. Jellema (Grand Rapids: Eerdmans, 1962), and my *Created in God's Image* (Grand Rapids: Eerdmans, 1986).

in 2 Corinthians 3:18, "And we, who with unveiled faces all reflect the Lord's glory, are being transformed into his likeness with ever-increasing glory, which comes from the Lord, who is the Spirit." We who are God's people today, Paul is saying, are continually reflecting the glory of the Lord Jesus Christ with unveiled faces. Since each of us is "a letter from Christ . . . written not with ink but with the Spirit of the living God" (v. 3), people should be seeing something of the glory of Christ when they look at us. While we are continually reflecting that glory, however, we are also being transformed into the same image—that is, into the likeness of Christ —from one degree of glory to another. This transformation, further, is brought about in us by the Lord, who is also the Spirit.

Secondly, however, we also have a responsibility in this matter, namely, to seek to become more like Christ by following his example. Renewal in the image of God, in other words, is not just an indicative; it is also an imperative.

Jesus himself taught us that we should follow his example. After he had washed his disciples' feet—a menial task that none of the disciples had offered to do—Jesus said to them, "Now that I, your Lord and Teacher, have washed your feet, you also should wash one another's feet. I have set you an example that you should do as I have done for you" (John 13:14-15). In saying this Jesus was not necessarily instituting a ritual of ecclesiastical footwashing. But he was directing his disciples, and thus all believers, to follow his example of lowly service (cf. Luke 22:25-27).

Though Paul laid great stress on the work of Christ as our Savior from sin, he also taught that we must follow Christ's example and that we must seek to be more and more like God. In Ephesians 5:1, for instance, he writes, "Be imitators of God, therefore, as dearly loved children." While God is indeed transforming us more and more into his likeness, we who are his people must also keep on trying to imitate God. There are, of course, many ways in which we cannot be like God: for example, in his omniscience, omnipresence, or omnipotence. But there are also ways in which we can and should be like God. One of these ways is described in the immediately preceding verse: "Be kind and compassionate to one another, forgiving each other, just as in Christ God forgave you" (4:32). We must follow God's example in forgiving those who hurt us. Another way of imitating God is to "live a life of love, just as Christ loved us" (5:2). It is not enough just to love others; we must love others as Christ loved us.

In 1 Corinthians 11:1 Paul writes, "Be imitators of me, as I am of Christ" (RSV). One is amazed at Paul's willingness to hold himself up as an example. But Paul, in turn, was trying to pattern his life after that of Christ, who is our ultimate example.

Another way in which Paul teaches the imitation of Christ is in the well-known "mind of Christ" passage (Phil. 2:5-11). Paul urges his readers to "have this mind among yourselves, which you have in Christ Jesus" (v. 5, RSV). He goes on to describe this mind of Christ as an attitude of humble service like that exemplified by Jesus when he was on earth.

Peter makes a similar point: "To this you were called, because Christ suffered for you, leaving you an example, that you should follow in his steps" (1 Pet. 2:21). It is clear, therefore, that following Christ's example is not an incidental but an essential aspect of the Christian life.[10] It is also clear that likeness to God and to Christ is the pattern of sanctification.

GOD AND HIS PEOPLE IN SANCTIFICATION

Whose work is sanctification? In looking at the pattern of sanctification, we have observed that it is both the work of God and the responsibility of his people.

Scripture plainly teaches that God is the author of sanctification. The work of sanctification is ascribed to all three persons of the Trinity. Jesus prays to the Father, "Sanctify them by the truth" (John 17:17), thereby ascribing sanctification to the Father. The author of Hebrews makes a similar point: "Our fathers disciplined us for a little while as they thought best, but God disciplines us for our good, that we may share in his holiness" (Heb. 12:10). "Disciplines" (Gk. *paideuō*, literally, "child training") suggests such things as suffering, adversity, and persecution. Since the purpose of this discipline is that we may share in God's holiness, we conclude that the process here described is what we have been calling *sanctification*, and that God may use such things as suffering and pain as means of sanctification. Of this disciplining, God, identified in the previous verse as "the Father of our spirits," is here said to be the author.

Sanctification, however, is also ascribed to the Son, as we learn from Ephesians 5:25-27. Here Paul tells his readers that husbands should love their wives

> just as Christ loved the church and gave himself up for her to make her holy [or to sanctify her, RSV], cleansing her by the washing with water through the word, and to present her to himself as a radiant church, without stain or wrinkle or any other blemish, but holy and blameless.

Christ, the Second Person of the Trinity, is identified as the agent of sanctification, cleansing the church "by the washing with water through the word." Most commentators understand the first part of this expres-

---

10. On following Christ's example, see Berkouwer's chapter, "The Imitation of Christ," in his *Faith and Sanctification*, trans. John Vriend (Grand Rapids: Eerdmans, 1952), pp. 135-60.

sion as referring to the sacrament of baptism; the passage thus suggests
that the sacraments (baptism and the Lord's Supper) are also means of
sanctification. The phrase "through the word" should be connected with
the verb "cleansing." Christ cleanses his church from sin by means of the
Scriptures. It is exciting to know that, according to this passage, the church
will someday be "without stain or wrinkle or any other blemish."

Though the word *sanctification* is not used in Titus 2:14, this text also
sees Jesus as the author of our sanctification: "who [Christ] gave himself
for us to redeem us from all wickedness and to purify for himself a people
that are his very own, eager to do what is good." In 1 Corinthians 1:30,
as noted above, Christ is said to have become our holiness, or our
sanctification.

Sanctification is also commonly ascribed to the Holy Spirit. Peter says
that God's people "have been chosen according to the foreknowledge of
God the Father, through the sanctifying work of the Spirit, for obedience
to Jesus Christ" (1 Pet. 1:2). Paul tells us in Romans 15:16 that he was sent
to proclaim the gospel "so that the Gentiles might become an offering acceptable to God, sanctified by the Holy Spirit." He also thanks God that
he chose the Thessalonians "to be saved through the sanctifying work of
the Spirit" (2 Thess. 2:13). And Titus 3:5 states that God saved us "through
the washing of rebirth and renewal by the Holy Spirit."

The work of the Trinity, however, cannot be divided. It is not surprising, therefore, that we find sanctification ascribed to the triune God
without any designation of persons: "May God himself, the God of peace,
sanctify you through and through" (1 Thess. 5:23).

It is most important for us to realize that sanctification is not something we do by ourselves, with our own efforts and in our own strength.
Sanctification is not first of all a human activity but a divine gift.

Sanctification, however, also involves our responsible participation.
To the members of the Corinthian church, designated in an earlier epistle
as "those sanctified in Christ Jesus," Paul says, "Since we have these promises, dear friends, let us purify ourselves from everything that contaminates body and spirit, perfecting holiness out of reverence for God"
(2 Cor. 7:1). The promises are those mentioned in the preceding verses,
embodying particularly the great covenant promise, "I will be their God,
and they will be my people" (6:16). Since we are God's covenant people,
Paul is saying, we have a solemn responsibility. We must fight against sin,
both of the body and of the mind. The Greek word *epitelountes,* translated
"perfecting," is based on the noun *telos* ("end" or "goal"), and means
"progressively bringing to its goal." What we usually think of as God's
work is here vividly described as the believer's task: to bring holiness to
its goal.

> I urge you, brothers, in view of God's mercy, to offer your bodies as living sacrifices, holy and pleasing to God—this is your spiritual act of worship. Do not conform any longer to the pattern of this world, but be transformed by the renewing of your mind (Rom. 12:1-2).

Paul here appeals to his readers to show their gratitude for God's mercy by offering themselves to God as living sacrifices, in contrast to the dead sacrifices offered in Old Testament times. Think of your bodies, Paul is saying, as belonging to God as totally and irrevocably as did the bulls and goats offered to the priest by Old Testament worshipers. Stop conforming yourselves outwardly *(syschēmatizesthe)* to the pattern of this evil age, but rather continue to be transformed within *(metamorphousthe)* through the renewal of your total attitude toward life. Although it is God who brings about our inner transformation (2 Cor. 3:18), we must yield our hearts, minds, and wills to the Holy Spirit, who is remaking us.

The author of Hebrews puts it this way: "Pursue peace with all men, and the sanctification [or holiness, Gk. *hagiasmos*] without which no one will see the Lord" (Heb. 12:14, NASB). Sanctification is here described as something we must continually pursue. According to Scripture, therefore, though sanctification is primarily God's work in us, it is not a process in which we remain passive but one in which we must be continually active.

J. C. Ryle puts it vigorously:

> Sanctification . . . is *a thing for which every believer is responsible.* . . . Whose fault is it if they [believers] are not holy, but their own? On whom can they throw the blame if they are not sanctified, but themselves? God, who has given them grace and a new heart, and a new nature, has deprived them of all excuse if they do not live for His praise.[11]

These two aspects of sanctification are mentioned together in a remarkable passage: "Therefore, my dear friends, as you have always obeyed . . . continue to work out your salvation with fear and trembling, for it is God who works in you to will and to act according to his good purpose" (Phil. 2:12-13). Since Paul is addressing "saints in Christ Jesus" (1:1), the command "work out your salvation" must be understood not as an evangelistic appeal to the unsaved but as a word to believers. Paul is asking his readers to continue to "work out" what God in his grace has "worked in." The word *katergazesthe,* translated "work out," is commonly used in the papyri (short Greek manuscripts, dating from 200 B.C. to A.D. 200, which illustrate the usage of New Testament words) to describe the cultivation of land by farmers.[12] We could therefore paraphrase Paul's words as follows: "Keep on cultivating the salvation God has given you."

---

11. *Holiness* (London: James Clarke, 1956), pp. 19-20.
12. Moulton and Milligan, VGT, pp. 335-36.

Believers must continually seek to apply the salvation they have received to every area of life and to make it evident in every activity. Verse 12, in other words, must be understood as describing the believer's responsibility to advance his or her sanctification.

The basis for this exhortation, as given in verse 13, is not that this working out of our salvation depends entirely on us. Instead, surprisingly, Paul states, "For it is God who works in you to will and to act according to his good purpose." God works in us the entire process of our sanctification—both the willing of it and the doing of it. The harder we work, the more sure we may be that God is working in us.

How, then, shall we describe the relationship between God's working and our working? Should we say, as some have done,[13] that sanctification is a work of God in which believers cooperate? This way of stating the doctrine, however, wrongly implies that God and we each do part of the work of sanctification. According to John Murray,

> God's working in us is not suspended because we work, nor our working suspended because God works. Neither is the relation strictly one of cooperation as if God did his part and we did ours. . . . God works in us and we also work. But the relation is that *because* God works we work.[14]

Summing up, we may say that sanctification is a supernatural work of God in which the believer is active. The more active we are in sanctification, the more sure we may be that the energizing power that enables us to be active is the power of God.

DEFINITIVE AND PROGRESSIVE SANCTIFICATION

Reformed theologians commonly assert that sanctification continues throughout a believer's life, in distinction from justification, which is a definitive act of God, occurring once for all.[15] Though the New Testament often describes sanctification as a lifelong process, there is also an important sense in which New Testament authors depict it as an act of God that is definitive, occurring at a specific time rather than during an extended period.[16] John Murray, in fact, observes: "It is a fact too frequent-

---

13. Berkhof, ST, p. 534.

14. *Redemption—Accomplished and Applied* (Grand Rapids: Eerdmans, 1955), pp. 184-85.

15. Bavinck, *Dogmatiek*, 4:286; Charles Hodge, *Systematic Theology* (1871; Grand Rapids: Eerdmans, 1940), 3:212; Berkhof, ST, p. 534.

16. This aspect of sanctification is incisively set forth by John Murray in his chapters "Definitive Sanctification" and "The Agency in Definitive Sanctification," in *Collected Writings of John Murray* (Carlisle, PA: Banner of Truth, 1977), 2:277-93. Cf. Chester K. Lehman, *The Holy Spirit and the Holy Life* (Scottdale, PA: Herald, 1959), pp. 108-20. Lehman uses the word *punctiliar* (as distinguished from *linear*) to describe definitive sanctification.

ly overlooked that in the New Testament the most characteristic terms that refer to sanctification are used, not of a process, but of a once-for-all definitive act."[17]

Passages that describe sanctification in the definitive sense include 1 Corinthians 1:2. Paul here addresses the believers in Corinth as "those sanctified in Christ Jesus"; the Greek verb is in the perfect tense, which describes completed action with continuing result. Protestant theologians usually understand justification to be a declarative act of God by which he pronounces the believing sinner righteous in Christ—an act, therefore, which is not continuing or progressive but once for all. In 1 Corinthians 6:11, however, sanctification is coordinated with justification as a definitive act of God: "But you were washed, you were sanctified, you were justified in the name of the Lord Jesus Christ and by the Spirit of our God." In the Greek text the three verbs are in the aorist tense, which usually describes instantaneous action (sometimes called "snapshot" action). Just as these believers have been justified once for all at a certain point in time, so, Paul says here, there is also a sense in which they have been sanctified once for all. Furthermore, both Acts 20:32 and 26:18 speak of believers as "those who are sanctified"; in both cases the verb is in the perfect tense.

The definitive aspect of sanctification is expressed most vividly and sharply in Romans 6. When Paul says in verse 2 of this chapter, "We died to sin," he is expressing in unambiguous language the truth that the person who is in Christ has made "a definitive and irreversible breach with the realm in which sin reigns."[18] Paul further underscores this decisive, once-for-all break with sin by telling us that if we are in Christ, our old self has been crucified with him (v. 6, the aorist tense again suggesting definitive action), sin shall no longer lord it over us, because we are now under the reign of grace (v. 14), and we now obey from the heart the pattern of Christian teaching to which we have been made subject (v. 17). The main thrust of this entire chapter is that the believer has been placed in a new relationship—one that can never be undone. Murray summarizes this position: "This means that there is a decisive and definitive breach with the power and service of sin in the case of every one who has come under the control of the provisions of grace."[19]

Not only does Paul teach that those who have come to faith in Christ have died to sin; he also affirms that they have been decisively and definitively raised with Christ. Using verb tenses that describe instantaneous,

17. *Collected Writings,* 2:277.
18. Ibid., p. 279.
19. Ibid., p. 280.

or snapshot, action, Paul asserts that "God . . . made us alive with Christ even when we were dead in transgressions. . . . And God raised us up with Christ" (Eph. 2:4-6). Though we were by nature dead in sin, God mercifully made us who are believers one with the risen Christ, thus raising us up with him; this "raising" is described here not as a long process but as something that happened at a certain point in time: the point at which we were regenerated. The Colossians, furthermore, are not told that they must progressively be raised with Christ; they are told, "Since, then, you have been raised [aorist tense] with Christ, set your hearts on things above, where Christ is seated at the right hand of God" (Col. 3:1). In the light of these texts, we conclude that definitive sanctification means not only a decisive break with the enslaving power of sin but also a decisive and irreversible union with Christ in his resurrection, a union by means of which the believer is enabled to live in newness of life (Rom. 6:4) and because of which he or she has now become a new creature (2 Cor. 5:17). As a result of our definitive sanctification, therefore, we who are in Christ must now count ourselves "dead to sin but alive to God in Christ Jesus" (Rom. 6:11).

Clearly, therefore, the New Testament teaches definitive sanctification. We now ask, When did believers die to sin and arise with Christ? To this question no simple answer can be given; there is both an objective and a subjective side to this matter. In the objective sense, believers died with Christ when he died on the cross and were raised with Christ when he arose from the dead in Joseph's garden. Since believers were chosen in Christ before the creation of the world, they were, at least in one sense, in Christ when he died and arose. Christ must never be thought of apart from his people, nor his people apart from him. When Christ died, he made the decisive break with sin, a break that accrues to our benefit; and when Christ arose, he brought into existence the new life into which we may enter by faith.

But we must not disregard the subjective aspect of our oneness with Christ in his death and resurrection. Paul says that God made us alive with Christ when we were dead in transgressions (Eph. 2:5), and that we died to sin when we were baptized into Christ Jesus (Rom. 6:2-3). In our own experience we arose with Christ when we became one with the risen Lord (Col. 3:1). Paul reminds the Colossians that at a certain point in their lives (presumably, the time of their conversion) they voluntarily put off their old selves and put on their new selves (3:9-10). To do full justice to biblical teaching, therefore, we must stress both aspects of this question: the past historical and the present experiential. In one sense we died to sin and arose to new life when Christ died and arose; in another sense, however, we died to sin and arose to new life when, having been regenerated by the Holy Spirit, we grasped by faith our oneness with Christ in his death and resurrection.[20]

Biblical teaching on definitive sanctification suggests that believers should look upon themselves and each other as those who have died to sin and are now new persons in Christ. To be sure, the newness that believers have in Christ is not equivalent to sinless perfection; as long as they are in this present life, they must struggle against sin, and they will sometimes fall into sin. Believers, therefore, should see themselves and each other as persons who are *genuinely* new, though not yet *totally* new. But the doctrine of definitive sanctification helps us to see that those who are in Christ have made a decisive and irreversible break with sin. Murray expresses this point eloquently:

> As we cannot allow for any reversal or repetition of the resurrection [of Christ], so we cannot allow for any compromise on the doctrine that every believer is a new man, that the old man has been crucified, that the body of sin has been destroyed, and that, as a new man in Christ Jesus, he serves God in the newness which is none other than that of the Holy Spirit of whom he has become the habitation and his body the temple.[21]

It should be added that definitive sanctification does not mean an experience separate from or subsequent to justification, as a kind of "second blessing." In its experiential sense, definitive sanctification is simultaneous with justification, as an aspect of union with Christ. It is also simultaneous with regeneration, the initial bestowal of spiritual life, by which we are enabled to believe. Though regeneration is causally prior to faith, justification, and definitive sanctification, it is not chronologically prior.

A word remains to be said about "positional sanctification." Many theologians mean by "positional sanctification" the same thing that I have called "definitive sanctification." Stanley M. Horton, a Pentecostal theologian, describes positional sanctification as follows: "There is also an instantaneous aspect to sanctification whereby at the time we are born again we are set apart from the world to follow Jesus and are saints in this sense."[22] The view of positional sanctification held by dispensational theologians is also virtually identical with the concept of definitive sanctification described above. Lewis Sperry Chafer put it this way: "That there is a *positional* sanctification which is secured by union with Christ has too often been overlooked."[23] In *The New Scofield Reference Bible*, which represents recent dispensational teaching, the following statement can be

20. See ibid., pp. 289-93.
21. Ibid., p. 293.
22. In Melvin E. Dieter et al., *Five Views on Sanctification* (Grand Rapids: Zondervan, 1987), p. 115.
23. *Systematic Theology* (Dallas: Dallas Seminary Press, 1948), 3:244.

found: "In position, believers are eternally set apart for God by redemption. . . . Positionally, therefore, believers are 'saints' and 'holy' from the moment of believing."[24] And Article 9 of the Doctrinal Statement of Dallas Theological Seminary includes the following description: "It [sanctification] is already complete for every saved person because his position toward God is the same as Christ's position. Since the believer is in Christ, he is set apart unto God. . . ."[25]

There are, however, other understandings of positional sanctification which are not the same as the doctrine of definitive sanctification. Henry C. Thiessen, for example, speaking of positional sanctification, says, "He [the believer] is an heir to the righteousness and holiness of Christ, these being imputed to him because of his relationship to Christ. . . ."[26] And J. Robertson McQuilkin says that the second step or aspect of positional sanctification is justification, calling it a judicial transaction between the Father and the Son that "declares the sinner forgiven and made right with God."[27] The understanding of positional sanctification advanced by these authors introduces concepts such as *imputation* and *declaration*—concepts that belong to the doctrine of justification and should therefore not be thought of as aspects of sanctification.[28]

As was mentioned, however, the Bible also teaches that there is a sense in which sanctification is a lifelong process and is therefore progressive. Rather than nullifying what Paul and Luke have said about definitive sanctification, this teaching supplements it. John Murray explains: "It might appear that the emphasis placed upon definitive sanctification leaves no place for what is progressive. Any such inference would contradict an equally important aspect of biblical teaching."[29]

The progressive aspect of sanctification is evident, first of all, from biblical statements that assert that sin is still present in the believer. We may think of Old Testament passages like 1 Kings 8:46; Psalms 19:12; 143:2; Proverbs 20:9; and Isaiah 64:6. The New Testament also is quite clear

24. C. I. Scofield, ed., *The New Scofield Reference Bible* (New York: Oxford University Press, 1967), p. 1377.

25. From the 1987-88 catalog of Dallas Theological Seminary. Cf. also John F. Walvoord in *Five Views*, p. 212; Charles C. Ryrie, "Contrasting Views on Sanctification," in *Walvoord: A Tribute*, ed. Donald K. Campbell (Chicago: Moody Press, 1922), pp. 189-90; and Robert P. Lightner, *Evangelical Theology* (Grand Rapids: Baker, 1986), pp. 204-205.

26. Henry C. Thiessen, *Lectures in Systematic Theology*, rev. by Vernon D. Doerksen (1949; Grand Rapids: Eerdmans, 1979), p. 286.

27. In *Five Views*, pp. 158-59.

28. See also J. Sidlow Baxter, *Our High Calling* (Grand Rapids: Zondervan, 1967), p. 205, where, in his "Excursus on Positional Sanctification," he speaks of "imputed holiness."

29. "Sanctification (The Law)," in *Basic Christian Doctrines*, ed. Carl F. H. Henry (New York: Holt, Rinehart and Winston, 1962), p. 229.

on this point. When discussing our need to be justified by faith, Paul vividly describes the universal sinfulness of humankind: "There is no difference, for all have sinned and fall short of the glory of God" (Rom. 3:22-23). "The glory of God" here can perhaps best be understood as meaning "glorifying God"; since the verb "fall short" is in the present tense in Greek, we may render the second half of the verse, "and continue to fall short of glorifying God." In an incidental but revealing comment, James, writing to believers, says, "We all stumble in many ways" (James 3:2). Probably the clearest New Testament statement of the truth under discussion is found in 1 John 1:8. Addressing those who claim to have fellowship with God, John writes, "If we claim to be without sin [literally, if we say that we have no sin], we deceive ourselves and the truth is not in us." The conclusion is inevitable: because sin continues to be present in those who are in Christ, the sanctification of believers must be a continuing process.

The New Testament goes on to describe both a negative and a positive aspect of progressive sanctification, involving the putting to death of sinful practices and the growth of the new self. In Romans 6, as we have seen, Paul vividly sets forth the definitive aspect of sanctification. In Romans 8:13, however, he points out that sanctification must also be progressive: "For if you live according to the sinful nature, you will die; but if by the Spirit you put to death [literally, keep on putting to death] the misdeeds of the body, you will live." Believers, whom he has previously described as having died to sin, he now enjoins to keep on killing the sinful actions to which they might be inclined. Paul's readers have definitively broken with sin as the realm in which they live, move, and have their being, yet they must continue to fight against sin as long as they live. Since they can do so only through the strength of the Spirit, this struggle against sin must be understood as an aspect of their sanctification.

Paul tells the Colossians that they have both died with Christ (Col. 3:3) and been raised with him (v. 1); that is, they have definitively and irreversibly entered into new life in fellowship with Christ. Yet in verse 5 of this chapter he enjoins them: "Put to death, therefore, whatever belongs to your earthly nature: sexual immorality, impurity, lust, evil desires and greed, which is idolatry." Though they have died to sin, they must still put sin to death; as he often does, Paul here combines the indicative and the imperative. The putting to death of these sinful practices, which can only be done through the strength of the Spirit, involves the strenuous and lifelong activity of the believer.

From 2 Corinthians 7:1, quoted above, we learned that believers must still contend with and seek to purify themselves from defilements of body and spirit. A similar injunction is found in 1 John 3:3. After having affirmed that when Christ appears we shall be like him, John goes on to say, "Everyone who has this hope in him purifies [literally, continues to purify] himself, just as he is pure." Christians are not simply to sit back and wait for the time when they will be totally like Christ; they must be constantly and energetically active in the struggle to overcome evil with good. Continuing purification implies continuing sanctification.

The progressive nature of sanctification is also shown in passages dealing with its positive aspect: the growth of the new self. In Colossians 3:9-10 Paul, as we saw, reminds his readers that they have taken off the old self and have put on the new self; the new self they have put on, however, is described as one "which is being renewed in knowledge in the image of its Creator" (v. 10). Since the new self is here said to need renewal, it obviously does not yet exist in a state of sinless perfection. The participle *anakainoumenon*, translated "being renewed," is in the present tense, indicating that this renewal of the new self is a lifelong process. Interestingly, this passage presents both facets of sanctification: once and for all believers have taken off the old self and put on the new (definitive sanctification; here the tense is aorist), but the new self that they have put on must be continually renewed (progressive sanctification; the tense here is present).

The most striking description of the progressive nature of sanctification is in 2 Corinthians 3:18, "We, who with unveiled faces all reflect the Lord's glory, are being transformed into his likeness with ever-increasing glory, which comes from [or, as from, NASB] the Lord, who is the Spirit." As believers reflect the glory of the Lord, they are being continually and progressively transformed into the likeness of Christ by the Lord himself, who is also the Spirit. The word *metamorphoumetha*, here rendered "we are being transformed," describes a change not just of outward form but of inner essence. Both the present tense of this verb and the words "from one degree of glory to another" (RSV) indicate that this transformation is not instantaneous but progressive.

Sanctification, therefore, must be understood as being both definitive and progressive. In its definitive sense, it means that work of the Spirit whereby he causes us to die to sin, to be raised with Christ, and to be made new creatures. In its progressive sense, it must be understood as that work of the Spirit whereby he continually renews and transforms us into the likeness of Christ, enabling us to keep on growing in grace and to keep on perfecting our holiness. One could think of definitive sanctification as the beginning of the process, and of progressive sanctification as the continual maturing of the new person who was created by definitive sanctification. While sanctification in its totality is the work of God from beginning to end, the active participation of the believer is also required. Not only must believers appropriate their definitive sanctification by faith; they must likewise continue to be active in their progressive sanctification, bringing holiness to its goal.

IS THE BELIEVER BOTH AN "OLD SELF" AND A "NEW SELF"?

We turn next to another problem involved in our sanctification, namely, the question of the relation between our so-called old self and our new self (or old person and new person). These expressions are found only in Paul. The term *old self* is found in Romans 6:6, Colossians 3:9, and Ephesians 4:22.[30] The term *new self* is found in Colossians 3:10 (where the Greek word *neos* is used for "new") and in Ephesians 4:24 (where the Greek word *kainos* is used for "new").[31]

In these passages Paul contrasts the old self associated with the life of sin with the new self that we have put on, now that we are in Christ. On the question of the relation between these two selves, Reformed theologians differ. Most of them, particularly those who taught and wrote some years ago, hold that the old self and the new self are distinguishable aspects of the believer. Before conversion believers had an old self; at the time of conversion, however, they put on the new self—but without totally losing the old self. The Christian, in this view, is understood to be partly a new self and partly an old self—something like a Dr. Jekyll and Mr. Hyde. At times the old self is in control, but at other times the new self is in the saddle; the struggle of life, according to this view, is the struggle between these two aspects of the believer's being.

By way of example, consider how one of the ablest proponents of this view describes the fight against sin in believers:

> The struggle [in the Christian life] . . . is between the inner man of the heart, which has been created to be like God in true righteousness and holiness, and the old man who, though driven out of the center, still wants to maintain his existence, and who fights all the more fiercely the more territory he loses. . . . This is a struggle between two people in the same person. . . . In every deliberation and deed of the believer, therefore, good and evil are as it were mingled together; . . . in all his thoughts and actions something of the old and something of the new man is present.[32]

30. In Greek the expression is *palaios anthrōpos*, rendered "old man" in the KJV and the ASV, but in newer versions often as "old nature" (RSV, NEB) or "old self" (RSV, JB, NASB, NIV). Since the word *anthrōpos* means "human being" and not "male human being," the rendering "old self" is to be preferred to "old man."

31. Here again, whereas the older versions (KJV, ASV) have "new man," the newer versions have "new nature" (RSV, NEB) or "new self" (JB, NASB, NIV).

32. Herman Bavinck, *Magnalia Dei* (Kampen: Kok, 1909), pp. 561-62 [trans. mine].

John Murray, who for many years taught systematic theology at Westminster Seminary, summarizes but then rejects this understanding of the old and the new self (or man):

> The contrast between the old man and the new man has frequently been interpreted as the contrast between that which is new in the believer and that which is old. . . . Hence the antithesis which exists in the believer between holiness and sin . . . is the antithesis between the new man and the old man in him. The believer is both old man and new man; when he does well he is acting in terms of the new man which he is; when he sins he is acting in terms of the old man which he also still is. This interpretation does not find support in Paul's teaching.[33]

I believe that Murray is correct. Let us turn to some Scripture passages that teach that the person who is in Christ is no longer an old man or old self, but is now a new self.

We begin with Romans 6:6, "For we know that our old self was crucified with him so that the body of sin might be rendered powerless, that we should no longer be slaves to sin." What does Paul mean here by the "old self"? Murray suggests that this expression designates "the person in his unity as dominated by the flesh and sin."[34] In other words, Paul is here talking about a totality: the total person enslaved by sin—what we all are by nature, and what we all were before our conversion. That "person enslaved by sin," he is saying, was crucified with Christ. When Christ died on the cross, he dealt a deathblow to our old self. Given the meaning of "crucified," Romans 6:6 states with unmistakable clarity that we who are in Christ, who are one with him in his death, are no longer the old selves we once were.

Other passages in Paul's epistles confirm this understanding of the death of the old self. Colossians 3:9-10, for example, considered above in connection with definitive sanctification, teaches us also about the old and the new self: "Do not lie to each other, since you have taken off your old self with its practices and have put on the new self, which is being renewed in knowledge in the image of its Creator." Paul tells the Colossian believers not that they now (or daily) *should* take off the old self and put on the new self, but that they *have already done so!* They made this

---

Similar interpretations of the roles of the old and the new self in the believer can be found in comments on Romans 6:6 by John Calvin, *The Epistle to the Romans and the Thessalonians*, trans. Ross Mackenzie (Grand Rapids: Eerdmans, 1979); Charles Hodge's comments on Ephesians 4:22 in his *Commentary on the Epistle to the Ephesians* (Grand Rapids: Eerdmans, 1950); William Hendriksen, *New Testament Commentary on Ephesians* (Grand Rapids: Baker, 1967), pp. 213-24, n. 124; Gordon Girod, *The Way of Salvation* (Grand Rapids: Baker, 1960), pp. 137-38; and Berkhof, ST, p. 533.

33. *Principles of Conduct* (Grand Rapids: Eerdmans, 1957), pp. 211-12.
34. Ibid., pp. 217-18, n. 7.

change when, at the time of their conversion, they appropriated by faith what Christ had done for them when he died and arose again.

The Greek participles *apekdysamenoi* and *endysamenoi*, rendered "taken off" and "put on," are in the aorist tense, which describes snapshot action; Paul is referring to something these believers have done in the past. You ought not to lie, he says, nor to lust, be sinfully angry, or slander, *because* you have taken off your old self and *because* you have put on your new self.[35] You must stop committing these sins because such conduct is obviously inconsistent with your having put on the new self. And the very figure Paul uses strengthens this thought: one does not wear two sets of clothes at the same time—one takes off one set and puts on another. Paul here pictures believers as people who are now clothed with the new self and no longer with the old.

Ephesians 4:20-24 is closely parallel but seems to offer some difficulty:

> (20) You, however, did not come to know Christ that way. (21) Surely you heard of him and were taught in him in accordance with the truth that is in Jesus. (22) You were taught, with regard to your former way of life, to put off your old self, which is being corrupted by its deceitful desires; (23) to be made new in the attitude of your minds; (24) and to put on the new self, created to be like God in true righteousness and holiness.

The Greek text of verses 22-24 has three main infinitives (*apothesthai, ananeousthai,* and *endysasthai*), which mean "to put off," "to be made new," and "to put on," and which in many versions are translated as imperatives, as if Paul were telling the believers in Ephesus what they should now do (cf. "put off . . . be renewed . . . put on," RSV). Following this rendering, the passage would convey a command, which would indeed be inconsistent with the position just defended (that believers have already taken off the old self and put on the new).

Though the translation found in the Revised Standard Version is not grammatically incorrect, there is another possibility. These infinitives can also be understood as so-called "explanatory infinitives"—that is, as simply giving the content of the teaching referred to in verses 20-21. In this analysis, Paul is assuming that his readers have done what they were taught to do. This understanding of the text makes its teaching parallel to that of the similar passage from Colossians, commonly considered a twin epistle to Ephesians. The rendering found in the New International Version (quoted above) is therefore to be preferred to that of the Revised Stan-

---

35. Presumably, the new self is "the person in his or her unity," or totality, ruled by the Holy Spirit. This new self, as we saw before, is being continually renewed after the pattern of the image of God. In other words, we must not expect to experience sinless perfection on this side of the resurrection. The new self is new but not perfect.

dard Version. So interpreted, Ephesians 4:22-24 tells the believers in
Ephesus that they should not continue to live as the unconverted Gentiles
do (vv. 17-19), since, as they were taught, they have put off the old self and
have put on the new self. The new self they have put on has, in fact, been
created like God in true righteousness and holiness.[36]

From the passages just considered, therefore, it is clear that, according to the New Testament, consistent with its teaching on the definitive
aspect of sanctification, believers are no longer the old selves they once
were. They are not, as has often been taught, both old selves and new
selves, but are indeed new selves in Christ. Paul highlights this important
point in the stirring words of 2 Corinthians 5:17, "Therefore, if anyone is
in Christ, he is a new creation; the old has gone, the new has come!" We
must not minimize the importance of this teaching and of its bearing on
our sanctification. John Murray again says it well:

> The old man is the unregenerate man; the new man is the regenerate man
> created in Christ Jesus unto good works. It is no more feasible to call the
> believer a new man and an old man, than it is to call him a regenerate man
> and an unregenerate. And neither is it warranted to speak of the believer as
> having in him the old man and the new man. This kind of terminology is
> without warrant and it is but another method of doing prejudice to the
> doctrine which Paul was so jealous to establish when he said, "Our old man
> has been crucified."[37]

Though believers are new persons, however, they have not yet attained sinless perfection; they must still struggle against sin. In Colossians
3:10 the new self that believers have put on is described as a self that is
being renewed; this renewal is a lifelong process. In Ephesians 4:23 Paul
reminds his readers that, although they have put off the old self and put
on the new, they are *being made new* in the attitude of their minds. The in-
finitive *ananeousthai*, rendered "made new," is in the present tense, suggesting a continuing process. Believers who have become new creatures in
Christ are still told to put to death the misdeeds of the body (Rom. 8:13), to
kill whatever is sinful in them (Col. 3:5), to rid themselves of such sins as
lust, greed, rage, malice, and filthy language (vv. 5, 8), and to purify themselves from everything that contaminates body and spirit (2 Cor. 7:1).[38]

The new self described in the New Testament, therefore, is not equivalent to sinless perfection. The newness of the new self is not static but dy-

36. Note that both Colossians 3:9-10 and Ephesians 4:22-24 confirm the point developed earlier, namely, that the pattern of sanctification is likeness to God.
37. Murray, *Principles of Conduct*, p. 218.
38. Note that, according to 2 Corinthians 7:1, believers must still fight against defilements (RSV) or contaminations (NIV) of the spirit—refuting those Christians who teach that
after conversion the human spirit becomes sinless.

namic, needing continual renewal, growth, and transformation. A believer deeply conscious of his or her shortcomings does not need to say, Because I am still a sinner I cannot consider myself a new person. Rather, he or she should say, I am a new person, but I still have a lot of growing to do.

The believer must still struggle against tendencies to sin which remain within. The author of Hebrews, writing to believers, puts it this way: "Since we are surrounded by such a great cloud of witnesses, let us throw off everything that hinders and the sin that so easily entangles" (or, "that clings so closely," RSV; Heb. 12:1). Paul exhorts the Christians in Galatia: "Walk by the Spirit, and you will not carry out the desire of the flesh" (Gal. 5:16, NASB). By "the flesh" Paul here means the inclination that is still in us to rebel against God's will. Whatever we may call this tendency ("indwelling sin,"[39] "remnants of corruption,"[40] "vestiges of sin,"[41] or "my sinful nature"[42]), we must remember that even after we have been regenerated we still have such sinful impulses, and must still fight against them as long as we live.

The New Testament often describes the Christian life as a constant battle against sin. Believers are enjoined to put on the full armor of God so that they may be victorious in their struggle against evil powers (Eph. 6:11-13), to fight the good fight of the faith (1 Tim. 6:12; cf. 2 Tim. 4:7), not to gratify fleshly desires (Gal. 5:16), and to resist sin to the point of shedding their blood (Heb. 12:4). In 1 Corinthians 9:26-27 Paul describes his own fierce struggle against sin as if he were a boxer: "I do not fight like a man beating the air. No, I beat my body and make it my slave so that after I have preached to others, I myself will not be disqualified for the prize."[43]

Bishop J. C. Ryle is insistent on this point:

> Sanctification . . . *does not prevent a man having a great deal of inward spiritual conflict.* By conflict I mean a struggle within the heart between the old nature and the new, the flesh and the spirit, which are to be found together in every believer (Gal. 5:17). A deep sense of that struggle, and a vast amount of mental discomfort from it, are no proof that a man is not sanctified. Nay, rather, I believe they are healthy symptoms of our condition, and prove that we are not dead, but alive.[44]

39. John Murray, *Principles of Conduct*, p. 219.
40. Westminster Confession, XIII,2.
41. *Inst.*, III.iii.11.
42. Heidelberg Catechism, Q. 56.
43. I do not here adduce Rom. 7:13-25, since I understand this passage to be a description, seen through the eyes of a regenerate person, of the struggle found in an unregenerate person (e.g., an unconverted Pharisaic Jew) who is trying to fight sin through the law alone, apart from the strength of the Holy Spirit. For a biblical defense of this interpretation, see my *The Christian Looks at Himself*, pp. 61-67; cf. also Herman Ridderbos, *Paul: An Outline of His Theology*, trans. John R. De Witt (Grand Rapids: Eerdmans, 1975), pp. 126-30.
44. *Holiness*, p. 21.

Yet, though the struggle against sin is very real, believers are no longer enslaved to sin. The crucifixion of the old self with Christ, Paul teaches, implies that we have been freed from the slavery of sin (Rom. 6:6); because we are not under law but under grace, sin shall no longer be our master (v. 14). "The sin which still inheres in the believer and the sin he commits does not have dominion over him."[45]

At this point it might be helpful to introduce a distinction between "the old and new self" and "the old and new nature." I have argued that according to New Testament teaching the person who is in Christ is no longer an old self but is now a new self. But in saying this I do not mean to deny that the believer still has an old or sinful nature, meaning a continuing tendency to sin or rebel against God. In regeneration the believer received, in addition to his or her old nature, a new nature, by which he or she is now enabled to do what pleases God. Believers do, therefore, have both a sinful nature (against which they must struggle) and a new nature (according to which they should now live). But they are no longer old selves or old persons, since this concept describes human beings as totalities: the old self is the total person enslaved by sin, whereas the new self is the total person ruled by the Holy Spirit (though not yet perfectly). Believers, in other words, are new persons, who must still struggle against their old natures.

Summing up, we may say that Christians are no longer old persons but new persons who are being progressively renewed. They must still battle against sin and will sometimes fall into sin, but they are no longer slaves of sin. In the strength of the Spirit they are now able to resist sin, since for every temptation God will provide a way of escape (1 Cor. 10:13).

One important implication of this teaching is that believers should have positive images of themselves. The basis for such a self-image is not sinful pride in our own achievements or virtues but seeing ourselves in the light of God's redemptive work in our lives. Christianity not only means believing something about Christ; it also means believing something about ourselves, namely, that we are indeed new creatures in Christ.[46]

THE QUESTION OF "PERFECTIONISM"

Some Christian groups hold that it is possible for believers to attain "perfection" in this present life. Among the denominations that teach this the

45. John Murray, *Principles of Conduct*, p. 220.
46. See *The Christian Looks at Himself*, particularly pp. 13-76.

following may be noted: the Wesleyan Methodist Church, the Free Methodist Church, the Salvation Army, the Church of God (Anderson, Indiana), the Christian and Missionary Alliance, the Nazarene Church, and the Pilgrim Holiness Church.[47]

The first question we need to face is this: What do these groups mean by "perfection"? They usually claim that they do not believe in the possibility of "sinless perfection." John Wesley, the founder of Methodism and the best-known proponent of what is commonly called "perfectionist" teaching, is somewhat equivocal on this point. At one place he says, "By perfection . . . I do not contend for the term *sinless,* though I do not object against it."[48] Elsewhere, however, he says, "*Sinless perfection* is a phrase I never use, lest I should seem to contradict myself."[49] Other teachers of "perfectionism" are unequivocal. J. Sidlow Baxter, for example, says, "Nowhere does our New Testament promise or even suggest complete sinlessness either of nature or conduct in this present life, yet it *does* teach a true holiness, inwrought by the Holy Spirit."[50] Donald Metz puts it this way: "Because of finite qualities which still bear the scars of sin, this same believer [one who lives in the state of perfection] will *not perfectly* fulfill God's law."[51] Another Nazarene writer, J. Kenneth Grider, makes a similar qualification: "The phrase 'perfect love' . . . is misleading to many people who suppose that we mean that our expressions of love to God and others are absolutely flawless. We only mean, however, that such love is not mixed with carnal motivations."[52] Writing about the Wesleyan view, Melvin E. Dieter affirms, "We should note that Wesleyanism . . . certainly does not imply sinless perfection; it is probably more misrepresented at this point than at any other."[53]

Despite these qualifications, however, these writers still use the words "perfection" and "perfect." Wesley certainly did. Scriptural perfection, he wrote, is "perfect love";[54] he also said, "A Christian is so far perfect, as not to commit sin."[55] On another page he declared that what he called "the circumcision of the heart" is "the being so 'renewed in the image of our mind,' as to be 'perfect as our Father in heaven is perfect.' "[56]

---

47. George M. Marsden, *Fundamentalism and American Culture* (New York: Oxford University Press, 1980), p. 75.

48. John Wesley, "Brief Thoughts on Christian Perfection," in *The Works of John Wesley*, 3rd ed. (1872; Peabody, MA: Hendrickson Publishers, 1984), 11:446.

49. John Wesley, "A Plain Account of Christian Perfection," *Works*, 11:396.

50. *A New Call to Holiness* (Grand Rapids: Zondervan, 1973), p. 121.

51. *Studies in Biblical Holiness* (Kansas City: Beacon Hill, 1971), p. 228.

52. *Entire Sanctification* (Kansas City: Beacon Hill, 1980), p. 36.

53. *Five Views*, p. 91.

54. "A Plain Account," *Works*, 11:442.

55. Ibid., p. 376.

56. Ibid., p. 367.

Melvin Dieter also uses these words. He speaks of "Christian perfection,"[57] "perfection in love,"[58] "perfect consecration to God,"[59] and "perfect love to God and others."[60]

We must therefore conclude that in writings by these authors the
word "perfection" is used in a qualified sense. The "perfection" which,
according to these writers, believers can attain is not sinless,[61] not Adamic,
nor angelic; it is not resurrection perfection, and it is not the perfection of
Christ.[62] This perfection, further, does not exclude "ignorance, or mistake,
in things not essential to salvation, . . . manifold temptations, or . . . num-
berless infirmities."[63] One spokesman for this position, in fact, calls the
holiness which is attainable by believers in this life "imperfect perfection."[64] So "perfection" as described by these authors is not perfection in
the full or even literal sense of the word but a qualified, limited, and defec-
tive type of perfection.

What, now, do these groups teach?

(1) They teach that it is possible for believers in this life to reach a state
called "entire sanctification" (a common name for the "Christian perfection" which is said to be attainable). Dieter defines "entire sanctification"
as follows: "A personal, definitive work of God's sanctifying grace by
which the war within oneself might cease and the heart be fully released
from rebellion into wholehearted love for God and others." Quoting Wesley, he goes on to say that this is a "total death to sin and an entire renewal
in the image of God."[65]

(2) "Entire sanctification" is said to be an experience distinct from and
subsequent to justification—that, in fact, a person may not be "entirely
sanctified" until many years after he or she has been justified. Sanctification is therefore often called "the second blessing" (after justification). In
churches teaching "perfectionism," therefore, there are two types of Christians: merely justified believers, and believers who are both justified and
sanctified.

(3) "Entire sanctification" is said to be an instantaneous experience
that is received by faith. After this "second blessing" has been received,

57. "The Wesleyan Perspective," in *Five Views*, p. 36.
58. Ibid., p. 30.
59. Ibid., p. 18.
60. Ibid.
61. Though on p. 376 of his "Plain Account" Wesley does claim that an "entirely
sanctified" person is so perfect as not to commit sin.
62. Donald S. Metz, *Biblical Holiness*, pp. 229-30.
63. John Wesley, "A Plain Account," *Works*, 11:383.
64. Metz, *Biblical Holiness*, pp. 228, 243.
65. Dieter, *Five Views*, p. 17.

believers are able to continue to reveal the kind of "Christian perfection" that has been described above—a life of wholehearted love for God and others.[66]

(4) "Entire sanctification" is said to involve the eradication of our sinful nature. Wesley said that at the time of "entire sanctification" "all inward sin is taken away."[67] H. Orton Wiley affirms that our holiness is "perfected by the cleansing at a single stroke from inbred sin. . . ."[68] The *Manual* of the Church of the Nazarene states that through "entire sanctification" believers "are made free from original sin."[69] Metz asserts that in "entire sanctification" the carnal nature is destroyed,[70] and Grider contends that in "entire sanctification" the carnal mind is expelled.[71]

(5) The sin which those who are "entirely sanctified" are said to be able to avoid is always carefully circumscribed. Wesley defined sin "properly so called" as "a voluntary transgression of a known law."[72] He went on to say that sin "improperly so called" is "an involuntary transgression of a divine law, known or unknown." Such transgressions, he added, "you may call sins, if you please: I do not."[73] "Entire sanctification," therefore, means that one is now able to avoid voluntary transgressions of known laws. Implied in this description is the thought that only if you recognize something to be sin is it a sin; and also that if you do something wrong without realizing that it is a sin, it is not a sin for you.

(6) The "perfection" which, it is said, believers can attain is always qualified. This point has been discussed above.

On what do these groups base their teachings?

(1) *Alleged biblical examples of "perfect" people.* Wesley, for example, states that perfection is attainable since "justified persons are to 'go on unto perfection' (Heb. 6:1)," and since "Paul speaks of living men that were perfect (Phil. 3:15)."[74] H. Orton Wiley mentions the following as "personal examples which confirm the doctrine of evangelical perfection": Noah, Job,

---

66. It should be noted, however, that "perfectionists" commonly present the doctrine of sanctification in three stages: the process of sanctification begins in regeneration (Dieter, *Five Views*, pp. 16-19), then comes the crisis of "entire sanctification" (ibid., p. 17), and after this the believer must still continue to grow in grace (ibid., p. 41). So the sequence would seem to be "process—crisis—process."

67. "A Plain Account," *Works*, 11:387.

68. *Christian Theology* (Kansas City: Beacon Hill, 1958), 2:446.

69. Kansas City: Nazarene Publishing House, 1968, p. 31.

70. *Biblical Holiness*, p. 250.

71. *Entire Sanctification*, p. 27.

72. "A Plain Account," *Works*, 11:396.

73. Ibid. Similarly, Donald Metz defines sin as "a voluntary transgression of a known law of God by a morally responsible agent" (*Biblical Holiness*, p. 79).

74. "A Plain Account," *Works*, 11:441-42.

Zacharias and Elisabeth, Nathanael, and persons referred to by Paul in 1 Corinthians 2:6 and Philippians 3:15.[75]

It must be remembered that "perfection" is defined by these groups as the ability to refrain from voluntary transgressions of known laws. But does the Bible give us any clear examples of people who were "perfect" in this sense, apart from Jesus Christ? Wiley mentions Job. Yet Job himself confessed, "I despise myself and repent in dust and ashes" (42:6). Though Noah is said in Genesis 6:9 to have been "a just man and perfect in his generations" (KJV; NIV has "blameless"), the ninth chapter of Genesis reports Noah's drunkenness. In 1 Corinthians 2:6 Paul says, "Howbeit, we speak wisdom among them that are perfect" (KJV). The word here translated "perfect," *teleios,* is rendered "mature" in the Revised Standard and New International Versions. Paul speaks here of believers who have obtained spiritual maturity, in distinction from those who are still babes in Christ. He certainly does not necessarily imply that these "mature" believers have never voluntarily sinned against known laws of God. In Philippians 3:15 we read, "Let us therefore, as many as be perfect, be thus minded" (KJV; again the adjective is *teleios,* and again both RSV and NIV have "mature"). "Perfection" in the sense these groups define it is definitely excluded here by the context. For to be "thus minded" in this passage means to know that one has not attained perfection (see v. 12), and that therefore one must continually press on toward the goal (v. 14).

J. C. Ryle expresses the point unforgettably:

> What saint can be named in God's Word, of whose life many details are recorded, who was literally and absolutely perfect? Which of them all, when writing about himself, ever talks of feeling free from imperfection? On the contrary, men like David, and St. Paul, and St. John, declare in the strongest language that they feel in their own hearts weakness and sin.[76]

(2) *Passages in 1 John stating that the regenerate do not sin: 1 John 3:9; 5:18.*[77] These two passages were dealt with on pp. 100-101 above. I there pointed out that in these texts the verbs for "sinning" are in the present tense and therefore describe continued action. What John is saying here is that a person who has been born of God does not keep on doing and enjoying sin with complete abandon—in other words, does not live in sin. But that these passages do not teach that a born-again person can never voluntarily transgress a known law of God is clear from what John says earlier in his epistle: "If we say we have no sin, we deceive ourselves, and the truth is not in us" (1:8, RSV).

75. *Christian Theology,* 2:515.
76. *Holiness,* p. XI.
77. See Wesley, "A Plain Account," *Works,* 11:375; Metz, *Biblical Holiness,* p. 250; Richard Taylor, *Exploring Christian Holiness,* Vol. 3 (Kansas City: Beacon Hill, 1985), p. 62, n. 14.

(3) *The teaching of 1 Thessalonians 5:23.*[78] The passage reads as follows:

> May God himself, the God of peace, sanctify you (*hagiasai*, aorist optative) through and through (*holoteleis*). May your whole (*holoklēron*) spirit, soul and body be kept (*tērētheiē*, also aorist optative) blameless at (*en*, or "in connection with") the coming of our Lord Jesus Christ.

Note that this is a prayer, and that Paul expects the prayer to be answered (v. 24). The first half of the text is a prayer for the total sanctification of Paul's readers; the adjective *holoteleis*, derived from *telos*, meaning "end" or "goal," suggests "whole in such a way as to reach the goal." But the fact that the verb is in the aorist tense does not necessarily imply that this total sanctification is expected to occur at a specific moment in a person's life;[79] in view of the second half of the verse it should be understood as a summary aorist, which summarizes what God does in a believer's life looked at as a whole. That second half is a prayer that these readers may be kept or preserved in their totality (*holoklēron* means "complete in all its parts"), in spirit, soul, and body, without blame, in connection with the Second Coming of Christ.

To understand the second half of the text, we should look at a parallel passage earlier in this epistle, where Paul writes, "May he [God] strengthen your hearts so that you will be blameless and holy in the presence of our God and Father when our Lord Jesus comes with all his holy ones" (3:13). There Paul prays that the believers in Thessalonica may be kept by God in such a way that they will be blameless in God's presence at the time when Jesus comes again. Similarly, in 5:23 Paul is praying that God will preserve the people to whom he is writing in such a way that they will be found blameless in connection with or at Christ's return.[80] 1 Thessalonians 5:23, therefore, does not prove that "entire sanctification" will occur at a certain moment in the lives of God's people. Rather, this prayer clearly implies that their perfection will not be complete until Jesus Christ returns.

B. B. Warfield makes the following comment about this passage:

> Paul, though promising this perfection as the certain heritage of every Christian man, presents it as a matter of hope, not yet seen; not as a matter of experience already enjoyed. . . . Can we learn from Paul *when* we can hope for it? Assuredly, he has not left us in ignorance here. [At this point 1 Thessalonians 5:23 is quoted]. You see it is on the second advent of Christ—and

---

78. This passage is adduced as a prooftext for "entire sanctification" by J. Sidlow Baxter, *A New Call to Holiness*, pp. 107, 115, 147; J. K. Grider, *Entire Sanctification*, pp. 96, 140; and W. T. Purkiser, *Exploring Christian Holiness*, Vol. 1 (Kansas City: Beacon Hill, 1983), p. 205.

79. Grider, *Entire Sanctification*, p. 96.

80. It is significant that the Greek phrase translated "when the Lord Jesus comes" in 3:13 (*en tou parousia tou kyriou hēmōn Iēsou*) is the same as that rendered "at the coming of our Lord Jesus" in 5:23.

that is the end of the world, and the judgment day—that the Apostle has his
eyes set. There is the point of time to which he refers the completeness of our
perfection.[81]

(4) *Passages in which believers are commanded to be perfect.*[82] Texts such
as these are often quoted: Matthew 5:48, Colossians 1:28, and Hebrews 6:1.

Do passages such as these teach that "perfection," in the sense defined
above, can be reached by believers in this life? I do not think so. Let us
look, for example, at Matthew 5:48, where Jesus is quoted as saying, "You,
therefore, must be perfect, as your heavenly Father is perfect" (RSV). The
word "perfect" in both instances translates the Greek word *teleios;* as we
saw, this term when applied to people commonly means "mature" or
"fully developed." Verse 48 occurs at the end of a section of the Sermon
on the Mount in which Jesus has been teaching his hearers to love their
enemies. By showing love even to our enemies, Jesus is saying, we are to
reveal our God-likeness, since our heavenly Father also shows love
toward his enemies (by making his sun rise on both the evil and the good).
We are thus to be complete, full-grown, mature in our love, thus imitating
the Father. Surely Jesus was not here trying to prove that human beings
can in this life be as sinlessly perfect as the Father, or can even approach
such perfection. Rather, he is holding before his disciples and before us
the ideal of Christian maturity in loving even the enemy—in contrast to
the Pharisaic ethic which justified hating the enemy.

Arguments against Wesleyan teachings[83]

I take up first some general considerations:

(1) *Wesleyans weaken the definition of sin.* Sin is defined in Question 14
of the Westminster Shorter Catechism as "any want of conformity unto,
or transgression of, the law of God."[84] Wesleyans, however, as we have
seen, define sin as "a voluntary transgression of a known law." According to this definition only deliberate wrongdoing is recognized as sin.
What is not recognized as sin is not considered sin. But how easy it is not
to recognize sin as sin! Often what we call "sinful anger" in others we
deem "righteous indignation" in ourselves. Our sins, as someone has said,
are like notes pinned to our backs; others see them but we don't. Did not
David say, "Who can discern his errors? Forgive my hidden faults" (Ps.

81. *Perfectionism,* ed. Samuel C. Craig (Philadelphia: Presbyterian and Reformed, 1958), pp. 462-63.

82. See Metz, *Biblical Holiness,* pp. 136-39; Grider, *Entire Sanctification,* p. 34; Purkiser, *Exploring Christian Holiness,* 1:82-85; and Dieter, *Four Views,* pp. 31, 33.

83. I use the term "Wesleyan" here to describe the view of sanctification developed in this section of the chapter—a view often described by the word "perfectionism."

84. Schaff, *Creeds of Christendom* (New York: Harper, 1877), 3:678.

19:12)? Did not Paul affirm, "My conscience is clear, but that does not make me innocent" (1 Cor. 4:4)? How, then, can we be sure that when we avoid what we think are known sins we are really doing God's will?

Stephen Neill's observations on this point are particularly perceptive:

> In certain circles, perfection is interpreted as meaning no more than the avoidance of all known or conscious sin. This is by no means a contemptible ideal. But how far short it falls of an understanding of the depths and realities of our problems! . . . How often we find that we have done wrong, without at the time being aware that we were doing it! . . . To go one stage deeper yet, which of us will venture to claim that the motives which impel us to action are always free from an admixture of dross, perhaps unobserved at the time, but painfully evident to us when we have leisure to be completely honest with ourselves? Over nearly forty years there comes back to me a beautiful description of a preacher returning from the University Church at Oxford with a bulky manuscript under his arm, bursting with pride because he had just preached so excellent a sermon on humility![85]

(2) *Wesleyans dilute the concept of perfection.* According to Wesley, "the highest perfection which man can attain, while the soul dwells in the body, does not exclude ignorance, and error, and a thousand other infirmities."[86] Again, according to Wesley, perfection does not exclude "involuntary transgression of a divine law, known or unknown."[87] In the words of Donald Metz, what the "entirely sanctified" believer can attain in this life is "imperfect perfection"[88]—surely a contradiction in terms. But this use of the word, it seems to me, is confusion worse confounded. Webster defines the word "perfect" as "being entirely without fault or defect: flawless."[89] Why should conduct be called "perfect" when it isn't? Why should "perfection" be described as imperfect? Why should people claim to be "perfect" when, according to their own admission, they are not?

Benjamin B. Warfield was certainly right when he said,

> Nothing can be more important than that the conception of perfection be maintained at its height. . . . The habit of conceiving of perfection as admitting of many imperfections—*moral* imperfections, glossed as infirmities, errors and inadvertences—not only lowers the standard of perfection and with it the height of our aspirations, but corrupts our hearts, dulls our discrimination of right and wrong, and betrays us into satisfaction with attainments which are very far from satisfactory.[90]

85. *Christian Holiness* (London: Lutterworth Press, 1960), pp. 37-38.
86. Wesley, "Sermon 76. On Perfection," *Works*, 6:412.
87. "Plain Account," *Works*, 11:396.
88. Biblical Holiness, p. 228.
89. *Webster's Ninth New Collegiate Dictionary* (Springfield, MA: Merriam-Webster, 1983).
90. Benjamin B. Warfield, *Perfectionism*, Vol. 2 (New York: Oxford University Press, 1932), pp. 457-58.

(3) *Wesleyans claim that the "carnal nature" is eradicated in "entire sancti-fication."* This has been shown above.[91] The New Testament, however, teaches that the believer has a continuing struggle with the flesh or "the sinful nature" (Gal. 5:16-17). Paul enjoins his Christian readers that they must continue to put to death whatever belongs to their earthly nature (Col. 3:5), and to cleanse themselves from every defilement of body and spirit (2 Cor. 7:1, RSV). If the "carnal nature" has been eradicated, why should there still be "defilement of spirit" in the believer? The New Testament also teaches that sanctified people can still be tempted from within as well as from without (Rom. 7:7; James 1:14; 1 Pet. 2:11; 1 John 2:16).

(4) *According to Wesleyan teaching, "entire sanctification" is "a second work of grace" after justification.* But the New Testament keeps justification and sanctification together. In 1 Corinthians 1:30 Christ is said to have been made "our righteousness [here Paul is presumably referring to our justification] and sanctification and redemption" (RSV); we cannot, in other words, have Christ as our justification without at the same time having him as our sanctification (cf. also 1 Cor. 6:11). Though justification and sanctification must be distinguished from each other, they may never be separated; both are essential aspects of our union with Christ. Whereas our definitive sanctification occurs at a point in time, this is not an experience separate from or subsequent to our justification; the two are simultaneous. Progressive sanctification, as we saw, continues throughout life. We are therefore to look not for a specific, dated "second blessing" or "second work of grace," but for continuing renewal, growth, and advancement in the way of sanctification (Rom. 12:2; Eph. 4:15; 1 Pet. 2:2; 2 Pet. 3:18).

In rejecting the teaching that "entire sanctification" is a second work of grace after justification, I do not mean to deny that Christians may have "peak experiences" or "mountaintop experiences" after they have been converted. We must all continue to grow spiritually after conversion, and such growth may well at times take the form of what we might call a "second blessing" experience. In fact, there is no reason why a believer might not also have a "third," "fourth," or even "fifth blessing." We must certainly expect in the lives of God's people times of deeper commitment and fuller consecration to God's service.

But we should not insist that every Christian must have such an experience as is looked for in Wesleyan circles, since God does not save all his people in exactly the same way. Further, to demand that every believer must have a definite "second blessing" experience implies that the church is divided into two groups of Christians: those who have attained this

91. See point (4) on p. 217.

higher level of spirituality and those who have not. Such a division might well leave some believers feeling quite inferior to others and possibly depressed, while exposing other believers to the danger of complacency or pride.[92]

We now go on to look at some Scriptural teachings that militate against the Wesleyan view.

(1) *Passages which teach that no one can claim to be free from sin.* Such texts as these come to mind: 1 Kings 8:46; Psalm 130:3; Proverbs 20:9; Romans 3:23; and James 3:2. It will be helpful to look particularly at 1 John 1:8, "If we say we have no sin *(harmartian ouk echomen)*, we deceive ourselves, and the truth is not in us" (RSV). The verb *echomen*, translated "we have," is in the present tense, ruling out the interpretation that would apply these words exclusively to sin in one's past life. John says specifically that if we claim to have no sin at the present time we are deceiving ourselves. In the light of this passage, and others like it, we must conclude that no believer, however far advanced in sanctification, may ever claim to be living a sinless life. In this connection it is highly significant that Paul, surely one of the most consecrated Christians of all time, confessed, not just that he had been in the past, but that he still was, the *chief* of sinners (1 Tim. 1:15).

(2) *Passages which require of believers confession of sin and prayer for forgiveness.* The Bible consistently describes even the holiest of believers as confessing their sins and asking for forgiveness: Job 42:6; Psalms 32:5; 130:3-4; Isaiah 6:5; 64:6; Daniel 9:15-16; Micah 7:18-19; 1 Timothy 1:15; 1 John 1:9. After having told us in 1 John 1:8 that no believer can claim to be without sin, John goes on to say in verse 9, "If we confess our sins, he is faithful and righteous to forgive us our sins and to cleanse us from all unrighteousness" (NASB). Although those who have fellowship with God (v. 3) and with fellow believers (v. 7) do still sin, they should not become disheartened; John here invites them to confess their sins to God and to receive his forgiveness. The verb translated "confess" *(homologōmen)* is in the present tense, suggesting that such confession should occur frequently. "This [the fact that the verb is in the present tense] teaches that the constant attitude of the saint towards sin should be one of a contrite heart, ever eager to have any sin in the life discovered for him by the Holy Spirit, and ever eager to confess it and put it out of the life by the power of that same Holy Spirit."[93]

In the Lord's Prayer Jesus taught us to pray, "Forgive us our debts, as we also have forgiven our debtors" (Matt. 6:12). The fourth petition of this

---

92. On this matter, see Chapter 2, "The Question of the 'Order of Salvation,'" particularly pp. 17-27.

93. Kenneth S. Wuest, *In These Last Days* (Grand Rapids: Eerdmans, 1954), p. 104.

prayer suggests that this petition, or its equivalent, is to be uttered daily: "Give us *today* our daily bread." Since Jesus taught us to pray daily for forgiveness, surely he never envisaged the possibility that any one of his followers could live even for one day without sin!

(3) *Passages which depict the struggle between the old and the new nature in the believer.* Earlier in the chapter I referred to a number of New Testament passages which describe this struggle. Here we look more closely at Galatians 5:16-17:

> But I say, walk [literally, keep on walking] by the Spirit, and you will not carry out the desire of the flesh. For the flesh sets its desire against the Spirit, and the Spirit against the flesh; for these are in opposition to one another, so that you may not do the things that you please (NASB).[94]

What does Paul mean here by "flesh"? Though the word "flesh" as used in the New Testament may have various meanings, here it means the tendency within human beings to disobey God in every area of life.[95] We must not restrict the meaning of this word as if it referred only to what we commonly call "fleshly sins," or "sins of the body"; "flesh" designates sins committed by the whole person. In the list of "deeds" or "works" of the flesh given in verses 19-21, only five out of 15 describe what we usually call bodily sins; the rest are "sins of the spirit" (hatred, discord, jealousy, and the like).

We learn from Romans 8:9 that believers are not in the flesh but in the Spirit—that is, they are no longer enslaved to the flesh but are now being ruled by the Spirit. Nevertheless, Galatians 5:16-17 implies that believers must still fight against sinful impulses coming from the flesh, since the desires of the flesh are opposed to the desires of the Spirit. God promises us in this passage that if we keep on walking by the Spirit, we will not carry out or fulfill the desire of the flesh (v. 16). But it is clear that Christians must continue to battle against evil tendencies within them until their final breath.

To be sure, Galatians 5:24 teaches that believers have crucified the flesh. Yet they must continue to struggle against the desires of the flesh (vv. 16-17). Similarly, believers are dead to sin (Rom. 6:2, 11) but must still put to death the misdeeds of the body (Rom. 8:13); they have been crucified to the world (Gal. 6:14), yet must no longer be conformed to the pattern of this world (Rom. 12:2); they are unleavened, yet must still be told to "cleanse out the old leaven" (1 Cor. 5:7). Passages of this sort il-

94. The NASB rendering is here used because it translates the Greek word *sarx* literally as "flesh." The NIV translates *sarx* as "sinful nature."
95. "Flesh" as here used is therefore synonymous with what I have earlier called our "old nature."

lustrate the tension Paul saw in himself and in his fellow believers.[96] The presence of this tension rules out the claim that believers can attain in this life the kind of "perfection" claimed by the Wesleyans.

What, finally, can we learn from the Wesleyans? We must admire and emulate their passion for holiness. There is among these fellow Christians a deep concern for holy living which we cannot but praise. Stephen Neill makes a good point when he says, "Whenever the Church sinks down into the placid acceptance of mediocrity, the perfectionists appear as gadflies to sting it again into alertness."[97]

Do we of Reformed persuasion sometimes fail to do full justice to the Scriptural injunction, "Be holy, because I am holy" (1 Pet. 1:16)? Are we persistently contending for peace with all, "and for the holiness without which no one will see the Lord" (Heb. 12:14)? Do we remember that we are called to no less a goal than that of "perfecting holiness out of reverence for God" (2 Cor. 7:1)? That goal will never be reached in this life; nevertheless, we must daily try to reach it. As Robert Browning once said, "Man's reach must exceed his grasp, or what's a heaven for?"

The fact that Bible writers often tell us that they have failed to reach the goal of perfection must be accepted as their personal testimony but should not be used as a hindrance in our striving for perfection. Paul's words in Philippians 3:13-14 may well serve as our motto:

> Brothers, I do not consider myself yet to have taken hold of it [perfect fellowship with and likeness to Christ]. But one thing I do: Forgetting what is behind and straining toward what is ahead, I press on toward the goal to win the prize for which God has called me heavenward in Christ Jesus.

SANCTIFICATION AND THE LAW

Many Christians claim that when a person becomes a believer, he or she has nothing more to do with the law. "Free from the law—O blessed condition!" would seem to describe their attitude toward God's law in all its functions.

In one sense, to be sure, the believer is free from the law. Romans 6:14 says it plainly: "For sin shall not be your master, because you are not under law, but under grace." "Not under law" here means that we are no longer under condemnation because of our failure to keep the law. Paul points out in Galatians 3:10 that all who fail to do everything that is written in the book of God's law are under a curse—the curse of everlasting punish-

96. On this point see F. F. Bruce, *Commentary on Colossians*, in *Commentary on the Epistles to the Ephesians and the Colossians* (Grand Rapids: Eerdmans, 1957), pp. 268-69.

97. *Christian Holiness*, p. 27.

ment. But he goes on to say that "Christ redeemed us from the curse of the law by becoming a curse for us, for it is written: 'Cursed is everyone who is hung on a tree.' He redeemed us in order that the blessing given to Abraham might come to the Gentiles through Christ Jesus" (vv. 13-14). Christ, that is, bore the "curse of the law" for us so completely that he became a curse for us—by suffering the results of the curse throughout his life, particularly on the cross. The blessing of Abraham (that is, the blessing of justification by faith; see v. 8) has therefore become ours. In the sense that believers no longer need to keep the law as a way of earning their salvation, they have indeed been delivered from it.

In another sense, however, believers are not free from the law. They should be deeply concerned about keeping God's law as a way of expressing their gratitude to him for the gift of salvation. Calvin identified this use of the law as its third and chief function in the lives of believers:

> The third and principal use [of the law], which pertains more closely to the proper purpose of the law, finds its place among believers in whose hearts the Spirit of God already lives and reigns.... Here is the best instrument for them to learn more thoroughly each day the nature of the Lord's will to which they aspire.... Again, because we need not only teaching but also exhortation, the servant of God will also avail himself of this benefit of the law.[98]

The Bible itself teaches this "third and principal" use of the law. For example, at the very beginning of the Sinaitic law God said, "I am the LORD your God, who brought you out of Egypt, out of the land of slavery" (Exod. 20:2), thereby reminding his people of his gracious act of delivering them from Egypt—that deliverance to which they owed their existence as a nation. "Now keep these commandments," God was saying, "in thankfulness for all my mercies shown to you."

The law was to be kept out of gratitude to God, which explains the delight that Old Testament saints had in God's law. So, for example, after speaking of the blessedness of the man who does not walk in the counsel of the wicked, the author of Psalm 1 goes on to say, "But his delight is in the law of the LORD, and on his law he meditates day and night" (v. 2). Here "law" means the precepts of God, given not only in the Ten Commandments but in other parts of his written revelation as well—precepts that give guidance for the believer's life. The same delight is expressed in Psalm 19:7-8,

> The law of the LORD is perfect, reviving the soul.
> The statutes of the LORD are trustworthy, making wise the simple.
> The precepts of the LORD are right, giving joy to the heart.
> The commands of the LORD are radiant, giving light to the eyes.

98. *Inst.*, II.vii.12.

All of Psalm 119, the longest psalm in the Bible, is a paean of praise to the beauty and sweetness of God's law and to the joy the Psalmist finds in keeping it: "Direct me in the path of your commands, for there I find delight" (v. 35).

The New Testament, which further amplifies Old Testament teaching, similarly urges believers to keep God's law in gratitude for blessings received. We find this directive first of all in the words of Jesus. In his Sermon on the Mount he said, "Anyone who breaks one of the least of these commandments [those found in the Law or the Prophets] and teaches others to do the same will be called least in the kingdom of heaven, but whoever practices and teaches these commands will be called great in the kingdom of heaven" (Matt. 5:19). On another occasion Jesus told his disciples, "If you obey my commands, you will remain in my love, just as I have obeyed my Father's commands and remain in his love" (John 15:10). Jesus' command, however, is not different from what the Ten Commandments require, for he went on to say, "My command is this: Love each other as I have loved you" (v. 12); at another time he taught that the entire content of the last six commandments of the Decalogue is "Love your neighbor as yourself" (Matt. 22:39). It is clear that New Testament believers must still keep the Ten Commandments; they have, however, the example of Christ as a kind of "visual aid" (cf. "as I have loved you," John 13:34).

Paul, often cited as one who puts law and grace into sharp contrast, also considers the law (in Calvin's third use) still binding on Christians. In Romans 8:3-4 he indicates that the purpose of Christ's incarnation was to enable his people to fulfill the law:

> For God has done what the law, weakened by the flesh, could not do: sending his own Son in the likeness of sinful flesh and for sin, he condemned sin in the flesh, in order that the just requirement of the law might be fulfilled in us, who walk not according to the flesh but according to the Spirit (RSV).

Some Christians see a sharp contrast between law-keeping and living by the Spirit. According to this passage, however, these two expressions describe the same thing: Spirit-led believers are precisely the ones doing their best to keep God's law.

The thought that the believer has nothing more to do with the law is far from Paul's mind. He describes love for our neighbor as a debt that we continually owe to one another, indicating that such love is the fulfillment of the law:

> Let no debt remain outstanding, except the continuing debt to love one another, for he who loves his fellow man has fulfilled the law. The commandments, "Do not commit adultery," "Do not murder," "Do not steal," "Do not

covet," and whatever other commandment there may be, are summed up in this one rule: "Love your neighbor as yourself." Love does no harm to its neighbor. Therefore love is the fulfillment of the law (Rom. 13:8-10).

Paul here not only instructs believers to continue to fulfill the law; he also implies that, contrary to the opinion of some, there is no conflict between law-keeping and love.

In 1 Corinthians 9:20-21 Paul discusses his missionary approach as well as his relation to the law: "To the Jews I became like a Jew, to win the Jews. . . . To those not having the law [the Gentiles] I became like one not having the law (though I am not free from God's law but am under Christ's law)." Paul here clearly sees himself as always subject to the law of Christ —as always "under law to Christ" (ASV).

Similar statements are found in the Catholic Epistles. James teaches that law-keeping, rather than holding us in bondage, brings true freedom: "But the man who looks intently into the perfect law that gives freedom, and continues to do this . . . , will be blessed in what he does" (James 1:25). John connects the law with knowing God and experiencing the fullness of his love: "We know that we have come to know him if we obey his commands. The man who says, 'I know him,' but does not do what he commands is a liar, and the truth is not in him. But if anyone obeys his word, God's love is truly made complete in him" (1 John 2:3-5; cf. also 1 John 5:3).

The Christian life, we conclude, must be a law-formed life. This does not mean a rigoristic observance of the letter of the law, but rather a living by the Spirit, who "helps Christians make their way safely between legalism and lawlessness."[99] Though believers must not try to keep God's law as a means of earning their salvation, they are nevertheless enjoined to do their best to keep the law as a means of showing their thankfulness to God for the salvation they have received as a gift of grace. For believers, law-keeping is an expression of Christian love and the way to Christian freedom; it is equivalent to walking by the Spirit. Since the law mirrors God, living in obedience to God's law is living as image-bearers of God. The law, therefore, is one of the most important means whereby God sanctifies us.[100]

THE SOCIAL DIMENSION OF SANCTIFICATION

Sanctification is often thought of as concerning only the individual Chris-

---

99. Gary N. Weisinger III, *The Reformed Doctrine of Sanctification*, No. 9 in "Fundamentals of the Faith," published by *Christianity Today* (Washington, D.C., n.d.), p. 24.

100. On this aspect of sanctification, see also Berkouwer's chapter "Sanctification and Law," in *Faith and Sanctification*, pp. 163-93.

tian. But this is a serious mistake. Sanctification has an important social dimension.

It must be remembered, first of all, that we are not sanctified merely as individuals but as members of the body of Christ. In Romans 12:4-5 Paul says, "Just as each of us has one body with many members, and these members do not all have the same function, so in Christ we who are many form one body, and each member belongs to all the others." The purpose of our sanctification, therefore, is "to prepare God's people for works of service, so that the body of Christ may be built up" (Eph. 4:12). We must therefore live in such a way as to advance and enrich the sanctification of the fellow believers whom our lives touch.

But this enrichment works both ways. Earlier it was pointed out that our fellowship with other Christians is one of the more important means of our sanctification. We grow more fully into Christ, not just by ourselves, but in and through the communion of the saints.

We are sanctified, further, not only as members of Christ's body but also as citizens of the Kingdom of God. The Kingdom of God is the reign of God over the entire created universe, dynamically active in human history through Jesus Christ. To be a subject of that kingdom means obedience to God in every area of life. This involves a kingdom vision: a world-and-life view which sees all of life and all human endeavors as under the lordship of Christ. Abraham Kuyper, the renowned Dutch theologian and statesman, once put it unforgettably: "There is not a thumb-breadth of the universe about which Christ does not say, 'It is mine.'"

Jesus described the citizens of the Kingdom as follows:

> You are the salt of the earth. . . . You are the light of the world. A city on a hill cannot be hidden. Neither do people light a lamp and put it under a bowl. Instead they put it on its stand and it gives light to everyone in the house. In the same way, let your light shine before men, that they may see your good deeds and praise your Father in heaven (Matt. 5:13-16).

These words imply that we who are Kingdom citizens must, like salt, try to let our influence count so that the evil in the world may be checked. They also imply that by our witness and example we are to let our light shine in such a way that God may be praised. And they suggest that our Christian influence ought to be as conspicuous as a city on a hill.

So sanctification means more than just making individuals holy. Albert Wolters, in his helpful recent book *Creation Regained*, gives a definition of sanctification which reflects this broader dimension: "Sanctification is the process whereby the Holy Spirit, in and through the people of God, purifies creation from sin. . . ." Expanding on this definition, he adds, "The 'Spirit of holiness' seeks to permeate our creaturely lives, making a qualitative difference in the internal workings of family, business, art, government, and so on."[101]

The Bible clearly teaches that sanctification concerns not just individuals in isolation from others but also involves social dimensions. What Jesus calls the second most important commandment of the law obliges us to be constantly concerned for the welfare of our fellow human beings: "Love your neighbor as yourself" (Mark 12:31; cf. Lev. 19:18; Rom. 13:10; Gal. 5:14). The Apostle John, in fact, puts it as strongly as this: "If anyone says, 'I love God,' yet hates his brother, he is a liar. For anyone who does not love his brother, whom he has seen, cannot love God, whom he has not seen" (1 John 4:20).

In the judgment scene depicted in Matthew 25 Jesus taught that our sanctification involves duties toward our neighbors: giving food to the hungry, drink to the thirsty, and clothing to the needy; inviting the stranger, looking after the sick, and visiting the prisoner. And our Lord added, "I tell you the truth, whatever you did for one of the least of these brothers of mine, you did for me" (Matt. 25:35-36, 40).

The Bible frequently mentions God's concern for the poor. Believers are told that they must maintain the rights of the poor and oppressed (Ps. 82:3); they are instructed to be kind to the poor (Prov. 19:17) and to care about justice for the poor (Prov. 29:7). Jesus told the rich young ruler to sell what he had and to give to the poor (Luke 18:22), and the apostles made remembering the poor one of their major concerns (Acts 24:17; Rom. 15:26; Gal. 2:10). James, in fact, surprises us when he says, "Has not God chosen those who are poor in the eyes of the world to be rich in faith and to inherit the kingdom he promised those who love him?" (2:5).

Bible writers severely condemn those who mistreat the poor. Isaiah denounces the elders and leaders of God's people who "are grinding the faces of the poor" (3:15), and Amos fulminates against Israelites who "buy the poor with silver and the needy for a pair of sandals" (8:6). The author of Proverbs affirms that he who oppresses the poor shows contempt for their Maker (14:31), and goes on to make a dire prediction: "If a man shuts his ears to the cry of the poor, he too will cry out and not be answered" (21:13).

The Old Testament prophets cry out for justice: "I, the LORD, love justice; I hate robbery and iniquity" (Isa. 61:8). Micah's words are often quoted: "He has showed you, O man, what is good. And what does the LORD require of you? To act justly and to love mercy and to walk humbly with your God" (6:8). Amos sounds a trumpet call from the high cliffs of vision: "Let justice roll down like waters, and righteousness like an ever-flowing stream" (5:24, RSV). But the demand for justice is not limited to the Old

101. Albert M. Wolters, *Creation Regained* (Grand Rapids: Eerdmans, 1985), p. 74.

Testament. One can almost see James's eyes flash with indignation when he writes, "Now listen, you rich people, weep and wail because of the misery that is coming upon you. . . . Look! The wages you failed to pay the workmen who mowed your fields are crying out against you. The cries of the harvesters have reached the ears of the Lord Almighty" (5:1, 4).

We conclude that sanctification is not complete without social concern. Sanctification means that we must seek to promote justice for all, through legislation, political action, and the use of the media. We must oppose all forms of injustice: racism, the oppression of minorities, the treatment of workers as machines instead of people, and the like. Sanctification means opposition to abortion on demand, since it causes the murder of millions of potential image-bearers of God. Sanctification means concern for the education of our children; this implies not only the establishment and maintenance of Christian schools, but also regard for the welfare of public schools.

Growth in sanctification requires concern for the environment — using our influence to oppose air pollution, water pollution, irresponsible use of land, irresponsible harvesting of forests, and the like. It means being burdened about world hunger, and working for the alleviation of poverty. It means involvement in the war against drugs, in drug rehabilitation, and in the restoration of alcoholics. It includes concern for better prisons and for programs aimed at reducing crime. It means diligence in working for world peace and for an end to the disastrous nuclear armament race.

All such concerns are an aspect of our sanctification. We must conscientiously seek to implement Christian principles in every area of life. This is what it means to be a loyal subject of Christ our King.[102]

THE GOAL OF SANCTIFICATION

The goal of sanctification may be viewed from two perspectives: its final and its proximate goal. The final goal of sanctification can be nothing other

---

102. On the social dimension of sanctification, see also Abraham Kuyper, *Calvinism* (Grand Rapids: Eerdmans, 1931); David O. Moberg, *Inasmuch* (Grand Rapids: Eerdmans, 1965), and *The Great Reversal* (New York: Lippincott, 1972); Richard J. Mouw, *Called to Holy Worldliness* (Philadelphia: Fortress, 1980). An important current approach to Christian social concern can be found in what is commonly called "Liberation Theology." This movement, which arose in Latin America, where the gap between rich and poor is wide and deep, understands salvation as liberation from oppression and injustice. Though the emphases of various theologians of this school vary, and though evangelical Christians have serious problems with some of their concepts, we must appreciate the genuine concern of these writers to apply Christian principles to the burning issues of poverty, oppression, and injustice in today's world. For a brief but helpful overview, see Harvey M. Conn, "Theologies of Liberation," in *Tensions in Contemporary Theology*, ed. S. N. Gundry and A. F. Johnson, rev. ed. (Chicago: Moody Press, 1979), pp. 327-434.

than the glory of God. As we think about this gracious divine activity, we should consider primarily not our own future happiness but the glory of our wonderful God.

The Bible indicates that the glory of God is the final end of our sanctification. After having written in Ephesians 1:4-5 that God has chosen us in Christ before the foundation of the world and that he has predestined us to be adopted as his children, Paul adds, "to the praise of his glorious grace" (v. 6)—a thought that is repeated in verses 12 and 14 ("for the praise of his glory" and "to the praise of his glory"). Elsewhere Paul prays that the love of his fellow Christians may abound more and more, so that they may be pure and blameless, filled with the fruit of righteousness, "to the glory and praise of God" (Phil. 1:9-11). Why did God raise us up with Christ and seat us with him in the heavenly realms? "In order that in the coming ages he [God] might show the incomparable riches of his grace, expressed in his kindness to us in Christ Jesus" (Eph. 2:7). In other words, all the amazing blessings of our salvation, including our sanctification, have as their final goal the praise of the glory of God. Nothing in all of history will reveal the fullness of God's perfections as brilliantly as will the completed glorification of his people.

In the Book of Revelation the Apostle John pulls aside the curtain of mystery and gives us a glimpse into heaven. He hears voices—the voices of the redeemed—singing, "To him who sits on the throne and to the Lamb be praise and honor and glory and power, for ever and ever!" (Rev. 5:13). The ultimate goal of all of God's wondrous works, including the sanctification of his people, is that he shall be given praise, honor, and glory forevermore.

The proximate goal of sanctification is the perfection of God's people. This perfection will be the final stage in the history of the image of God, for in the life to come God's people will perfectly image him and Christ, who is "the exact representation of his being" (Heb. 1:3). Paul says in 1 Corinthians 15:49, "Just as we have borne the likeness of the earthly man, so shall we bear the likeness of the man from heaven." This "man from heaven" is obviously Jesus Christ, whose glorified image we shall fully bear and reveal in the resurrection.

John says something similar in 1 John 3:2. Though it has not yet been made known, John affirms, what we who are God's children will be in the future, "we know that when he [Christ] appears, we shall be like him, for we shall see him as he is." The goal of our sanctification, as here described, is perfect and total likeness to Christ, and therefore to God. This total likeness will not entail the loss of personal identity, since we shall retain our individuality; it will, however, mean a completely sinless existence (see also Eph. 5:27; Heb. 12:23; Rev. 22:14-15).

Such future perfection is the purpose for which God has predestined us: "For those God foreknew he also predestined to be conformed to the likeness of his Son" (Rom. 8:29). God's purpose for us, in other words, is not just future happiness or a guaranteed entrance into heaven but perfect likeness to Christ and therefore to himself. God could not, in fact, have designed a higher destiny for his people than that they should be completely like his only Son, in whom he delights.

The future perfection of God's people will be a sharing of the final glorification of Christ. We are not only heirs of God, Paul tells us in Romans 8:17, but fellow heirs with Christ, "provided we suffer with him in order that we may also be glorified with him" (RSV). We must never think of Christ apart from his people, nor of Christ's people apart from him. So it will be in the life to come: the glorification of Christ's people will occur together with the final glorification of Christ (Col. 3:4). When our sanctification will have been completed, we shall be wholly like Christ in his glorification. Then we shall not only see him face to face, but shall totally and undividedly live to the praise of the glory of his grace, world without end.[103]

103. On the doctrine of sanctification, in addition to books already referred to, see also Robert N. Flew, *The Idea of Perfection in Christian Theology* (London: Oxford, 1934); William E. Hulme, *The Dynamics of Sanctification* (Minneapolis: Augsburg, 1966); Adolf Köberle, *The Quest for Holiness* (New York: Harper, 1936); Hans K. La Rondelle, *Perfection and Perfectionism* (Kampen: Kok, 1971); Harald Lindström, *Wesley and Sanctification* (London: Epworth Press, 1946); Arthur W. Pink, *The Doctrine of Sanctification* (Grand Rapids: Baker, 1955); Kenneth F. W. Prior, *The Way of Holiness* (Chicago: InterVarsity Press, 1967); W. T. Purkiser, *Sanctification and its Synonyms* (Kansas City: Beacon Hill, 1963); Peter Toon, *Justification and Sanctification* (Westchester: Good News, 1983); Laurence W. Wood, *Pentecostal Grace* (Wilmore, KY: Francis Asbury, 1980); Mildred B. Wynkoop, *A Theology of Love: The Dynamic of Wesleyanism* (Kansas City: Beacon Hill, 1972).

CHAPTER 13

The Perseverance of True Believers

A PASTOR WAS CALLING ON AN AGED PARISHIONER WHO WAS SERIOUS-
ly ill. When asked how he was feeling, the sick man replied, "I feel very
weak. In fact, pastor, sometimes I'm too weak to pray. And I worry about
this. I'm afraid—so afraid—that one of these days I may in my weakness
let go of Christ and be lost." The pastor then quoted Jesus' words recorded
in John 10:28, "I give them [my sheep] eternal life, and they shall never
perish, and no one shall snatch them out of my hand." "What keeps us
secure to the end," the pastor went on to say, "is not finally our hold on
Christ but Christ's hold on us. And, praise God, he will never let us go!"

One could call this a pastoral way of describing the comfort involved
in the doctrine of the perseverance of true believers. In this chapter we
shall be looking at the biblical basis for this teaching, together with the
chief objections that have been advanced against it.

The Concept of Perseverance

The meaning of this doctrine must be clearly understood. It does not mean
that every churchgoer or even every church member is certain to persevere
to the end in his or her faith, or that everyone who has made a public
profession of faith is eternally secure, or that all who seem to us to be true
believers will never fall away from the faith. Neither does the doctrine
mean that everyone who has been incorporated into the covenant of grace
as it reveals itself in history is eternally secure, since the Bible clearly
teaches that there may be covenant breakers.

What the doctrine of the perseverance of true believers does mean is
this: those who have true faith can lose that faith neither totally nor finally. The real question at issue, therefore, is this: Can a person who has true
faith ever lose that faith? To this question the person of Reformed persuasion says: No. It should immediately be added, however, that the Calvinist gives this answer not on the basis of the superior spiritual strength

of the believer, but on the ground of God's faithfulness to his promise. The Calvinist believes that God will never permit those to whom he has given true faith to fall away from that faith. True believers persevere not because of their strength but because of God's unchangeable mercy.

A good definition of the doctrine can be found in the Westminster Confession of Faith:

> They whom God hath accepted in his Beloved, effectually called[1] and sanctified by his Spirit, can neither totally nor finally fall away from the state of grace; but shall certainly persevere therein to the end, and be eternally saved.[2]

We may note that those who are here said not to fall away are those who are in Christ, who have been regenerated, and who are being sanctified by the Spirit. These, the Confession goes on to say, can neither *totally* nor *finally* fall away from the state of grace—that is, they can never completely lose their salvation, nor can they reach the end of their lives in an unsaved condition. The Confession further states that they will persevere in the state of grace, thus rejecting a common caricature of this doctrine which describes it as teaching that believers are certain to be saved no matter how they live. Believers, the statement concludes, will be "eternally saved"—that is, their salvation will last forever.

What this definition does not say, however, is that believers can only persevere through the power of God.[3] Left to themselves, to their own strength, to their own resources, they would undoubtedly fall away and lose their salvation. But God will not permit this to happen to those who are his own, whom he has chosen in Christ from the creation of the world (Eph. 1:4) and whom he has predestined to be conformed to the likeness of his Son (Rom. 8:29). This is a most important point, and it is really the heart of the doctrine. Believers persevere only because God in his unchangeable love enables them to persevere.

This brings up the question of terminology. Is the expression "the perseverance of true believers" the most apt designation of this doctrine, or would it be better to speak of "the preservation of the elect"? It is significant to note that the Canons of Dort use both expressions: "Concerning this preservation of those chosen to salvation and concerning the perseverance of true believers in faith. . . ."[4] The Canons here look at this teaching from two sides. When we look at it from God's side, the Canons

---

1. By "effectual calling" is meant the gospel call made effective to salvation in the lives of God's people (see Chapter 6). In the Westminster Standards, "effectual calling" is used as a synonym for regeneration.

2. Westminster Confession, XVII,1.

3. This point *is* made in Section 2 of Chapter XVII.

4. Canons of Dort, V,9 (1986 trans.).

are saying, we think of it as God's preservation of those he chose to salvation. But when we look at it from the human side, we think of it as describing the fact that true believers persevere in the faith.

John Murray makes a strong plea for retaining the expression "perseverance" rather than "preservation." The term "perseverance," he says, guards against the notion that believers are spiritually secure regardless of the extent to which they may fall into sin or become careless about their way of life. It is simply not biblical teaching to say that believers are secure regardless of how they live. The doctrine we are considering is the doctrine that believers *persevere;* it is only through the power of God that they are able to persevere, to be sure, but they do persevere. The security of believers is inseparable from their perseverance; did not Jesus say, "He who stands firm to the end will be saved" (Matt. 10:22)? Murray, in fact, puts it as strongly as this: "Perseverance means the engagement of our persons in the most intense and concentrated devotion to those means which God has ordained for the achievement of his saving purpose."[5]

For the reasons just advanced, I prefer to use the expression "the perseverance of true believers" to designate this doctrine. Though this teaching is commonly known as "the perseverance of the saints," the term "saint" is capable of various meanings and is therefore ambiguous.

THE SCRIPTURAL BASIS FOR THIS DOCTRINE

It is often said, by those who oppose this teaching, that the Reformed doctrine of perseverance is a logical deduction from other Calvinistic doctrines, rather than a teaching based on Scripture. I. Howard Marshall, for example, observes, "The point which impresses one when reading some Calvinist authors is that they tend to accept the doctrine of final perseverance on philosophical and dogmatic grounds. For the Calvinist the doctrine of perseverance can be regarded as a corollary of the doctrine of the predestination of particular individuals to salvation."[6] This is not so, however. The doctrine of the perseverance of true believers has not been merely deduced from other doctrines and is not based on philosophical and dogmatic grounds, but is clearly taught in Scripture. We go on now to examine the Scriptural basis for this doctrine.

Passages from the Gospels:
1. Luke 22:31-32, "Simon, Simon, Satan has asked to sift you [plural] as wheat. But I have prayed for you [singular], Simon, that your faith may not

5. John Murray, *Redemption — Accomplished and Applied* (Grand Rapids: Eerdmans, 1955), pp. 192-93.
6. *Kept by the Power of God* (Minneapolis: Bethany Fellowship, 1975), p. 26.

fail. And when you have turned back, strengthen your brothers." Jesus is here telling Simon Peter that Satan had asked and received permission from the Father to subject the disciples to a severe strain, to "sift them like wheat." Satan's purpose would be to break up the group, to take away their loyalty to Christ, and thus to bring to nought the Savior's work. But Jesus also reveals that he has prayed specifically for Peter that his faith might not fail.

In the expression "that your faith may not fail," the verb rendered "fail" is *eklipē*, from *ekleipō*, which means "to come to an end," or "to give out." The English word *eclipse*, in fact, is derived from this verb. Kenneth Wuest, therefore, has caught the flavor of this word when he translates, "that your faith should not be totally eclipsed."[7] Jesus prayed that Peter's faith might not utterly disappear, might not be wiped out without a trace. So, though Peter certainly became faithless in the sense of disloyalty, he did not utterly lose saving faith. His prompt repentance ("he went outside and wept bitterly," v. 62) indicated that Jesus' prayer for him had indeed been answered.

Here, then, we have an example of a believer who fell deeply into sin and yet whose faith was not eclipsed, because of Jesus' intercession. Believing as we do that our Lord intercedes for all who are his own, should we not also trust that Christ will not permit the faith of any of his people to fail, though they should fall into grievous sin? This passage from Luke must be read in connection with Hebrews 7:25, "He [Jesus] is able to save completely those who come to God through him, because he always lives to intercede for them."

2. John 5:24, "I tell you the truth, whoever hears my [Christ's] word and believes him who sent me has eternal life and will not be condemned; he has crossed over from death to life." Those who listen to my word and keep on believing him who sent me, Jesus here teaches, will not be condemned for their sins, but have been permanently transferred from death to life. The verb rendered "crossed over" is *metabebēken*, from *metabainō*, meaning "to go or pass over." The verb is in the perfect tense, a tense which describes past action with abiding result. The action pictured is final and irrevocable, like that of a person who has burned his bridges behind him. The possibility that a true believer could cross back again from life into death is contrary to the finality of the passage.

In this connection, listen to Jesus' words to the Samaritan woman: "whoever drinks the water I give him will never thirst. Indeed, the water I give him will become in him a spring of water welling up to eternal life" (John 4:14). How can a spring welling up to eternal life dry up and disappear? Note also what Jesus said to the Jews on the shore of the Lake of

---

7. *The New Testament, An Expanded Translation* (Grand Rapids: Eerdmans, 1961), p. 197.

Galilee: "I am the living bread that came down from heaven. If anyone eats of this bread, he will live forever" (John 6:51). By "eating of this bread" Jesus meant believing that his flesh had been given "for the life of the world." How, now, could it be possible for someone to be living forever and then to lose that life? Is not such a possibility a sheer contradiction in terms? Again, hear Jesus' words to Martha: "I am the resurrection and the life. He who believes in me will live, even though he dies; and whoever lives and believes in me will never die" (John 11:25-26). Surely the language could not be more clear: "whoever believes in me *will never die*"! He or she may die physically, as Lazarus had just done, but will never die spiritually or eternally. Those who truly believe in Christ will live forever. This is Jesus' unchangeable promise!

3. In John 6:39 Jesus says, "And this is the will of him who sent me, that I shall lose none of all that he has given me, but raise them up at the last day." Here Christ refers to his people as those whom the Father has given him—a point touched upon earlier in this book.[8] To those the Father gave him, Jesus teaches, he, their Savior, has given eternal life (John 17:2). Is "eternal life" something one can have for a time and then lose? If that could happen, how could it be called *eternal* life? Is the "eternal salvation" of which Christ is said to be the source in Hebrews 5:9 a salvation which could in some cases be only temporary?

Jesus says that all those whom the Father has given him will come to him in faith (John 6:37). In verse 39 he assures us that he will keep those the Father has given him in such a way that none of them will be lost. Lest there be any misunderstanding of what he means, Jesus affirms, "I will raise them up at the last day." This, he adds, is precisely the will of my Father in heaven: "For my Father's will is that everyone who looks to the Son and believes in him shall have eternal life, and I will raise him up at the last day" (v. 40).

Could anyone ask for stronger assurance? Those whom the Father has given me, our Lord avows, who come to me in true faith, will receive eternal life, and I will lose none of them but will preserve them in the salvation that has been granted them in such a way that they will all be raised to a life of glory on the day when I come again on the clouds of heaven.

4. Most emphatically Jesus teaches that true believers will persevere in John 10:27-28, "My sheep listen to my voice; I know them, and they follow me. I give them eternal life, and they shall never perish; no one can snatch them out of my hand." Those whom the Father has given him Jesus here calls his sheep. To these sheep—those who keep listening to his voice, and who keep on following him—Jesus gives eternal life, a life that will

8. See above, p. 58.

never end. "And they shall never perish." In the Greek we have here the strongest possible way of expressing a negation: *ou mē* with the aorist subjunctive. Literally the text reads, "And they shall not by any possible means perish throughout eternity."

"No one," Jesus continues, "can snatch them out of my hand."[9] The security of believers is thus not dependent on their hold of Christ, but on Christ's hold of them. Arminian interpreters have tried to evade the thrust of Jesus' words by saying that, though no outside force can snatch believers out of Christ's hand, believers themselves can still give up their hold on Christ and be lost.[10] Against this interpretation it must be said that surely the "no one" to whom Jesus alludes must include believers themselves. Our hold on Christ may sometimes be very weak, but Christ's hold on us is strong and unbreakable. Further, does it make sense to understand Jesus' words as meaning, My sheep, some of whom may indeed perish, will never perish?

As if what he has said so far is still not eloquent enough, Jesus goes on to say, in verse 29, "My Father, who has given them to me, is greater than all; no one can snatch them out of my Father's hand." The Father, too, will keep hold of my sheep, Christ here teaches, and no one can possibly pluck them out of the Father's hand. And so believers are doubly secure. The hand of the Son and the hand of the Father clasp the weak and feeble hand of the believer, clasp him or her so tightly that no one will ever be able to snatch that believer away from the double handclasp of God.

Passages from the Epistles

1. In Romans 8:29-30 Paul writes: "For those God foreknew he also predestined to be conformed to the likeness of his Son, that he might be the firstborn among many brothers. And those he predestined, he also called; those he called, he also justified; those he justified, he also glorified." Here Paul tells us that God foreknew and predestined certain people to be conformed to the likeness of Christ. Those so predestined, he goes on to say, God also called, justified, and glorified.[11] "Called," as was

9. The Greek text reads, "no one will snatch them out of my hand." The NIV rendering here is not strictly literal, though it does not change the point Jesus is making.

10. Cf. Robert Shank, *Life in the Son* (Springfield, MO: Westcott Publishers, 1960), pp. 56-60; Grant R. Osborne, "Exegetical Notes on Calvinist Texts," in *Grace Unlimited*, ed. Clark H. Pinnock (Minneapolis: Bethany Fellowship, 1975), p. 179; Dale Moody, *The Word of Truth* (Grand Rapids: Eerdmans, 1981), pp. 356-57.

11. I. Howard Marshall seems unwilling to accept Paul's statement, "those he justified, he also glorified." He quotes John Wesley, who said, "And whom he justified [KJV] — provided they continue in his goodness, Rom. 11:22, *he* in the end *glorified . . .*" (*Kept by the Power of God*, p. 103). But this is not what Paul said. What Paul said was: "whom he justified, them [not just some of them] he glorified." Wesley and Marshall must add something to the text to make it mean what they think it means. On this passage, see also n. 7 on p. 84 above.

shown earlier,[12] here designates effectual calling. "Justified" means to be declared righteous in Christ; only those who have true faith are justified. Does Paul now leave room for the possibility that persons who have been effectually called, who have true faith, and who have been justified can still lose their salvation? The answer is a decisive *No!*

> A true Christian cannot be defined in lower terms than one who has been called and justified. And therefore the question is: May one who has been called and justified fall away and come short of eternal salvation? Paul's answer is inescapable—the called and the justified will be glorified.[13]

In considering Paul's teaching on perseverance, we must not forget the triumphant conclusion of Romans 8, in verses 38-39, "For I am convinced that neither death nor life, neither angels nor demons, neither the present nor the future, nor any powers, neither height nor depth, nor anything else in all creation, will be able to separate us from the love of God that is in Christ Jesus our Lord." In these unforgettable words Paul again highlights the security of true believers. If we have genuinely experienced and still do experience God's love in Jesus Christ, the apostle assures us, we shall continue to be kept in that love throughout eternity.

Particularly significant are the words "neither the present nor the future." Sometimes we wonder whether something might happen to us which could take away our fellowship with God in Christ. Life is so uncertain—who knows what tomorrow may bring? What seductive temptation might threaten to sweep us off our feet? What undreamed-of disaster might shake us to our foundations? Paul's answer dissolves our fears: Nothing that can happen to us who are in Christ—nothing that is happening today, and nothing that might happen to us tomorrow—can possibly separate us from the love of God in Christ Jesus. Once we are truly in Christ, we are in him forever!

2. After having thanked God because of the grace given them in Christ Jesus, Paul goes on to say to the Corinthians, in 1 Corinthians 1:8-9, "He will keep you strong to the end, so that you will be blameless in the day of our Lord Jesus Christ. God, who has called you into fellowship with his Son Jesus Christ our Lord, is faithful." Though the members of this congregation had many faults, and were guilty of carnal behavior (3:3), nevertheless Paul assures them that God will keep them strong (or firm or steadfast) until the end—will keep them, in fact, in such a way that they will be blameless on the Day of Judgment. Their continuing steadfastness in the faith, in other words, will finally depend, not on

---

12. See above, pp. 82-84.
13. Murray, *Redemption*, p. 195. It is significant to note that the Canons of Dort call Romans 8:30 the "golden chain of our salvation" (I, Rejection of Errors, Par. 2).

their own strength, but on the sustaining power of God—the God who always remains faithful.

3. In Ephesians 4:30 Paul enjoins his readers, "Do not grieve the Holy Spirit of God, with whom [or in whom; Gk. *en hō*] you were sealed for the day of redemption." Paul is warning the believers to whom he is writing against grieving the Spirit—that is, wounding him by their shameful conduct. Perhaps he has in mind particularly the kind of unwholesome talk he mentioned in the previous verse. But he probably intended to include impure, self-centered, or ungrateful thoughts as well as loveless or dishonest deeds. All such behavior, he is saying, wounds or grieves the Holy Spirit who lives in us as his temple.

Such grieving of the Spirit is all the more reprehensible because by or in that same Spirit we have been sealed for the day of redemption. Sealing stands for security. In New Testament times shepherds often marked their flocks with seals so as to distinguish their own sheep from those of others.[14] This would suggest that when applied to believers, sealing is a mark of ownership.

In 2 Corinthians 1:22 the thought that God has sealed us is paralleled by the thought that God has given us his Spirit "as a deposit, guaranteeing what is to come." In Ephesians 1:13-14 Paul indicates that it is by means of the Spirit that God has sealed us: "Having believed, you were marked in him [Christ] with a seal, the promised Holy Spirit, who is a deposit guaranteeing our inheritance until the redemption of those who are God's possession." In both passages the figure of being sealed with the Spirit is joined to another figure, that of the Spirit as a "deposit guaranteeing" *(arrabōn)* our future redemption. G. Fitzer observes, "The Holy Spirit as the pledge of the inheritance is now the seal with which the believer is marked, appointed and kept for the redemption. It shows that he is God's possession to the day of redemption."[15]

When Paul states, therefore, in Ephesians 4:30 that in or with the Holy Spirit we have been sealed for the day of redemption, he is telling us that though true believers may indeed grieve the Spirit, they will not be ultimately lost. Through the Spirit with whom they are sealed God will again lead them to repentance and amendment of life, as he did in the cases of David and Peter. In the light of New Testament teaching, to be sealed with the Spirit means to be eternally secure. Just as no one can ever snatch us out of the hand of Christ or out of the hand of the Father, so no one can ever break the seal of the Spirit.

4. Another significant Pauline passage is found in Philippians 1:4-6,

---

14. G. Fitzer, *"sphragis,"* TDNT, 7:950, n. 86.
15. Ibid., p. 949.

"I always pray [for you] with joy because of your partnership in the gospel from the first day until now, being confident of this, that he [God] who began a good work in you will carry it on to completion until the day of Christ Jesus." What does Paul mean by "a good work"? He remembers the Philippians' partnership in the gospel with him from the first day he met them until now. But surely the "good work" God has begun in them is more inclusive than this: it must include their union with Christ, their true faith, and their growing Christian joy (see 1:1, 25-26, 29). Paul now expresses his confidence that the God who has begun this good work in them will carry it on to completion[16] until the day of Christ's return. On that day, the day of resurrection, the goal will have been reached.

Paul's confidence in the final perseverance of the saints at Philippi does not ultimately rest on their continued faithfulness to Christ (though he expects this—see v. 27) but on God's faithfulness to them. God does not do things by halves. What man begins he often leaves unfinished (think of Schubert's "Unfinished Symphony"), but what God begins he finishes. And what Paul says about the Philippians we may apply to all in whom God has begun the good work of salvation. Paul's confidence must also be ours:

> The work thou hast for me begun
> shall by thy grace be fully done.

5. In 2 Timothy 4:18 we read, "The Lord will rescue me from every evil attack and will bring me safely to his heavenly kingdom." The verb *sōzō* used here commonly means "to save," in the sense either of salvation from sin or of rescue from physical danger; in this text it means "to keep safe for," or, as in the NIV, "to bring safely into," God's heavenly kingdom. God's kingdom is heavenly in both its origin and its essence. Paul is again expressing his confidence that the one who will keep him secure until the final glorious manifestation of the heavenly kingdom is not himself but God.

6. The doctrine of the perseverance of true believers, however, is taught not only by Paul but also by the author of the Book of Hebrews. In Hebrews 7:23-24 the point is made that, although the ministry of Old Testament priests was limited because their term of office was cut short by death, Christ, since he lives forever, has a permanent priesthood. "Therefore he [Christ] is able to save completely those who come to God through him, because he always lives to intercede for them" (7:25).

Christ is here said to save completely (*eis to panteles*) those who come to God through him. These must be true believers since, as Jesus himself

---

16. Literally, bring it to its goal: *epitelesei*, derived from *telos*, end or goal.

taught us, "No one comes to the Father except through me" (John 14:6). *Eis to panteles* may mean either "completely" or "forever, for all time." The second meaning is illustrated in a third-century papyrus which reports a man selling some property *apo tou nyn eis to panteles* ("from now on forever").[17] If we opt for this second meaning, the passage would be saying that Christ is able to save true believers for all time or forever, since he always lives to intercede for them. If we choose the first meaning, the passage teaches that Christ is able to save his people completely, totally, or "to the uttermost." The words "he is able" are not intended to suggest: "this is something Christ might do but will not necessarily do." The point is rather that since Christ lives forever he is able to do this, and since he is our perfect high priest he does indeed do it.

What is meant by the intercession of Christ? The word here used, *entynchanō*, means "to plead for someone." This pleading is an aspect of Christ's work as priest. Having brought his perfect sacrifice on the cross while he was on earth, and having ascended to heaven, Christ now continually makes intercession for his people on the basis of that sacrifice (see also Rom. 8:34). What is included in Christ's intercession? Christ pleads with the Father that the sins of his people may be forgiven (1 John 2:1). He also prays that his people may be progressively sanctified (John 17:17), that the work they do for God may be accepted by the Father (1 Pet. 2:5), and that they may all at last be with him eternally so that they will be able to see his glory (John 17:24).[18]

Surely Jesus' prayers for his people will be heard. Did he not once say, "Father, I thank you that you have heard me. I knew that you always hear me" (John 11:41-42)? Is it now possible that those for whom our faithful high priest continually intercedes, on the basis of his all-sufficient sacrifice, will yet fail to attain to heavenly glory? The answer must be a resounding *No!*

7. One of the most eloquent biblical passages describing the eternal security of true believers is found in 1 Peter 1:3-5:

> Blessed be the God and Father of our Lord Jesus Christ, who according to His great mercy has caused us to be born again to a living hope through the resurrection of Jesus Christ from the dead, to *obtain* an inheritance *which is* imperishable and undefiled and will not fade away, reserved in heaven for you, who are protected by the power of God through faith for a salvation ready to be revealed in the last time (NASB).

We who are believers, Peter is saying, have become partakers of Christ's new resurrection life. We have been born again to a living hope,

---

17. Moulton and Milligan, VGT, p. 477.
18. On the intercession of Christ, see Berkhof, ST, pp. 400-405.

a hope that will never die, a hope that is "an anchor for the soul" (Heb. 6:19). We have also been born again into a glorious future inheritance which, in contrast to the kinds of inheritance with which we are familiar, will never be destroyed, spoiled, or withered. This inheritance, in fact, has been reserved in heaven for us—not like a hotel reservation which may unexpectedly be cancelled, but permanently and unchangeably. The inheritance of New Testament believers is the fulfillment of the inheritance of the land of Canaan promised to Old Testament believers (see Heb. 11:8-10); it means "the city which has foundations, whose builder and maker is God" (v. 10). In other words, our future inheritance will mean eternal fellowship with God in glorified bodies on the new earth, which will then have merged with heaven (Rev. 21:2).[19]

But Peter says more. Believers have a double security: not only is the inheritance being kept for them; they are also being kept for it, by nothing less than the almighty power of God. The word rendered "protected" in the New American Standard Bible is *phrouroumenous*, from the verb *phroureō*, which means "to guard" or "to keep." The power of God, the strongest power in the universe, is ceaselessly protecting, guarding, and keeping us for the final stage of our salvation, which is ready to be revealed when Christ comes again. And it is significant that it is Peter who writes these words—that same Peter who had learned an unforgettable lesson about the weakness of unaided human nature when he denied that he had ever known Jesus.

We must, however, not overlook the significant words, "through faith." Why were these words added? To make the point that this security is ours only as we continue to grasp it by faith. Earlier we observed that the spiritual security of believers is inseparable from their continued perseverance in the faith. Peter puts it vividly: We are kept by the power of God *through faith*—a living faith, which expresses itself through love (Gal. 5:6). In other words, we may never simply rest on the comfort of God's preservation apart from the continuing exercise of faith.

But this fact does not overthrow the doctrine of the perseverance of true believers. The inheritance we look for, Peter says, is *reserved* for us in heaven, and will *never fade away*. What we continue to grasp by faith is that it is God who keeps us true to him. And even that faith, as we saw earlier,[20] both in its beginning and in its continuation, is a gift of God. God preserves us, therefore, by enabling us to continue in our faith. Our

19. See Chapter 20, "The New Earth," in my *The Bible and the Future* (Grand Rapids: Eerdmans, 1979); also G. C. Berkouwer, "The New Earth," *The Return of Christ*, trans. James Van Oosterom (Grand Rapids: Eerdmans, 1972), pp. 211-34.

20. See above, pp. 143-45.

perseverance is ultimately grounded not in ourselves but in God; we are kept, not by the power of man, but by the power of God. To him be all the praise!

> No other work save Thine,
>   No other blood will do;
> No strength save that which is divine
>   Can bear me safely through.

OBJECTIONS CONSIDERED

The Doctrine of Perseverance Leads to Complacency and Moral Laxity

This is an objection commonly voiced by those who reject the doctrine. It is said that those who believe that their perseverance in the faith is guaranteed by God will tend to become careless about the way they live, to stop fighting against sin, and to become self-centered, worldly, and lukewarm.

It is, of course, true that this doctrine could be misconstrued in such a way as to lead to complacency or moral and spiritual laxity. If one would hold this doctrine in a speculative and abstract way, one might imagine that he or she could rest in the comfort of this teaching without daily battling against sin, unbelief, and worldliness. But this would be accepting a caricature of the doctrine, not the doctrine itself. The Scriptures constantly warn us against such complacency. "Let anyone who thinks that he stands take heed lest he fall" (1 Cor. 10:12, RSV).

As we have noted, the Bible teaches that God does not preserve us apart from our watchfulness, prayer, and persevering faith. The expression "once saved, always saved" is therefore not an accurate way of stating the doctrine of the perseverance of true believers. Such an expression could easily be understood to mean "once saved, always saved" regardless of how we live, and such a notion is clearly contrary to Scripture. On this point I quite agree with Robert Shank when he says,

> There is no warrant in the New Testament for that strange at-ease-in-Zion definition of perseverance which assures Christians that perseverance is inevitable and relieves them of the necessity of deliberately persevering in faith, encouraging them to place confidence in some past act or experience.[21]

The doctrine of perseverance has to do with true believers. And a true believer, one in whom the Holy Spirit dwells and works, desires to live for God, in gratitude for the priceless gift of salvation. If there is no such desire in a person's heart, such a person is not a true believer.

21. *Life in the Son,* p. 64.

John L. Dagg, a Baptist author, has put it well:

They who understand the doctrine of perseverance to imply that God's people will obtain the crown without the struggle [against sin], totally mistake the matter. The doctrine is, that God's people will persevere in the struggle; and to suppose that they will obtain the crown without doing so, is to contradict the doctrine. It is a wretched and fatal perversion of the doctrine, if men conclude that, having been once converted, they will be saved, whatever may be their course of life.[22]

The Doctrine of Perseverance Is Contrary to Scripture

Three types of Scripture passages are commonly adduced as militating against the doctrine of the perseverance of true believers:

Exhortations to continue in the faith

Passages such as these are commonly cited: "He who stands firm [or endures] to the end will be saved" (Matt. 10:22); "If you continue in my word, you are truly my disciples" (John 8:31, RSV); "If a man remains in me and I in him, he will bear much fruit" (John 15:5); "Be on your guard; stand firm in the faith" (1 Cor. 16:13); "For we share in Christ, if only we hold our first confidence firm to the end" (Heb. 3:14, RSV); "Be faithful, even to the point of death, and I will give you the crown of life" (Rev. 2:10); "Hold on to what you have, so that no one will take your crown" (Rev. 3:11).

Do passages of this sort, and others like them, overthrow the doctrine of perseverance? No, they do not. But they warn us against a misunderstanding of this teaching. They underscore our responsibility in our perseverance. They tell us that it is only as we prayerfully endure to the end, hold fast to what we have, continue in Christ's word, and remain in Christ that we can enjoy the blessing of perseverance. And they also remind us that God, in preserving us, uses means. Those means include the exhortations, threatenings, and promises of his word.

We may find an illustration of the way God uses means to preserve people in the story of Paul's shipwreck. When it looked as if the ship in which they were sailing would be wrecked by the storm, Paul told the others on the ship that an angel had informed him that none of them would be lost. Sometime later, as the ship was approaching land, the sailors tried to escape in the lifeboat. But Paul told the centurion, "Unless these men stay with the ship, you cannot be saved" (Acts 27:22, 31). The certainty of deliverance did not rule out the indispensability of the means.

22. *Manual of Theology* (1857; Harrisonburg, VA: Gano Books, 1982), p. 144.

Warnings against apostasy

Under this heading passages like the following are quoted: "Once you were alienated from God . . . but now he has reconciled you by Christ's physical body through death to present you holy in his sight, without blemish and free from accusation—if you continue in your faith, established and firm, not moved from the hope held out in the gospel" (Col. 1:21-23); "We must pay more careful attention, therefore, to what we have heard, so that we do not drift away" (Heb. 2:1); "Therefore, dear friends, since you already know this, be on your guard so that you may not be carried away by the error of lawless men and fall from your secure position" (2 Pet. 3:17).

The comment made above also applies here: God keeps his people from falling away through means, and these means include warnings against apostasy. By giving heed to warnings of this sort believers persevere.

Keeping in mind the passages just cited, we may put it this way: The true believer will reveal the genuineness of his or her faith by continuing in the faith (Col. 1:23), by not drifting away from what has been heard (Heb. 2:1), and by neither being carried away by error nor falling from his or her secure position (2 Pet. 3:17). These verses again emphasize the responsibility of believers in their perseverance. 2 Peter 3:18, in fact, expresses the same warning in positive terms: "But grow in the grace and knowledge of our Lord and Savior Jesus Christ."

G. C. Berkouwer aptly describes the relationship between the doctrine of perseverance and the warnings found in Scripture:

> The doctrine of the perseverance of the saints can never become an *a priori* guarantee in the life of believers which would enable them to get along without admonitions and warnings. . . . For the correct understanding of the correlation between faith and perseverance, it is precisely these admonitions that are significant, and they enable us to understand better the nature of perseverance.[23]

Cases of actual apostasy

Some of the passages cited under this heading contain indications that the individuals involved never had true faith. In the Parable of the Sower, for example, Jesus, describing a hearer who falls away when tested or tempted, qualifies the faith of this hearer as being only temporal: "Those on the rock are the ones who receive the word with joy when they hear it, but they have no root. They believe for a while, but in the time of testing they fall away" (Luke 8:13). Whereas true faith endures to the end, these hearers believe only "for a while" *(pros kairon)*.

---

23. *Faith and Perseverance,* trans. Robert D. Knudsen (Grand Rapids: Eerdmans, 1958), pp. 110-11.

John pictures a similar situation: "They [the antichrists described in the previous verse] went out from us, but they did not really belong to us. For if they had belonged to us, they would have remained with us; but their going showed that none of them belonged to us" (1 John 2:19). The departure of these people, John is saying, revealed that they never really belonged to us in the first place. Their faith was obviously not genuine.

The Bible clearly teaches that there always have been and still are those who seem to belong to the fellowship of God's people but are not true believers. In Old Testament times, as Paul points out, not all who were descended from Israel were true, believing Israelites (Rom. 9:6). Among those who are at least outwardly associated with the church in New Testament times, there is chaff among the wheat (Matt. 3:12), and there are non-fruitbearing branches on the vine (John 15:2).[24] There are also those who have only a form of godliness but who deny its power (2 Tim. 3:5), who claim to be apostles but are not (Rev. 2:2), and who have a reputation for being alive but are dead (Rev. 3:1). The problem is, we do not always know who these people are; we cannot read the heart. If some whom we had thought to be true Christians do become apostate, we must assume either that the Lord will still bring them back to his fellowship, or that their faith was not genuine. For, as the Bible teaches, those who have true faith will persevere, not in their own strength, but through the power of God.

There is a passage that speaks of "falling away from grace." In Galatians 5:4 Paul says, "You are severed from Christ, you who would be justified by the law; you have fallen away from grace" (RSV). However, Paul is not speaking here about the possibility that true believers may lose their faith, but about a disastrous doctrinal error. John Murray's comment on the passage is helpful:

> Paul is here dealing not with the question as to whether or not a believer may fall out of the favour of God and finally perish but with defection from the pure doctrine of justification by grace as opposed to justification by works of law. What Paul is saying in effect is that if we seek to be justified by the works of the law in any way or degree whatsoever then we have abandoned or fallen away entirely from justification by grace.[25]

Some New Testament texts do indeed mention a "falling away from the faith." In the New American Standard Bible 1 Timothy 4:1 reads as follows: "But the Spirit explicitly says that in later times some will fall away

---

24. The words "every branch in me that bears no fruit" do not imply that someone can truly be in Christ without bearing fruit, or that genuine believers can fall away. This figure is part of the imagery of the cultivation of the vine. True believers remain in Christ and thus bear much fruit (v. 5).

25. *Redemption*, p. 194.

from the faith." The expression "fall away" translates the Greek verb *apostēsontai*, a word from which our English term "apostasy" is derived. Instead of "fall away" the Revised Standard Version has "depart from the faith," and the New International Version gives "abandon the faith." The word "faith," however, as is common in the Pastoral Epistles, is here used in the objective sense, as meaning the truth which is believed *(fides quae creditur)* rather than the act which appropriates Christ and his merits *(fides qua creditur).* What Paul is saying here is that in later times many will fall away from a profession of the Christian religion. Such a defection would not imply that these defectors had true faith to begin with. In the same way we are to understand a passage like 1 Timothy 6:10, "Some people, eager for money, have wandered from the faith."

In John 17:12, in Jesus' so-called High-Priestly Prayer, we hear him praying, "While I was with them [the disciples], I kept them in thy name, which thou hast given me; I have guarded them, and none of them is lost but the son of perdition, that the scripture might be fulfilled" (RSV). This passage is often quoted by those who do not accept the doctrine of perseverance to prove that even persons who are kept and guarded by Christ can perish or be eternally lost.

Jesus here calls Judas a "son of perdition"—that is, one doomed to perdition. The purpose of Christ's keeping and guarding, however, is to keep his own from perdition. Repeatedly Jesus assures us that those whom he guards cannot perish or be lost. John 6:39 and 10:28 have already been discussed. In the very prayer with which we are dealing Jesus says, "You granted him [the Son] authority over all people that he might give eternal life to all those you have given him" (John 17:2), and also, "Father, I want those you have given me to be with me where I am, and to see my glory" (v. 24). Did Jesus guard Judas in this way? If this should be so, the entire text would make no sense: "I guarded Judas so that he would not perish, but he did perish."

Judas's defection came as no surprise to Jesus. Earlier Jesus had said to his disciples, "There are some of you who do not believe." And the evangelist added, "For Jesus had known from the beginning which of them did not believe and who would betray him" (John 6:64). In the passage now under consideration Jesus says that Judas would be lost "that the scripture might be fulfilled." Christ was not here suggesting that Judas was not responsible for his unbelief, but was indicating that Judas's unbelief and subsequent perdition, having been predicted by Scripture, had been included in the plan of God. Jesus, therefore, far from implying that he had tried to guard Judas from perdition but had been unsuccessful, affirms that Judas's unbelief happened so that the Scriptures might be fulfilled.

I conclude, therefore, that the "but" *(ei mē)* of John 17:12 describes an exception, not just to the "not being lost" but also to the keeping and guarding. Those whom Jesus keeps and guards are all saved, without exception. But Judas was not included among those whom Jesus kept in the Father's name.[26] The Bible nowhere teaches that Judas had a true and living faith.

Probably the most difficult passage under this heading is Hebrews 6:4-6:

> (4) It is impossible for those who have once been enlightened, who have tasted the heavenly gift, who have shared in the Holy Spirit, (5) who have tasted the goodness of the word of God and the powers of the coming age, (6) if they fall away, to be brought back to repentance, because to their loss they are crucifying the Son of God all over again and subjecting him to public disgrace.

At first reading it seems as if the people here described must have been true believers who fell away. Grant R. Osborne, in fact, in commenting on this passage, puts it as strongly as this: "There is no more powerful or detailed description of the true Christian in the New Testament."[27]

Others, however, have a different interpretation. John Owen, in his commentary on Hebrews, gives four reasons why the people here described (assuming that they are actual people, and not just hypothetical cases) are not true believers: (1) No mention is made of their faith. (2) Despite all that is said about them, they are not said to have been regenerated, sanctified, or to be sons of God. (3) They are compared, in verse 8, to land that produces thorns and thistles, and that is therefore ready to be burned. (4) They are distinguished from true believers on the following counts: (a) the author says to those whom he is addressing, "We are confident of better things in your case—things that accompany salvation" (v. 9); (b) he ascribes to his readers a "love you have shown him [God] as you have helped his people and continue to help them" (v. 10), while attributing no such work of love to those who have apostatized; (c) he assures his readers of their preservation in the faith on account of the justice of God (v. 10) and on account of the unchangeable nature of God's purpose (vv. 17-18), though this preservation will not take place apart from their own diligence (vv. 11-12). In fact, the very description of hope as an anchor of the soul in verse 19 strongly underscores the security of the true believer. For of what value is an anchor which does not hold?

To Owen's comments I would add a reference to Hebrews 7:25, a pas-

---

26. This thought is confirmed by what Jesus said about Judas in John 6:65, "This is why I told you that no one can come to me unless the Father has enabled him."

27. "Soteriology in the Epistle to the Hebrews," in *Grace Unlimited,* ed. Clark H. Pinnock, p. 149.

sage we looked at earlier in this chapter: "Therefore he [Christ] is able to save completely [or forever] those who come to God through him, because he always lives to intercede for them." Here we have a description, in the next chapter of this epistle, of the "true Christian." A true Christian, the author of Hebrews affirms, is someone for whom Christ, the ever-living high priest, is always interceding, in such a way as to save him or her *completely* and *forever*. Is it then conceivable that the author who wrote these words could possibly imagine that the people described in 6:4-6 were genuine Christians — persons who had truly "come to God through Christ," and for whom Christ was continually interceding?

The real difficulties of the passage, however, concern, first, the meaning of the various phrases used in verses 4 to 5 to describe these people. Those who teach that true believers can fall away interpret them as describing the fruits of a true faith. In the light of the context, however, as we have seen, this cannot be the right interpretation.

F. F. Bruce suggests that "once enlightened" (v. 4) may refer to the baptism of these people, since in the second century baptism was often called "enlightenment."[28] Even if we do not accept this interpretation, however, we have no particular difficulty here, since the people described in this passage had obviously been enlightened by the gospel.

"Tasted the heavenly gift." Bruce here sees a reference to the Lord's Supper.[29] This is a possible interpretation. These words could also refer to the spiritual blessings for which Christianity stands. These people had had a taste of these blessings, as for many years they had associated themselves with the people of God.

"Have shared in the Holy Spirit." The clue to these words, I believe, is found in 10:29, where we read about a man who has "insulted the Spirit of grace" by profaning and making light of the spiritual blessings he had received. If so, he must have had some contact with the Holy Spirit. To "have shared in the Holy Spirit," therefore, can be interpreted as meaning that these people had experienced a certain working of the Spirit which they nevertheless rejected. We may think in this connection of the sin against the Holy Spirit described in Matthew 12:31-32.

"Have tasted the goodness of the word of God" (v. 5). These people had heard the word of God and tasted its goodness, but had never fully accepted it.

"And the powers of the coming age [or age to come]." Here we think of certain miraculous signs, which indicated that "the age to come" was al-

28. F. F. Bruce, *The Epistle to the Hebrews* (NICNT; Grand Rapids: Eerdmans, 1964), p. 120.

29. Ibid., pp. 120-21.

ready present. In 2:3-4 we read that the message of the gospel was confirmed by those who heard the Lord, "while God also bore witness by signs and wonders and various miracles and by gifts of the Holy Spirit distributed according to his will" (RSV). The word here translated "miracles" *(dynameis)* is the same word which is rendered "powers" in 6:5. These miracles or powers had been tasted by the people described in chapter 6. They had seen amazing miracles happen—and yet they fell away. We think of Jesus' words about people who had not only witnessed miracles but had even performed them, to whom he will say, on the day of days, "Away from me, you evildoers; I never knew you!" (Matt. 7:22-23).

The other major difficulty concerns the meaning of "it is impossible [for those described in these verses] . . . if they fall away, to be brought back to repentance." The Greek has *palin anakainizein eis metanoian,* "renew again to repentance." These words at first glance seem to give the impression that the people here referred to were once repentant, but now have lost that true repentance and cannot be renewed in it. If this were the right interpretation, the doctrine of the perseverance of true believers would indeed be disproved.

True repentance, however, is spoken of in Scripture as being unto life (Acts 11:18), for the forgiveness of sins (Mark 1:4), and as leading to salvation (2 Cor. 7:10). In agreement with the prevailing testimony of the New Testament, therefore, the repentance which the word *again* implies that these people once displayed cannot have been genuine. It must have been a mere outward profession of repentance, comparable to the temporal faith described in Luke 8:13.

Consider again what the author of Hebrews says he is going to do. He says that he is not going to lay again a foundation of repentance from acts that lead to death and of faith in God (6:1). We have done this once, the author continues, and do not need to do it again. In your case (the addressees of this epistle, who are assumed to be believers) the laying again of that foundation is unnecessary. In the case of those who were once enlightened and then fell away, however, the laying again of that foundation is utterly useless. For it is impossible to renew them again to repentance. Once we, their spiritual leaders, led them to what we thought was a profession of faith and repentance; but by now it is obvious that that profession was not sincere. Now they have gone beyond the point where even an outward profession of repentance is possible.

We find a somewhat similar passage in Hebrews 10:26-29, the first two verses of which read, "If we deliberately keep on sinning after we have received the knowledge of the truth, no sacrifice for sins is left, but only a fearful expectation of judgment. . . ." Those here pictured had obviously been instructed in the Christian faith, but had turned away from even an outward adherence to Christian truth. For them there is no possibility of forgiveness, but only a "fearful expectation of judgment." Most interpreters understand these words as a description of the so-called "unpardonable sin."[30] But can a true believer commit this sin? Or, in different words, can a true believer "fall away from the living God" (Heb. 3:12, RSV)? Again, in the light of Hebrews 7:25, the answer must be No.

We look, finally, at a passage from Peter's second epistle:

> If they [the false teachers described in the preceding verses] have escaped the corruption of the world by knowing our Lord and Savior Jesus Christ and are again entangled in it and overcome, they are worse off at the end than they were at the beginning. It would have been better for them not to have known the way of righteousness, than to have known it and then to turn their backs on the sacred command that was passed on to them (2 Pet. 2:20-21).

Here again we are looking at people who have had some knowledge of Christ and who have known the way of righteousness. But they have again become entangled in the corruption of the world and have now turned their backs on God's laws—so much so that, as Peter says, they are now worse off than they were at the beginning. Were these men ever true believers? Was their knowledge of Christ ever a true and saving knowledge? There is no indication in the text that they were ever true believers. Besides, earlier in this epistle Peter had described true believers as those who, by adding to their faith goodness, knowledge, self-control, perseverance, godliness, brotherly kindness, and love, will make their calling and election sure, adding the promise, "If you do these things, you will never fall" (2 Pet. 1:5-11). And in his first epistle, as we have seen, the same author had said that true believers not only have an inheritance that can never perish but are being shielded or guarded by God's power through faith until the coming of the salvation ready to be revealed in the last time (1 Pet. 1:3-5). Is it not obvious that those described in 2 Peter 2:20-21 do not fit into these descriptions?

THE CANONS OF DORT ON PERSEVERANCE

No Protestant creed has a better or more complete statement of the doctrine of the perseverance of true believers than the Canons of Dort (1618-19). Set forth as the Fifth Main Point (or Head) of Doctrine, this statement is not only clear and balanced, but it is also comforting and pastorally helpful.

---

30. On the unpardonable sin, see G. C. Berkouwer, "The Sin Against the Holy Spirit," *Sin*, trans. Philip C. Holtrop (Grand Rapids: Eerdmans, 1971), pp. 323-53.

After the first two articles of this Fifth Point have described the inclination of believers to fall into daily sins of weakness, Article 3 states that the converted, if left to their own resources, would not be able to remain standing in the grace of God. "But," the article continues, "God is faithful, mercifully strengthening them in the grace once conferred on them and powerfully preserving them in it to the end."[31]

Article 4 goes on to indicate that true believers may indeed fall into serious sins if they fail to watch and pray. But Article 6 affirms that

> God, who is rich in mercy, according to his unchangeable purpose of election does not take his Holy Spirit from his own completely, even when they fall grievously. Neither does he let them fall down so far that they forfeit the grace of adoption and the state of justification, or commit the sin which leads to death (the sin against the Holy Spirit), and plunge themselves, entirely forsaken by him, into eternal ruin.

In Article 7 the Canons maintain that God will by his Word and Spirit certainly and effectually renew to repentance those of his people who have fallen into serious sins. Then follows Article 8, which underscores the fact that the preservation of God's people is due entirely to God's grace:

> So it is not by their own merits or strength but by God's undeserved mercy that they [true believers] neither forfeit faith and grace totally nor remain in their downfalls to the end and are lost. With respect to themselves this not only easily could happen, but also undoubtedly would happen; but with respect to God it cannot possibly happen, since his plan cannot be changed, his promise cannot fail, the calling according to his purpose cannot be revoked, the merit of Christ as well as his interceding and preserving cannot be nullified, and the sealing of the Holy Spirit can neither be invalidated nor wiped out.

It would be hard to compose a more beautiful statement of this doctrine. Once again the thought is repeated that the perseverance of true believers is due not to their merits or strength but only to God's undeserved mercy. And once again the real heartbeat of this doctrine comes home to us: God's unchanging faithfulness to his promises. This is what we lean on—weak, changeable, and fickle sinners that we are—when we profess to believe in the perseverance of God's true people.

It should further be observed, however, that the Canons of Dort do not in any way support the erroneous understanding of this doctrine that some seem to have: namely, "Once saved, always saved, regardless of how we live." Articles 12 and 13 make clear that the assurance of our preser-

---

31. Quotations from the Canons of Dort are from the 1986 text.

vation by God, far from being an occasion for carelessness in living or laxity in morals, is actually an incentive to godliness:

> This assurance of perseverance, however, so far from making true believers proud and carnally self-assured, is rather the true root of humility, of childlike respect, of genuine godliness, of endurance in every conflict, of fervent prayers, of steadfastness in crossbearing and in confessing the truth, and of well-founded joy in God. Reflecting on this benefit provides an incentive to a serious and continual practice of thanksgiving and good works, as is evident from the testimonies of Scripture and the examples of the saints.
>
> Neither does the renewed confidence of perseverance produce immorality or lack of concern for godliness in those put back on their feet after a fall, but it produces a much greater concern to observe carefully the ways of the Lord which he prepared in advance.

A SUMMARIZING STATEMENT

The doctrine of the perseverance of true believers is one of the most comforting teachings of Scripture. We learn from it that God by his power keeps his people from falling away from him, that Christ will never permit anyone to snatch them out of his hand, and that the Holy Spirit seals them for the day of redemption. Our heavenly Father holds us securely in his grasp; that is our ultimate comfort in life and death. We rest finally not on our hold of God but on God's hold of us.

Yet this doctrine also urges us to persevere in the faith—and this is our challenge. We can only persevere through God's strength and by his grace. But to teach this doctrine in such a way as to present only its comfort and not its challenge, only the security and not the exhortation, is to teach it one-sidedly. And the Bible constantly warns us against such one-sidedness.

We remember how Paul, despite his ringing affirmations of the preservation of believers by God, says about himself in 1 Corinthians 9:26-27, "I do not run like a man running aimlessly; I do not fight like a man beating the air. No, I beat my body and make it my slave so that after I have preached to others, I myself will not be disqualified for the prize." Only as he thus continued to discipline himself did Paul feel justified in claiming his spiritual security in Christ. He did not dare to claim this blessing while being careless and indolent in his daily battle against sin. And neither may we.

In 2 Corinthians 13:5 Paul, as it were, fixes his piercing eyes upon us as he says, "Examine yourselves to see whether you are in the faith; test yourselves." How can we know that we are in the faith? We can know this only from our continuation in the life of faith, our perseverance, our standing firm to the end. John Murray has put it well: "We may entertain the faith of our security in Christ only as we persevere in faith and holiness to the end."[32]

The doctrine of the perseverance of true believers, therefore, is both a comfort and a challenge. But the challenge is based on the comfort. We can be certain that we shall persevere to the end only because God has promised to enable us to do so. And so we rest in him, for time and eternity, knowing that he will never let us go.

> I've found a friend, oh such a friend,
>   He loved me ere I knew him;
> He drew me with the cords of love
>   And thus he bound me to him.
>
> And round my heart still closely twine
>   Those ties which nought can sever;
> For I am his and he is mine,
>   Forever and forever.[33]

32. *Redemption*, p. 193.

33. On the doctrine of perseverance, in addition to sources already referred to, see Loraine Boettner, "The Perseverance of the Saints," in *The Reformed Doctrine of Predestination* (Grand Rapids: Eerdmans, 1932), pp. 182-201; Robert Gromacki, *Is Salvation Forever?* (Chicago: Moody Press, 1973); H. A. Ironside, *The Eternal Security of the Believer* (Neptune, NJ: Loizeaux, 1923); Edwin H. Palmer, "Perseverance of the Saints," in *The Five Points of Calvinism* (Grand Rapids: Baker, 1972), pp. 68-80; and Arthur Pink, *Eternal Security* (Grand Rapids: Baker, 1974).

Bibliography

Augustine. *On the Predestination of the Saints*. In *Nicene and Post-Nicene Fathers*, ed. Philip Schaff, First Series. Vol. 5. Grand Rapids: Eerdmans, 1956.

Adair, James R., and Ted Miller, eds. *We Found Our Way Out*. Grand Rapids: Baker, 1964.

Barth, Karl. *Church Dogmatics*, Vols. I/2; IV/2. Edinburgh: T. & T. Clark, 1956.

Barth, Markus. *Justification*. Trans. A. N. Woodruff III. Grand Rapids: Eerdmans, 1971.

Bavinck, Herman. *The Certainty of Faith*. Trans. Harry der Nederlanden. (1901) St. Catharines: Paideia Press, 1980.

_____. *Gereformeerde Dogmatiek* (abbr. *Dogmatiek*). 3rd ed. 4 vols. Kampen: Kok, 1918.

_____. *Our Reasonable Faith*. Trans. Henry Zylstra. (1909) Grand Rapids: Eerdmans, 1956.

_____. *Roeping en Wedergeboorte*. Kampen: Zalsman, 1903.

Baxter, J. Sidlow. *Divine Healing of the Body*. Grand Rapids: Zondervan, 1979.

_____. *A New Call to Holiness*. Grand Rapids: Zondervan, 1973.

_____. *Our High Calling*. Grand Rapids: Zondervan, 1967.

Belgic Confession (1561), new translation adopted by the 1985 Synod of the Christian Reformed Church. CRC Publications, 2850 Kalamazoo Ave., SE, Grand Rapids, MI.

Berkhof, Hendrikus. *Christian Faith*. Rev. ed. Trans. Sierd Woudstra. Grand Rapids: Eerdmans, 1986.

_____. *The Doctrine of the Holy Spirit*. Richmond, VA: John Knox, 1964.

Berkhof, Louis. *The Assurance of Faith*. Grand Rapids: Smitter, 1928.

_____. *Systematic Theology* (abbr. ST). (1938) Rev. and enl. ed. Grand Rapids: Eerdmans, 1941.

Berkouwer, G. C. *Conflict with Rome*. Trans. David H. Freeman. Grand Rapids: Baker, 1958.

_____. "Election and the Certainty of Salvation." In *Divine Election*. Trans. Hugo Bekker. Grand Rapids: Eerdmans, 1960.

_____. *Faith and Justification*. Trans. Lewis B. Smedes. Grand Rapids: Eerdmans, 1954.

_____. *Faith and Perseverance*. Trans. Robert D. Knudsen. Grand Rapids: Eerdmans, 1958.

_____. *Faith and Sanctification*. Trans. John Vriend. Grand Rapids: Eerdmans, 1952.

_____. *Man: The Image of God.* Trans. Dirk W. Jellema. Grand Rapids: Eerdmans, 1962.

_____. *The Return of Christ.* Trans. James Van Oosterom. Grand Rapids: Eerdmans, 1972.

_____. *Sin.* Trans. Philip C. Holtrop. Grand Rapids: Eerdmans, 1971.

_____. *The Work of Christ.* Trans. C. Lambregtse. Grand Rapids: Eerdmans, 1965.

Best, W. E. *Regeneration and Conversion.* Grand Rapids: Baker, 1975.

Bittlinger, Arnold. *Gifts and Ministries.* Trans. Clara K. Dyck. Grand Rapids: Eerdmans, 1973.

Boehl, Edward. *The Reformed Doctrine of Justification.* Trans. C. H. Riedesel. (1890) Grand Rapids: Eerdmans, 1946.

Boettner, Loraine. "The Perseverance of the Saints." In *The Reformed Doctrine of Predestination.* Grand Rapids: Eerdmans, 1932.

Bonar, Horatius. *God's Way of Holiness.* London: Nisbet, 1886.

Bonhoeffer, Dietrich. *Life Together.* Trans. John W. Doberstein. New York: Harper and Row, 1954.

Brakel, W. à. *Redelijke Godsdienst.* Ed. J. H. Donner. 3 vols. Leiden: D. Donner, 1893.

Bromiley, G. W. "Conversion," ISBE, 1:768-70.

Brown, Colin. *That You May Believe.* Grand Rapids: Eerdmans, 1986.

Bruner, Frederick D. *A Theology of the Holy Spirit.* Grand Rapids: Eerdmans, 1970.

Brunner, Emil. *The Christian Doctrine of the Church, Faith, and the Consummation.* Trans. D. Cairns. Philadelphia: Westminster, 1960.

Buchanan, James. *The Doctrine of Justification.* (1867) Grand Rapids: Baker, 1955.

Bultmann, Rudolf. "The Concept of Life in the New Testament," TDNT, 2:861-72.

Burkhardt, Helmut. *The Biblical Doctrine of Regeneration.* Trans. O. R. Johnston. Downers Grove: InterVarsity, 1978.

Calvin, John. "Antidote to the Canons of the Council of Trent." In *Tracts and Treatises in Defense of the Reformed Faith.* Trans. Henry Beveridge. Vol. 3. (1851) Grand Rapids: Eerdmans, 1958.

Calvin, John. *Commentaries on the Old Testament.* 30 vols. (1843-55) Grand Rapids: Eerdmans, 1948-50.

_____. *Institutes of the Christian Religion* (abbr. *Inst.*). Ed. John T. McNeill. Trans. Ford Lewis Battles. 2 vols. Philadelphia: Westminster, 1960.

_____. *New Testament Commentaries.* Ed. David W. Torrance and Thomas F. Torrance. 12 vols. Grand Rapids: Eerdmans, 1963-73.

Canons of Dort (1618-19), new translation adopted by the 1986 Synod of the Christian Reformed Church. CRC Publications, 2850 Kalamazoo Ave., SE, Grand Rapids, MI.

Chafer, Lewis Sperry. *Systematic Theology.* 8 vols. Dallas: Dallas Seminary Press, 1948.

Chamberlain, William D. *The Meaning of Repentance.* Philadelphia: Westminster, 1943.

Charnock, Stephen. *The Doctrine of Regeneration.* (1840) Grand Rapids: Baker, 1975.

The Church Teaches, Documents of the Church in English Translation. By John F. Clarkson et al. St. Louis: B. Herder, 1955.

Citron, Bernhard. *The New Birth*. Edinburgh: University Press, 1951.

Clarke, Adam. *The New Testament of Our Lord and Savior Jesus Christ*. 2 vols. New York: Mason and Lane, 1837.

Conn, Harvey M. "Theologies of Liberation." In *Tensions in Contemporary Theology*. Ed. S. N. Gundry and A. F. Johnson. Rev. ed. Chicago: Moody, 1979, pp. 327-434.

Cook, James. "The Concept of Adoption in the Theology of Paul." In James Cook, ed., *Saved by Hope*. Grand Rapids: Eerdmans, 1978.

Coppes, Leonard J. *Are Five Points Enough? The Ten Points of Calvinism*. Manassas, VA: Reformation Educational Foundation, 1980.

Crabtree, Arthur B. *The Restored Relationship. A Study in Justification and Reconciliation*. Valley Forge: Judson, 1963.

Dabney, Robert L. *Lectures in Systematic Theology*. (1878) Grand Rapids: Zondervan, 1972.

Dagg, John L. *Manual of Theology*. (1857) Harrisonburg, VA: Gano Books, 1982.

De Ferrari, T. M. "Baptism (Theology of)." In *The New Catholic Encyclopedia*. New York: McGraw Hill, 1967, 2:62-68.

Deissmann, G. Adolf. *Die Neutestamentliche Formel "In Christo Jesu."* Marburg: N. G. Elwert, 1892.

De Jong, Alexander C. *The Well-Meant Gospel Offer: The Views of H. Hoeksema and K. Schilder*. Franeker: T. Wever, 1954.

Dieter, Melvin E., et al. *Five Views on Sanctification*. Grand Rapids: Zondervan, 1987.

Dodd, C. H. *The Bible and the Greeks*. London: Hodder and Stoughton, 1935.

Dowey, Edward A., Jr. *The Knowledge of God in Calvin's Theology*. New York: Columbia University Press, 1952.

Dunn, James D. G. *Baptism in the Holy Spirit*. Naperville, IL: Allenson, 1970.

Ehrlich, Rudolph J. *Rome: Opponent or Partner?* London: Lutterworth, 1965.

England, R. G. *Justification Today: The Roman Catholic and Anglican Debate*. Oxford: Latimer House, 1979.

Erickson, Millard J. *Christian Theology*. 3 vols. Grand Rapids: Baker, 1983-85.

Evangelical Dictionary of Theology (abbr. EDT). Ed. Walter A. Elwell. Grand Rapids: Baker, 1984.

Flew, Robert N. *The Idea of Perfection in Christian Theology*. London: Oxford, 1934.

Gaffin, Richard B., Jr. *Perspectives on Pentecost*. Phillipsburg, NJ: Presbyterian and Reformed, 1979.

Girod, Gordon. *The Way of Salvation*. Grand Rapids: Baker, 1960.

Godwin, Johnnie C. *What It Means to be Born Again*. Nashville: Broadman Press, 1977.

Graafland, C. *De Zekerheid van het Geloof*. Wageningen: Veenman, 1961.

Green, Michael. *I Believe in the Holy Spirit*. Grand Rapids: Eerdmans, 1975.

Grider, J. Kenneth. *Entire Sanctification*. Kansas City: Beacon Hill, 1980.

Gromacki, Robert. *Is Salvation Forever?* Chicago: Moody, 1973.

Grounds, Vernon C. "The Postulate of Paradox," *Bulletin of the Evangelical Theological Society*, Vol. 7, No. 1 (Winter 1964), pp. 3-21.

Grudem, Wayne A. *The Gift of Prophecy in 1 Corinthians*. Washington, D.C.: University Press of America, 1983.

Gruss, Edmond C. *We Left Jehovah's Witnesses*. Philadelphia: Presbyterian and Reformed, 1974.

Hamilton, Neill Q. "The Holy Spirit and Eschatology in Paul," *Scottish Journal of Theology Occasional Papers No. 6*. Edinburgh: Oliver and Boyd, 1957.

Harrison, Everett F. "Life," ISBE, 3:129-34.

Heidelberg Catechism (1563), new translation adopted by the 1975 Synod of the Christian Reformed Church. CRC Publications, 2850 Kalamazoo Ave., SE, Grand Rapids, MI.

Hillis, Don W. *Tongues, Healing, and You*. Grand Rapids: Baker, 1969.

Hills, A. M. *Fundamental Christian Theology*. 2 vols. (1931) Salem, OH: Schmul, 1980.

Hodge, Archibald A. *Evangelical Theology*. (1890) Carlisle, PA: Banner of Truth, 1976.

Hodge, Caspar Wistar. "Imputation," ISBE, 2:812-15.

Hodge, Charles. *Systematic Theology*. 3 vols. (1871) Grand Rapids: Eerdmans, 1940.

Hoekema, Anthony A. *The Bible and the Future*. Grand Rapids: Eerdmans, 1979.

_____. *The Christian Looks at Himself*. Grand Rapids: Eerdmans, 1975.

_____. *Created in God's Image*. Grand Rapids: Eerdmans, 1986.

_____. *Holy Spirit Baptism*. Grand Rapids: Eerdmans, 1972.

_____. "Karl Barth's Doctrine of Sanctification." Inaugural Address. Grand Rapids: Calvin Theological Seminary, 1965.

_____. "Two Types of Preaching," *Reformed Journal*, Vol. 5, No. 5 (May 1955), pp. 5-7.

_____. *What About Tongue-Speaking?* Grand Rapids: Eerdmans, 1966.

Hoeksema, Herman. *The Protestant Reformed Church in America*. 2nd ed. Grand Rapids, 1947.

_____. *Reformed Dogmatics*. Grand Rapids: The Reformed Free Publishing Association, 1966.

_____. "Whosoever Will." Grand Rapids: Eerdmans, 1945.

Hoyt, Herman A. *Expository Messages on the New Birth*. Grand Rapids: Baker, 1961.

Hulme, William E. *The Dynamics of Sanctification*. Minneapolis: Augsburg, 1966.

International Standard Bible Encyclopedia (abbr. ISBE). Rev. ed. Ed. Geoffrey W. Bromiley. 4 vols. Grand Rapids: Eerdmans, 1979-88.

Ironside, H. A. *The Eternal Security of the Believer*. Neptune, NJ: Loizeaux, 1923.

Kasdorf, Hans. *Christian Conversion in Context*. Scottdale: Herald Press, 1980.

Kelsey, Morton T. *Healing and Christianity*. New York: Harper and Row, 1973.

Kerr, Hugh T., and John M. Mulder, eds., *Conversions*. Grand Rapids: Eerdmans, 1983.

Köberle, Adolf. *The Quest for Holiness*. New York: Harper, 1936.

Kuiper, Herman. *By Grace Alone: A Study in Soteriology*. Grand Rapids: Eerdmans, 1955.

Küng, Hans. *Justification: The Doctrine of Karl Barth and a Catholic Reflection*. Trans. Thomas Collins et al. New York: Thomas Nelson, 1964.

Kuyper, Abraham. *Calvinism*. Grand Rapids: Eerdmans, 1931.

_____. *Dictaten Dogmatiek*. 2nd ed. 5 vols. Kampen: Kok, 1910.

_____. *The Work of the Holy Spirit*. Trans. Henri De Vries. New York: Funk and Wagnalls, 1900.

Ladd, George E. "Eternal Life." In *A Theology of the New Testament*. Grand Rapids: Eerdmans, 1974, pp. 254-59.

Lane, Anthony N. S. "Calvin's Doctrine of Assurance," *Vox Evangelica*, Vol. 11 (1979), p. 32.

La Rondelle, Hans K. *Perfection and Perfectionism*. Kampen: Kok, 1971.

Law, William. *A Serious Call to a Devout and Holy Life*. Philadelphia: Westminster, 1948.

Lawrence, Roy. *Christian Healing Rediscovered*. Downers Grove: InterVarsity, 1980.

Lawson, J. Gilchrist. *Deeper Experiences of Famous Christians*. (1911) New York: Pyramid Books, 1970.

Lehman, Chester K. *The Holy Spirit and the Holy Life*. Scottdale, PA: Herald Press, 1959.

Lewis, C. S. *Mere Christianity*. New York: Macmillan, 1960.

Lindström, Harald. *Wesley and Sanctification*. London: Epworth Press, 1946.

Link, H. G. "Life." In *New International Dictionary of New Testament Theology*, ed. Colin Brown. Grand Rapids: Zondervan, 1976, 2:480-84.

Luther, Martin. *Lectures on Romans*. Vol. 15 of *The Library of Christian Classics*. Trans. and ed. Wilhelm Pauck. Philadelphia: Westminster, 1961.

Machen, J. Gresham. *What Is Faith?* Grand Rapids: Eerdmans, 1946.

MacNutt, Francis. *Healing*. Notre Dame: Ave Maria Press, 1974.

Marshall, I. Howard. *Kept by the Power of God*. Minneapolis: Bethany Fellowship, 1975.

Metz, Donald. *Studies in Biblical Holiness*. Kansas City: Beacon Hill, 1971.

Moberg, David O. *The Great Reversal*. New York: Lippincott, 1972.

_____. *Inasmuch*. Grand Rapids: Eerdmans, 1965.

Moody, Dale. *The Word of Truth*. Grand Rapids: Eerdmans, 1981.

Mouw, Richard J. *Called to Holy Worldliness*. Philadelphia: Fortress, 1980.

Morris, Leon. *The Apostolic Preaching of the Cross*. Grand Rapids: Eerdmans, 1956.

_____. *The Cross in the New Testament*. Grand Rapids: Eerdmans, 1965.

_____. "Propitiation," EDT, p. 888.

Moulton, J. H., and G. Milligan. *The Vocabulary of the Greek Testament Illustrated from the Papyri* (abbr. VGT). Grand Rapids: Eerdmans, 1957.

Murray, John. "Assurance of Faith." In *Collected Writings of John Murray*. Carlisle, PA: Banner of Truth, 1977, 2:264-74.

_____. "Definitive Sanctification" and "The Agency in Definitive Sanctification." In *Collected Writings of John Murray*. Carlisle, PA: Banner of Truth, 1977, 2:277-93.

_____. "Justification." In *Collected Writings of John Murray*. Carlisle, PA: Banner of Truth, 1977, 2:202-22.

_____. *Principles of Conduct*. Grand Rapids: Eerdmans, 1957.

_____. *Redemption—Accomplished and Applied*. Grand Rapids: Eerdmans, 1955.

_____. "Sanctification (The Law)." In *Basic Christian Doctrines,* ed. Carl F. H.
      Henry. New York: Holt, Rinehart and Winston, 1962, pp. 227-33.
Murray, John, and N. Stonehouse. *The Free Offer of the Gospel.* Phillipsburg, NJ:
      Lewis J. Grotenhuis, 1948.
Neill, Stephen. *Christian Holiness.* London: Lutterworth, 1960.
Nettles, Thomas J. *By His Grace and For His Glory.* Grand Rapids: Baker, 1986.
Nicole, Roger. "C. H. Dodd and the Doctrine of Propitiation," *Westminster
      Theological Journal,* Vol. 17, No. 2, pp. 117-57.
Osborne, Grant R. "Exegetical Notes on Calvinist Texts." In *Grace Unlimited,* ed.
      Clark H. Pinnock. Minneapolis: Bethany Fellowship, 1975.
_____. "Soteriology in the Epistle to the Hebrews." In *Grace Unlimited,* ed. Clark
      H. Pinnock. Minneapolis: Bethany Fellowship, 1975.
Owen, John. *The Doctrine of the Saints' Perseverance Explained and Confirmed.* In *The
      Works of John Owen,* Vol. 11. Edinburgh: T. and T. Clark, 1862.
_____. *The Holy Spirit.* Grand Rapids: Sovereign Grace Publishers, 1971.
_____. *Justification by Faith.* Grand Rapids: Sovereign Grace Publishers, 1959.
Packer, James I. *Evangelism and the Sovereignty of God.* Chicago: InterVarsity, 1961.
_____. *Keep in Step with the Spirit.* Old Tappan, NJ: Revell, 1984.
_____. *Knowing God.* Downers Grove: InterVarsity, 1973.
_____. "Justification," EDT, pp. 593-97.
_____. "What Did the Cross Achieve? The Logic of Penal Substitution," *Tyndale
      Bulletin,* Vol. 25 (1974), pp. 3-45.
Packer, James I., et al. *Here We Stand: Justification by Faith Today.* London: Hodder
      and Stoughton, 1986.
Palmer, Edwin H. "Perseverance of the Saints." In *The Five Points of Calvinism.*
      Grand Rapids: Baker, 1972.
_____. *The Person and Ministry of the Holy Spirit.* Grand Rapids: Baker, 1974.
Pieper, Francis. *Christian Dogmatics.* 3 vols. St. Louis: Concordia, 1950-53.
Pink, Arthur W. *The Doctrine of Salvation.* Grand Rapids: Baker, 1975.
_____. *The Doctrine of Sanctification.* Grand Rapids: Baker, 1955.
_____. *Eternal Security.* Grand Rapids: Baker, 1974.
_____. *Regeneration or the New Birth.* Swengel, PA: Bible Truth Depot, n.d.
Plantinga, Cornelius, Jr. *A Place to Stand.* Grand Rapids: CRC Publications, 1979.
Pope, William B. *A Compendium of Christian Theology.* New York: Hunt and Eaton,
      1889.
Prior, Kenneth F. W. *The Way of Holiness.* Chicago: InterVarsity Press, 1967.
Purkiser, W. T. *Exploring Christian Holiness.* Vol. 1. Kansas City: Beacon Hill, 1983.
_____. *Sanctification and its Synonyms.* Kansas City: Beacon Hill, 1963.
Rahner, Karl. "Justified and Sinner at the Same Time." In *Theological Investigations.*
      Trans. K. and B. Kruger. Baltimore: Helicon Press, 1969, 6:218-30.
Rahner, Karl, and Herbert Vorgrimler. *Dictionary of Theology.* 2nd ed. New York:
      Crossroad, 1981.
Rees, Thomas, "Adoption; Sonship," ISBE, 1:53-55.
Reisinger, Ernest C. *What Should We Think of "The Carnal Christian"?* Carlisle, PA:
      Banner of Truth, n.d.

Ridderbos, Herman. *Paul: An Outline of His Theology.* Trans. John R. De Witt. Grand Rapids: Eerdmans, 1975.

Routley, Eric. *The Gift of Conversion.* London: Lutterworth, 1957.

Ryle, John C. *Holiness.* London: James Clarke, 1956.

Schaff, Philip. *The Creeds of Christendom.* 3 vols. New York: Harper, 1877.

Schilder, Klaas. *Heidelbergsche Catechismus.* Vol. 2. Goes: Oosterbaan and Le-Cointre, 1949.

Schnell, William J. *Thirty Years a Watchtower Slave.* Grand Rapids: Baker, 1956.

Scofield, C. I., ed. *The New Scofield Reference Bible.* New York: Oxford University Press, 1967.

Shank, Robert. *Life in the Son.* Springfield, MO: Westcott, 1960.

Shedd, William G. T. *Dogmatic Theology.* 3 vols. (1889-94) Grand Rapids: Zondervan, n.d.

Smedes, Lewis B. *All Things Made New.* Grand Rapids: Eerdmans, 1970.

_____. *Union With Christ.* Grand Rapids: Eerdmans, 1983.

Smilde, E. *Een Eeuw van Strijd over Verbond en Doop.* Kampen: Kok, 1946.

Steele, David N., and Curtis C. Thomas. *The Five Points of Calvinism Defined, Defended, Documented.* Philadelphia: Presbyterian and Reformed, 1965.

Stewart, James S. *A Man in Christ.* New York: Harper, [1935].

Stott, John R. W. *Baptism and Fullness.* Downers Grove: InterVarsity, 1976.

_____. *The Cross of Christ.* Downers Grove: InterVarsity, 1986.

_____. *Men Made New.* Downers Grove: InterVarsity, 1966.

Strong, Augustus H. *Systematic Theology.* 3 vols. Philadelphia: Griffith and Rowland, 1907-1909.

Swete, Henry B. *The Holy Spirit in the New Testament.* (1909) Grand Rapids: Baker, 1964.

Taylor, Richard. *Exploring Christian Holiness.* Vol. 3. Kansas City: Beacon Hill, 1985.

Theological Dictionary of the New Testament (abbr. TDNT). Ed. G. Kittel and G. Friedrich. Trans. G. W. Bromiley. 10 vols. Grand Rapids: Eerdmans, 1964-76.

Thiessen, Henry C. *Lectures in Systematic Theology.* Rev. by Vernon D. Doerksen. (1949) Grand Rapids: Eerdmans, 1979.

Toon, Peter. *Born Again.* Grand Rapids: Baker, 1987.

_____. *The Emergence of Hyper-Calvinism in English Nonconformity, 1689-1765.* London: The Olive Tree, 1967.

_____. *Justification and Sanctification.* Westchester: Good News, 1983.

"U.S. Lutheran–Roman Catholic Dialogue on Justification by Faith," *Origins, N.C. Documentary Service,* Vol. 13, No. 17 (October 6, 1983), pp. 279-304.

Vos, Johannes G. *The Separated Life: A Study of Basic Principles.* Philadelphia: Great Commission Publications, n.d.

Wagner, C. Peter. *What Are We Missing?* Carol Stream: Creation House, 1978.

Warfield, Benjamin B. "Faith." In *Biblical and Theological Studies.* Ed. Samuel C. Craig. Philadelphia: Presbyterian and Reformed, 1952, pp. 404-44.

_____. *Miracles Yesterday and Today* (earlier title, *Counterfeit Miracles*). (1918) Grand Rapids: Eerdmans, 1953.

_____. *Perfectionism.* Vol. 2. New York: Oxford University Press, 1932.

_____. *Perfectionism,* ed. Samuel C. Craig. Philadelphia: Presbyterian and Reformed, 1958.

_____. *The Plan of Salvation.* Grand Rapids: Eerdmans, 1984.

Watson, Richard. *Theological Institutes.* 2 vols. New York: Carlton and Porter, 1857.

Webb, R. A. *The Reformed Doctrine of Adoption.* Grand Rapids: Eerdmans, 1947.

Weisinger, Gary N., III. *The Reformed Doctrine of Sanctification.* No. 9 in "Fundamentals of the Faith," published by *Christianity Today,* Washington, D.C., n.d.

Wesley, John. "Brief Thoughts on Christian Perfection." In *The Works of John Wesley.* 3rd ed. (1872) Peabody, MA: Hendrickson, 1984, 11:446.

_____. "A Plain Account of Christian Perfection." In *The Works of John Wesley.* 3rd ed. (1872) Peabody, MA: Hendrickson, 1984, 11:366-446.

Wiley, H. Orton. *Christian Theology.* 3 vols. Kansas City: Beacon Hill, 1958.

Wilkinson, John. "Healing in the Epistle of James," *Scottish Journal of Theology,* Vol. 24, No. 3 (August 1971), pp. 338-40.

Wimber, John. *Power Evangelism.* San Francisco: Harper and Row, 1986.

Wolters, Albert M. *Creation Regained.* Grand Rapids: Eerdmans, 1985.

Wood, Laurence W. *Pentecostal Grace.* Wilmore, KY: Francis Asbury, 1980.

Wynkoop, Mildred B. *A Theology of Love: The Dynamics of Wesleyanism.* Kansas City: Beacon Hill, 1972.

Zodhiates, Spiros. *The Patience of Hope.* Grand Rapids: Eerdmans, 1960.

Index of Subjects

Adoption as children of God: creedal statements on, 185; role in justification, 181, 185; Scriptural basis for, 185-87; Westminster Confession on, 185; work of the Spirit, 30

Already–not yet tension, 9, 10, 17

Assurance of salvation: biblical teaching on, 149; Calvin's view on, 147-48; Heidelberg Catechism on, 150; Holy Spirit's role in, 30; Roman Catholic view on, 146

Baptismal regeneration, 108

Carnal Christian, 20-26, 82, 232

Charisma, defined, 32

Charismata, 32, 33, 44

Conversion: and covenant children, 119, 120; defined, 113; as gift of the Spirit, 29; national, 116; paradox of, 115; post-conversion experience, 26, 27, 50; second, 27, 116, 117; temporary, 115; types of, 115-17; variations in patterns of, 118-19; work of both God and man, 114

Decree: of Christ as Savior, 56; that Christ would save his own, 57

Depravity: biblical teaching on, 94-95; total or pervasive, 94

Effectual call, 80-81; biblical basis, 81-86; Calvin on, 87-88; defined, 86; goal of, 86-87; objections to, 89, 90; Westminster Confession on, 88

Eschatology: inaugurated, 9; future, 9, 10

Faith: aspects of, 140-43; assurance of salvation in, 146-51; biblical descrip-

tion of, 134-38; Calvin's view of, 139-40; dead without works, 136; gift of God, 145; gift of the Spirit, 29; importance of, 132-33; mystery or paradox of, 143; Roman Catholic view of, 146-47; Scholastic view of, 139

Gospel call: all included in, 68-71; biblical teaching on, 73-77; Calvin's view on, 74; Canons of Dort on, 77-78; command as well as invitation, 69; defined, 68; implications for missions, 79; internal call, 81; offensive to some, 68; rationalistic view, 78-79; seriously meant, 72-77

Grace of God, irresistible, 104-105

Healing: biblical teaching on, 36; cautions regarding, 40-41; new emphasis on, 36; result of prayer, 38-40

Heart, biblical view as core of being, 81

Holiness: biblical concept of, 193; election and, 56

Holy Spirit: baptism with, 19, 27-29; fruit of, 44-47; fullness of, 49-53; gifts of, miraculous, 32-35; non-miraculous, 32, 33, 35; power of in biblical texts, 42-43; power of in Wimber's view, 41; role in salvation, 28-31; role in soteriology, 9; role in union with Christ, 54

Interrelations between soteriology and other doctrines, 7-10

Irresistible grace, 104; objections to, 105

Justification: benefits of, 185-88; Calvin on, 177, 184; concept of, 172-78; con-

Index of Proper Names

Gill, John, 78
Godwin, Johnnie C., 112
Girod, Gordon, 210
Graafland, C., 151
Grider, Kenneth, 215, 217, 219
Gromacki, Robert, 256
Grounds, Vernon C., 7
Grudem, Wayne A., 35

Hendriksen, William, 210
Henry, Carl F. H., 206
Hillis, Don W., 35
Hills, A. M., 102, 182, 183
Hodge, A. A., 19, 181
Hodge, Charles W., 3, 88, 107, 175, 180, 202, 210
Hoekema, Anthony A., 4, 35, 75, 81, 95, 178, 192, 195, 197, 213, 214, 244
Hoeksema, Herman, 71, 79, 88, 91
Horton, Stanley M., 192
Hoyt, Herman A., 112
Hughes, Philip E., 77
Hulme, William E., 233
Hussey, Joseph, 78

Ironside, H. A., 256

Kasdorf, Hans, 120
Kelsey, Morton T., 36
Kerr, Hugh T., and Mulder, John M., 113, 118
Köberle, Adolf, 233
Köster, Helmut, 136
Küng, Hans, 167, 168
Kuyper, Abraham, 88, 101, 109, 115, 231

Ladd, G. E., 188
La Rondelle, Hans K., 233
Lawrence, Roy, 36, 39, 43
Lawson, James Gilchrist, 26
Lehman, Chester K., 202
Lenski, R. C. H., 38
Lewis, C. S., 93, 105, 118, 143
Lightner, Robert P., 206
Lindström, Harald, 233

Link, H. G., 188
Luther, Martin, 130, 152, 153, 161, 170, 175, 184

Machen, J. Gresham, 146, 151
MacNutt, Francis, 36
Marsden, George M., 215
Marshall, I. Howard, 236, 239
Maslow, Abraham, 26
McKenzie, Ross, 210
McQuilkin, J. Robertson, 21, 192, 206
Menninger, Karl, 153
Metz, Donald, 215, 217, 221
Moberg, David O., 231
Moody, Dale, 239
Morris, Leon, 98, 158, 173, 175
Moulton, J. H., and Milligan, G., 30, 60, 201, 243
Mouw, Richard, 231
Murray, John, 11, 13, 14, 54, 77, 87, 88, 97, 123, 148, 151, 153, 164, 187, 189, 190, 202, 203, 205, 210, 212, 213, 214, 236, 240, 248

Neill, Stephen, 221, 225
Nicole, Roger, 158

Olevianus, Caspar, 170
Osborne, Grant R., 239
Owen, John, 191

Packer, James I., 6, 153, 162, 169, 173, 175, 176, 187, 189, 191
Palmer, Edwin H., 104, 256
Pascal, Blaise, 27
Pelagius, 80
Phillips, J. B., 46
Pieper, Francis, 108
Pierard, R. V., 27
Pink, Arthur W., 112, 233, 256
Pinnock, Clark H., 239, 250
Plantinga, Cornelius, Jr., 105, 114
Pope, William B., 86
Prior, Kenneth F. W., 233
Purkiser, W. T., 219, 233

Index of Scriptures